CASES IN IRISH BUSINESS STRATEGY AND POLICY

Cases in Irish Business Strategy and Policy

Thomas N. Garavan
Barra O Cinneide
Mary Garavan
Anna Cunningham
with
Ambrose Downey
Trevor O'Regan
Briga Hynes

Oak Tree Press

Dublin

Oak Tree Press
Merrion Building
Lower Merrion Street
Dublin 2, Ireland

A catalogue record of this book is
available from the British Library.

ISBN 1-86076-014-7

Printed in Ireland by Colour Books Ltd.

Contents

About the Authors

THOMAS N. GARAVAN is a lecturer in human resource development at the University of Limerick. He is also editor of the *Journal of European Industrial Training*, an international human resource development journal. His research interests include the analysis of how companies structure and deliver training functions, continuing professional development and the effectiveness of company graduate training and development programmes. He is a Fellow of the Irish Institute of Training and Development, a member of the American Society of Training and Development and co-author of *Training and Development in Ireland: Context, Policy and Practice*, published by Oak Tree Press.

DR BARRA O CINNEIDE is Professor of Entrepreneurship and Course Leader of the Agribusiness Programme at the University of Limerick. His research interests include analysis of Irish sectoral development, including the effects on agriculture and tourism following Ireland's membership of the EC, and emergent indigenous enterprises — the subject of over 80 case studies since 1979.

MARY GARAVAN lectures in human resource management at HSI College in Limerick. Her research interests include the analysis of trainer competencies, the roles of training and development specialists and health and safety law and practice.

ANNA CUNNINGHAM lectures in strategic management and marketing at the Shannon College of Hotel Management. She also lectures in tourism marketing at the University of Limerick. Her research interests include hospitality marketing and services marketing and management development in the hospitality industry.

AMBROSE DOWNEY is a research student at the Graduate Centre of Business, University of Limerick. His current research specialism focuses on the human resource implications of transformative organisational change and strategic development in the Irish context, with particular reference to the automotive supply industry.

BRIGA HYNES is a Lecturer in Entrepreneurship in the Department of Management and Marketing at the University of Limerick. In this role Briga is responsible for the design, delivery and evaluation of entrepreneurship modules to undergraduate, graduate and post-experience students. Before joining this Department, Briga was Manager of the Marketing Centre for Small Business at the University. Her main research interests and published works concentrate on entrepreneurship education, management practices and decision-making in the small firm, the role of training and development in the small firm and its impact on employment and growth of the firm.

TREVOR O'REGAN lectures in Business Policy at the University of Limerick. His research interests lie in looking at the experience of Irish companies in Eastern Europe and the former Soviet Union (EEFSU).

Preface

A major problem of studying the strategic process is that academics and students can become detached from the reality of the business organisation. Many business policy and strategy courses suffer from concentrating on the major big issues without adequate consideration of operational and organisational details. Effective business strategy relies on analysis of company specifics and consideration of the realities of the organisation.

Cases are not the perfect way to understand strategic processes but they are a useful way of introducing practice into the classroom. They can involve the student in actively analysing a situation and making a set of decisions. The cases in this volume are both descriptive and prescriptive. They provide background material on how major business decisions were made while at the same time allowing the student to apply strategic concepts and understand the dynamics of the modern organisation.

The cases presented in this book are not intended to emphasise any particular theories, nor are they intended to illustrate examples of either weak or exceptionally good management/ strategic practices. In each case you will find several sets of issues considered. Furthermore, each case provides a description of the organisation in question, the types of strategic decisions that it made, a description, or in some cases implied, of the strengths and weaknesses of the organisation. The information provided will allow the student and the teacher to consider what could have been done differently. What issues are left to be resolved? What types of strategic alternatives are now available to the organisation? Almost all of the cases present a combination of qualitative and quantitative data. Both sets of data need consideration in order to formulate an integrated solution.

In this cross section of cases we have tried to capture the mix of Irish business enterprises that exists: product and service organisations, non-technological cases, small and large business situations. The cases try to capture some of the more important concepts within the field of business strategy: managing change, industry structure analysis, competitor analysis, TQM/continuous improvement initiatives and the management of human and financial resources. There is no "correct" answer to any case. The purpose of a business strategy course should be to provide the student with an understanding of the issues but also to ensure that they remember that the total number of variables in a real strategy situation is typically beyond the control of any one person or group. Many of the companies presented in this book may have succeeded or failed not because of specific decisions that they took but rather because of luck or some other external event. Such is the nature of business.

The authors wish to thank all those organisations who provided information and granted interviews. The authors, however, accept responsibility for any errors of fact which appear in the book and will seek to correct them in later editions.

A large number of people provided support and direct assistance during the production of this book. Specifically the authors would like to thank the following at the University of Limerick for their encouragement: Professor Noel Whelan, Dean, College of Business; Dr Paddy Gunnigle, Head, Department of Personnel and Employment Relations; Dr David McKevitt, Head, Department of Management and Marketing; Professor Donal Dineen, Associate Dean, College of Business. We would also like to thank Mr Philip Smyth, Director, Shannon College of Hotel Management; and Michael McNamara, Director HSI College Limerick.

Other individuals who provided support include Joseph Wallace, Michael Morley, Noreen Heraty, Sarah Moore, Gerard Fitzgerald, Colette Noonan, Helena Lenihan, Paul Sweeney, Rita Garavan, Juliet McMahon, Bernard Delaney, Jim Dalton, Joseph McDonnell, Derry McMahon and others too numerous to mention.

It is customary to give thanks to the person who helped type the manuscript, but rarely can so much be owed to one person. Our heartfelt thanks go to Kim O'Neill, University of Limerick, whose skill helped to create graphics and keep track of the numerous changes made to the cases as the material took shape. We would have been lost without her.

To our families, our thanks for being so understanding about and supportive of this project that took away much of our time with them.

Note: The data presented in the cases represents the situation in each company at the time of writing.

Introduction

Business Policy and Corporate Strategy, as part of an education programme, can be a challenging experience for the student. Essentially, the student of strategy is one who seeks to develop critical thinking in a way that promotes a wider understanding and appreciation of organisational and strategic development. Because no one definition can be universally ascribed to strategy, it is best to view that strategy process in an abstract way, as an approach that encompasses the totality of the organisation acting in an environment that is characterised by complex and turbulent change. Analysis is a key feature of this process, as it is incumbent on management to develop a clear understanding of the organisation's current position in the context of both the internal and external business environments. Such an analysis will enable organisational decision-makers to make a rational assessment of the potential success of any future strategic options adopted. It will also facilitate the management of strategic change. By advancing the current strategic orientation of the organisation, it becomes possible to understand the key beliefs, attitudes and values that inform and sustain the culture of the organisation. An accurate culture definition will permit the promotion of conditions whereby the prevailing corporate culture becomes initially receptive, and subsequently willing, to sustain the desired change objectives. Corporate strategy, in this context, is pervasive in its influence on the general direction and scope of organisational activities.

The study of business policy and strategy has been the subject of much debate since it emerged as an academic discipline during the 1960s. Traditionally, the teaching of the subject focused on the needs of the graduate student, where previous academic achievement, maturity and often previous work experience have provided a sound foundation for the assimilation of advanced, participatory learning techniques such as those afforded by business-case analysis. However, in recent years, the discipline has been included in many undergraduate study programmes as a capstone course that integrates the application of interdisciplinary business skills. As is often the case, undergraduate students lack the practical experience necessary to appreciate wholly the scope of the subject area, thus making it imperative to create classroom conditions that closely approximate the strategic circumstances of the organisation. By promoting experiential learning, the case-study method enables students to improve their analytical skills by applying key concepts and theories to specific case scenarios. Accordingly, business-case analysis makes up for a deficiency of real world experience and provides an opportunity for "discovery learning", an approach that is based on independent student analysis, interpretation and rationalisation.

The Case as a Learning Strategy

The case method can be described as a non-directive approach to learning, and can be used principally to highlight the practical application of theories and concepts. The role of the tutor in this context is one of facilitation, providing information sources when appropriate, maintaining the course of the discussion, posing specific questions and encouraging the participation of students. Because of its heuristic character, the method aims to teach students how to identify and analyse complex problems and formulate possible solutions. It exposes the student to a wide variety of approaches and perspectives and provides for the derivation of principles that can be appropriately applied in a subsequent real-life situation.

The boundary between the case as a learning strategy and other instruments of learning is generally explicit. Principally, the case method is an inductive learning strategy. The focus is one of developing knowledge through empirical observation rather than through theorising based on the testing of hypotheses. In general, inductive strategies assume that learning occurs through shared experiences leading to generalisations. It involves not only doing things but also talking about them in order to abstract the key learning points. This strategy leads to high-level learning outcomes, enabling students to take ownership of the process. Yet in the context of business policy and strategy teaching, the case method represents the practical application of an earlier, but perhaps more fundamental, didactic learning strategy. Didactic strategies provide the student with the necessary theoretical support for the more organic inductive learning afforded by the case method. Didactic strategies are located in the academic domain and are developed through deductive thinking. They are therefore more appropriate to instruction than facilitation.

As a learning strategy, the case study presents the student with a written description of an actual situation facing an organisation. It will usually describe how the present position developed and what problem a key personality in the case is currently facing. Tables of data and other diagrams may be included to help provide a more complete picture, while appendices may also be used to incorporate large amounts of data that would otherwise clutter the text. The case study can vary in length from a few pages to, perhaps, several hundred. Normally students who are new to case-study analysis associate length with difficulty. This, however, is a dangerous principle to follow, as many short cases can often prove to be very demanding in that all of the trivial detail has been stripped away, leaving the student to tackle core issues head on. Case studies can also be described as "dead" or "live" or indeed somewhere in between. A "dead" case is one in which all the case information is presented to students at the start of the case analysis. To make a case "live", further information is injected during the course of analysis. This approach allows a case to develop in a more realistic way. Students can thus build up their knowledge of the organisation and its problems, and develop increasingly sophisticated solutions.

The Business Policy and Strategy Case

The business policy and strategy case study details facts about the events and circumstances surrounding a strategic event or situation facing the organisation. Ideally, the case will be clear and understandable, providing an interesting and enjoyable narrative that is different in its presentation of the organisation or a contemporary business issue. According to Thompson (1995), a good case study will:

- Enable students to learn by doing — diagnosing, assessing, evaluating, recommending

- Improve students' analytical skills — by their applying theories and concepts to particular (case) situations

- Improve students' critical judgment-forming and decision-making skills and, in some cases, but not always, make up for a lack of a real world experience

- Provoke discussion about strategic issues

- Force individuals to take a stance — by recommending a strategy for the company, the student must be in a position to defend their proposed strategy

- Provide enough information to enable the evaluation of the feasibility of potential strategic options: for example, can the organisation manage a particular point, given its resource capability?

- Enable students to determine the desirability of any chosen strategy — would the organisation itself select the strategy? Desirability, however, emphasises the influence of strategic leadership and culture on strategic choice. Because of the inherent subjectivity involved in the formulation and implementation of corporate strategy, the student, as an objective analyst, may obtain a different solution from that of the organisation.

It is important to realise that organisations are made up of people, and that people by their very nature are indeterminate and subjective in their outlook and interpretation of events affecting themselves, and by extension, the organisation. Because students are also subjective in their interpretation, implicitly, there cannot be any one absolute "best" solution. Accordingly, any proposed solution is susceptible to open interpretation. Who therefore is to say that an alternative solution would not have been more efficient, more effective, or both? The course tutor, in this context, acts in a facultative capacity, with a responsibility for the development of advanced judgment skills in the student. The student will, as a result, acquire a personal perspective on what constitutes effective strategic management. Exposure to real issues — and to the views of other people in a class, people who come from a variety of backgrounds, people with a range of different options and beliefs — can help to build a diversity and richness in the student's perspective.

Primarily, the focus of most case studies is one of analysis.

They begin by summarising the actions taken by a company, and then, in the appendices, pack in high amounts of basic data — financial results, market statistics, etc. Students thus tease out key trends and ratios in order to generate the broad strategic performance of the organisation. However, just as important is the ability to incorporate techniques such as SWOT (Strengths, Weaknesses, Opportunities and Threats) analysis, and perhaps some form of portfolio matrix, to clarify the strategic situation, thus providing a sound foundation for a debate on possible alternatives and future strategic direction. Yet many of the cases in this publication will not advance a strong financial perspective — rather, they will provide a straightforward description of a strategic challenge that is currently facing the organisation, or perhaps an explanation of how the organisation has previously dealt with a key strategic issue. These cases may be quite short, thus promoting a useful forum for the discussion of strategic issues and challenges.

Business-Specific Skills Developed by the Case Method

The strategy case method is primarily a vehicle for developing a range of business-specific skills. However, these skills of themselves, are not sufficient wholly to develop a good business decision-maker. Learning strategies other than the case method can just as well afford the student the opportunity to develop skills befitting a well-rounded strategy decision-maker. Inductive learning strategies such as the discussion and project method, and a range of management aims, simulations and exercises can promote the wider acquisition of strategy decision-making skills. Yet specifically, the strength of the case method as a learning strategy lies in its ability to generate "creative" problem-solving skills. Easton (1982) explores this "creativity" dimension and suggests that six major skill areas form the focus of business problem solving:

- *Analytical Skills*: Case studies comprise information, or more approximately, data. Data do not become information until they have meaning and relevance for the analyst. One of the analytical skills developed by the case method therefore is that of information handling. The student learns to classify, organise and evaluate information. Also learned is the ability to recognise when vital information is missing, as is the ability to know how this information may alternatively be obtained. Using this information, the student will learn to understand the situation as described. In so doing, a clear and logical pattern is initiated, which can be appropriately developed and improved upon through consistent practice.

- *Application Skills*: At a slightly lower level of difficulty, the case method provides the student with practice at applying key concepts, techniques, and principles. For example, techniques such as value-chain analysis, portfolio analysis and Porter's five-force model can be used to help students in developing their analysis. The key word is help, as techniques like these cannot provide a solution by themselves. The student will also learn to judge where techniques are appropriate, and when they may be used to support their interpretation.

- *Creative Skills*: Cases cannot be solved by logical processes alone. Creativity is vital to good-quality case presentations. However, this principle is not widely understood. Many students who are afraid of quantitative methods but who nonetheless pride themselves on their creativity, are frightened of cases. These students must realise that they have a vital skill necessary for good work. Creativity is particularly important in generating alternative solutions to the problems uncovered by logical analysis. It also helps when trying to predict the outcomes that could result from following a particular course of action.

- *Communication Skills*: The communication skills developed will depend to a certain extent on the way in which the course tutor chooses to run the class. The student may be required to present findings orally, to use visual aids and other media, to co-operate in group presentations, or to write clear, well-constructed case reports.

- *Social Skills*: Case discussions are essentially social process. Students will accordingly learn to communicate, listen, support and direct and control their argument. Principally, students will learn to gain a better understanding of their own behaviour and of that of others in a loosely structured social context. In ways, case discussions can provide students with the opportunity to learn more about human behaviour than, perhaps, about strategy problem-solving.

- *Self-Analysis Skills*: Disagreements can frequently occur in case discussions over opinion-driven judgments rather than analytical judgments. Accordingly, case discussions provide a useful forum for analysing student opinions in a simulated business context. Issues of a moral and ethical nature can complicate otherwise simple business decisions. For example, if a bribe were necessary to get a contract, would the student as decision-maker pay it? These issues therefore, can pose ethical dilemmas for the student, the type which usually generate active, and often, heated participation in classroom discussions.

Problems with the Case Method

Because of its non-directive approach, the case method is not a formally structured learning situation in the same way as the classroom lecture or tutorial is. This characteristic can be intimidating, thus creating problems for the student who is not familiar with the case-study approach. Making the successful transition between these two learning situations requires careful deliberation, particularly in respect of three key problem areas identified by Easton (1982). These problem areas can be summarised in the following way:

- *What is the student supposed to do?* Students in the case study are not told by the tutor what the problem is, leaving them in a position to find it out for themselves. Where previously they were informed of the goals or objectives of the exercise, they are now required to define the goals for themselves. When they finally arrive at an answer, students are unaware as to whether it is the correct answer or not. This process is further compounded by the ambiguous nature of the information contained in the case to begin with. It is therefore not unusual for students to describe their first case experience as disheartening.

- *What is the student learning?* In a lecture situation, students feel confident with the concrete nature of the facts presented. They will feel that they have learnt something of substance, much of which can be reinforced through further reading. In the case situation, however, students may feel insecure and uncomfortable with the seemingly inefficient direction of the case discussion. Student improvement, therefore, may not be forthcoming in an explicit way, as it is often difficult to detect the higher-level skills promoted by the case discussion. Students, in this context, should take a longer-term perspective in their acquisition of case-study skills.

- *Why doesn't the teacher teach?* A major problem for case students relates to the method of teaching employed by the course tutor. Students may have difficulty coming to terms with the fact that the tutor doesn't teach in the traditional sense. Accordingly, the tutor can be perceived as being ambiguous in approach, offering little or no concrete advice on the nature of the case solution. This, however, should not alarm the student as the tutor will most probably offer guidelines on the general direction and scope of the solution. The tutor therefore will be acting in a facilitating way, encouraging students to discover for themselves the appropriateness or otherwise of their proposed solution.

A Step-by-Step Approach to Business Strategy Case Analysis

The use of practical guidelines in business strategy case analysis, can provide a facilitating framework for the student developing a case solution. Such an approach will enable the student systematically to frame the scope, context and content of a proposed solution, and determine the direction of the analysis generated as a result. Easton (1982) proposes the following step-by-step process as being useful in this respect:

- *Understanding the Situation*: Essentially, the body of a case study is one of information. In this first step, the student must become familiar with the information provided and begin to work on it immediately. The information should be logically organised in a way that promotes understanding and order. It also needs to be wholly evaluated, as not all of it will be valid, precise or relevant. Vital pieces are probably missing, requiring the student to extrapolate from what is provided if any decision is to be made properly.

- *Diagnosing Problem Areas*: A problem can be defined as the difference between a current (or expected future) situation and some desired situation. Problem identification therefore is the search for these differences. In the case situation, the student will be attempting to uncover them. Yet this is not altogether an easy task. Sometimes problems are simply symptoms of more fundamental problems. Problems may, for instance, be caused by a number of different factors, while basic problems can have any number of symptoms. The student will therefore try to unravel these relationships, determining probable cause in the process. Problems, when identified, should be stated as accurately and explicitly as possible by the student. Note, however, that not all problems are equally important, thus creating difficulties for the student in deciding on their priority. In general, however, there are four sources of problems.

The first kind of problem is the more or less obvious one that is either pointed out to the student, or else is recognised from a straightforward reading of the case. The second type is less obvious because it is only uncovered by using the analytical frameworks of the varying business disciplines studied by the student evaluating the case situation. The third type of problem has to do with the future. Potential future problems are created almost invariably by threats or opportunities that may be currently identified by the organisation but may not yet have occurred and, of course, may not do so. The fourth kind of problem results from the fact that people in organisations perceive problems in ways which differ from each other, and from the case analyst. Because people have different motivations, and are singular in seeking and implementing possible solutions, the student as case analyst, may find it difficult to determine how the problem is perceived in the organisation, and to whom in the organisation it relates. To overcome this difficulty, students need to clarify the role they will play as case analysts, and determine what the people in the case perceive their problems to be. Role clarification will focus student analysis on providing specific insights into the problem, thus obviating the tendency to offer vague and general recommendations.

The recommendations offered by the student, therefore, should obviously change depending on the role adopted — whether it is, for example, as managing director or graduate trainee. Determining the perceptions of key individuals in the case situation, however, is not easily achieved. The definition of what constitutes an organisational problem, in this context, thus becomes a problem in itself for the student case analyst.

One individual's problem may be another individual's perfectly satisfactory situation. For instance, if no problem is perceived, no action will result, or if a problem is seen where none exists (at least according to the case analyst), then unnecessary actions will result. Students in this instance, should incorporate any "problem perception" problems into their overall case analysis.

- *Generating Alternative Solutions*: This is the creative step in the solution-formulation process. While many strategy textbooks would advocate a logical approach to generating any number of alternative solutions, it is perhaps the flair and chance creativity of the case analyst that will produce the elusive and singular solutions. Possible solutions can be generated through use of a number of creative techniques. This approach essentially denies critical thinking, while promoting in its place a free-flow of contemplation, which can be subsequently appraised in a more formal sense. Accordingly, brainstorming can be explained in the following practical way: write everything down, no matter how irrelevant it seems at the time; relax and let ideas come to mind rather than trying to concentrate on logical progressions of thought. Use the list created to generate new ideas. Following this, the second stage of brainstorming involves an evaluation of the ideas generated. Many of the ideas will be discarded, some will be retained for further scrutiny, while others will become possible solutions. Each of these solutions, in turn, can be evaluated in respect of its generality. Thus, the more general solutions are examined first, followed by solutions which can be explored more specifically.

- *Predicting Outcomes*: The first stage in choosing among alternatives is to predict what would happen if a particular alternative solution were put into action. Two particular warnings are important here. The first is to be sure to predict all the possible outcomes. It may be that a particular solution solves one problem, only at the expense of creating another. Secondly, predicting is a difficult and uncertain business. Not all outcomes are equally likely to occur. The student should be aware of the techniques which attempt to cope with the risk and uncertainty associated with a particular action, i.e. decision-tree analysis — an approach which allows the decision-maker to asses the probabilities associated which each alternative outcome.

- *Evaluation Alternatives*: In this case, the student will choose among the alternative solutions generated. This is a process which lists the merits and demerits of each alternative. Choosing among alternatives is, in principle, a straightforward process. Each alternative is first evaluated, with a value assigned to it. This value may be quantitative (profit expressed in pounds) or qualitative (achievement of personal satisfaction). However, each alternative, if implemented, would create a stream of outcomes. The value of all these outcomes must somehow be totalled to get a value for each alternative. This implies a two-stage evaluation process: firstly, assigning values to outcomes; secondly, totalling these values to provide an overall index of values for each alternative. When each alternative has been evaluated, the choice falls upon the alternative with the highest value.

- *Rounding out the Analysis*: This step links the case analysis with communicating the results of that analysis. It may involve a reiterative process through stages 4 and 6 of the step-by-step analysis. The student in this context must know when to stop the process, and work with the solutions generated thus far. An important question that also needs to be asked is whether to concentrate on breadth or depth in developing analyses. A broad analysis is one that seeks to generalise, in an extensive way, on the number of competing solutions or strategies that can be chosen. It, however, does not detail the specifics involved in implementing the solution. An in-depth analysis, on the other hand, would devote less time to the choice of solutions at the general level, and concentrate specifically on the details of implementation. Because students who are new to case analysis may, understandably, concentrate on developing breadth in their analysis, the course tutor should encourage students to tease out the issues and to become more specific in their approach. Conversely, students with previous industrial experience may ignore the generalities of the case, and focus their attention on the specifics of implementation. These latter students are presumably repeating the behaviour of the workplace, and are therefore not properly attuned to appreciate fully the significance of the broader perspective. Again, the course tutor should intervene by directing students to adopt a more general focus in their analysis.

  The student as case analyst and decision-maker may also be

faced with the probability that the chosen solution may not work in practice. Rarely, if ever, are business decisions made in a once-off, transcendental way. Rather, they are made incrementally, with management thus making a small decision, observing the effects of it, making another decision, and so on. The decision process is therefore linear and sequential in its character. If a problem decision were to be made, management would then be in a position to reverse the decision before its consequences became profound. Accordingly, it is only fair that the case analyst be given appropriate discretion in developing a case solution. This discretion should approximate the scope of real-world decision-makers, which can be afforded through a process of contingency planning. By planning for contingencies, the case analyst is in a position to make conditional "if/then"-type decisions. Thus the original decision of the analyst becomes subject to any emerging strategic scenarios in the organisation and, in a pre-programmed way, the decision can be modified to fit the "new" strategic circumstance in which the organisation finds itself.

- *Communicating the Results*: Presenting the case analysis is the final stage in the solution-formulation process. No matter how logical, creative and detailed the analysis is, it will fail in its intent if it is not communicated properly to its target audience. To ensure that the results are properly communicated, the case analyst needs to ask five key questions:

    1. What is to be communicated?

    2. To whom is it to be communicated?

    3. Through what channels will the communication proceed?

    4. Who will deliver the communication?

    5. What effect will the communication generate?

These questions will help the case analyst to frame the presentation of their results in a focused and cogent way. A factor to be considered in this process is the context in which the results will be presented. Generally speaking, these contexts can range from informal case discussions to the highly formal case examinations. More specific, however, is the type of communication channel required of the presentation. These channels can be classified as being either oral or written. By combining the contexts and channels of communication, four possible presentation formats can be identified: case discussions; oral presentations, written case analyses; written case examinations.

1. *Case Discussions*: These form the least-structured context for communicating the findings of the case analysis. The amount of structure involved is largely at the discretion of the course tutor. Some tutors, for instance, choose to keep their intervention to a minimum, while others prefer to act as facilitators, asking questions that will stimulate problem-solving behaviour. Despite the freedom afforded by the case discussion, and the unseemly difficulties associated with presenting long and complex arguments orally, the approach does help to present key conceptual and cognitive arguments in a way that will develop artificial thinking and decision-making skills.

2. *Oral Presentation*: In general, these presentations involve an individual or a group. Most of the teaching period is devoted to the delivery of the presentation, with the course tutor and the rest of the class forming the audience. Perhaps using some visual aids, individuals (or groups) communicate their findings within a structure that is largely determined by themselves. Problems associated with this approach include the inability of some audience members to comprehend what is being communicated because of an over-inclusive and elaborate use of language by the individual making the presentation.

3. *Written Case Analyses*: The audience in this instance is almost exclusively confined to the course tutor. Accordingly, the tutor will set formal parameters such as length, structure, style, submission date, assessment criteria, etc. Important factors to be considered by the student include the general layout of the report in its sequence of main headings, subheadings and paragraph descriptions. The content and context of the report may be changed as the report is drafted.

4. *Written Case Examinations*: This format requires students to answer questions in the examination room based upon a case study given out some time previously.

This approach gives the student an opportunity to study the case in detail, taking note of any key trends or strategic developments that may be useful in answering the examination questions. The questions in the examination are not known in advance by the student.

Cases in Business Strategies and Policy

This publication presents a collection of cases on business strategies and policy in the Irish context. Each of the 26 cases has been specifically written so as to illustrate a particular dimension of strategic formulation and implementation, and to uncover the difficulties and challenges associated with the strategy process. The cases are designed to promote critical thinking and analysis, while generating debate as to the nature and scope of corporate strategy in Ireland. The collection covers a diversity of themes, many of which include the notion of strategic change. The global development of world markets in recent years is also explored — generally in respect of its implications for competitive advantage, and more specifically, how organisations are responding to the challenges of a complex and turbulent business environment. Various structural configurations and organisational cultures are profiled, as are a number of key individuals who have shown considerable strategic leadership in their contribution to organisational change and development. Figure 1 (pp. 26–27) presents an outline of the areas examined by each case study.

In the following sections, a brief overview of each case study will be made. Each case study will be outlined in a contextual way, and will pinpoint the key themes and strategic issues considered therein.

The Agribusiness/Food Sector

Avonmore Foods plc

This case recounts the evolution of an international food company in a context of strategic change and development. Principally, the case focuses on a critical juncture in the company's strategic development to date. In 1984, when faced with EU restrictions on its milk output, the company sought to explore alternative strategic development routes. It obtained a stock exchange quotation in 1988, and since then has pursued an expansionist development policy. One such expansion involved a proposed joint-venture partnership with a group of Polish co-operatives which subsequently became known as the Wielkopolska Dairy Group (WDG). Specifically, the case examines how best to employ the experience and expertise of an Irish food company in a developing central-European economy. The strategic synergy of the proposed partnership is discussed, as are the attributes and the probable success of the venture. The role of the project champion is explored, particularly in respect of the commitment shown to the WDG transition process. The case concludes by suggesting that Ireland has a number of core competencies that could successfully be employed in a wider international context.

Bailey's Irish Cream

This story of Bailey's is one that examines the various strategies adopted in the company's 20-year history. As part of the drinks giant, Grand Metropolitan, Bailey's is now established as a premium global brand. However, in establishing itself in international markets, the company experienced a number of difficulties that could only be overcome through developing logical and systematic import-distribution networks. The case is very specific on the marketing strategy employed by the company, and on recent new product developments. The importance of product perception is also discussed, as are the implications of emerging healthy drinking patterns. The case commands the creativity and stamina of the company's marketing team, principally their focus on the company's core business. Several future growth strategies are also explored, as is the company's policy of manufacturing in Ireland.

Waterford Foods plc

The case of Waterford Foods plc focuses on its structural and strategic development over the past 30 years. It generally describes the various amalgamations that brought the company into being, while detailing how its milk volume grew substantially in the enlarged consolidated group. Notable in the company's evolution to date has been its diversification into high value-added dairy foods. The case also examines Waterford's strategic focus, organisational structure and corporate culture. A brief mention is made of the group's commitment to Total Quality Management, and there is a discussion on the group's current strategic positioning. Passable future strategic options are also examined. The case concludes with a review of the group's recent financial performance.

Ritz

The Ritz case examines the new product development process of the Clonmel-based company, Showerings (Ireland) Limited. The company has been quite successful at introducing new products in the past, a fact that becomes all the more apparent when one considers the number of new products that fail each year. In developing a new product concept, the company used several techniques to analyse the market to determine if a gap existed. Accordingly, the research showed that women were more willing to try new products, and that they were less loyal to existing products. On this basis, and considering that Showerings had experience in this particular segment of the market, it was decided to develop a product that reflected the taste characteristics of a singular and sophisticated female market segment. The case pays particular attention to the nature of the market research undertaken by the company. More specifically, it documents the selection of the "Ritz" brand name, and the role of advertising and product distribution in securing market penetration.

The Pig Industry in Ireland

The case is introduced by a brief overview of the principal characteristics of the Irish pig industry. The recent rationalisation of the industry at producer level is examined, focusing on the improvements in production efficiency. In profiling the dimensions of the Irish pig producer, the case explores the scope of production capability in Ireland. The pig industry is contrasted with four European competitors: Denmark, Holland, France and England. An interesting discussion on the pigmeat market examines the changing international consumption and production patterns over the past 25 years. Government support for the industry is reviewed, particularly in respect of product processing and marketing. The case ends with a general note on the future of the industry.

The Irish Horse

The case on the Irish horse presents an interesting discussion on the nature and scope of the Irish horse industry. The Irish horse population is comprehensively examined, as is the development of the Irish racing and bloodstock industry. The notion of sponsorship is discussed, focusing in particular on the difficulties and challenges experienced by many Irish racecourses. The contribution of Bord na gCapall (the Irish Horse Board) is considered over an 18-year period from its inception in 1970, to its abolition in 1992. The challenges facing the Irish Sport horse provide and interesting account of an industry optimising its core resource capability. The case ends with a specific focus on the pricing and market potential of the Irish Sport horse.

The Tourism/Hospitality Sector

Castletroy Park Hotel

This short case reviews the recent evolution of an Irish corporate-sector hotel development. The Castletroy Park Hotel, in its brief four-year history, has experienced a number of discrete phases of turbulence and growth. The case examines each of these phases, and illustrates a number of structural and contextual dimensions that are unique to the venture. Specifically, the case focuses on business strategy formulation. It also discusses the cultural characteristics of the organisation, focusing in its analysis on the human resource management dimensions. A market review is also included. The case concludes with an exploration of future growth strategies.

Bunratty Banquet

This case examines the conceptualisation and subsequent development of a mid-west tourism attraction at Bunratty, Co. Clare. The case tells of how, at a time when an increasing number of airlines were overflying Shannon Airport, it became apparent that a tourism innovation was necessary to generate much-needed tourism revenue in the region. The contribution of the key players to the proposed project are discussed, with particular attention focused on the "genesis" of one individual, Brendan O'Regan. The idea of a banquet at Bunratty is considered in a commercialisation context, as is the extension of the concept to include a separate form of banqueting entertainment at Knappogue Castle near Quin, Co. Clare, and at Dún Guaire Castle near Kinvara, Co. Galway. The case ends with a short discussion on possible future tourism strategies for the region.

Jury's Hotel Group

This case begins by discussing the evolution and growth of this leading Irish hotel group. It examines in detail the factors that have contributed to its success to date. The organisation's structure and culture are explored, as are possible future growth strategies. A detailed account of the group's Total Quality Management strategy is made, specifically in respect of the ISO9002 Quality Management Standard. The case includes a brief overview of the Irish hotel industry. The market outlook for Jury's is also examined, principally in a UK context. The case considers the recent financial performance of the group, and concludes with a review of the current key trends.

Campbell-Bewley Group

This case describes the development of Campbell Catering, and the substantial acquisition and integration of the Bewley's café chain in 1986. It examines the difficulties encountered by Campbell Catering in its initial growth phase, focusing on its industrial relations strife and off-share catering contracts. Learning from its experience, the catering company sought to develop through acquisitive growth and expansion. In this context, the case explores the Bewley acquisition, probing specifically on the funding and complex ownership of the café chain. The restructuring of the combined organisation is also examined. The group's recent joint ventures are appraised, while some of the group's acquisition and franchising strategies are also discussed. There is an interesting account of how the group managed to procure the lucrative channel tunnel catering contract. Total Quality Management and ISO9000 also feature significantly in the case, which concludes with a review of the group's very recent financial performance.

Berkeley Court Hotel

The case on the Berkeley Court begins by describing the development of this exclusive Dublin five-star hotel. The appeal of the hotel's location, and the décor and general ambience found within, provides an interesting prelude to the more concrete discussions found later in the case. In a very specific way, the case reviews the five-star hotel market in Dublin, thus providing a valuable insight into the nature of immediate competition for the Berkeley Court. The hotel's marketing strategies are extensively appraised, as is its current market outlook.

Mosney Holiday Centre

The case on Mosney Holiday Centre begins by recounting the development of this Co. Meath-based holiday attraction. Consisting of accommodation facilities and numerous fun attractions, the holiday centre has experienced mixed fortunes throughout its 47-year history. Originally opened as Butlins holiday camp, the centre went through a period of decline during the 1970s before it was purchased by its current owner, Phelim McCloskey, in 1981. With investment in new attractions and accommodation facilities, the centre has experienced consistent growth in sales and profitability since. The case examines the target market served by the centre, and reflects on the nature of the Mosney product mix. The organisational structure is examined. Product pricing policies are discussed, as is the promotion and marketing of the centre. Explored also are the various elements contributing to the recent success of the resort. The case concludes with a short note on the future of the organisation.

CIE Tours International

Beginning with a brief history of the company, the case on CIE Tours International examines the organisational and strategic development of this state-sponsored coach tourism operator. Formally established in 1929, the company has since provided a very high standard of personalised service — one that has been suitably tailored to meet the demands of an affluent and discerning customer base. The case discusses the international dimension of the organisation, as well as documenting the mission, structure, and marketing strategies of the product packages on offer. In a specific way, the international marketing strategies of the company are examined, as is the approach adopted in an Irish market context. The recent financial performance is reviewed, including a note on the positive implications of current strategies implemented by the organisation. The case ends with a brief discussion on the future of the organisation.

The Semi-State Sector

Aer Lingus

The Aer Lingus story is one of success, setback and possible future recovery. In recounting the evolution of the organisation, the case tells of how the company developed its transatlantic operations, and of how it diversified into aircraft brokerage and maintenance. There is a detailed discussion of the company's four business groupings. Also examined is the development of TEAM Aer Lingus as a subsidiary specialising in high-quality, quick turnover and cost-effective maintenance. The recent difficulties experienced by the airline are discussed, particularly in respect of the amendment to the Shannon stop-over. The Cahill Rescue Plan is examined, as are the implications of its implementation. A brief discussion of recent non-core asset disposal is also included in the case. The proposed transatlantic strategic alliance with US airline, Delta, is examined, as is the recent financial performance of the company. The case concludes with a discussion on the future of the airline.

The Electricity Supply Board

This case begins with an overview of the business activities of the ESB, paying particular attention to the structure of the organisation. There follows a piece on the evolution of the organisation over three discrete phases in its development to date. The implications of the world recession during the period 1973–78 reflects on the dependency of the company on oil, and on how the organisation managed subsequently to adapt its operations to fit with a changing business environment. The case includes a detailed discussion on the organisational reforms undertaken during the 1980s, and examines the workings and recommendations of a joint-steering committee established in the aftermath of the 1991 strike. The eight key issues identified by the committee as being central to the achievement of quality working relationships in the company are explored, specifically because they frame the formulation context of the organisation's future strategic direction. The appointment of McKinseys Inc., the international business consultants, to work with senior management on a dynamic blueprint for the future of the organisation is examined. Also discussed is the proposal to restructure the organisation radically, so as to make it comparably efficient with other European producers and suppliers of electricity. A section of the case reviews the recent financial performance of the company. The ancillary activities of the ESB as a diversified organisation are also examined, as is the human resource dimension of the business activities. The external business environment is analysed, while the case ends with a note on the future of the company in a competitive European context.

Telecom Éireann

The case on Telecom Éireann begins with a general evaluation of the organisation's activities to date. The contention that the national telecommunications service is now a fundamentally different operation from what it was a decade ago, is discussed, with particular attention paid to the development of the organisational structure, and the infrastructural investment in telecommunications technology. There is a brief note on the chief executive of the organisation, and on his predecessor. The strategy for the future of the organisation is examined, with a specific focus on the implications of European telecommunications deregulation. The international competitive environment is analysed to determine the potential feasibility of a strategic alliance for Telecom. The company's diversification strategy is reviewed, as is the recent financial performance of the company. A considerable part of the case focuses on a number of ethical issues raised by the decision to purchase the former Johnson, Mooney and O'Brien site in Dublin. The implications of the decision are discussed, as are the findings of the formal inquiry set up to examine the bona fides of the purchase.

Shannon Airport: The Aeroflot Connection

Beginning with a brief overview of the strategic significance of the airport, the case on Shannon Airport focuses on a specific innovative development in Irish civil aviation, namely a strategic alliance with the Russian airline, Aeroflot. Because of the combined recessionary effects of the 1970s fuel crises, Shannon experienced a decline in technical transit traffic, which, since the airport's inception, has directly influenced the profitability performance of the airport. Responding to this decline, the airport entered into an operational agreement with Aeroflot. The case examines the cost implications, the project planning process, and the operational and financial benefits accruing to both Shannon and Aeroflot. In a brief way, the case discusses the possible future development of commercial enterprises built around the Shannon experience.

Multinational Companies and Manufacturing

Waterford / Wedgwood

Beginning with a discussion on the group's evolution to date, this case examines an Irish multinational company in the context of turbulence and change. It describes the structural development of Waterford Glass, and the strategic expansion initiated at various stages in the company' development. The labour-intensive nature of the crystal industry is undermined, as are the implications of the company's concentric diversification strategy. The decline in the company's profitability is traced to the recessionary business environment of the 1980s. Specifically, the case focuses on the acquisition of the Wedgwood group in 1986. Accordingly, the acquisition is reviewed in respect of the synergistic benefits afforded to both companies. The case critically examines the 1987 restructuring programme implemented in both the Waterford and Wedgwood divisions. Operating and marketing strategies in both divisions are also reviewed. An appraisal of the recent financial performance is made, while the case concludes with a discussion on business strategies for the future.

Guinness Peat Aviation

This case is introduced by a brief description of the world's largest operating leaser of modern commercial aircraft, GPA. It describes the nature of the group's business up to the end of 1992, and considers the development of GPA in the context of a dynamic and turbulent external business environment. GPA was founded in 1975 by Dr Tony Ryan, a former employee in the leasing department of Aer Lingus. Ryan found that, because Aer Lingus was operating with aircraft surplus to requirements, it could capitalise on this position by leasing the surplus to other airlines. Guinness Peat Aviation came into being on this basis of this leasing concept. The case examines the growth patterns experienced by the company over the years, particularly the 1980s, when the group generated phenomenal increases in profitability. Through the efficient use of tax-effective packages for its investors, the company managed to insulate itself, to some extent, against the turbulence of the marketplace. The case discusses the various business activities undertaken by the company. Principally, these activities are organised in three business units: leasing; capital; and technologies. The case also contains a profile of key directors and shareholders in the company. Financial policies and performance indicators are reviewed. Because the company has an extensive knowledge of the airline industry, it can use this information as an industry-competitive advantage. The internal characteristics of the organisation are also discussed. The failed flotation attempt in June of 1992 is examined, as are the implications of this failure for future capital requirements. The subsequent "white knight" intervention in the form of General Electric (GE) is also examined. The case concludes with a brief discussion on the future prospects for the company, particularly in view of the competence and experience capability it has built up over the years.

Analog Devices (Ireland)

The case on Analog Devices introduces the company in a global context. There follows a general description of the integrated circuits (ICs) produced by the company. The Irish subsidiary is examined, highlighting in particular the cultural and structural development of the company. The corporate strategy process is comprehensively reviewed, as is the nature of the Irish semiconductor industry. A detailed examination of the competitive factors affecting Analog is made, with particular reference to new product development and the manufacturing process. Key factors contributing to the success of the company are explored: computer integrated manufacturing; artificial intelligence; subcontracting. The case concludes with a review of recent financial performance.

Irish Distillers Ltd.

This case begins by recounting the amalgamation of three renowned Irish distillers. It describes how the new organisation managed to overcome the difficulties associated with such a move, particularly in respect of operational and cultural expectations. The strategic focus of the organisation is examined, as are the various restructuring programmes undertaken by the company in response to challenging environmental pressures. A detailed account is provided of the GC&S takeover bid, and of how the French Pernod Ricard subsequently managed to acquire the company. Accordingly, the implications of the Pernod takeover are discussed in three contexts: brand distribution; management restructuring; marketing strategy. A review of the company's recent financial performance is made, while the case concludes by examining a number of possible strategies for the future.

Irish Chemical Industry

The case begins by defining the nature of the chemical industry in Ireland. It reviews the economics of the industry and examines the contribution of Irish subsidiaries to worldwide operations. The general business environment is discussed, while a profile of five industry performers provides specific insights into the development of business competitive advantage in the industry. The focus of this discussion is on core-competence development, flexible manufacturing systems, and speed. Workforce management policies are explored, with particular attention paid to decentralised responsibility and teamwork. The training needs of the industry are discussed, as is the strategic importance of total quality management.

Jefferson Smurfit Group

The case begins by profiling the evolution of this successful Irish multinational company. A very detailed account is provided on the development of the packaging industry in Ireland. The company's acquisition and diversification strategies are examined over a three-decade period. The effects of the recessionary economic conditions of the 1980s are described, focusing in particular on the extensive integration and re-organisation programmes implemented by the company. A section of the case discusses the flotation of the Jefferson Smurfit Corporation (JSC) in the United States. The key factors contributing to the company's success to date are also explored. The structural development of the company is examined in great detail, as are the management control systems in place. The company's human resource management strategies are considered, while attention is also focused on the total quality dimensions of operations. The case concludes with a review of the company's recent financial performance.

Kerry Group plc

The introduction to this case provides a brief introduction to the activities of Kerry Group plc. There follows a brief discussion on the plc status of the group, and the diversification of the group into the poultry and pigmeat markets. The various strategies implemented by the group are discussed, as are the structural and cultural characteristics of the organisation. Particular attention is paid to the management style and strategic leadership of the group's managing director, Denis Brosnan. The group's recent financial performance is also reviewed. The case concludes with a discussion on potential future strategies for the organisation.

Kentz Corporation

The Kentz case begins with an overview of the group's activities. There follows a comprehensive review of the factors leading to the group's collapse in early 1994. The implications of the collapse are discussed at length, as is the rescue plan drawn up by the group's examiner following the collapse. A financial overview of the group's financial performance prior to the collapse is also included. The case includes a detailed environmental analysis of the group. Kentz personnel/human resource policies are examined in the concluding sections of the case.

Allergan Pharmaceuticals (Ireland) Ltd.

The Allergan case represents one of the few cases in this book which focuses on a foreign multinational company operating in Ireland. The case outlines the establishment of Allergan and describes its main competitors in the Irish market. There is also a focus on the internal strengths of the company and how it has to adapt to manage its external environment effectively.

References

Easton, G. (1982): *Learning from Case Studies*, London: Prentice Hall.

Thompson, L. (1995): "What Goes into a Management Case Study?", in Richardson, B., Montanheiro, L. and O Cinneide, B. (eds.), How to Research, Write, Teach and Publish Management Case Studies, Sheffield: PAVIV Publications.

Figure 1

Case Study	Organisation Structure	Organisation Culture	Business Environment Analysis	Overall Strategic Analysis	Diversification Strategy	Acquisition Strategy	Financial Management	HRM	Marketing Strategy	Total Quality	Managing Change
Avonmore Foods plc		*	*								
Bailey's Irish Cream				*			*		*		
Waterford Foods plc	*	*		*	*	*	*			*	
Ritz			*						*		
The Pig Industry in Ireland			*						*		
The Irish Horse			*	*					*		
Castletroy Park Hotel	*	*	*					*	*		
Bunratty Banquet			*						*		
Jury's Hotel Group plc	*	*	*	*			*			*	
Campbell-Bewley Group	*					*	*			*	
Berkeley Court Hotel			*						*		
Mosney Holiday Centre	*								*		
CIE Tours International	*		*	*			*		*		
Aer Lingus	*		*	*	*		*				*

Figure 1 (continued)

Case Study	Organisation Structure	Organisation Culture	Business Environment Analysis	Overall Strategic Analysis	Diversification Strategy	Acquisition Strategy	Financial Management	HRM	Marketing Strategy	Total Quality	Managing Change
ESB	*		*		*		*	*			*
Telecom Éireann			*		*	*	*				
Shannon Airport			*								
Waterford/Wedgwood					*	*	*	*	*		
GPA/General Electric		*	*	*			*				*
Analog Devices (Ireland)	*	*	*	*			*	*			
Irish Distillers Ltd	*					*	*	*	*		*
Jefferson Smurfit Group	*			*	*	*	*	*		*	
The Irish Chemical Industry			*					*		*	*
Kerry Group plc	*	*		*	*	*	*				
Kentz Corporation	*	*	*				*	*			*
Allergan Pharmaceuticals (Ireland) Ltd.			*	*						*	

Part 1

The Agribusiness/Food Sector

1

Avonmore Foods plc: Involvement in Poland

Introduction

Avonmore's history begins back in the 1960s at a time when the Irish dairy industry was very much underdeveloped. In 1967, no fewer than 36 co-operatives, which were operating around the Kilkenny area in the south east of Ireland, came together to form Avonmore Creameries Federation, with Britain's Unigate taking a 23 per cent stake in the new company. This new company was based in Ballyraggett, Co. Kilkenny, where the milk would be centrally processed for the former independent co-ops. This was followed six years later by a merging of 21 of the co-ops into a single society to form Avonmore Co-Ops in 1973, the year Ireland joined the EEC. The new society had 13,000 farmer shareholders and 7,500 milk suppliers.

In 1978, the company bought out Unigate's 23 per cent interest in the processing plant, making it a wholly Irish concern for the first time, although marketing links between the two partners to the joint venture remained. A series of further amalgamations and mergers subsequently took place. The new society provided all the necessary services to farmers to help them expand milk production — for example, farm advisory services and the financing of milking machines. This resulted in a dramatic expansion of milk production in the late 1970s and early 1980s.

A critical juncture in Avonmore's history came on 31 March 1984 when, with the introduction of milk quotas and the super levy, the opportunity or right to expand milk production ended. According to group Managing Director, Pat O'Neill:

> We had been increasing our milk throughput by between 10 and 14
> per cent a year during the 70s and early 80s and, but for the im-
> position of the super levy we would have doubled it again before
> the end of the decade ... we had no choice but to look for alternative
> routes to develop (*Co-Op*, 1993: 22).

These changes culminated in the company deciding to take a de-
cisive step along the expansionist road in 1988, when Avonmore
Foods plc was established with a view to obtaining a Stock Exchange listing. This was one way of attracting outside investment
into the group without having to alter its fundamental status as a
co-op. Avonmore Foods acquired control of all the assets and undertakings in Avonmore Foods plc, and currently holds 63.5 per
cent of the company. According to Group MD, Pat O'Neill, in the
process of going public they had set out a five-point plan:

> The strategy we set out for the investment institutions involved a
> five-point plan: adding-value on milk and grain, developing the
> cheese business, developing the liquid milk side, particularly outside
> Ireland, developing in meat processing, which we had just started in
> Roscrea and developing food ingredients (*Co-Op*, 1993: 22–3).

Figure 1.1: Turnover of Avonmore Foods plc, 1988–94

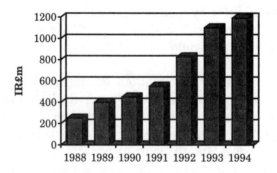

Source: Avonmore Foods plc, Annual Report 1994.

As a result of a continued decline in total milk intake, resulting
from the EU's continued quota restriction policy, Avonmore would
have to acquire new sources of the raw material, milk, if it was to
maintain its dramatic growth. This has resulted in Avonmore

pursuing an expansionist policy since 1988. This aggressive expansionist policy has resulted in an outstanding performance between 1988 and 1993.

Figure 1.2: Avonmore Foods Profit Before Tax, 1988–94

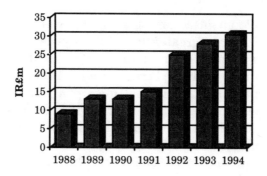

Source: Avonmore Foods plc, Annual Report 1994.

History of Avonmore's Involvement in Poland

The Irish Co-Operative Society (ICOS), the umbrella group for the Irish co-ops, in a prelude to the internal market of 1992, had been encouraging the larger co-ops to consider merging in preparation for the inevitable competition that would result in a boundary-free Europe after 1992.

Meanwhile, two of Ireland's largest co-ops, Avonmore Foods plc and Waterford Foods plc were having talks about merging in anticipation of the new internal market. Avonmore realised that there would be inevitable job losses resulting from the proposed merger, and decided to set up a consultancy that would try to find alternative outlets for the skills and experiences of its employees. This led soon after to the setting up of Avonmore Consultancy Services (ACS), by Hugh O'Rourke, Development Manager for the Milk Products Division and Kevin O'Boyle, an independent management consultant on contract to Avonmore.

The idea behind ACS was to offer consultancy to organisations and governments, both at home and abroad, on all aspects of agribusiness: from the farm level through processing to the consumer marketplace. According to the ACS brochure, Avonmore's key skills and competencies lay within two parallel areas.

> The combination of technical excellence at all levels and the ability to organise resources on the ground to create maximum benefit for our shareholders, is complimented by a comprehensive understanding of the need to apply structural management processes, to ensure the consistency of quality throughout our organisation (ACS brochure).

A second development occurring at a time when western Europe was moving towards greater integration, was the collapse and disintegration of the former Centrally-Planned Economies (CPE) of Eastern Europe and the Former Soviet Union (EEFSU). This situation resulted in the EU setting up a number of aid programmes to help the fledgling democracies to make the transition from a CPE to a Market-Oriented Economy (MOE). One of the main programmes set up to help with the transformation process was the Poland-Hungary Assistance for the Restructuring of their Economies (PHARE) programme.

Initial Visit to Poland

ACS believed that there might be a number of opportunities to gain consultancy experience in eastern Europe, in their attempt to establish an international consultancy task record. With this in mind, Kevin O'Boyle and Hugh O'Rourke, the people responsible for setting up ACS, made an initial fact-finding visit to Poland in June 1991. The first problem they encountered was finding out how to get involved in the PHARE programme. Their first course of action involved contacting the Irish Embassy in Warsaw, which was very accommodating towards the Avonmore party, but was unable to give a lot of advice regarding PHARE projects. The second course of action was more informal. Kevin approached a friend of his, Mr Tony Doran, who was on contract from the International Finance Corporation (IFC), an offshoot of the World Bank, as a special adviser to the Polish Prime Minister. Tony advised them of two possible ways forward. First, to contact the Ministry of Agriculture, and secondly, to contact the Chief Liquidator of the Central Union of Dairy Co-Ops (CUDC), Mr Wladna.

On approaching the Ministry of Agriculture, the Avonmore party met with the typical bureaucratic response that might be expected from a state body — which basically amounted to the details of ACS being taken from them and put on file. The next approach was to meet Mr Wladna, Chief Liquidator of the CUDC.

Mr Wladna was interested in showing the group a milk processing facility in a place called Kozygowa, outside Poznan in the
western part of Poland. During the days of the Centrally Planned
Economy, it was intended that a state-of-the-art super plant be
built in Kozygowa, which had been designed for a capacity of up to
800,000 litres of milk per day, although the physical size of the
plant would indicate an output capacity way in excess of this. This
interested Kevin and Hugh, in theory, as it sounded very like
what Avonmore had done in Ballyraggett, Co. Kilkenny, when it
built one of the most modern and largest dairy-processing plants
in western Europe at the time.

Second Visit to Poland

Kevin O'Boyle, Hugh O'Rourke and the Farm Services manager
from Avonmore, Michael O'Reilly, made a second visit to the Polish market during the summer of 1991. The three men were taken
on a fact-finding visit to the Kozygowa plant. However, there were
some inherent problems with Kozygowa. First of all, lack of finance meant that the plant was only half completed by 1988, and
in the process had also accumulated a huge debt. Secondly, there
was the problem of organised milk supply — basically there
wasn't any. As the men in the Avonmore party walked around the
plant, they were increasingly losing interest in Kozygowa as any
sort of viable initiative with which to proceed.

Yet, a number of interesting points emerged later from talks
with one of the managers from Poznan Co-Op, the largest supplier
of liquid milk in the area, and the principal promoters of the super plant. First of all, a Japanese corporation, Marubenni, had
been interested in Kozygowa for the manufacture of cheese curd
for onward processing in Japan, but lost interest in the idea when
it had been unable to secure sufficient assurances as to the continuity of supply for quality milk. Secondly, most of the co-ops in the
region were over 30 years old and were in need of some kind of
immediate investment if they were to survive in the short to medium term.

At the back of the Avonmore team's minds was the fact that
Kozygowa was never really going to take off as such, but at least it
was a good catalyst for talks with Marubenni. Avonmore and Marubenni met, and it was agreed by both parties that some sort of development plan should be drawn up for the region's dairy industry.

The Project Proposal was written and submitted to the Ministry of Agriculture, where it would receive the attention of Mr Lonc, who was in the process of setting up the Foundation for Assistance Programmes for Agriculture (FAPA). FAPA, an EU-funded aid-assistance programme, was primarily being set up to prioritise and decide on the level of aid-assistance that each proposal would receive. Having submitted the Project Proposal to FAPA, Mr Lonc assured ACS that its proposal would be high up on the list of priorities for funding.

In October of 1991, two months after the Project Proposal was submitted, Kevin O'Boyle returned to Poznan to make a presentation to the co-ops of the Poznan Wojevod. O'Boyle communicated the idea that Avonmore was in the process of looking for funding in Warsaw to carry out a development plan for the region. The presentation was about the Irish co-op system and how it has progressed from a starting point similar to the current Polish one, to a modern, competitive and efficient dairy industry. The goal of the presentation was to encourage interested co-ops to participate in the proposed development plan for the region.

It was in October of 1992 that Avonmore learned from FAPA that its Development Plan was to be aid-assisted under the PHARE programme. Avonmore initially thought that it would have people on the ground in Poland to undertake the development study in January of 1992.

The Development Plan

The principal objective of the study was as follows:

> To prepare an analysis of the sectors of milk production and processing in the vovoidships of the Wielkopolska region and an integrated action plan for the development of these sectors (PHARE Project No. P9105, s. 1.1: 2).

The principal findings of the report may be summarised as follows:

- The Dairy Industry is at present in a continuing decline because of lack of affordable investment funds at farm and processing levels. Herd slaughters, resulting from disease and fodder shortages, are not being replaced. Some state farms are going out of business, and private farmers do not have confidence in the continuation of a stable industry.

- The industry in the area is very fragmented with a large number of small co-ops, each with one or more processing plants. All have suffered declines in milk supply over the past four years from 20 per cent to 40 per cent. Consequently, there is a large overcapacity chasing a shrinking milk supply.

- The shortages of milk lead to processors paying relatively high prices for poor quality milk because of a focus on butterfat quantity instead of milk quality. Hence there is a knock-on effect to the consumer products, with shelf lives of only one day being common. This compares to 7 or 8 days in Ireland.

- At the market level there is a multitude of products with little specialisation being adopted by individual co-ops. Competition between co-ops is conducted mainly on a price basis.

- The fragmented nature of the milk pool and the marketplace is at present unattractive to investors.

The problems outlined above are primarily caused by what are perceived to be structural deficiencies in the organisation of a viable milk pool in order to create a climate for investment. The report recommends consolidation of the existing co-ops of the region into one or more strong farmer-owned bodies representing milk pools of 250–400 million litres, in order to be of a competitive scale and to be attractive to international sources of finance as prospective joint-venture partners. Further, the suggested scale would enable the aid agencies to focus their activities on a local recipient in such a way that long-term sustainable results could be achieved following initial pump-priming interventions.

A model for a future dairy industry within the region is outlined below, and this has been used as a basis for discussion between all the interested parties, receiving general acceptance as the stated vision for the future structure of the Wielkopolska dairy industry.

Following completion of the development plan, a series of meetings was held with the dairy co-operatives of the region on an individual and joint basis, at which the contents of the development plan and the Irish dairy co-operative experience were discussed. The co-ops of the region were invited to join the Wielkopolska Dairy Group (WDG) by entering into a legal agreement, committing themselves to work together with Avonmore and the Polish Business Advisory Service (PBAS) to develop a workable business and restructuring plan. On 25 November 1993, the representatives of a group of 23 co-ops, having received the approval of their supervisory boards, came together in Poznan to sign the co-operation agreement which underpins the Wielkopolska Dairy Group. At the same time, the members nominated three farmers from each co-op to form a Farmers' Council, which will have specific functions as part of the Business Planning Process.

Figure 1.3: Future Model for the Wielkopolska Dairy Industry

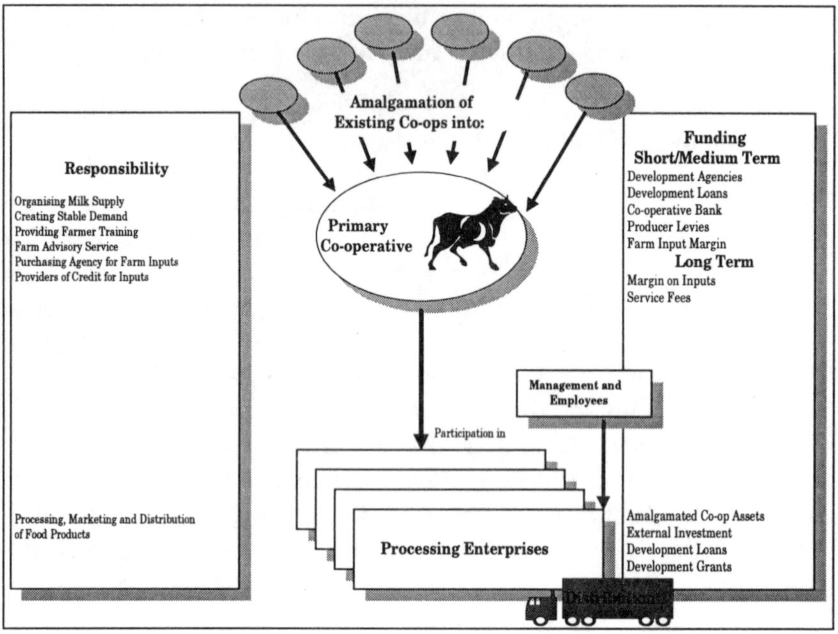

Since the beginning of 1994, the participants in the Business Planning Process have been working towards the completion of this process in order to achieve a number of objectives, primarily though to define the funding requirements of a restructured amalgamated co-operative, and to develop a modern processing venture to meet current needs within chosen local and national markets capable of consuming the production capacity of the participating WDG members.

Choosing the Polish Market

Environmental Analysis

Choice of Market: The primary reason for choosing Poland was not a strategic decision in the traditional sense. Entering the Polish market was not the result of some formal planning process by top management. According to Mr Kevin O'Boyle:

> In general, top management weren't all that interested in the project, at least nothing more than a "coffee morning interest" (O'Boyle, 1994c).

On the contrary, the process may be described as an informal one, in which Avonmore Consultancy Services (ACS) went to Poland to gain consultancy experience through the many EU-funded assistance programmes that existed. However, having made contact with a number of co-operatives in the Wielkopolska region, Avonmore realised that the problems facing the Wielkopolska dairy region were very similar to those that Avonmore had faced more than 25 years previously.

This would suggest that two levels of strategic planning exist within the organisation, which can be approximately described as visible and invisible planning. Visible strategic planning occurs when top management decides in a formal process its long-term goals and objectives, and allocates the necessary resources in order to attain these goals. Invisible strategic planning occurs when top management is aware of a project, such as Avonmore's proposed involvement in Poland, but does not highlight or incorporate such a venture into its formal planning process. However, the project may become operationalised into the formal planning process at a later stage.

Pace of Reform: Five successive governments have committed themselves to a pace of reform that is unprecedented in eastern Europe. The relative success of this course of action can be seen in the following statistics: the government's budget deficit has fallen from 7 per cent of GDP in 1989 to below 3 per cent in 1993. Inflation has fallen from a peak of 640 per cent in 1989 to 38 per cent in 1993. Most significantly, Poland's economy grew by 4 per cent in real terms in 1993, the fastest growth in Europe, east or west. In this context, Avonmore realises that if the ongoing commitment to the current pace of reform continues, the prospects for the long term in Poland are good.

Poland is in a transitional stage at the moment. There is a certain amount of disillusionment at the moment, because the people of Poland are disappointed that the utopia they thought a western-style system would bring has not yet been realised. There is still a lot of work to be done before this change materialises. However, the potential long term is good (O'Reilly, 1994).

Furthermore, Kevin O'Boyle has received the commitment of a number of key politicians regarding Avonmore's proposed venture:

They understand that there will be a need for rationalisation and consolidation in the short term (O'Boyle, 1993).

Therefore, an Irish food company intending to enter an eastern European market should not focus primarily on quantitative criteria such as current rate of inflation or GDP per capita per se, but rather on qualitative criteria such as pace of reform and commitment to sustaining that reform in the future. Evidence of quantitative criteria as outlined should determine the suitability of the market in question.

Role of the European Union: There are several factors to consider here. First, the various aid agencies supported by the European Union, such as PHARE, have helped Avonmore to progress from the original project proposal through a development plan on the Wielkopolska region to the business planning stage, which is on-going. Secondly, the EU's priorities regarding Poland should be trade and not aid-oriented. However, Kevin O'Boyle feels that:

To simplify an argument to trade and not aid is to oversimplify the current situation. It is necessary in the short term to have more aid than trade in order ultimately to increase Poland's ability to trade in the longer term (O'Boyle, 1994b).

The level of EU commitment, measured by criteria such as market access and aid assistance, will make one eastern European market relatively more attractive than another, depending on this commitment.

The Common Agricultural Policy (CAP): The CAP is likely to have little or no effect on Avonmore's proposed venture into the Polish market in the short term. Avonmore is likely to focus its resources on the Wielkopolska market in the short to medium term. However, the venture will not find it easy to gain access into the EU market if Avonmore decides to enter in the longer term, as it is likely to find that the powerful farming lobby will not be receptive to cheaper produce from eastern Europe. Therefore, the concerning factor for an Irish food company here is to decide whether it intends to make the domestic Polish market the focus of its selling activities or if it intends to use Poland as a base to export into the EU. The CAP will have a varying effect on an Irish food company in Poland depending on the venture's selling costs.

Polish Agri-Sector: The Polish agri-sector is currently in a position similar to Ireland's agri-sector 30 years ago. First, Polish farms are small and fragmented, the industry is labour intensive, and available machinery is often inefficient and obsolete. Secondly, the physical make-up of the country is in many ways quite similar to Ireland — being generally flat and favourable to farming. Thirdly, as regards the climate, it could again be described as similar to Ireland; however, it is more prone to extremes in the summer and winter. Thus, the Avonmore experience of dealing with a similar set of opportunities and threats in the Irish agri-sector has made Poland a suitable candidate for a potential investment by Avonmore:

> Our own late development and our current surplus of skills, may allow us to help the Polish industry accelerate through the transition stages, from a "production-driven" to a "market-led" focus (O'Boyle, 1994a).

Polish Dairy Sector: The Polish dairy sector faces a number of inherent problems at present. Again, similar to the problems faced by the Polish agri-sector in general, dairy farms are dominated by small private holdings, which has resulted in too many inefficient producers. Furthermore, the Polish farm structure has resulted in a number of local problems when it comes to the collection and quality of milk, with over 10,000 collection points. Moreover, average milk yields per cow are relatively poor. Again, Avonmore has the technical know-how and experience to help the Wielkopolska region to overcome these threats.

Joint-Venture Partner Assessment

Search for Prospective Partners

On arriving in Poland for the first time, Avonmore Consultancy Services (ACS) approached the Irish embassy, where staff were very accommodating towards the Avonmore party, but were unable to give a lot of relevant advice. The second course of action was even more informal. Kevin approached a friend of his, Mr Tony Doran, who was on contract from the International Finance Corporation (IFC) as a special economic adviser to the Polish Prime Minister. Tony advised them of two possible ways forward. First, to contact the Ministry of Agriculture, and secondly, to contact the Chief Liquidator of the Central Union of Dairy Co-Ops (CUDC). The Minister for Agriculture took Avonmore's details, but very little else was proposed. The Chief Liquidator of the CUDC took the group on a visit to a half-finished milk-processing facility near Poznan in western Poland. It was here that Avonmore met, and began initial talks with, local dairy co-ops of which the Wielkopolska Dairy Group (WDG) now comprises.

Screen those Partners Identified

When selecting a partner, there should be strategic synergy between the prospective partners. Strategic synergy exists when one organisation's weaknesses are compensated by the prospective partner's strengths, and vice versa. In this regard, Avonmore possesses strengths in several areas in which the WDG is weak, and the reverse is also the case.

Table 1.1: Strategic Synergy between Avonmore and the WDG

Avonmore's Strengths	WDG's Weaknesses
Strong Marketing Skills	Weak Marketing Skills
Investment Funding	Lack of Investment Funding
Organisational Know-how	Lack of Organisational Know-how
Avonmore's Weaknesses	**WDG's Strengths**
No Milk Pool	Sizeable Milk Pool
Lack of Local Market Knowledge	Local Market Knowledge

In the analysis of the proposed synergy, the issue of searching for a prospective partner is secondary to that of screening potential partners. In ways, finding a potential joint-venture partner is similar to finding a marriage partner, in that what is important is not how you met the prospective partner but that both partners are compatible, and this compatibility can be measured by the level of strategic synergy between the two prospective partners.

Partnership Success

In determining the probability of partnership success, it is useful to develop a theoretical model that will consider the factors associated with partnership success. The underlying premises giving such a model are twofold. Firstly, that partnerships tend to exhibit certain behavioural characteristics that tend to differentiate them from more conventional organisational relationships. Secondly, while partnerships in general tend to exhibit these characteristics, successful partnerships will exhibit these with more intensity than less successful partnerships. However, before examining these behavioural characteristics, it is necessary to point out the limitations of doing so in respect of Avonmore's involvement in Poland.

Although Avonmore has been involved with the Wielkopolska Dairy Group for nearly three years, a joint venture has yet to be formed. This implies that the model can only be applied to the extent that the two prospective partners, Avonmore and the WDG, have worked together, and may possibly continue doing so in the longer term.

Attributes of the Partnership

The Business Planning stage, carried out and due to be completed by September 1994, is the first example of a co-ordinated effort between Avonmore and the WDG. The project team (primarily Avonmore and the WDG) will carry out the research, assessment, modelling and specification of action/implementation plans in teams addressing specific modules or "workstreams". Each team will have a team leader responsible for specifying the detailed work plans and co-operating with, and reporting to, the project managers on the output plans from their workstream.

Interdependence: Avonmore needs the co-operatives of the Wielkopolska Dairy Group for regular access to their milk pool in order to develop and expand upon the current market for dairy products in the region. Similarly, the WDG co-operatives need Avonmore to help them produce and market milk that is of a sufficiently high quality, enabling the venture to compete both regionally and internationally.

Trust: One of the first problems facing Avonmore was that the dairy co-operatives had an archaic image of large corporations wanting to extract as much as they could from them. Furthermore, Dr Nico Nissen of PBAS, project managers to the proposed venture, feels that:

> There is a fear that Avonmore could be seen as too eager by the dairy co-ops and thus there must be some ulterior motive if they are this eager (Nissen, 1994).

This concept is further articulated by one of the dairy managers:

> Because there is no precedent for this kind of thing, there is a feeling that someone is being altruistic, and that the old motto, beware of Greeks bearing gifts, might be the attitude of many of the farmers towards Avonmore (Szczepaniak, 1994).

However, Avonmore feels that to overcome these issues and to gain the trust of the prospective partners requires time:

> This is the most important thing in order that you understand their expectations as well as their capabilities. Invest time (Cronin, 1994).

Communications Behaviour: There is little or no knowledge of English among the dairy managers. This requires that anything that Avonmore has to communicate to the managers must be translated into Polish. There are several inherent problems with this. First, it is expensive in terms of time and money. Secondly, there is always the problem that some of the meaning or idea is lost in the translation process. According to Michael O'Reilly, Avonmore's Farm Services manager:

> Language is a major problem, one of the biggest problems. It makes it difficult to operate on the ground with a language barrier. For example, there are four or five full-time translators needed for the Avonmore operation in Paszto, Hungary (O'Reilly, 1994).

Information Sharing and Participation: Avonmore Foods plc has been building a sound working relationship and sharing knowledge with the dairy co-operatives of the Wielkopolska region.

Participation: On the issue of participation, Tom Cronin of Prozan made the following statement:

> It's important that the expectations of each partner are clearly understood by the other, before the joint venture takes place. If expectations and capabilities are known beforehand, then you can avoid a lot of disillusionment that can be experienced by both partners in the future (Cronin, 1994).

Conflict Resolution: One of the central issues to emerge from Avonmore's proposed venture in Poland is building partners and partnerships in the Polish Dairy Industry (Agribusiness Conference, 1994). This simply means that in order to achieve its goals, Avonmore needs to have a strong Polish partner — in other words, it is in Avonmore's interest to ensure that the WDG is structured so that it can produce a high-quality, cost-effective product. Currently, the WDG is not in a position to do this, as it does not have the necessary structures, finance and technical know-how to become a strong partner. Avonmore can act as the catalyst, however, to enable the Polish partner to become strong. So a mutual dependency exists, in that Avonmore needs a strong Polish partner, while the WDG needs Avonmore to make it strong. A mutual dependency will invariably produce a certain amount of conflict; however, it is knowing how to deal with this conflict that will determine the eventual success or failure of the partnership.

There are two points here that need to be highlighted with regard to Avonmore's approach to conflict. The first, a general point regarding co-operatives, is that co-ops were founded on the democratic principle that it is the members of the co-op who will ultimately decide on the direction of the co-op. This is still the case in Ireland's largest food company and Ireland's seventh largest company. The second point relates to the WDG and is that Avonmore has adopted a constructive approach to conflict resolution — that is, Avonmore will try to persuade its Polish partners that it is in their mutual interest to form a joint venture rather than trying to coerce the Polish into a venture.

Critical Factors in the Venture

Project Champions

The original idea behind Avonmore Consultancy Services was to provide opportunities for those employees who were likely to be affected by a possible merger between Avonmore and Waterford Foods at the end of the 1980s. ACS went to Poland looking for an opportunity to get involved in one of the PHARE programmes that would allow them to build a consultancy track-record. Poland was not seen by Avonmore as a strategic market — that is, the Polish project is not the result of any formal planning. The Polish project has achieved its current status because of the presence of a champion. Kevin O'Boyle has been championing the project since the beginning, back in June of 1991.

First of all, it was Kevin O'Boyle who wrote and submitted the original project proposal to the Ministry of Agriculture in August 1991. O'Boyle was also responsible for ensuring that the project proposal received sufficient attention so that FAPA eventually grant-aided the development plan for the Wielkopolska dairy region. This was partly achieved by the fact that Avonmore, in an unprecedented move, was willing to bear a substantial portion of the costs of carrying out the development plan by contributing 50,000 ECU. Kevin O'Boyle can also be accredited with receiving grant assistance from the Agricultural Development Fund (ADF), which is part of the British know-how fund. He was able to revive support from the British government for the business-planning stage of the project by arguing that "We're (Avonmore) British as we are Irish" (O'Boyle, 1993), to the extent that half of Avonmore's 7,000 employees were based in the UK, and that Avonmore was also listed on the London Stock Exchange.

Building Strong Partners and Partnerships

Avonmore has taken a long-term view of its proposed investment in Poland with the Wielkopolska Dairy Group. This long-term view consists of ensuring that there are two strong partners to the venture. Avonmore, as one of the strong partners, can provide the necessary marketing skills to sell the end-product to the consumers. However, Avonmore also realises that its marketing skills can only provide a competitive advantage in the short term. The second part of the equation in sustaining a long-term competitive advantage is to ensure that milk is processed at the highest quality level.

It is in Avonmore's interest to ensure that the processing half of the joint venture, the Polish partner, is equally as strong as the Irish partner. Therefore, the appropriate structures have to be put in place, at both the farm level and the processing level, to ensure that there is an incentive for producers and processors alike to produce the highest quality milk in the most cost-effective manner. Kevin O'Boyle believes that in order for the Polish partner to be made strong, it will need the involvement of the various international aid agencies to provide the necessary development capital that will be needed for pump-priming activities at the beginning.

The Importance of Strong Leadership

> You have to act definite and communicate in a certain way which leads people to believe that within certain parameters, things can be done (O'Boyle, 1994d).

The Polish dairy industry is in a difficult transition period at present. It is having to face the reality of market forces for the first time, resulting in some difficult decisions having to be made. The dairy industry cannot make the transition to a market-oriented economy by itself.

The Avonmore Development Plan identified a number of key problems facing the Wielkopolska dairy industry. Primarily, the farms are too fragmented, while the co-ops lack the necessary scale and ability to compete. As a result of these ongoing problems, therefore, the industry has been unable to attract the necessary investment in order to overcome these deficiencies.

Avonmore has proposed a new model of the Wielkopolska Dairy Industry which will allow it to overcome these deficiencies in partnership with the Irish food company. However, Avonmore also realises that among the farmers there is a lot of resistance towards the new model. One dairy manager suggests two possible reasons for this resistance:

> First, the farmers are free from the Communists controlling their destiny for the first time in 40 years, and along arrives this foreign multinational who is asking them to give up this freedom and become part of their idea (Szczepaniak, 1994).

However, Mr Szczepaniak goes on to argue that even though there is a certain amount of resistance to change, there are two things that Avonmore will have to convey:

> Confidence in what we are doing and confidence in the end result. They want to hear that this is the right thing — that everything will be OK. They want to hear strong reasons for why it will succeed. Farmers will be looking to those who will face them, and tell them that this WILL happen — for definite — they need guidance and leadership (Szczepaniak, 1994).

A further example of this was seen during a meeting between Avonmore's representative in Poznan, Mr Tom Cronin, and the manager of Srem Co-Op:

> The farmers realise that there is probably no other way forward at present other than what Avonmore proposes. The farmers will follow if you show them the way (Cronin, 1994).

There is an almost biblical theme underlying this message in that the dairy plant manager is calling on Avonmore to be the Moses that will lead the Wielkopolska dairy to the Promised Land.

Acceleration of Transition through Application of Experience

> The Irish dairy sector has been notoriously fragmented over the years. At one stage literally hundreds of co-ops controlled our relatively tiny national milk quota of around one billion gallons ... Avonmore's history is an excellent example of how our dairy and food industry should have developed over the past 25 years (*The Irish Exporter*, 1991: 5).

There are several parallels to be drawn between the Avonmore experience over the past 28 years and that of the proposed venture between Avonmore and the Wielkopolska Dairy Group in Poland. Avonmore has achieved its success recognising that:

- The milk had to be produced on farms which would be, on average, larger than existing holdings.

- The cost of producing and collecting milk would be reduced by improving the methods used by dairy farmers.

- The quality of milk at all stages needed dramatic improvement in order to meet market requirements.

- The changes required could only come about through strong, dynamic leadership by the Board of Directors and Senior Management.

Similarly, there are parallels to be drawn between the Irish dairy industry in the 1960s and the Polish dairy industry in the 1990s. Twenty-five per cent of Ireland's population was engaged in the agricultural sector in 1966, while there were over 150 dairy co-ops in the same year. By 1991 this figure was reduced to 30. Avonmore believes that its experience is uniquely similar to the development path that Poland's dairy industry now has to travel. Accordingly, Avonmore is convinced it has a major contribution to make to the development of Poland's dairy industry.

The one fundamental difference between Avonmore's experience and that of the Polish Wielkopolska Dairy Group (WDG) is that the Polish do not have a similar period of time, as Avonmore did, to make the transition. The Polish dairy industry faces imminent collapse if a similar transition is not made within the short to medium term. Avonmore's experience can act as the catalyst that will allow the WDG's transition to a market-oriented economy within such a time scale.

Some Important Lessons

EU's Commitment to the Visegrad Region

The EU has committed itself through various aid and trade programmes to assisting some former Centrally Planned Economies (CPEs) more than others. For example, the EU's priorities for the shorter term in eastern Europe are towards the Visegrad countries (Poland, Hungary, the Czech and Slovak Republics). Similarly, Irish companies should be more favourably oriented to these economies when deciding on a market to enter in eastern Europe.

The CAP

The Common Agricultural Policy (CAP) is unlikely to deter an Irish food company's entry into Poland in the short term, especially if the Irish company intends to sell the products of the venture on the domestic market, as Avonmore does. However, there may be longer-term problems in trying to gain access to the EU's market, as resistance to cheaper produce from the East is likely to be intense.

Opportunities and Threats in the Polish Agri-Sector

The opportunities and threats facing Avonmore in the Polish market are similar to those that they faced in Ireland during the 1960s. Their experience of having dealt with this will be crucial in determining the eventual success of the venture.

Joint-Venture Criteria

The joint venture is considered a suitable market-entry strategy for Avonmore's proposed entry into the Polish market. Strategic synergy exists between the two partners, where one partner's weaknesses are compensated by the other's strengths and vice versa. In the case of Avonmore, its strength is in marketing, while the Wielkopolska Dairy Group's is that it has a relatively large milk pool of 250 million to 400 million litres of milk per annum. Partnership success criteria, having been applied to Avonmore, would suggest that the proposed joint venture in the longer term is more likely to be a success than a failure.

Concluding Remarks

Avonmore Foods, having concluded the business planning stage in September 1994, had reached the point where it had to decide whether or not to commit substantially more resources to the proposed venture. According to Gerry Howhey, Corporate Affairs Director:

> We decided not to proceed any further at this stage, not because of any one single reason, but because of a number of factors. We felt that we weren't getting the kind of support we needed from the Polish Government, and the international finance agencies, so we decided not to proceed any further.

As for the future:

> We don't see Poland as a potential place for investment in the immediate future.

References

Co-Op (1993): "Co-Op Ownership Ensures Irish Control", May.

Cronin, T. (1994): an interview with Mr Szczepaniak, manager of Srem Co-Op, Poznan, 9 March.

Irish Exporter, The (1991), 5.

Nissen, N. (1994): interview, PBAS Office, Poznan, 9 March.

O'Boyle, K. (1993): interview, 1 December.

O'Boyle, K. (1994a): "Towards 2000: Agriculture, Agribusiness and the Food Industry in Central and Eastern Europe", Conference Budapest, Hungary, 3–4 March.

O'Boyle, K. (1994b): meeting with the author, 12 May.

O'Boyle, K. (1994c): interview with author, 19 November.

O'Boyle, K. (1994d): interview with author, 1 December.

O'Reilly, M., Farm Services Manager of Avonmore (1994): telephone interview, 10 May.

Szczepaniak, Manager of the Poznan Co-Op (1994): interview with Kevin O'Boyle, Poznan, 8 March.

"Towards 2000: Agriculture, Agribusiness and the Food Industry in Central and Eastern Europe", Conference (1994): Budapest, Hungary, 3–4 March.

Questions

1. Discuss the role played by a project champion such as Kevin O'Boyle in the case of Avonmore in Poland.

2. How does this case illustrate the concept of emergent strategy? What potential gains and pitfalls are associated with an emergent strategy in the context of Avonmore in Poland?

2

Bailey's Irish Cream

Introduction

Bailey's Original Irish Cream Liqueur is currently believed to be the most profitable product within the International Distillers and Vintners Group (IDV) portfolio, the drinks division of Grand Metropolitan and the top-earning non-aged spirit drink in the world. It ranks fifteenth in the world's top 100 spirit brands, and for 1992 it achieved profits of £102.6 million. It is the Dublin-based R&A Bailey & Co. that manufactures and markets the product, and R&A Bailey recently launched a new brand, "Sheridan's", which it is hoped will emulate the success of Bailey's.

The company has extended its product range to include Bailey's Light for the US market, Bailey's Gold for Japan, and other cream liqueurs such as Emmet and O'Darby, and the new product, Sheridan's, which has sold more than 100,000 cases in its first year. Gilbeys of Ireland (Manufacturing) Ltd., which is part of the Gilbeys Group and which is also the Irish wine and spirits subsidiary of Grand Metropolitan International Distillers and Vintners, produces Bailey's and Sheridan's for R&A Bailey & Co. With turnover of over £180 million, R&A Bailey & Co. is the largest element within the Gilbeys of Ireland Group.

Product Growth and Development

The growth and development of Bailey's Irish Cream can only be described as phenomenal, and it is a success story that continues to flourish. For instance, the 1992 annual sales of the product reached 3.8 million cases, and to facilitate this continued growth and to accommodate new brand development a new £14 million state-of-the-art manufacturing plant was opened in 1992. Launched in 1975, Bailey's is now sold in over 160 countries worldwide, with the most important market up to five years ago being the US, which accounted for up to 50 per cent of sales. Since Bailey's first took off in the US, this figure has fallen to 30 per cent, but this has been compensated for by the faster growth rate being achieved in Europe and other markets. Up to a million cases are sold in the US and a further 2 million cases are sold in Europe every year. The success of Bailey's Irish Cream was not achieved overnight — for instance, in the Italian market it was only after six years of hard graft that sales of Bailey's took off, reaching its present level of 200,000 cases per year. Much of the product's growth is a result of the considerable amount of money invested in the brand every year, with a budget of £50 million available, funded equally between R&A Bailey and its international distributors.

R&A Bailey advertises and promotes the brand very heavily: the company is in the top five advertising spend of spirit brands in the world, which accounts for much of the success of the product. Also, the growth of the product has been helped by IDV's strategy of gaining ownership of its worldwide distribution network, which has allowed the company to exercise more control over Bailey's marketing and development, leading to higher profit margins. IDV now controls more than 95 per cent of its distribution network worldwide. One of the major strengths of IDV, and of considerable benefit to its subsidiaries like R&A Bailey, is the fact that it has about 50 marketing companies spread around the globe, with the result that there is a vehicle already in place to take up new products and to develop further existing ones. Bailey's Irish Cream benefited from this system when it was launched, and the new brand Sheridan's has also benefited.

Bailey's is very much a premium global brand and, despite inflation rates in many of its markets working against it, has still been able to increase profitability. It has been the policy of management to add value to the brand through top-quality advertising, packaging and promotions, thus, it is hoped, achieving the company's aim of a value/price balance so that any price increase will be reflected in added value to the product for the consumer.

As noted, Bailey's is one of the most lucrative products within the IDV portfolio and the world's most profitable non-aged spirit drink; some would even consider it the world's most successful dairy product. The cream base for the product is produced by Virginia Milk Products, formerly part of the Express (Grand Met) group and now part of Waterford Foods, where up to 40 million gallons of milk are used annually in the process. Bailey's is distributed in all of its key markets by Grand Met subsidiaries, but the global marketing strategy is controlled and directed from Ireland. Although R&A Bailey is a subsidiary of Grand Met-owned IDV, the company is allowed considerable autonomy. While Grand Met exercises considerable control over financial reporting procedures, R&A Bailey is given substantial leverage as regards managing the brand, including formulating the marketing strategy.

Strategy behind the Success of Bailey's Original Irish Cream

Bailey's was launched in Ireland in 1974 and on the international market in 1975. Backed by the resources of the British-owned giant, Grand Metropolitan, it has enjoyed phenomenal success, with R&A Bailey using a marketing strategy which has made the product the most successful new Irish brand of the past 20 years. The original goal for the product was to sell about 100,000 cases per year, but this was a major underestimation of the product's success because, within five years, up to a million cases were being sold and the company currently sells just under 4 million cases per year. Translated into retail terms that is nearly 50 million bottles of Bailey's a year coming off the production line in Dublin. The product's explosive growth was helped in part by the marketing of Bailey's as an "on the rocks" drink.

As a new product, establishing the brand in the international markets was a considerable challenge for the company, and one that had to be achieved within a short space of time. If R&A Bailey had not established its presence quickly, competitors would have been quick to cash in on the company's product success. The company went about establishing the product in a logical and systematic manner with a focus on building a distribution network by gaining support and help from distributors to import and sell to their local markets. The next step was to introduce the product physically to the markets using the tasting method, which the company believed was the key to the successful development of the brand. R&A Bailey still uses the method to remind the market of the product and to introduce the drink to new consumers.

While the company was working on gaining international success, it did not neglect the home market. It believed that it was important to have a strong home base and to let the international world know that Bailey's had a strong profile in its home territory. Another marketing strategy of the company was the adoption of central brand building, thus ensuring that the marketing and promotional efforts were the same in all of the product's markets, leading to greater consistency of brand image and continuous reinforcement. All aspects of the marketing strategy are controlled from Dublin, with the result that the same advertisement is seen in Canada, America and across Europe, and global consumers are purchasing Bailey's Irish Cream for the same reasons everywhere — namely, its taste, and its relaxed and easygoing image. These are features of the product that the company's advertising continuously seeks to reinforce.

The strategy of selling the product at a premium price is a deliberate move on the company's part — it is sold at twice the price of its Irish competitors in its various markets. When Bailey's was originally launched in 1974, it was positioned as a mainstream spirit brand, but through advertising and packaging the company was gradually able to position Bailey's as a premium product. Patience has also played a major part in the ground work for Bailey's worldwide assault, which is overseen by three regional directors and eight area managers. Ninety-nine per cent of the company's business is abroad and the company looks to the mainstream spirit brands as its benchmark of excellence, with the aim of being the best in its field.

The company's marketing strategy owes much of its success to Ned Sullivan, who joined the company in 1980 and who worked on the marketing, brand positioning, and pricing of Bailey's Original Irish Cream, and until recently acted as chief executive of the company. Ned Sullivan spent almost six years with Córas Tráchtála (now An Bord Tráchtála) in Milan and London. He joined R&A Bailey as European marketing manager and was made managing director in 1989, on the retirement of David Dand.

David Dand was the mastermind behind Bailey's Irish Cream when he introduced it in 1974, and was very much the hand behind its success. Along with being head of R&A Bailey, he was also chairman of Gilbeys of Ireland and executive chairman of Gilbeys Northern Ireland. He also held a seat on the IDV export board based in London, a move seen by many as recognition of his success with the Dublin-based subsidiary. Under his guidance as chief executive and chairman of Gilbeys of Ireland, he transformed Gilbeys from a £1 million turnover operation, with Ireland as its main market, into a £250 million business by 1992 with markets all over the world. He retired from executive duties in early 1992, and, following this, the management of Gilbeys of Ireland was restructured. David Dand remained a non-executive chairman, thus ensuring a smooth transfer of control, and Gary McCann took over as chief executive with Tom Keaveney as chairman of Gilbeys of Ireland.

New Product Development

The introduction of Sheridan's in October 1992 was part of R&A Bailey's policy to move away from being a single-branded company into a multi-brand one. Sheridan's is the first of its kind and an innovative product, and the company has used this as a selling point. It is unique not just in terms of the drink itself, but also because of its packaging, which features the concept of a split black and white bottle, one part containing Irish cream and the other Irish spirit, with overtones of vanilla ice cream. The idea for the product originated in the early 1980s and the man responsible was Pat Rigney, a director of R&A Bailey. Production got underway in 1989 at Nangor in Co. Dublin, where to date up to £2 million has been invested in the building of new facilities for its production. This new plant is fully automated and contains top-class production facilities. Like Bailey's, Gilbeys launched Sheridan's in Ireland, and spent up to £250,000 on a national advertising and promotional campaign.

Sheridan's retails at £12.99 per bottle. Its success was helped by the fact that its inventors work for one of the few Irish companies, albeit with a foreign parent, with the financial resources to allow for an investment of over £1 million in research and development of a product that might not work. Although all the ingredients are sourced in Ireland, R&A Bailey was unable to find an Irish glass manufacturer to make the very distinctive bottle for Sheridan's. In fact, it is two separate bottles of different size, with the glass blown separately but moulded together by hand, and so the original bottles were made in Italy, and bottles are now made in France and England. The company is pleased that Sheridan's has expanded the Irish liqueur market rather than taking customers from the Bailey's market, which is reflected in the fact that in

Ireland, 1993 sales increased for Bailey's by 14 per cent, and in Britain they increased by 7 per cent.

With such a highly successful product as Bailey's Irish Cream it would be easy to believe that it could not be improved upon. Instead, R&A Bailey discovered that by making slight adjustments the product could be tailored to suit a particular market and so lead to even greater success. Bailey's Light is a very good example of this — it was specifically tailored for the US market with slight modifications being made, enhancing its success.

A similar strategy was adopted for the newly entered Japanese market where Bailey's Original Irish Cream is starting to make a name for itself. Bailey's Gold was specially created for this new market, targeting the "gift-giving" sector of the Japanese market. Following extensive research, the taste, packaging and appearance of the product were changed to suit the requirements of this market. The main difference between Bailey's Original and Bailey's Gold is that in the latter, malt whiskey is used, which makes for a product more suited to Japanese tastes. Research showed that the Japanese had a liking for ten-year-old malt whiskey, and its inclusion in the cream liqueur enabled the retail price to be pushed to twice its usual figure. The name "Gold" was chosen because of the positive aspects this metal has for Orientals, and especially Japanese people. The colour of the product has been changed to give it a "golden" appearance. Considerable attention was paid to packaging, with a slimmer bottle used to give it a more oriental look. There is a new quality opening device, and the Bailey's seal is gold.

The company focused its marketing strategy on the Yokohama area initially, with its tasting sessions carried out using the Bailey's warm, friendly and relaxed concept. The company is targeting upmarket department stores, like Harrods and Brown Thomas, hence the emphasis on packaging includes the presentation box. Bailey's Gold is aimed at the older segment of the market where higher disposable incomes are to be found, which explains the rationale for charging a premium price, while Bailey's Original is priced more reasonably, as Japanese consumers will purchase the product for their own personal use.

New Facilities

In its aim to become a multi-brand company, R&A Bailey recently invested in a new manufacturing facility. This modern 300,000 square foot facility will be used for the production of Bailey's Original Irish Cream Liqueur, Bailey's Light, Sheridan's and any other brand developed by R&A Bailey. It will also be used to make Smirnoff Vodka for the Gilbeys of Ireland group. The idea behind the £14 million investment in new production facilities was to equip the company for future growth and to have the production capacity and technology to lead it into the twenty-first century. Bailey's is reaching sales of 4 million cases and the new facilities will allow another million cases to be produced. Moreover, such facilities give the company the capacity and flexibility to develop new brands and move away from being a single-brand company. Future growth is expected to come from new brand introductions such as Sheridan's, and also from increased sales of the existing brands, with Bailey's leading the way. Furthermore, the company hopes to see increased sales as a result of the addition of the R&J Emmet and J.J. O'Darby labels, two drinks businesses which it acquired in 1991. In total, £36 million was spent in acquiring these two companies and, in the process, R&A Bailey gained two valuable brands to add to its portfolio. The production of Emmet's and O'Darby's is carried out at a separate production site located at Bailieboro in Co. Cavan.

The company sees great room for development in many as yet untapped markets such as the Far East, Latin America, Africa, and also in existing markets in Europe, North America and Australia. The company is viewing the potential of the 120 million Japanese market as its next area for growth and sales, and it has just begun promoting the Bailey's brand in China. The new plant facility in Dublin has increased capacity by 50 per cent, and it has also allowed for improved customer service, considerably increased productivity and reduced product loss, but the most important factor from the company's viewpoint is that quality is assured. About 80 per cent of the £14 million spent on the facility went on plant and equipment. Facilities include a fully automated processing plant; the latest in hardware and software technology; high-speed bottling lines, which enable the production of high-quality consistent packaging; and a plant designed to the latest risk-management standards. The processing plant is unique to Gilbeys of Ireland and Bailey's, and was custom built and designed to maximise product integrity and security. Within the IDV group, Gilbeys of Ireland Manufacturing is recognised as a worldwide centre of excellence for cream liqueur technology, and these new facilities can only add to its high standing.

Sponsorship Deal

In 1995, following a three-year search for a suitable event, the company entered one of the largest sports sponsorship commitments undertaken by any Irish company. At a cost of £5 million, the company signed a five-year contract with the international skating union to sponsor the World and European Ice Skating Championships.

This move fitted in with R&A Bailey's marketing strategy for its core product — Bailey's — because the concept of "Bailey's on Ice" was used in its advertising. It was felt, therefore, that there was an obvious synergism with the events in question. The sponsorship will corner a significant share of the annual marketing budget spent on the product. Such events have considerable audience numbers, which should aid the company in its endeavours to reach new customers.

Financial Results

Bailey's is ranked the world's number one liqueur brand and is placed number 15 in the world's spirit league. It has just short of 4 million cases in sales, worth over £180 million. It accounts for 1 per cent in value of total Irish exports and over 47 per cent in terms of all Irish beverage exports. It is available on most world markets. Because R&A Bailey is part of the international group IDV, its financial results for the year are not separate from its parent company, so it is not possible to determine exactly how well it performed. However, for its half-year results to 31 March 1993, IDV, the drinks division within the group, saw operating profits slip by £26 million sterling to £254 million on turnover down £14 million at £1.66 billion.

In the North American market, sales of Bailey's have been adversely affected by declines in drinks industry volumes, as well as deteriorating trade conditions in some parts of this region. Also, a process of consolidation among wholesalers has resulted in a reduced stock requirement from trade customers. Overall, Grand Met's half-year results showed pre-tax profits increased by 9.6 per cent to £446 million. The group's gearing fell from 83 per cent to 62 per cent because of the sale of assets. Earnings per share were up 14.5 per cent at 15p. While growth for Bailey's itself reached 3.8 billion cases in 1991, the two subsequent years showed how

Table 2.1: Financial Analysis of R&A Bailey

	1989 £m	1990 £m	1991 £m	1992 £m	1993 £m
Turnover	9,298	9,393	8,748	7,913	8,120
Trading Profit	949	1,059	1,063	937	810
Profit Before Tax	732	919	448	913	810
Profit After Tax	516	640	225	618	419
Net Income	1,068	1,069	218	616	164
Retained Profit	901	871	—	370	164
Business Analysis					
Turnover					
• Food	2,872	3,506	2,618	2,647	3,066
• Drinks	2,784	3,000	2,471	2,858	3,418
• Retailing	2,040	2,531	2,531	1,070	1,153

	1989 £m	1990 £m	1991 £m	1992 £m	1993 £m
Profit (Loss) Before Tax					
• Food	245	309	257	186	227
• Drinks	389	473	451	493	561
• Retailing	230	278	187	129	170
Net Assets					
• Food	—	1,651	1,800	1,992	2,131
• Drinks	—	1,427	1,534	1,725	1,778
• Retailing	—	1,869	2,278	1,505	1,751
Geographical Analysis					
Turnover by Origin					
• UK & Ireland	4,668	3,658	2,940	1,872	1,343
• Continental Europe	471	661	862	1,292	1,550
• US	3,720	4,537	4,433	4,184	4,499
• Rest of N. America	174	216	216	185	214
• Africa & Middle East	126	138	145	155	182
• Rest of World	139	157	152	225	332

	1989 £m	1990 £m	1991 £m	1992 £m	1993 £m
Profit (Loss) Before Tax					
• UK & Ireland	424	451	354	319	245
• Continental Europe	66	81	104	117	137
• US	395	475	504	445	576
• Rest of N. America	20	21	20	19	26
• Africa & Middle East	10	10	10	7	15
• Rest of World	52	44	35	30	36
Net Assets					
• UK & Ireland	—	2,500	1,816	1,356	1,312
• Continental Europe	—	427	557	557	630
• US	—	3,149	3,466	3,644	4,048
• Rest of N. America	—	148	128	152	151
• Africa & Middle East	—	11	21	29	31
• Rest of World	—	80	65	77	136

sales have remained static. Yet it would appear that Bailey's is not alone, as sales of the top spirit brands in the world have remained static since 1990. And while Bailey's is the flagship product of R&A Bailey, the company does have other brands in its portfolio that are also putting in an impressive performance. For instance, the acquired brands have justified their purchase. Emmet Classic sells up to 300,000 cases each year, while O'Darby Irish Cream is performing almost as well, with sales of 280,000. Dubliner Irish Cream is proving to be very popular in Italy where sales have reached 50,000 and where sales of Caymana are at 60,000 cases.

Strategy for the Future

The Bailey's brand has a rather unique position in the marketplace. In recessionary times, consumers either go for the value brands or the well-established premium brands, and the company has maintained its high level of spending on advertising of the product through good times and bad. There is less scope for price increases now than in the 1980s, so the key for the future is to add value to the brand through better advertising, promotion, etc. From an advertising point of view, the strategy will be not so much creating awareness and gaining distribution, as concentrating on reinforcement of the image of the product by stressing its quality, authenticity and great taste. It will then focus on uniting these concepts through the company's advertising in all of the product's markets. The aim for the 1990s and the future will be to maintain consistency of message in a contemporary and fashionable manner.

Keeping the product on a growth cycle is difficult when the world market for alcohol is shrinking and the product is already being sold in most countries around the world, though from the company's viewpoint many of these markets are underexploited. Moreover, the company has undertaken a major campaign over the years to "deseasonalise" the product — 75 per cent of the company's business for Bailey's was done between October and December because the customers' perception was that it was a warm "friendly" type of drink. R&A Bailey is trying to change this by targeting the customer who likes long drinks during the warm weather, promoting the product using a concept of "Bailey's Fizz", which essentially means adding to it either soda and ice, or some other mix.

The drinks industry has changed considerably since the late 1980s. People are drinking less and in many countries there is a strong anti-drink policy which has affected the sales of various drink manufacturers. Added to this has been the increased interest in health and fitness. The anti-drinks lobby has been very strong in the US, which in the 1980s was Bailey's major market. For instance, in a five-year period the American market shrank by 4–5 per cent per annum, which represented 25 million cases disappearing from the market. This trend was prevalent in many other markets also such as Australia, Germany and France. On the other hand, there is an increasingly strong demand among consumers for good quality beverages. For Bailey's this is a positive trend because it is a premium brand, with a premium price and an image of quality in all of its markets.

If people are drinking less but drinking better, the aim for the big players in the industry will be to take control of as many of the brand leaders as possible. R&A Bailey is fortunate in this sense in that its parent, the UK-based Grand Met, is becoming one of the leaders in the world brand business. In 1987, for instance, it bought the US company Heublein for £1.2 billion, and in the process took control of the world's biggest-selling vodka, Smirnoff. Just as brands are falling into fewer hands, the same trend is occurring with the distribution networks which can determine the success of a product. Again, R&A Bailey is fortunate in that Grand Metropolitan was at the forefront in the race for the rationalisation of worldwide distribution links, and others have followed its example. The end result of these strategic moves is that 20 per cent of the people are responsible for 80 per cent of the business, and in a shrinking market this degree of concentration is necessary to ensure volume or critical mass. J&B and Malibu supply Grand Met with some of the volume levels required.

With the high level of brand failure, a little luck goes a long way, but to be a success and sustain that success much more than luck is required. For R&A Bailey, extensive market research has played a major part in its new product development, and the Irish company has a brand-development team and manager. It is the group's policy to have over 20 ideas in process at the same time, and of these about three or four are identified as leaders. It also helps to have a good team of people behind a brand and R&A Bailey has at its disposal a team of high-performing, high-quality people with the capacity, ability, creativity and energy to handle all the brands in the company's portfolio, while at the same time maintaining a strong focus on what it considers its business now and in the future — Bailey's Irish Cream. With the long hours and the amount of travelling required, the team also possesses another vital ingredient, namely youth — most managers are in their thirties.

The company's strategy is to recruit the best people, regardless of how long it takes. One of the chief executive's major tasks is to act as a facilitator, to ensure that the culture is there to foster, encourage and develop people's abilities, in order to maximise performance. Being located under the one roof ensures a high degree of communication among team members, with the result that any good ideas developed are transferred rapidly throughout the organisation. The company maintains a good working relationship with its parent company, Grand Metropolitan.

R&A Bailey is optimistic for its future success. It has a good portfolio of brands, to which it is adding all the time, and a strong team to allow the company to grow and prosper. One concern is that, at present, R&A Bailey's product growth is restricted in some countries by quota impositions, tariffs, and a combination of tariffs and restrictive practices. These restrictions have prevented the company exporting the volumes that are achievable, or it has had to price its product at an uncompetitive rate against domestic products in various markets. Accordingly, much attention is being given to the GATT trade agreement which could mean a lift in sales of 10 per cent within five years.

At present, 55 per cent of the product's sales are in Europe, 30 per cent in North America, 5 per cent in Australia/New Zealand and 10 per cent in the rest of the world — only 1 per cent of the sales of Bailey's are in Ireland. For future growth, R&A Bailey is looking to other markets such as South East Asia, and the company hopes to increase sales to Japan and also enter the Indian, Vietnamese and Chinese markets.

Source: Interviews with company personnel.

Questions

1. Analyse the factors that have led to development and growth of Bailey's. Discuss the features of New Product Development that the case illustrates.

2. Develop a model of the cream liqueur market. Comment on the appropriateness of the brand management strategies adopted by Bailey's.

3. Critically assess Marketing's role within the company's business planning. Develop a marketing plan for Bailey's into the next century.

3

Waterford Foods plc

Introduction

Waterford Co-Operative was formed in 1965, resulting from the amalgamation of five co-op societies based in Waterford — Dungarvan Co-Op Creamery Ltd., Kilmeaden, Gaultier, Milvale, and Rathcormack Co-Ops Ltd. These co-ops had been in operation for some years. Dungarvan started operations in 1921, and by 1936 was twice its original size, manufacturing baby foods for the UK-based company Cow & Gate. By 1949, it had diversified into the chocolate crumb and grain market. By 1969, the current structure of Waterford Foods had been put in place. The events of 1965 were of major significance not only for local co-operatives, but also at national co-operative level. A climate of change was appearing and future membership of the EEC was a possibility. Waterford Foods resulted from one of the first major amalgamations of the co-operative movement of the period, one that has been copied successfully since.

Evolution of the Organisation

The 1970s

The new grouping that emerged from the amalgamation of local co-ops had doubled its combined milk intake, and processing capacity was much greater than prevailing supply levels, with the result that a new joint venture was formed with Unigate in order to put this excess capacity to good use, and growth on the dairy side was accompanied by increasing volume in the farm-trading end of the enlarged business. A new chief executive, Stephen O'Connor, was appointed in 1972 as Waterford Co-Op faced the opportunities afforded by Ireland's entry to the EEC. In the same year, Waterford Co-Op expanded by amalgamating with three other co-ops — Castle Lyons Creamery, South East Farmers' Co-Op and IDA Co-Op. Later that same year, Glenmore Co-Op joined this new grouping. The impact of the amalgamation was that milk volume increased substantially in the consolidated group to 53 million gallons, 10 times the volume handled by Dungarvan 10 years previously. What was required at this stage in the company's development was the development of a sales team and distribution network, as the company had to start from scratch in building up a market image for itself. Waterford Co-Op was fortunate in having a management team capable of handling such problems.

Franchising Strategy

A positive development for the company in 1973 was its first efforts to diversify into high value-added dairy foods, with the Yoplait range of yogurt being launched in Ireland. This move was brought about through negotiating a franchise agreement with Sodima, a French Co-Op group which marketed Yoplait.

The franchise agreement entered into with Sodima provided Waterford Co-Op with more outlets for its milk supplies and helped it to become a market-led organisation, something which without the Sodima alliance, would have taken the company years to achieve. Management also benefited from the strategy because it acquired more sophisticated marketing techniques, and the production technology required to produce the yogurt gave the company a new competitive edge which would help in future growth efforts, such as in 1975 when Waterford Co-Op made an arrangement with General Foods (USA) to produce dairy-based desserts for export to the UK, with the products produced at Waterford Co-Op's subsidiary, Castle Lyons Foods. Although this venture met with mixed success and was discontinued in 1979, it allowed Waterford to tap into and utilise the extensive knowledge and expertise that General Foods had acquired in such areas as product design, development, market skills, and production technology. The alliance, although temporary, has helped Waterford Co-Op in its development and, like its other ventures, has enabled the organisation to capitalise and utilise the extensive knowledge gained.

The overall result of all this diversification for Waterford was a huge growth in the volume of milk supplied, and also an increase in the agricultural trading sector in which the company also participated. In fact, the latter growth was so significant that Waterford Co-Op's volume and market share increased to the point where, by 1979, it outsold the competition in the animal food sector, which included such UK companies as Rents and Unilever. In 1976, Knockneal milk producers became direct suppliers to Waterford Co-Op, and two years later the Shelbourne Co-Op Society became part of the group. However, one side effect of all of this activity was that facilities already in place could not cope with demand. There was a growing need for major investment in new production facilities. The Co-Op responded to this need in 1977, when a £20 million investment programme was undertaken, which included the building of manufacturing facilities at Dairyland for new fresh products; a new automated computerised dairy process control system at the Dungarvan plant, and a new casein plant. A new central group laboratory was also provided for farm services. On the trading side, some mills were modernised and a new mill costing £4 million was built at Clónroche, Co. Wexford to manufacture the "Gain" brand of animal feed.

The 1980s

In 1980 the company received the franchise to distribute Yoplait in Northern Ireland and, like the earlier expansion, considerable market share was quickly established. In 1995 it stood at 46 per cent. New products were developed and distributed along the Yoplait network, such as chilled salad foods and flavoured milk drinks. Also in the same year, through an association with Irish Distillers Ltd., Waterford Cream, the whiskey-based cream liqueur, was launched. By 1982, Waterford Co-Op had received the franchise to distribute Yoplait in the UK, resulting in a new subsidiary being set up there, Waterford Foods Ltd., to handle the marketing and distribution and to provide a base for future expansion in this market.

At about this time, the company proceeded into the fertiliser sector. A joint venture was formed with Avonmore Co-Op, with each taking a 30 per cent stake in the Grassland Holdings fertiliser plant in Kilkenny, which resulted in both companies securing a strategic amount of the combined annual fertiliser supplies. In 1983, another joint venture saw the company entering the malting barley export business, this time with Avonmore and H. Hittall. Initiatives that year included acquiring 20 per cent of Ballyfree Farms. Developments since then include the 1984 modernisation of Snowcream Dairies at Waterford and Wexford.

In 1985, Waterford was incorporated as a private limited company under the name Alevtian Ltd., and by 1986 the company entered a partnership with the Duf Food company, Wessanen, to manufacture continental cheeses for the European market. In 1987, a 100 per cent natural Yoplait yogurt was introduced into the Irish market. The trading division of the company opened a chain of retail outlets under the name Shopwell and it also acquired the feed division of Davis Moss, Enniscorthy, Co. Wexford. The year 1988 saw the opening of the continental cheese plant at Kilmeaden, Co. Waterford, and the acquisition of Trynors of Tagham, Co. Wexford. The same year the company acquired Eatwell Ltd., a fresh and frozen food pie manufacturer.

The biggest event for the company to date happened in the summer of 1988 when the board unanimously recommended the establishment of a public company, which was endorsed by the shareholders at two extraordinary general meetings. This was looked upon as a new beginning for the company, which now operated under the name Waterford Foods plc. In 1989, Gallow West in the US and Healds Foods in the UK were acquired by the company. These two acquisitions added over £200 million to the group's turnover. In the same year, the group acquired a 50 per cent stake in Premier Tír Laighean, which is Ireland's biggest retail milk business.

The 1990s

The year 1990 saw further integration of Gallow West and Healds Foods into the group. This move gave Waterford Foods plc much needed international expansion, and there was a positive blending of cultures. Greater cost control during 1990 saw the group invest in high-performance market segments and the latest new technology while continuing to pursue product development. As a result of the drive for lower costs, there was some level of rationalisation. In December 1991, United Co-Operative Dairies in Manchester was acquired, providing a significant boost to the existing liquid milk business. It added some 36 million gallons of milk per annum to Waterford Foods plc output and has two major processing centres. It is to be combined with Healds Foods operations, resulting in the second largest milk business in the north west of England, with a market of 7 million people.

July 1992 saw the acquisition of Express Foods Ireland and Premier Dairies. The group completed the acquisition from Grand Metropolitan plc of Express Foods Ireland, the principle businesses of which are Virginia Milk Products, Ltd. (Virginia Co. Cavan) and Express Foods Northern Ireland Ltd. The core business of these companies is the manufacture and marketing of food ingredients. The facility at Virginia is a modern high-performance facility. It manufactures the cream base for Bailey's Original Cream Liqueur and a wide range of milk supplied from Premier Dairies. The company has co-operated closely with Gilbeys of Ireland in the development of the processing technology for the cream base.

Express Foods at Magheralin in Co. Armagh manufactures and markets a range of dairy products including cheddar cheese, mozzarella cheese and whey protein concentrate (WPC). It is the largest such facility in the UK. Premier Dairies was acquired in July 1992. It controls in excess of 30 per cent of the national liquid milk market, while its share of the Dublin market is over 70 per cent. The company supplies products under the Premier and Dealgan brand names, with processing plants in Dublin and Dundalk.

Associated Enterprises

Over the years, through strategic investment, the group has gained access to vital product supplies, management and costing information. Waterford Foods holds a 33 per cent share of Barley Exports Ltd., which handles exports of the product to the European market. A 30 per cent share is also held in Grassland Fertilisers (Kilkenny) Ltd., one of Ireland's major fertiliser companies. Co-Op Animal Health Ltd., of which Waterford Foods holds a 25 per cent share, distributes veterinary medicines and supplies. A 22 per cent share is held in Clasfern Holding Ltd., a southeast-based oil importation and distribution company. Waterford Foods also own a 50 per cent share in the forestry development company, Waterford Green Belt Forestry Ltd.

Today, Waterford Foods plc represents a £439 million multi-activity business. It is involved in the manufacturing, sale and distribution of a wide variety of commodity and consumer dairy produce, as well as top-quality animal feeds for the food industry in the US, North Africa, Middle East, South America and the European Union (EU). With subsidiaries located in the US and the UK, the group is able to produce, market and distribute products internationally and can be said to be a growing and very profitable company in the food processing and agri-trading industry.

Dairyland services the home market with all types of yogurt. Its biggest successes include Petit Filous which has 80 per cent of a greatly expanding market. Sales and profits have increased steadily over the years. Snowcream/Castle Lyons is the liquid milk operation of Waterford Foods. With a widening of its product range to include full market, light milk and buttermilk, the company has increased its sales and it is now one of the group's high-performing companies. Kilmeaden Foods (suppliers) operates in the North of Ireland, and supplies yogurt, packaged poultry meat and the star Petit Filous. This company is showing steady growth. Eatwell manufactures frozen meat and pies. Its main markets are in the US and UK. Western Cheese (Wiltshire, UK) joined the Waterford group in 1990, bringing with it the added-value cheese business which looks to have a bright future. Galloway West, a subsidiary in the US, supplies 41 per cent of the bulk sweetened condensed milk sold in the US, and 40 per cent of Wisconsin's Swiss Cheese output. This company is a leader in product development and a much valued asset for the group. Healds Foods UK, a Manchester-based company, operates five high-tech manufacturing plants, processing milk, dairy products and fruit juices. It also supplies the supermarket chains in England. Galloway West and Heald Foods together contribute £200 million turnover to the Waterford Group.

Evolution of Organisational Practices

In the early years, management strategy focused very much on two issues — encouraging the local farmers to supply milk and keeping the business solvent during the milk price wars of the late 1920s. On coping with these, Waterford's strategic emphasis shifted to developing a strong competitive focus and becoming the dominant business in the local market. It was then necessary to develop new markets for the increasing milk supply. During the 1930s, prominence was given to increasing the Irish market and turning to the UK potential. Also, with increasing suppliers and shareholders, and the change in farming patterns in the 1930s and 1940s, the focus was put on ancillary businesses such as agri-trading, which was brought about by development in technology. Greater free trade in the 1960s brought another change in strategy, with emphasis on market and economies of scale, as well as an urgent requirement for rationalisation of the industry and an improvement in efficiency.

The Dungarvan company took the lead in the merger movement in the South East in the 1960s and 1970s, leading to the consolidation in 1972. At this time, the organisation was not overly concerned with acquiring new markets, because it was able to capitalise on the European Community intervention programme up until 1984, which bought up any excess capacity. Thereafter, the focus of strategy was one of diversification into new markets, with higher value-added products using the company's marketing and distribution facilities. The result of this change in strategic focus was that there was less reliance on programmes such as that of EC intervention.

Organisation Structure

In most co-operative societies there are influences present which can often hinder the development and growth of the company. One such influence can be identified as the wishes of the members, which must be accommodated within a structure that allows for effective direction and a facility for introducing change as members desire it. Furthermore, the business of managing the affairs of the co-op requires a structure that permits proper task execution and accommodates any necessary change. In the early years, the organisation structure of any of the co-ops in existence reflected a lack of business complexity. All that was required was a structure to permit the division of limited management responsibility into self-contained tasks, largely based on production facilities in various locations. Because the operation was small, the general manager could exercise tight control, with the help of a specialist in the area of finance to look after administration and accounts. In the 1930s, with the move into new markets and the influence of training in dairy science, there resulted a greater awareness of product quality and the need arose for specialisation in this area. With the introduction of agri-trading, the need for a totally separate division was recognised. This division was managed by an assistant general manager and supported by the existing financial function. However, in over 40 years the organisation structure did not change considerably, reflecting Waterford's status as a dominant operator in a single market.

In the 1960s and 1970s, Waterford Co-Op's organisation structure was very much concerned with meeting the needs of the enlarged membership. The company resolved this at board level by offering directorship positions to the various societies, with a rotating chairperson. The management of the business was left to the former general manager of the Dungarvan Co-Op, Jim Foley, who was the company's first chief executive. However, a large board of directors can often be unyielding, and this can stifle the development of a company. The Waterford group prevented this by introducing a small board sub-committee to oversee the operations of the management team. With this system, management could manage, and at the same time, the interests of the shareholders would also be catered for.

Figure 3.1: Worldwide Operations of Waterford Foods plc Executive Committee

Group Managing Director	
Company Secretary	**Group Chairman**
Dairy Products Managing Director	**Consumer Products** Managing Director
Finance Group Finance Director	**Trading** General Manager
Waterford Foods (UK) Managing Director	**Waterford Food Products Inc. (USA)**
Human Resources Division Personnel and Strategic Planning	

Up to 1972 Waterford remained very much a production-oriented company, but greater complexity, diversification into new markets and movements into distribution necessitated a more effective planning system. The move from a product-oriented company to a market-oriented company has meant that the organisation structure has changed many times since 1972. The present structure is a divisionalised form, based on key functions. Integration of these functions is through a formal hierarchy cemented by way of a number of management committees. Further integration is provided through a division of the company-wide functional responsibilities — such as transport, personnel, planning, etc. — among the executives of these management committees. These responsibilities are in addition to their primary functions. Once a month, a planning and performance review by each executive is undertaken. This structure is supported by two product development committees comprising senior management. Monthly meetings are held and it is the responsibility of the committees to bring forward ideas on new products. One of the strengths of the company over the past few years has been its ability to adapt its structure to the changing business environment, which is essential for the growth of the group. This organisation structure is very much the prevailing form of most large global corporations.

Control System

In the early days control was a rather simple matter. The control system was confined to such things as market results, sales values, volume and quality standards for the milk intake. But on entering the cheese and milk powder business in the late 1930s, process and stock control systems had to be introduced, along with a simple financial control system. The greater efficiency drive of the 1960s led to the groups' use of consultants to design costing systems, which were then used as control devices, and in the 1970s this was developed further with strict budgeting and management accounting systems. Like most companies, Waterford Foods relied on an accurate management information system to highlight any inefficiency, so the production of computers has helped enormously with this development, dealing with purchasing, stock control, and other such areas. Corporate planning was introduced in 1972, and the success of this move can be observed in the company's successful diversification strategy. With EEC membership, control became an imperative, and the EEC intervention programme imposed quality standards requiring that quality-control systems and lab facilities be established.

Group Culture

When considering the history of the group from its origins to its present-day status as a major international enterprise, it is no surprise to discover the very distinct culture that is evident within the group. The development of this culture was largely determined by the management style of the group, and so falls into three distinct periods coinciding with the periods of office of the three chief executives of the group. The first managing director of the group, Ned Maher, exerted considerable personal influence on the organisation. Very much a task-master, the company's early rapid growth was a result of his driving influence. Under his management, the organisation developed a very competitive spirit and became pioneering in its endeavours — a hallmark of the company that still survives to this day. In 1954, Jim Foley was appointed chief executive. Coming to the post from a technological background, his appointment was seen as significant at the time because the dairy industry was on the brink of a technological revolution. With this change of leadership came a change in culture, with an emphasis on technological and product development. Yet another change in culture came about in 1972 with the appointment of a new managing director, Stephen O'Connor. A new emphasis was put on business development, marketing, international acquisitions and management development, and in the late 1980s came the major transformation of Waterford Co-Op to Waterford Foods Group plc.

Waterford Co-Op/Foods developed from a farmer's co-op in the late 1930s into a multinational corporation in the 1980s. Despite this transformation and the resultant cultural evolution, the group does not forget its roots. This is evident in its rural development policy, through which the organisation works with community-based groups to explore innovative ideas for the farming community, and to encourage the development of a more efficient agribusiness. The pioneering spirit of the early days still exists also. One detrimental effect of the culture changes has been the dilution of the co-operative spirit on which the organisation was founded. This is evidenced by the formation of segregated interest groups within the organisation. As a result, the labour unrest of large organisations is now a feature of the Waterford Group also. This resulted in a strike in 1988.

With the acquisition of overseas companies, Waterford Foods has now added new organisational and international cultures to its mix. So the challenge for Waterford Foods from a cultural point of view is one that requires the successive fusing of its international cultures, and the redevelopment of a co-operative culture to include its entire labour force.

Management Style at Waterford Foods

Stephen O'Connor was chief executive at Waterford Foods from 1972 to 1994. His vision and astuteness are considered to be largely responsible for the excellent results achieved by the company over this period. However, he is quick to point out that only a team effort could achieve such results. The perception that large boards make for difficulties in managing and small boards are the answer to the manager's prayer has not been borne out by Waterford Foods' experience.

Staff and customers are encouraged to air their views, with the management always prepared to listen, help and advise where necessary. Stephen O'Connor came up through the ranks and has seen the business in all its states, something that he considers an added advantage. While he has never attracted the plaudits that more "dynamic" chief executives, like Denis Brosnan, have enjoyed, it is unlikely that he harbours regrets. His original hunch that Dungarvan Co-Operative was a creamery with a future has proved correct and that has had much to do with the man himself. In December 1994, Stephen O'Connor retired as managing director and appointed in his place Matthew Walsh. The contribution by O'Connor has been indelible on the development of the group. Under his leadership, Waterford Co-Op, and more recently Waterford Foods, became one of the major players in the Irish food industry and a leading public company with a significant global presence.

Business Philosophy

On its agreement with H.J. Heinz subsidiary, Johma, to market prepared meals and salads, the company feels that this development is exactly in line with its business philosophy as a major food processor. It provides the company with the highest level of technology and connects it to a highly refined quality-control system. It also gives Waterford Foods access to a brand that has been proven in some of the most concentrated, most competitive markets in Europe. Waterford Foods has the potential to be the premier food-products company in Ireland, as well as being a very successful business, and the decision to go public in 1988 was part of the company's strategy aimed at achieving this goal. In its acquisition strategy, the companies taken over have been very carefully selected and bought on a reasonable price basis. Waterford Foods recognised in its development plan as far back as 1987 that, inevitably and in the short term rather than the long term, mergers would be part of its strategy.

The strategic move in 1989, which saw a shift away from the commodity market to the added-value market, was designed to build on Waterford's earlier success in moving into the consumer products area. This decision to expand with such vigour in 1989 owes a lot to the fact that the company had been actively seeking new businesses since it came to the market in 1988. The bottom line was that the organisation had limited expansion possibilities on an organic basis, so a decision to expand through acquisitions was taken and this entailed going to the market. Waterford Foods has tried to identify businesses that fit in with its own business. The key to the success for the company to date has been top management's long-held belief that quality branded products aimed at the consumer market are better than "commodities". The belief in consumer branded products can be traced back to 1973 when, one year into the job of chief executive, Stephen O'Connor signed a deal with Sodima of France to produce Yoplait yogurt under franchise at a plant in Inch, Co. Wexford. A spread of activities and products is central to Matthew Walsh's future strategy for Waterford, because the company possesses tremendous flexibility, especially in milk, and it has the excess capacity that allows it to move from one product to another, even at peak times. This flexibility has been very important to the company in the 1990s.

Commitment to Total Quality Management

Waterford Foods was awarded the ISO9002 international quality certification in 1991 for both its cheddar cheese and Leerdammer plant at Kilmeaden, and the butter plant at Dungarvan. For Waterford, the Kilmeaden plant represents an investment in product development, modern technology, flexibility, quality and a high degree of operational efficiency. At the Dungarvan plant, a full commitment to quality is in evidence at all levels, which has earned it the ISO9002 certificate for milk assembly, separation and butter production. At both plants an elaborate system of sampling and laboratory analysis is carried out to provide data for raw-material inspection, process control and finished-product monitoring. The emphasis of the quality system at Waterford Foods is on problem prevention and continuous quality improvement. The documentation and regular audits, together with the quality review meetings, ensure that potential problems are identified and remedied at the earliest possible stage in the process.

The Competitive Situation

Waterford Foods has developed into a business with international markets, as well as having its own home market in Ireland. It has achieved this position through a joint-venture and acquisition strategy. With its history and experience of continued growth in the food industry, Waterford Foods is ideally placed to capitalise on market growth and new markets. The possibility of new markets becoming available in Eastern Europe also results in greater growth potential for the company. Excellent earnings per share over the past number of years mean that the Waterford Foods can easily attract investment as and when required. This was apparent in 1989 when increased shareholdings successfully raised £11 million, which was required at the time to strengthen the capital base of the group. The group's profit performance has been consistent and impressive over the past few years.

Being based in the EU has a positive effect, since both consumer and agribusiness numbers continue to grow in EU countries. Healthy eating habits, an emphasis on fitness and a reluctance to tolerate artificial food additives are high on consumer agendas. Many dairy foods are not projected as "health" foods. These include yogurt, low-fat milk, cheese, etc. This type of market demand, and Waterford Foods ability to respond to it, is an important strategic consideration.

The seasonal nature of milk supply in Ireland is disadvantageous to the Waterford Foods Group in competing in the fresh products market with European competitors whose supply is much less affected by seasonal fluctuations. As a result, it is necessary for Waterford Foods to offer low seasonal bonuses to milk suppliers in order to level out milk-production patterns. The effect of the Common Agricultural Policy (CAP) in regard to restrictions in milk-production quotas can be seen as a threat to the Waterford Group. The quota system continues to be the largest single factor limiting milk production growth for Waterford.

Waterford Foods together with Kerry Group is a leader in the Irish dairy foods processing industry. Its history of being regarded as an industry leader dates back to the 1960s when technology was rapidly developing in the dairy industry. Waterford Co-Op (as it was at the time) pioneered the technology advancement which revolutionised the variety and quality of dairy food products available to the consumer. Today, with ever-increasing turnover, profits and market share, Waterford Foods has reinforced its position as an industry leader.

Waterford has also built up a top-class reputation for quality products. Each year its products have received a variety of quality awards, such as the Kerry Gold lactic butter award which the dairy industry won in 1990. Product quality has been copperfastened in latter years through the achievement of the ISO9000 standard in many of its divisions. The ability of Waterford Foods to produce high-quality continental-type cheeses such as Seerdammer underlines the high quality standard that it can achieve.

Product-development expertise is also a strength of the Waterford Foods Group. This is particularly evident in its development of various yogurt products and milk varieties. The ability to develop such products to meet market needs, together with good marketing strategies, makes such products runaway successes.

The vast range of products produced by Waterford Foods testifies to the ability of the group to diversify. This feature is yet another strength of the organisation. The products produced range from animal feeds, to milk products, to frozen-food products. The continuing policy of company acquisition has reinforced the ability to diversify through the cross-fertilisation of expertise. The rapid market growth and expansion of its organisation resulted in Waterford Group marketing efforts being in crisis in the 1970s. Increased emphasis on marketing in the 1980s culminated in outstanding marketing success with the launching of Yoplait yogurt and Petit Filous. In 1988, Petit Filous won the "New Product of the Year Award" from the trade magazine *Today Grocer,* and in the same year Waterford Foods won the prestigious American Express Marketing Award. The group stressed the importance of being a market-focused business, sympathetic to customer needs.

However, the group cost structure features as a weakness for the company. As an international trading company, high domestic energy and labour costs, coupled with currency fluctuations, militate against low-cost production. While Waterford Foods products are diverse, they are mostly dairy-based, and as such the group is vulnerable to dairy-related influences such as seasonal supply fluctuations and restrictive pressures on milk production.

Financial Performance of Waterford Foods

The year 1990 was one of substantial growth for Waterford Foods with turnover increasing from £278 million in the previous year to £439 million, an enormous jump of 57 per cent and yielding pre-tax profits of £11.3 million. This rise can be attributed to the full-year inclusion of results for two major acquisitions made towards the end of 1989. Healds Foods, based in Manchester, turned in record results in its first year in the Waterford Group. Galloway-West also had a good year but the benefit to Waterford of this performance was lessened by the weak dollar at the end of the year. Margins reached 4.8 per cent and earnings per share were 6.26p. The return on capital employed was 14.2 per cent. This is not a bad performance when one considers the dairy markets during this period. Waterford claims to have supported milk prices to farmers over the period to the tune of £6 million in excess of what market prices could justify. As a result, operating expenses showed a significant increase in the previous year. In percentage terms these costs represented 9.95 per cent of turnover, as against 9.14 per cent in the previous year. This increase was spread evenly over distribution and administration costs, with both recording significant increases. As a result of takeover activity during the year, Waterford's borrowings increased significantly, resulting in increased interest payments, which jumped from £1.5 million during 1989 to £9.9 million.

The year 1991 was also good for the company with profits before tax of £15.86 million, a 40 per cent growth on 1990 with £11.3 million. This resulted in a 48 per cent improvement in earnings per share to 9.27p. Record operating profits were achieved but there was a slight reduction in turnover caused by lower dairy prices in the US, reduced animal food prices, and the decision by the company not to renew the Yoplait franchise in the UK. Borrowings at the year end were £45.7 million or 55 per cent of shareholders' funds, which now stood at £82.3 million.

The following year saw record turnover, profits, and cash flows achieved, along with the acquisitions of Express Foods and Premier Dairies. Profit before tax increased by 29 per cent to £20.41 million, up on the 1991 figure of £15.86 million. Profits before tax and goodwill amortisation were £22.31 million, representing an increase of 41 per cent over the previous year (£15.86 million). Operating profit was £29.07 million, compared to the 1991 figure of £19.78 million, an increase of 47 per cent, and operating margins improved to 5.3 per cent over the previous year (4.7 per cent). Interest at £9.70 million was covered 3.30 times; 1991 interest was £6.85 million or 3.32 times. Earnings per share rose to 10.04p, an increase of 8 per cent on the previous year.

Table 3.1: Trading Record

	1990 £m	1991 £m	1992 £m	1993 £m	1994 £m
Turnover	439.0	423.8	551.4	693.7	710.62
Operating Profit	18.59	19.78	29.07	39.98	32.89
Other Income	2.62	2.92	2.93	0.60	1.38
Goodwill Amortisation	—	—	(1.90)	(3.38)	(3.59)
Exceptional Items	(1.94)	—	(1.75)	0	(14.50)
Interest, net	(9.92)	(6.84)	(9.65)	(12.72)	(10.41)
Profit on Ordinary Activities Before Taxation	9.36	15.85	18.65	24.48	5.77
Tax (charge)/credit	(1.13)	(0.49)	(0.90)	(2.06)	(0.94)
Profit for the Financial Year	8.23	15.36	17.74	22.42	6.79
Dividends					
• Ordinary	(1.45)	(4.11)	(5.10)	(5.29)	(5.53)
• Preference	(0.59)	(1.18)	(1.18)	(1.67)	(3.33)
Retained Profit/(Loss)	6.18	10.06	11.45	15.43	(2.165)

In 1993, the company saw pre-tax profits rise 32 per cent to £24.5 million as the large acquisitions of mid-1992 produced their first full-year contributions to the company. This represents an increase of £6 million over the previous year's figure of £18.6 million and the 1991 figure of £15.8 million. Operating profit increased by 37 per cent in 1993 to £39.9 million, against the 1992 figure of £27

million. Operating margins continued to improve to 5.8 per cent
for the year — £693.7 million compared to £551.4 million in 1992.
Earnings per share, after exceptional items and goodwill amortisation, were 11.1p, up from 9.08p in 1992. A dividend of 2.83p per
share was paid, up from 2.73 a year earlier. Over the past six
years the cash flow for Waterford Foods has increased by 300 per
cent to a present figure of £41.7 million. Net interest costs were
£13.07 million up from the 1992 figure of £9.35, but the interest
cover has been improved on since 1992 when it was 3.1 times. It
now stands at 3.2 times. Bank debt for the year rose to £114 million, up from £106 million a year earlier and considerably more
than the 1991 figure of £46 million. Shareholders funds also increased by almost £40 million on the previous year to £171 million.

Table 3.2: Waterford Foods Five-Year Financial Ratios, 1990–94

	1994	1993	1992	1991	1990
Operating profit as a percentage of turnover	4.6%	5.8%	5.3%	4.7%	4.2%
Interest cover (times)	3.3	3.2	3.3	3.3	2.1
Earnings per ordinary share (in pence)	1.8	11.1	9.1	9.3	5.0
Adjusted earnings per ordinary share (in pence)	10.2	12.9	11.1	9.3	6.3
Dividends per ordinary share (in pence)	2.93	2.83	2.73	2.63	2.50
Net assets per ordinary share (in pence)	66.6	66.1	61.8	40.6	34.4

According to the company's annual report, 1994 was a year of
"challenge and change" for Waterford Foods plc:

> A combination of factors, including an imbalance between Irish
> milk costs and market returns, structural changes in the UK milk
> markets and adverse trading conditions for our US business all
> put pressure on margins (Waterford Foods plc, 1994).

The group experienced a sharp decline in turnover, and more significantly, net profits fell from £22 million in 1993 to £7 million in
1994. A £14.5 million provision for restructuring and rationalisation was included in the 1994 financial statements to provide for
required redundancies, plant closures and related asset write
downs. In all, some 400 redundancies were involved and geo-

graphically were spread between the UK (250), Ireland (100) and US (50). The restructuring provision resulted in a retained loss for the year of £2.2 million. The net interest charge for 1994 amounted to £10.4 million, compared to £12.7 million in 1993. According to the annual report, this reduction is mainly the result of the issue of £25 million of preference shares during 1993, the reduction in net borrowings and the generally lower interest rates prevailing during 1994. Interest cover has increased to 3.3 times despite the reduction in operating profits. EPS before provisions and goodwill at 10.15p compared with 12.91p in the previous year, a decline of 21.3 per cent. The ordinary dividend (net) for the year increased by 5 per cent from 2.83p per share to 2.97p per share. The company's balance sheet shows a net worth of £166 million, including £81 million in goodwill and other intangibles.

Strategy for the Future

The year 1993 provided excellent end-of-year results for Waterford. This was because of the acquisitions undertaken by the group in 1992 — the total contribution of Express Foods and Premier Dairies to the group is estimated to be in the region of £17 million. Waterford has spent close to £240 million over the past four years alone on acquisitions, but only £17 million in 1993. However, 1994 directed group efforts at restructuring, an activity that the company will pursue in key markets where competitive pressures prevail. It believes that a focused and efficient dairy business with a record of product innovation, good operating cash flows and a well-structured balance sheet will put the group in a strong position to avail of any future opportunities that may arise.

The group will continue on the acquisition trail in order to increase turnover, which since 1987 has increased by some 204 per cent. The group's main goal over the next three years is to double sales to £1.4 billion, and most of this growth will come from acquisitions. At present there are no immediate plans, but the group is always actively looking at likely possibilities, especially in the UK where it hopes to increase its share of liquid milk market to 10 per cent. Other possible markets would include the US where the group wishes to increase its activities in the food ingredients and cheese sectors. Also, there are great opportunities in Europe for expansion, and Waterford is not as yet a major player in that market. As far as the home market is concerned, the group sees it as a limited area for growth in the future, so the aim here will be to maintain the 20 per cent share it holds in the overall milk market and the 45 per cent share it holds in the liquid milk market. Waterford Foods does not have any plans to follow Kerry Group by diversifying out of dairy processing into meat.

Source: Company reports and accounts.

Questions

1. Critically evaluate the growth and development of Waterford Foods plc to its present-day position.

2. How would you characterise the competitive situation which currently faces Waterford Foods plc?

3. Critically evaluate the organisation's culture and structure and indicate how they might facilitate its future strategic development.

4. What strategic options are now available to Waterford Foods plc if it is to remain competitive?

4

Ritz

We are here, today, to talk about a new brand — a very important new brand for the company. It all started two years ago, back in 1984, when we decided to place much greater emphasis on developing new products. The brief at the time was to look for a gap in the market for an alcohol product.

This was the opening comment by Tony Brophy, marketing manager at the wholesalers' conference organised by Showerings (Ireland) Limited, the Clonmel, Co. Tipperary firm, in April 1986.

History of the Product Introduction at Clonmel

Showerings has been quite successful at introducing new products and this is all the more apparent when one considers the number of new products that fail every year. The company prides itself on knowing its market and on being thorough about the products to develop and bring to the market.

- "Snowball", an advocaat, has been on the market for a couple of decades, and although in decline has managed to carve a very definite and profitable segment in the market.

- "Stag" was introduced in 1974 and has become a major force in the drinks industry with a turnover at retail level of well over IR£2 million.

- "Madison", introduced in 1977, was another brand which found a very profitable niche in the marketplace.

- "Hunters", introduced in 1980, was a cider-based drink with a beer-like "head" which did not receive sufficient consumer

[84]

acceptance to justify the necessary commitment to its continued support, and it was withdrawn from the market.

- "Britvic 55" a fruit juice product, introduced in 1981, developed a small but important franchise at the premium end of the soft-drinks market.

- "Bulmers Draught" was introduced in 1984 and has proved very successful.

So in 1984, the company decided that it would attempt to find a new market gap from which it was hoped a successful brand could be developed.

Concept Development for New Product

The brief was open-ended, with the only major limitation being that it should be in the alcoholic drinks market. Techniques such as brainstorming, market mapping and gap analysis were used to see if such a market gap existed. The team was broadly based, consisting of marketing and laboratory personnel as well as the company's advertising agency, Youngs.

From this analysis it became apparent that the market segment in which a gap might be found was among young women aged 20–30. Consequently, it was decided to concentrate on the development of a concept and product for this market segment.

But why young women? It was quite clear from research that women are more adventurous in their drinking habits. They are more willing to try new products and they are less loyal to existing products. They have a much larger repertoire of drinks than men. The market is a sizeable one amounting to approximately IR£200 million at retail level and is growing. Furthermore, within the company's product range the majority of brands — Madison, Babycham, Snowball and Stag — were aimed primarily at women. Consequently, Showerings had considerable experience in this particular segment of the market. The experience in developing Stag, with its unique imagery based on sophisticated advertising, would be of particular relevance to this product.

Showerings knew that Stag, which had been the company's most successful product, was very much a traditional brand. Although Stag was consumed both by men and women, Showerings began to realise that, increasingly, young females were beginning to dominate in the "regular drinker" category. Research showed that it was considered by many as a starter drink, in the sense that young women moving into alcohol for the first time find its taste very palatable and the imagery just right. However, many leave Stag at the age of 20 or 21, moving on to what they consider more sophisticated drinks such as Pils, vodka and white, etc. They associate this move with growing up and adulthood.

It was in April 1984 that the new product search, code-named "Product Elegant", was born. A number of qualitative research studies took place among groups of women in the 20–30 age group. The research looked at their attitudes to things in general, their habits, their leisure activities and, more specifically, what they were drinking and why, so that their attitudes to various drinks could be established. During these qualitative studies rough concepts were presented to each of the groups. Feedback was considered to be a fundamental part of the process in crystallising the type of concept and product that should be developed.

Desired Product Features

The research findings indicated that the product should have acquired-taste characteristics, dryness and bite. Sophisticated drinks such as Satzenbrau are seen to have acquired-taste characteristics. It was planned, therefore, that the new "Elegant" product should have a sophisticated taste and be fairly dry.

Alcohol delivery was also a very important factor to these young women. It is quite clear that the "kick" or "buzz" from a drink is a necessary element. Moreover, alcohol delivery is associated with value for money. Furthermore, products like Satzenbrau, with high alcohol delivery, unlike regular beer, are required to be consumed in lesser volume.

Use of a half pint amber bottle was considered to be an important component in positioning the product as a regular, mainstream and serious drink, i.e. among the beers, lagers, Pils, etc. It was apparent that the packaging should also be stylish and sophisticated since the target market was selected for being particularly style and fashion conscious. "After all, the psychologists believe that the drinks which people choose to some extent reflect what they are," said Tony Brophy

Since this product would not be a beer, although packaged in a half-pint beer bottle, its distinctiveness should be reflected in its packaging/label presentation to position it away from ales and lagers. Research indicated that prospective female consumers were unclear about the price of many of the products that they consumed regularly in pubs. This is quite understandable given the number of price increases that have taken place. However, despite this ambiguity it is apparent that "value for money" would be fundamental to the success of "Elegant". Consequently, since this product would be pitched at young women currently drinking products such as Satzenbrau, it would be critical that the price charged in pubs would not be more than Satzenbrau or other main competitive brands.

The qualitative studies also suggested that drinkers could broadly be split into two categories — "serious drinkers" and "light drinkers". In addition, drink types could be divided into three classifications — "session drinks" which could be consumed in quantity and with regularity, such as beers, stag, vodka and white; "occasional drinks" such as coolers, wine, brandy, "Martini" etc; and "special drinks" such as cocktails and champagne. "Elegant" was to be designed to appeal clearly to "serious drinkers". It would also be developed as a "session drink". These two preconditions were considered essential if significant volumes were to be achieved.

Following these research studies, Showerings had a very clear idea of the type of product that should be produced and the style of branding and packaging that should be developed.

Product Development

The company product-development team headed by Dr Peter Hatton, quality control manager, was briefed on the projected product. The most likely base was considered to be perry — this would enable the development of a product that was distinctly different from cider or lager. Being light and crisp it should appeal to young women.

The product should have acquired-taste characteristics, such as sophistication, challenge, and bite. It should be strong in alcohol and should have a character suitable for consumption in half-pint quantity. "Elegant" should be capable of being consumed over an evening — providing quantity without an unpleasant build-up. Being perry-based, it would be light in colour and in texture, almost reminiscent of sparkling wine.

While the brief given to the development team at Clonmel was wide-ranging, it was agreed that the desired product could be accommodated within a perry formulation. There is no strict legal interpretation of what constitutes a "perry" product, although since 1962 the European Union (EU) has provided a product description as follows:

> **Perry** (definition): A beverage obtained by complete or partial fermentation of the juice of fresh pears, or a mixture of the juice of fresh pears and fresh apples.

Pears come in many varieties and Showerings undertook an extensive search of pear types that would best suit the product brief. The variety finally selected was indigenous to South Tyrol. Sample shipments were obtained from a well-known supplier in Northern Italy who stored the juice in single strength for several months. The juice was concentrated just before shipment to prevent the discoloration of the consignment that would otherwise occur.

Working to a specification brief that "Elegant" should be distinctive, sophisticated and adult, the development team experimented with a series of fermentation formulae and an extensive selection of additives to give a wide range of taste options. From exhaustive internal testing, it was decided to eliminate additives and to concentrate on developing a distinctive product with a natural character, having the required alcoholic characteristics. This meant that "Elegant" had to be positioned away from traditional "fruit-type" drinks, while retaining its natural qualities as far as possible.

It was decided that, in taste terms, the new product should mirror Riesling wine, although it would have its own unique flavour, being perry-based. This was achieved through introduction into the fermentation process of a special yeast grain from the Alsace region of France. As the ultimate formulation was being finalised, the following qualities were pinpointed as essential for "Elegant":

- While perry-based, it must be positioned away from typical "pear" alcoholic drinks.

- It must compete with premium Pils and lager and yet be distinct from these products.

- It must be clear and light coloured.

- It must have a "body" equivalent to light dry wine.

Dryness, lightness and palatability were essential requirements. If the new product were to be too sweet or heavy, it would be limited to being an *occasional* drink and defeat the objective of creating a regular, *session* product. External product testing established a high level of acceptability of the proposed new product, and sessionability tests helped to define much more precisely the most acceptable taste qualities. The product-development team responded quickly to the consumer tests, and so "Elegant" was ready in its final formulation for commercial trials.

Pre-Launch Marketing Research

The initial role of market research was to provide the company with information on the attitudes of consumers to various drinks on the market and on the drinking behaviour of these consumers. As the project progressed, there was a steady flow of information from marketing research, undertaken by Colm Carey, senior research executive with Irish Consumer Research Ltd. Consumer attitudes and reactions to product initiatives were closely monitored to establish whether the product was moving in the right direction.

> Essentially our job in this, as in other projects on which we work, was to bring the voice of the consumer to management meetings and to relay what he was saying about the ideas developed by the company (Carey, 1986).

The marketing research programme for "Elegant" developed along a series of stages. Briefly they can be described as follows:

- Initial exploratory research
- Marketing-mix test
- Sessionability test
- Advertising test.

Initially, exploratory research was designed to look at the current drinking practices of young female drinkers. The objective was to try to understand their attitudes to drinking and the various drinks on the market. Through this understanding, Showerings hoped to identify gaps in the market and to see what type of drink could best fill these gaps.

Perhaps the most interesting thing to emerge from this initial work was that young women who started out by drinking Stag in their teens, felt the need to graduate to what they saw as a more sophisticated drink as they grew older. Pils seemed to be the most popular choice among these graduates, on the basis of value for money and the fact that it had a more sophisticated, adult image.

The movement to Pils, however, did not take place immediately. A young woman may chop and change between Stag and Pils for a period of over a year. She was also likely to try other drinks, such as "West Coast Cooler" and draught lager, in her search for the "right" drink. What a young woman drinks in the pub is an expression of her personality. The young female who drinks Guinness is making a statement that is different from that made by the girl who opts for a dry martini.

Many options exist in the female repertoire that can range between two extremes. Showerings was attracted to the concept of developing a product that would suggest femininity while creating a strong female imagery. It must reflect an element of independence and assertiveness that is modern.

It was apparent that a low-alcohol drink would not fit the bill. Young female drinkers aged under 30 want to get a kick from their drinks. Bitter, heavy tastes are not really suitable either. It was found that a light colour and a light dry taste were desirable, but that these properties should be coupled with a reasonably strong alcohol delivery. On the basis of this information a formulation of appropriate drink was attempted.

Next, Showerings examined how elements of the product, including package design, came together as a drink proposition. In other words, the company wanted to see how young female drinkers would react to the various elements, physical and image related, of the proposed new "Elegant" product. In order to do this, a marketing mix test was conducted.

This piece of research involved showing the proposed new bottle to a sample of 300 young women aged between 20 and 30 years, half of whom were regular drinkers of Stag and half regular drinkers of Pils. In addition to seeing the bottle, they were also allowed to taste "Elegant" and gave their opinions of it at interview sessions where a structured questionnaire was used. During this marketing mix test, attitudes to a range of other drinks were also examined in order to see where "Elegant" fitted into the current drinks market.

In image terms, "Elegant" emerged as a drink that:

- Appeals to women
- Would be found mainly in stylish pubs and bars
- Would be popular in continental Europe
- Would grow fast in popularity in Ireland
- Was sophisticated
- Was trendy.

These results were positive in that they related closely to earlier studies on the expressed preferences/attitudes of young drinkers.

In product tests on the physical properties of the new "Elegant" product, positive scores were recorded in key areas as illustrated in Table 4.1 below.

Table 4.1: Consumer Reactions to Product

	Percentage Response
Is refreshing	97
Has the right level of strength	89
Has the right level of sweetness	78
Has the right level of sparkle	74
Would buy the product when it comes on the market	85

Base: 300 young female drinkers.

Although encouraged by these results, there remained a slightly nagging question in the minds of Showerings' management: "How would the product perform in a session situation?"

It is one thing to have a taste of a drink, but the real test of its potential would come when people had a chance to drink it in quantity in a real drinking situation. For example, Showerings wondered whether consumers would reject it after one or two bottles. Or would it leave people with negative after-effects?

To answer these questions two sessionability tests were organised involving 65 Pils drinkers. Pils drinkers were chosen because it was felt that they would be an objectively critical set of consumers. They tend to be quite serious about their drinking and to be quite blunt in rejecting drinks that they find unappealing.

A hotel function room was chosen as the venue for the session-ability tests. It was laid out in an informal, lounge style. The young women invited along for the sessions were offered four bottles of "Elegant" each. They were asked for their opinions by means of a questionnaire after the first and third bottles, and by means of open group discussions at the end of the evening. Each participant was contacted the day after the session to see if she had any further comments to make.

Essentially, the results of the sessionability test reinforced the findings of the marketing-mix test and showed "Elegant" to be a suitable session drink that would fit in with other mainstream drinks such as lager and Pils. With regard to strength, there was a notable shift in consumer perceptions of the product's strength from the first bottle to the third. Many of the participants said that they believed at first that it would be quite weak but were pleasantly surprised to find that it had a "kick". The strength factor, which was said to be "about right", served to position it as being better value for money than low-alcohol fruity drinks.

The follow-up calls the next day produced a high level of positive comments. However, one point that caused some concern was that several people said that they found "Elegant" to be a bit too sweet and heavy, with the result that they felt they would not drink more than one or two bottles of it in an evening. This type of feedback was exactly what was sought from the sessionability tests as it was something that could not be picked up from people tasting small quantities, as in the marketing-mix test.

In an effort to solve this problem, the sweetness level was reduced for the next sessionability test. This had the required result. Sweetness was judged to be "about right", and reports that "Elegant" was too heavy to drink in quantity diminished.

Selection of Brand Name

Considerable attention was given to choice of a name for the new product. Many brainstorming sessions were held within the Showerings group before the final choice was made. Each of the proposed names on the final shortlist reflected concepts and themes around expressions such as "elegant", "style", "chic", "sophistication", "luxury" "cosmopolitan", "premium", etc.

In all, a couple of hundred names were considered. Among all the proposed options, one name stood head and shoulders above all the rest: "Ritz". In market tests, it was shown that this name had high acceptability, so Showerings quickly settled on branding the new product accordingly.

Distribution Plan

Showerings planned an intensive sales drive that would emulate the exposure level achieved by Guinness when launching "Kaliber", the non-alcoholic lager. Within two and a half months — that is, by the end of June 1986 — it was intended to achieve the following coverage:

Table 4.2: Planned Distribution

Area	Percentage
Dublin and Other Major Cities	84
Rest of Leinster	63
Munster	45
Connaught	40
Total	51

Sales would be concentrated on the largest outlets, over 2,500 pubs, bar and off-licences, while developing a strong presence in licensed supermarket chains. The salesforce was to impress on retailers that the product needed to be served chilled. Each sales representative was supplied with a "cool-box" capable of holding 24 bottles, so that Ritz might be presented and demonstrated to the trade at the correct temperature level. The salesforce was strongly encouraged to merchandise the product near Satzenbrau, if at all possible. Showerings had made representations to the trade associations, which it was hoped would ensure that the retail selling price of Ritz would be on par with that of Satzenbrau.

Role of Advertising

Showerings gave Young Advertising, Dublin, a detailed advertising brief as a result of which several concepts emerged for a multi-media programme. The campaign would ensure:

- That Ritz would be noticed — with a media-coverage rate of 95 per cent to be attained among the target group

- Strong positioning of the product in retail establishments, mainly in high turnover Irish licensed premises

- Correct "emotional" positioning — Ritz is for females but must not be perceived as effeminate.

It was planned to target sophisticated, self-possessed females who, at the same time, were in touch with the reality of everyday living. It was intended to promote the product as having a distinctive style, while remaining in the regular drink category and not being confined to special social occasions. "Ritz Catches the Light" was to be the central theme of the advertising campaign.

Given that the product was to be well-supported by a media campaign, it was decided that the theme developed by Young Advertising should be subjected to the rigours of consumer criticism before being finalised. A rough version of the television commercial was shown to 120 young female Pils drinkers to measure their reactions.

From the findings of this research it emerged that the television commercial clearly communicated the character of the new product in a way that appealed to the target audience. The drink came across as being cool, sophisticated and continental. Furthermore it was seen as a regular, rather than an occasional, drink.

The Ritz drinker was seen as pleasant, continental and beautiful with the kind of lifestyle a lot of young women would like to have. The commercial as a whole was considered to be interesting and enjoyable. The overall result gained from this research programme indicted that Ritz would hold substantial appeal for young female drinkers.

Communications-Support Programme

Both advertising and sales-promotion support programmes were devised to encourage trade participation. Packaging was designed so that the product would gain notice through its attractiveness. The product could, of itself, act as a strong Point of Sale (POS).

As Ritz was presented in a half-pint amber glass bottle, Showerings saw the need to reflect sophistication through providing a neck foil with front and back label. The back label contained factual information — alcohol/calorie/carbohydrate content — along with other relevant brand information.

The off-trade bottle was packed in an attractive premium style 3-pack. Subsequently, a 500 ml can with distinctive branding was developed to provide strong shelf impact for the off-trade.

Figure 4.1: Ritz Advertising Campaign

MEDIA SCHEDULE

- Television

  Mid-May–June 1986
  July 1986
  September 1986
  November 1986

  200 spots, approximately, in 4 bursts

- Consumer Press   June through December 1986

Image	*RTE Guide*
IT	*In Dublin*
U	*Hot Press*
Woman's Way	*Sunday Tribune*

- Trade Press   June/July/August 1986
  Vintner's World
  Checkout
  Today's Grocer

- Outdoor   June/July/August 1986
  National 48-sheet campaign
  70 Sites

- Bus Sides
  30 Dublin city-centre buses

Figure 4.2: Other Promotional Support for Ritz Launch

- Point of Sale (POS)
  Dripmats
  Walter Trays
  Counter Display Cards
  Till Stickers
  Window Stickers
  Cabinet Stickers

All POS material was available to Showerings' salesforce. Drip-mats and till stickers (with back adhesive) were sent directly to wholesalers with initial orders. An extensive sampling pro-gramme was planned for the off-licence trade.

Table 4.3: Ritz Marketing Communications Appropriation, May–December 1986

	IR£
Media Budget	375,000
Other Promotion	125,000
Total Marketing Communications	500,000

Role of Publicity

In addition to advertising and sales-promotion initiatives, Show-erings paid particular attention to the role of publicity in generat-ing awareness and interest in its new brand. Through its PR agency, Forman Dove, it developed a programmed series of press releases, highlighting background planning to the new product and its innovative features (particularly its dedication to "the modern young woman"). See Appendices 1, 2 and 3.

Post-Launch Marketing Research

As an integral component of its marketing plan, Showerings un-dertook extensive post-launch research on consumer perceptions and attitudes to Ritz, in particular the level of awareness of the new product among a representative cross-section of consumers within the Irish drinks sector. See Tables 4.4, 4.5 and 4.6.

The company realised that correct analysis and interpretation of the research data would have a significant bearing on the fu-ture direction to be taken with Ritz, "for better or worse" — and, indeed, the road ahead was to prove challenging, testing the mar-keting mettle of the Clonmel management team!

Table 4.4: Ritz Survey — Awareness x Demographics, 1986

Spontaneous Awareness*

	May %	June %	July %	November %
Sex				
Male	7	9	16	16
Female	7	14	23	26
Age				
Under 25	13	21	33	39
25–34	6	14	28	25
35–49	7	10	14	16
50–64	5	5	7	6
65+	2	2	5	2
Class				
AB	10	15	26	21
C1	8	15	19	26
C2	7	14	20	22
DE	6	8	19	17
F	6	6	12	11
Region				
Dublin	2	7	18	18
Rest of Leinster	10	14	23	18
Munster	15	15	17	20
Connaught/Ulster	1	10	18	24
TV Reception				
RTE only	12	14	17	17
RTE & Other (e.g. ITV)	5	10	21	21
Total				
All Alcohol Drinkers	7	11	19	20

Base: Alcohol drinkers.
*   **Unaided:** unprompted response in "Omnibus" question: "Have you *heard* of any new alcoholic drinks similar to bottled beer, cider or wine that have come on the market *this* year?"

Table 4.5: Ritz Survey — Awareness x Demographics, 1986

Total Awareness*

	May %	June %	July %	November %
Sex				
Male	26	37	52	68
Female	21	42	62	74
Age				
Under 25	36	56	79	89
25–34	25	49	73	88
35–49	25	35	55	69
50–64	15	24	29	52
65+	12	17	25	24
Class				
AB	24	40	65	79
C1	25	42	66	73
C2	23	43	61	76
DE	21	39	51	71
F	29	32	39	51
Region				
Dublin	15	35	55	71
Rest of Leinster	27	42	58	77
Munster	38	50	63	69
Connaught/Ulster	17	30	47	64
TV Reception				
RTE only	31	47	56	61
RTE & Other (e.g. ITV)	21	36	58	75
Total				
All Alcohol Drinkers	24	39	56	71

Base: Alcohol drinkers.

*   **Aided/Unaided:** including positive spontaneous responses, see Table 4.4 *plus* "Yes, heard of" answers from remaining interviewees to separate question: "Have you heard about or come across *this* particular drink, *Ritz* at all?" (on displaying *Ritz* show card).

Table 4.6: Ritz Survey — Awareness x Demographics, 1986 Trial*

	May %	June %	July %	November %
Sex				
Male	4	5	10	13
Female	2	9	19	31
Age				
Under 25	7	10	25	34
25–34	4	10	21	30
35–49	3	5	10	16
50–64	2	1	3	6
65+	—	5	1	2
Class				
AB	3	6	17	28
C1	4	10	17	26
C2	3	9	18	20
DE	4	5	10	19
F	3	2	5	10
Region				
Dublin	1	4	17	24
Rest of Leinster	3	9	14	21
Munster	7	9	14	19
Connaught/Ulster	—	4	6	16
TV Reception				
RTE only	7	10	12	16
RTE & Other (e.g. ITV)	6	5	15	23
Total				
All Alcohol Drinkers	3	7	14	20

Base: Alcohol drinkers.
*   Response to question: "Have you *tried* this drink, *Ritz*, at all?"

APPENDIX 1

Ritz Press Release No. 1 (Extract)

Forman Dove Public Relations, Harcourt Centre, Dublin 2
Date: May 14, 1986.   For further information contact: Jim Rowe.

"RITZ" SET TO BECOME MARKETING CLASSIC

"Ritz", the new drink from Showerings, is already selling in 5,000 pubs and every major supermarket group — well before the advertising campaign breaks on May 22.

The sell-in rate in the trade has been so high that Showerings have already had to double plan production volume at their Clonmel plant. This is the kind of problem any company would be happy to live with. In a sense, it demonstrates that Showerings got their initial thinking right and "Ritz" appears set to prove a classic marketing success story.

Further sweet music for the ears of Marketing Manager Tony Brophy and his team has been an enthusiastic report from one publican in a provincial town who jumped in well before the official launch. "Ritz" he said, was now the biggest selling bottled drink in his establishment. Also, out of the blue, came the letter from a young woman congratulating the company on their new product and assuring them that it would be her regular drink from now on.

That is what "Ritz" is all about. For up until now, most alcoholic drinks have been introduced primarily with the male drinker in mind. "Ritz" on the contrary, has been designed from the outset for the modern young woman of today.

Showerings' research also indicated that young women were more adventurous in their drinking habits and had a much wider repertoire of drinks than men. A latent demand was identified for a new, long mainstream drink with a bit of a bite, light in appearance, crisp to the palate and sophisticated in its appeal.

(ENDS)

APPENDIX 2

Ritz Press Release No. 2 (Extract)

Forman Dove Public Relations, Harcourt Centre, Dublin 2
Date: February 10, 1987.   For information contact: Jim Rowe.

"RITZ" BACKGROUND

In the past, most alcoholic drinks were introduced primarily with the male drinker in mind. "Ritz" was designed from the outset for the modern young woman of today.

Every aspect was assessed carefully. The yeast selected for the fermentation process, for example, comes from the top-quality, wine-producing region of Alsace.

Representatives of the target market themselves had a strong influence on the product, which cost over IR£100,000 to bring from the think-tank stage to fruition. The pack design alone, by international experts, cost IR£20,000.

In the final test, a rough of the television commercial created by Young Advertising was previewed to 120 young women who were regular Pils drinkers. It emerged that the commercial clearly communicated the character of "Ritz" in a way that appeals to the target audience. The drink came across as being cool, sophisticated and continental.

The IR£500,000 promotional launch and its follow-up included outdoor posters, Dublin bus sides, magazine advertising and a range of in-pub display material, as well as the 30-second TV commercial which has been the centrepiece of the marketing campaign.

The commercial features a beautiful and liberated "Ritz Girl" in a series of Paris scenes pursued by the paparazzi — the gossip photographers who concentrate on the rich and famous. Just who she is is left unanswered, but she is undoubtedly the kind of woman who drinks "Ritz". And that's the message.

(ENDS)

APPENDIX 3

Ritz Press Release No. 3 (Extracts)

Forman Dove Public Relations, Harcourt Centre, Dublin 2
Date: February 24 1987.   For information contact: Jim Rowe.

"RITZ" AN IRISH SUCCESS STORY

"Ritz" is the most dramatic success story of the Irish drinks industry for years.

The concept of the crisp, dry perry, developed exclusively by Showerings (Ireland) Ltd., is now being investigated with a view to marketing it in the USA. A considerable amount of market research will be required, but it is hoped that the concept may be introduced there in 1988.

"Ritz" has already broken all records for the Clonmel-based company since it was launched in May last year with a IR£500,000 advertising and promotional campaign. Forecasts have had to be repeatedly revised upwards and the latest projection is that retail sales in Ireland will exceed IR£7 million for the first year — five times the original target.

Recently named "Drink of the Year" by the authoritative trade magazine *Checkout*, "Ritz" is now a serious competitor for the top names in lagers and Pils — with an alcoholic strength and price to match — and also for vodkas and other spirits.

In its distinctive half-pint amber bottle and striking white, black and gold packaging, devised by an international specialist agency, it is now on sale at most licensed outlets throughout the country. Served chilled, it quickly established itself as a popular night-out drink among sophisticated young women in the 20–35 age group — its key target consumer group. However, "Ritz" has also proved to be a popular take-home drink with a wider public and, to encourage this off-trade demand, Showerings have recently introduced a 500 ml canned version.

Showerings, who celebrate their 50th anniversary this year, have had to expand their production facilities in Clonmel. Although they have had other major product performers with brands like "Stag", "Bulmers", "Madison", "Britvic" and "Cidona", they regard "Ritz" as their biggest instant success in their history.

Two years of secret planning, development and consumer research went into the Ritz launch. It was important to get the product and the taste right — the market for which "Ritz" caters in Ireland has IR£200 million buying power.

Says Marketing Manager Tony Brophy: "It has proved to be the most significant new drinks product launch in the second half of the 1980s. It is unique because it has created an Irish bottled drink category of its own. Although it ranks alongside the best premium lagers and Pils, it is quite distinct from them — and indeed is already outselling some brands in this sector. We are confident that the "Ritz" concept can be adapted successfully to overseas market also and will be a valuable export for Ireland".

Showerings already have considerable experience in export marketing through "Carolans Irish Cream Liqueur", "Irish Mist" and a number of other products which will in future be grouped under the new sister company, Grants of Ireland (International) Ltd. This summer, an IR£1.5 million bottling plant will be opened to cater for the growth in export business.

Another company in the group, Grants of Ireland (Sales) Ltd., is one of Ireland's leading wines and spirits importers and some of the products it handles are bottled in Clonmel. Showerings/Grants of Ireland are subsidiaries of the Cantrell and Cochrane group which is jointly owned by Guinness and the Allied Lyons Group.

(ENDS)

Source: Colm Carey at Showerings (Ireland) Ltd. wholesalers' conference, Clonmel, Co. Tipperary, April 1986.

Questions

1. Analyse Showerings' marketing research programme prior to and during the "Ritz" development process.

2. Critically assess Showerings' strategy of product planning and introduction to the market.

3. "... psychologists believe that the drinks which people choose show to some extent what they are" (Tony Brophy, quoted in the case). Comment.

4. If the management team were to undertake product development for the introduction of a new perry product oriented towards the UK and US markets, how might the plan and its execution differ from that described for "Ritz" in Ireland?

5

The Pig Industry in Ireland

Introduction

The pig industry in Ireland has seen radical changes over the past 30 years. Pigs were traditionally kept on most farms as a primary source of protein. They were fed on a combination of potatoes, some barley and skim milk which was returned to the farm by the creamery when the butter fat had been extracted. Traditionally two weaners were purchased — one for sale and one for home use. The pig for the house was usually slaughtered on the farm and this was an important social occasion for the household and the neighbours.

The past 20 years have seen major rationalisation within the pig industry. Pigs are now kept on larger units, the majority in excess of 200 sows producing in excess of 400 finished pigs per annum. At producer level, a rapid improvement in efficiency in production has survived. In terms of producer efficiency Ireland is now one of the most efficient pig producers in the world. These pigs are largely fed on compound feed supplied by the compound feed industry and processed in a small number of modern highly efficient slaughter houses.

This contrasts with the industry in Europe where pigs are still largely a farm enterprise as are other farm activities such as dairy, beef etc. However, the processing of the industry is much more efficient. On the Continent a large proportion of pigmeat (mainly pork) is sold as branded product and thus factories are able to deliver a better price to their producers.

The industry as a whole in Ireland is relatively small, employing 1,200 at farm level, 2,000 in processing, 500 in feed and

[104]

manufacture, and approximately 1,000 involved in providing services in one form or other.

The Pig Producers

There are three types of pig units in operation in Ireland: specialised breeding units breed and rear pigs up to 32 kg or approximately 11 weeks old; specialised finishing units then prepare these pigs for slaughter, which takes roughly a further 10 to 11 weeks; and integrated units carry out breeding and fattening activities.

Tables 5.1 and 5.2 present data on the structure of the production sector.

Table 5.1: Structure of Breeding and Integrated Units in Ireland

	Breeding Units		Integrated Units	
Unit Size Sows	No. Units	Total No. Sows	No. Units	Total No. Sows
20–49	35	1,235	53	1,585
50–99	65	4,745	49	3,425
100–199	112	16,110	58	7,790
200–499	116	34,575	28	8,430
500–999	40	25,330	11	6,955
1,000+	18	28,670	4	5,950
Total	386	110,665	203	34,135

Source: Tuite (1995).

Table 5.2: Structure of Finishing Units in Ireland

Unit Size	No. Units	Total Pig Places
150–499	16	5,200
500–999	19	12,870
1,000–1,999	14	20,330
2,000–4,999	22	72,000
5,000+	7	59,100
Total	78	169,500

Source: Tuite (1995).

The present trend within the industry is that of smaller producers getting out of pigs (during a particularly difficult period for
pigs, January 1991–93, 59 producers ceased to produce pigs). In
Ireland there are very few pigs kept in small units. There has
been great expansion of numbers in the integrated units, and
some of the specialist breeding and finishing units are becoming
more integrated. In 1994, for example, 2.7 million pigs were
slaughtered.

In comparing the structure of the Irish pig herd and that of our
main competitors we see that, in terms of herd size, the Irish pig
producer is well positioned. Table 5.3 shows the average herd size
in 1992. It has grown considerably since, and according to a Teagasc survey is close to 200 in 1995. The reason for this is that
many of the large finishing units have become integrated with
small suppliers.

Table 5.3: Average Sow Herd Size in EU

	Denmark	Netherlands	France	UK	Ireland
Average Herd Size	60	115	50	68	68

Source: MLC (1994).

In terms of productivity the Irish pig producer is one of the most
efficient in the world. Table 5.4 presents a comparison.

Table 5.4: Comparison of Critical Performance Factors in Ireland and the EU

	Denmark	Netherlands	France	UK	Ireland
FCE	4.12	3.81	4.21	3.74	3.77
P/S/Y	20.18	18.68	17.7	20.6	21.7

Source: MLC (1994).

In two important measures of efficiency, food conversion efficiency
(FCE) — that is, the number of kilos of feed, sow weaner and fat-
tener to get a kilo of carcass — and number of pigs sold per sow per
year (P/S/Y), Irish pig farmers can compete with the best. However, they are disadvantaged when compared on a cost per kilo
price. There are two basic reason for this: feed is more expensive

in Ireland and production costs are higher.

Irish slaughter weights are generally lower than those of our main competitors, and cheaper feeds can be fed to older and heavier pigs.

Table 5.5: Comparison of Pig Production Cost between Ireland and EU (1992 figures)

	Feed	Labour	Interest	Misc.	Total	Total ex-Labour
Ireland	75.4	10	6.9	9.5	101.8	91.8
Denmark	73.6	15.9	6.9	7.5	103.9	88.0
Netherlands	70.3	15.75	6.4	10.5	102.95	87.2
France	77.9	13.3	6.2	9.3	106.7	93.4
UK	75.7	12.94	8.16	9.7	106.5	93.56

Source: European Statistics, MLC (1994); Irish Statistics, Teagasc (1995).

The statistics in Table 5.5 are compiled from two sources. The Irish figures come from the Teagasc national recording scheme and are an average of the 1992 figures. They cover a large number of Irish pig herds. The remainder are MLC figures and cover roughly the same time period. All the figures are calculated in a similar fashion, with the exception of labour. The Teagasc labour figure is an estimate of the actual amount of money paid to labour. The MLC figure is a computed figure, and is calculated by estimating the number of labour hours per sow and multiplying it by local labour rates (for example, in Denmark 20 hours per sow at £11.50 per hour). However, with the exception of the Netherlands, the pig herds are small and the element of paid labour is minimal.

A recent study of European pig-feed costs found similar differences to those of the MLC. The costs are lower, reflecting the reduction in feed costs because of GATT.

The Dutch are considerably cheaper than anybody else. Focusing on our two main competitors on the export market, the Dutch produce pigs considerably cheaper than we do. The cost of producing pigs in Denmark is slightly higher. However, if the labour element is removed, they produce pigs nearly 4p per kilo cheaper than Ireland.

The industry at producer level has a number of major strategies. The Irish pig herd has an excellent disease status. In some large herds there has been a trend to destock and replace the herd with disease-free animals. These pigs perform better, and veterinary and medication costs are minimal. Pig herds on the Continent are currently experiencing major problems with Blue Ear and Swine Vesicular disease. In the case of the latter, a large number of pig herds have been depopulated in order to confine the disease to the southern states of Germany. This destocking is having a positive effect on pig prices. With the emphasis in the EU on free markets and deregulation, it is critical that Ireland protects the disease-free status of its herds.

The second major strength the Irish pig-producer has is the low density of pigs. Apart form the Lough Sheelin catchment area, slurry disposal does not present a major problem for pig farmers in Ireland. This contrasts with the Continent where slurry disposal is a major problem. In the Netherlands there are now limits on phosphorous levels in feeds, and a manure charge has been imposed. Enzymes must be added to increase the availability of phosphorous and thus reduce the requirement for added material.

A major problem facing both new and existing producers is the difficulty in obtaining planning permission both for expansion of existing units and the building of new units. No matter how well planned intensive pig units are, they do create a certain amount of pollution. However, in modern well-planned units, air pollution is minimal and only a problem when slurry is being pumped or moved out of the unit.

International Competitors

Denmark

Denmark is the largest exporter of pigmeat in the EU, slaughtering 19 million pigs and exporting 1.1 million tonnes of pigmeat annually. Pigs are largely produced on farms with other enterprises. Five co-operatives, which are farmer-owned, supply the feed and purchase the pigs.

The marketing of pigs in Denmark is highly organised with the five co-operatives slaughtering 97 per cent of all pigs. The producers receive a price for their pigs based on the market price received for pigmeat the previous week. All farmers are paid the same basic price regardless of processor, with an appropriate adjustment for carcass grading. The price is fixed weekly by the Federation Board, which has representatives from producers, processors and independent experts. Profits made by the processors are divided up into agreed amounts, which are then pooled to a consolidation fund, with the remainder being paid to producers as a bonus at the end of the year.

A very flexible taxation system operates in order to encourage investment in the industry. An important difference between the Irish and the Danish systems is the treatment of equipment and refurbishment in Denmark, with free depreciation allowed on a wider range of items such as feeders, slats, machinery and tractors. Corporation tax on profits is set at 34 per cent.

The Netherlands

The Netherlands has the highest density of pigs in Europe. The industry displays a high degree of integration, with the co-operative movement having a strong influence in the country. Many producers enter into long-term contracts with feed mills and processors (which are also co-operatives). This gives them some degree of security in terms of price and costs.

A price-stabilisation fund exists, with producers paying in or drawing out. This gives some degree of stability in terms of price. The tax system is similar in many respects to that which operates in Ireland.

Because of the size of the country and the volume of pigs produced, the Dutch have experienced considerable problems with manure disposal. There are now strict limits on the amount of phosphorous that can be applied to land, and in some instances slurry has to be shipped out of regions. A manure levy is now imposed on pig farmers. The levy equates to about £33 per sow and is used to fund environmental research and protection.

A loan scheme operates at low interest rates to pig farmers. It is guaranteed by the government. As well as encouraging banks to lend to farmers, the low interest rate acts as a stimulus to investment within the sector.

France

France currently consumes 2.2 million tonnes of pigmeat and is 90 per cent self-sufficient. The gap is made up by the import of live pigs mainly from the Netherlands.

Like many of the pig-producing countries on the Continent, the co-operative movement is particularly strong with 85 per cent of pigs produced within this structure. Farmers can avail of cheap compound feed and other necessary services from this source.

Prior to 1992, the French government heavily supported the industry through loans and grant schemes. However, loans are now only available to young farmers, or for renovations related to environmental protection. For young establishing farmers, loans of up to £50,000 are available to establish a business.

The co-operatives, through the banks, operate a price stabilisation scheme. The taxation scheme operates in a similar fashion to that in Ireland. However, items of plant and machinery can be written off slightly quicker. Corporation tax is a little lower at 33.5 per cent.

England

The UK consumes approximately 1.4 million tonnes of pigmeat per annum. Being only 72 per cent self-sufficient, it imports a considerable quantity of pigmeat products. Production over the past 10 years has been relatively static with the anticipated increase in production through the establishment of outdoor herds never materialising. Production in the UK has been affected in the past three years by Blue Ear disease, which affects the performance both of sows and of growing pigs.

New legislation has had a significant impact on the industry. This includes safety regulations, pollution control and new animal-welfare regulations. Currently, the majority of sows are kept in loose or tethered stalls. In the UK, it is stipulated that by 1999 all sows must be kept in loose sheds. For many farmers this will involve a considerable investment, and it is likely that many producers will not make the change and exit the industry.

The taxation system is similar to that which operates in Ireland; however, corporation tax is considerably lower. On the first £250,000 of profits a charge of 25 per cent is made, with the maximum rate set at 35 per cent.

The pig industry constitutes only a small proportion of the economy in the UK. Pig production has received very little help in terms of grants or cheap loans to help pig farmers to develop or comply with new legislation. Loans are available in the normal way; however, producers have often to pay a premium above commercial rates because of the perceived risk associated with the industry.

The Pigmeat Market

Along with the change in the home pig industry, the international production and consumption trends for pigmeat have changed over the past 25 years. On a global basis there has been a shift in production away from Europe and the USSR to Asia Pacific and USA/South America (see Table 5.6). The change in production patterns has followed consumption patterns. In the Far East consumption of pork has increased by 4 per cent per annum. The increase results from both increasing per capita consumption and increasing population. The increase in per capita income and population in many of these countries has led to an increased demand for food.

Many of the Pacific-Rim countries have adopted Western genetics and production technology. This has brought about a reduction in production costs, making them comparable to those of the West. However, some of those countries are now experiencing environmental problems — Taiwan, for example. Typically in hot countries water, rather than electrically driven fans is used as a method of cooling animals. This increases the volume of slurry produced and the associated disposal problems. However, governments are now starting to address such problems by introducing legislation similar to that of developed countries.

Table 5.6: World Pigmeat Production by Geographical Region

	% Share of World Pigmeat Production	
Region	**1970**	**1994**
Europe and Former USSR	50.4	33.0
Asia-Pacific	24.3	49.5
Africa	0.7	1.0
North/Central America	20.9	13.5
South America	3.7	3.0

Source: Pig International (1995).

In 1994 world meat production was estimated at 191.7 million tonnes. All meats experienced some degree of increase. Within the EU a total of 32 million tonnes of meat (excluding offal) are consumed annually (1992). Average per capita consumption within the EU is approximately 85 kg. This figure is substantially lower than those of the United States with 123 kg, Australia 102 kg, and Canada 96 kg.

Of the 32 million tonnes of meat consumed, 14.3 million tonnes or 44.7 per cent is pig. In Ireland approximately 174,000 tonnes of pigmeat were produced, of which 60 per cent was exported.

Table 5.7: Destination of Irish Pork and Bacon Exports (1994)

Country	Tonnes
UK	72,000
France	11,000
Germany	15,000
Italy	8,000
Japan	2,500
USA	3,000
Korea	2,500

Source: An Bord Bia (1995).

Over the past number of years, the market in Europe has had particular difficulties because of increases in production above those of consumption (within the EU, production is 3–4 per cent in excess of consumption). Because agricultural supports for grain and feed are the major cost of production, producers find it difficult to be competitive on the world market.

Two of Ireland's main markets have seen a drastic drop in production over the past year (UK 40,000, Germany 173,000 tonnes). Swine fever has had a major impact on the German pig herd; however, numbers should recover over the next 18 months. At the same time, in Germany there was a dramatic drop in meat consumption, owing to the BSE scare and associated adverse media publicity. In the UK new regulations regarding animal welfare and the cost of compliance with legislation have meant a reduction in the number of pigs produced. There has been a particularly buoyant market for Irish pigs in 1995 because of favourable fluctuation in currency.

Consumption of meat is expected to rise marginally over the next 10 years to reach close to 90 kg per capita at the close of the century. The current level of consumption, when compared to that of the United States, gives considerable scope for an increase.

Table 5.8: EC per Capita Meat Consumption (kg)

	1986	1992	1999
Pork	37.6	39.8	42.2
Poultry	16.2	18.9	21.5
Beef	23.2	21.9	21.5
Lamb	3.7	4.2	4.4
Total	80.7	84.8	89.6

Source: Healy (1994).

As we see from Healy's predictions (Table 5.8), beef and lamb consumption are going to remain more or less static with increases of the order of 6 per cent and 13.75 per cent for pork and poultry meat respectively.

However, it is difficult to predict where this extra consumption will come from. Complicating an assessment of the situation at the moment is the implementation of the GATT agreement. The meat element of the agreement started in 1995 and is due to be completed by 1999. The key elements of the meat agreement are:

- A reduction in domestic supports by 20 per cent (this includes such payments as headage payments, disadvantaged area payments, environmental protection schemes, retirement schemes, etc.)

- Border measures to be converted to tariffs and reduced by 36 per cent

- Minimum access of up to 5 per cent of domestic consumption to be provided on top of any access that is already permitted

- Subsidised exports to be reduced by 36 per cent in budgetary terms and by 21 per cent in volume terms.

To comply with the GATT agreement the EU has to reduce meat exports, reduce export subsidies, and allow increased market access for non EU countries. These restrictions cover beef, poultry and pigmeat.

Looking specifically at pigmeat, exports will have to be reduced by 107,000 tonnes or the equivalent of 1.25 million pigs, while at the same time allowing a minimum access for 76,000 tonnes of pigmeat. Under a similar arrangement there will be a reduction of 100,000 and 250,000 tonnes respectively for poultry meat and beef exported, with access being allowed for 29,000 and 20,000 tonnes respectively.

Overall, with the reduction in exports, the increase in import, and the reduction in intervention for beef, the price of other meats should become more competitive over the next number of years.

The Feed Suppliers

In terms of cost, the major suppliers to the pig industry are the grain merchants and the compound feed industry. In excess of 70 per cent of the cost of pig production is feed-related. Pig farmers purchase feed in two ways.

Home Mixers

Home mixers feed approximately 15 per cent of the pigs in the country. They secure their raw materials from grain merchant or feed millers, and then mill and mix this feed in their own units to provide a complete feed for their pigs. The main advantages of operating in this manner are: larger units can deliver feed to their pigs at a low cost; they pay a lower rate of tax if they are able to obtain classification as a manufacturing company (most are); they are in a position to utilise by-products such as whey and molasses more easily, which reduces the overall feed costs.

There is a capital cost involved in setting up a mill. However, a number of producers have availed of Business Expansion Scheme (BES) funding to do this.

Finished Feed

The majority of producers purchase finished feed from feed compounds. In 1994, 644,000 tonnes were produced and sold to pig farmers, making up 18.9 per cent of the total compound feed produced in the country. As well as availing of compound feed as a source of feed, many producers avail of credit (usually 3 months) making the compound-feed industry a major source of finance for the pig industry. Many millers provide some level of technical advice on pig production and are an important source of information on new technical development for pig producers.

Cost of Feed

As feed is the major cost of production, feed prices have a major bearing on the profitability of pig production. Farmers are very sensitive to feed prices and most treat feed as a commodity. In any event, because of the level of performance-monitoring, farm buyers can easily detect if inferior feed is being sold.

Many of the mills in operation are able to supply the level of service, feed quality and length of credit required by producers. Because there are many sources of supply, excess capacity and low levels of differentiation, farmers exhibit high levels of bargaining power and millers' margins are quite low.

Cereals are the main constituent of pig feed and thus have a major influence on feed prices. Unlike pigmeat, cereal producers are supported under the CAP régime. With the signing of the GATT, intervention for grain is now less significant as a means of price support. Cereal farmers in theory now receive a lower price for grain, and receive direct income support in the form of area aid. Under the GATT, cereal farmers are required to reduce the amount of grain produced to reduce the build up of grain mountains in the future. In order to achieve this, a setaside scheme was introduced. In this scheme, if they do not produce grain, farmers receive set payments from the EU on an area basis.

CAP reform and changes brought about by the GATT have both led to changes in the European grain markets. The reduction in grain intervention has brought about a reduction in grain prices and an increase in grain usage across Europe. The combination of reduced grain output (because of set aside) and increased grain usage caused by lower prices has meant that Ireland is now a deficit area for feeding grain. The drop of grain prices in Ireland relative to Europe has not been as significant, and the price of imported grain is becoming a significant determinant of cereal prices in Ireland. There has been a significant drop in the volumes of home-produced grain, with imports buoyant since 1992. The cost of transporting grain from the UK or the Continent is shown below and is now close to the grain price differential between Ireland and the Continent.

Table 5.9 demonstrates the disadvantage faced by Irish pig farmers. Feed prices are over £8 more expensive than on the Continent.

Table 5.9: Cost of Importing Grain from UK and France to Ireland

	EX UK	EX FRANCE
Haulage to Port	£4.00	£4.00
Port and Loading Charge	£3.00	£3.00
Shipping	£6.00	£9.00
Discharge and Port Charge	£3.00	£3.00
Total	£16.00	£19.00

Source: Torc (1995).

In a recent report for the Irish Grain and Food Association, Dr Tom Hanrahan estimates that Irish pig farmers may be at a disadvantage of between £6.50 and £9 per tonne in terms of feed costs. At £6.50 this equals an additional cost of £1.70 to produce an Irish pig. The difference in cost was estimated as follows:

- Different feeding régime in terms of diets for age and weight — £1

- Cheaper ingredients because of location close to major ports and better selection of ingredients because of same — £4 to £6

- More economical distribution because of proximity of feed mills to intensive production areas — £1.50 to £2.

In Ireland the introduction of the setaside scheme has meant that the country is now a net importer of grain. This means that grain prices in Ireland are relatively more expensive than in Europe. The grain price now is significantly influenced by the import price, which is the foreign price plus a carriage charge.

Government Support for the Industry

In all sectors of the economy, government intervention can have a beneficial effect on development. Within the pig industry government support has focused on the supply side and on processors. In the past four years, grants have been available to grain merchants and feed millers to develop their facilities. These grants were partly funded by the EU.

On the processing side, help is provided through a number of avenues. The major processors have received grants over the past number of years to develop their processing facilities. Assistance is also available for product development in terms of finance or facilities to carry it out.

On the marketing side An Bord Bia provides considerable support to the pig-processing industry. At a financial level, the Board plans to spend £1.8 million in 1995 on marketing and promotional activities. Support comes in the form of generic support for pig-meat promotion, as well as specific support for market research and branding activities for individual companies. The Board operates a dual focus. On the home market, promotion is the dominant feature of its support. Pork as a quality value-for-money product is a key activity. As well as an extensive media campaign, the Board also carries out food demonstrations and provides a comprehensive range of information leaflets for distribution at point of sale.

On the export market, Bord Bia's activities are more focused on specific markets. In the UK market, the focus is on expanding business with the multiple retail stores and increasing overall market share. On the Continental markets the focus is on increasing the quality of Irish pork that is used in the processing industry. The Board also provides marketing support for exports to Far Eastern countries such as Japan and South Korea.

As well as promotional activities, the Board provides support in a number of key areas such as:

- Organising tours and presentation for key foreign buyers to demonstrate the high quality of Irish pigmeat and the high standards within the industry

- Exhibiting food at all of the major European food exhibitions and introducing new customers to the range of available products

- Carrying out extensive market research in key markets and making this information available to the relevant companies

- Organising a pigmeat quality assurance scheme and promoting the quality Irish logo

- Providing direct support in the form of grants (up to 50 per cent for approved projects) for individual companies to enhance their marketing capabilities.

At producer level, very little assistance is offered. Grants are available for slurry-storage facilities; however, these can be difficult to secure and the uptake has been poor. Teagasc provides an advisory service at a nominal charge. A network of pig advisers keeps records and advises producers on how to improve performance. There is a significant uptake of this service among pig producers.

Within all sectors of the industry, government assistance is available for training and development. For pig producers a specialised course on pig production is run. The course involves attending lectures in pig production, as well as a block release programme to a number of different pig farms. The graduates are highly regarded by pig farmers and the majority find immediate employment. In the manufacturing sectors of the industry, training and development are supported by FÁS.

The Future

The pig industry in Ireland has experienced major changes over the past decade. At producer level there has been a rapid decline in the number of farmers producing pigs; however, this has been more than compensated for by the remaining farmers increasing productivity and herd size.

Feed costs make up a sizeable proportion of the cost of producing pigs in Ireland. However, the Irish producer is at a serious disadvantage because of higher feed costs relative to European competitors. The much-promised reductions in grain prices to result from the GATT agreement have not materialised.

The market situation for meat is ever-changing and unpredictable. The unpredictability has much to do with the volatile nature of pig supplies as well as a market that will have to change significantly as a result of the GATT agreement.

References

An Bord Bia (1995): "Meat Market and Renewal Outlook, 1994/95", Dublin.

Healy, S. (1994): *GATT and Its Impact on the Meat Industry*, Dublin: Department of Agriculture, Food and Forestry.

Milton Keynes Meat and Livestock Commission (MLC) (1994): "The Competitive Position of the British Pig Production Industry".

Pig International (1995): "25 Years of Achievement in Industry Growth", May.

Teagasc (1995): unpublished report.

Torc Grain and Feed Ltd. (1995): Personal Communication.

Tuite, P. (1995): "Concentration of Irish Pig Producers in Larger Units", *Irish Farmers' Journal*, 17 June.

Questions

1. Using Michael Porter's five forces model, analyse the Irish pig industry.

2. What can be done at the level of the State and at EU level to help the Irish pig industry to grow further?

6

The Irish Horse

Historical Background

The megalithic tombs at Newgrange, Co. Meath, date from the stone age, 5,000 years ago, a full half millennium before construction of the Egyptian pyramids. Excavation at the Boyne Valley prehistoric site revealed not only human remains but also evidence of the important role played by horses in Ireland's earliest civilisation.

From the Red Branch Knights era through the Celtic twilight to modern times, it is evident that the horse featured significantly in the rich pageant of Irish history, with heroic literature that refers to the particular horsemanship of the Tuatha De Danann.

The Celts, who came to Ireland from continental Europe, were skilled horsemen and brought with them a breed of Arab-like steeds. The ancient Irish pastime of horse racing enjoyed huge popularity, paving the way for the eventual emergence of the Thoroughbred. It is significant that "Byerly Turk", one of the three progenitors of the entire Thoroughbred breed, was ridden as a charger at the Battle of the Boyne in 1690 before finally being retired to stud in Ireland.

Ancient Irish charioteers tested the mettle of their steeds on the Curragh of Kildare at the dawn of history. "Cuirreach" is the old Gaelic work for racecourse. Appropriately, the Curragh racecourse is the venue for the Budweiser Irish Derby — one of the highlights of the Irish racing calendar, which incorporates a wide variety of meetings at 27 racetracks (two in Northern Ireland and the remainder in the Republic). Most of these cater primarily for flat events but jumping is a significant feature of the Irish racing calendar.

Jump Racing

Jump racing (also known as National Hunt) is an Irish speciality. The world's first recorded steeplechase took place in 1752 when Mr Edmund Blake and a Mr O'Callaghan rode a match of four-and-a-half miles from the Church at Buttevant to St Leger Church in Doneraile, Co. Cork, (*Horse Racing: Records, Facts and Champions*: 8). Irish jumpers were soon showing all-comers a clear pair of heels. An early nineteenth-century text described the local breed as "the highest and steadiest leapers in the world". The point has been well proven, since then, by Irish horses in the Aintree Grand National and other top events.

> Irish jumpers, point-to-pointers and hunters have the edge — and the track record to prove it. The crossing of sturdy Irish mares with well-bred Thoroughbred sires set a pattern for success — climaxing in the exploits of turf immortals like "Cottage Rake", "Arkle", and "Dawn Run". Modern jump racing now takes place on a global scale — and Irish breeds are setting the pace with horses like dual Breeders' Cup Steeplechase hero, "Morley Street" (*Irish Thoroughbred*, 1992).

The Irish Horse Population

Climate and soil type have bestowed many advantages with regard to horse breeding in Ireland. An island climate, tempered by the Gulf Stream and rich limestone soils, produces lush green pastures. This, combined with a high level of skills and an innate love of horses, makes Ireland a natural home for the horse.

Traditionally, horse-breeding has been a farm-based enterprise, involving the production of work and military horses. The advent of the tractor and the decline of the horse in the military had a profound effect on the horse industry. These developments are clearly illustrated by an analysis of the official livestock data (see Table 6.1 below).

Going back in time, the population of horses in 1939 was about 450,000. This figure remained remarkably steady until the 1950s. In the decade 1950–60, the number halved, roughly to just over 220,000 and, in broad terms again, it halved in each of the decades to 1980, also. Since 1980, the number has stabilised in the 50,000–60,000 range.

Table 6.1: Irish Horse Population — Selected Years

Year	Working Horses and Ponies	Thoroughbred Horses	Other Horses and Ponies	Total
1939	n/a	n/a	n/a	450,000
1950	n/a	n/a	n/a	390,614
1960	176,091	13,281	34,402	223,774
1969	86,900	17,800	19,100	123,800
1980	17,789	15,420	34,257	67,466
1985	7,800	16,100	33,700	57,600
1988	4,600	14,700	33,700	53,000
1990*	5,770	18,530	29,200	53,500

*   Castewriter estimate based on Department of Agriculture (1991), *The Saddle* (1992). All data except 1990 are quoted from Beecher (1989).

Source: "Agricultural Statistics", Central Statistics Office (CSO), Dublin.

The current horse population of Ireland, according to official CSO estimates, has been stabilised at approximately 53,000. The "other horses and ponies" category includes all horses and ponies used for leisure, hunting, jumping, eventing etc. and combined with "working horses" comprises the non-thoroughbred sector. The validity of the official statistics, particularly in relation to the young, unregistered equine stock, has been queried (Fitzgerald 1992).

It is somewhat ironic that horse sports only really began to flourish long after the horse had lost its practical utility. Increasing affluence has allowed more people to participate in horse sports, while modern transport facilities have allowed more competitors to travel abroad, and television has allowed many more people to become spectators at major events. Together, these factors have generated a demand for more international competitions and championships, and they have also ensured a steady improvement in standards.

The horse industry has, to a large degree, become part of the international entertainment and leisure business. The horse industry in Ireland is no exception in this regard, but, while the international market for leisure horses is expanding, it is highly competitive.

Ireland's Horsepower

The bloodstock industry represents a significant part of the Irish economy, with direct and indirect employment in the Thorough-bred industry estimated to be close to 25,000, according to a min-isterial statement in the Dáil on 12 February 1993, with as much as an additional 5,000 jobs ascribable to the non-Thoroughbred sector — although some commentators might argue that these estimates are excessive!

Much of the employment is generated in rural areas where there are unlikely to be alternative economic activities such as manufacturing industry.

The industry is a significant contributor to the balance of trade, with annual export sales in the region of IR£45–60 million in recent years, since over 80 per cent of Thoroughbreds are sold abroad. Currently, it is estimated by bloodstock-industry sources that Thoroughbred exports are in the region of IR£45 million, with National Hunt horses contributing up to IR£10 million to foreign earnings.

Today, many major international stud owners have established farms in Ireland — including H.H. the Aga Khan, the Maktoum family, Mr Walter Haefner and others. Several of the world's leading stallions now stand in Ireland. Native bloodlines have been crossed successfully with American and other influences. There are approximately 5,000 Thoroughbred breeders in Ireland, 4,000 of whom own only one or two mares. In 1992, the Thorough-bred horse population was over 19,000 as indicated in Table 6.2.

Table 6.2: Irish Thoroughbred Horse Population

	1986	1991	1992
Stallions	270	380	370
Mares	8,500	12,100	11,700
Foals	5,223	7,304	7,118
All Thoroughbreds	13,993	19,784	19,188

Source: Mitchell (1993a).

Note: The pedigree of the humblest Thoroughbred racehorse in any part of the world can be readily traced to its roots, in many cases for more than 30 generations, and we have access to the performance and breeding records of all its ancestors. No other animal species is better documented than the

Thoroughbred horse, no other organised sport has a longer recorded history than horse racing.

Successive governments have encouraged horse breeding as an enterprise vital to the national economy. The industry has benefited from special fiscal concessions over the past two decades. This has led to the emergence of world-class breeding establishments owned by both domestic and overseas interests.

The Thoroughbred sector has two main functions — racing and breeding. Within racing there is a further division, the flat for horses of between two and four years old, and National Hunt for horses of four years and older. The flat horses run distances of between five furlongs and two miles, whereas the National Hunt horses run longer distances over fences.

A unique aspect of the equine industry is the way in which the current year's demand for stud services depends, to a significant extent, on the previous year's sales results. In this way, the breeder uses historical information to predict trends, often inaccurately. Consequently, the boom period of the early 1980s has led to a significant level of overproduction in recent years. To combat this it may be necessary to promote such practices as: rebates for gelding male offspring, price discrimination in favour of quality mares, and limited stud bookings for stallions. Other alternatives include the development of overseas markets for breeding stock.

Table 6.3: Profile of Irish Racing Training Establishments, 1985

No. of Horses	No. of Trainers
1–5	144
6–10	104
11–15	50
16–20	19
21–30	21
31–50	15
50+	13
Total	366

Source: Report of the Commission of Equity into the Thoroughbred Horse Breeding Industry, 1987.

In response to the increasing international dimension of the Irish horse industry, high-class veterinary services are now provided for Irish stud farms. The Irish Equine Centre at Johnstown in Co. Kildare is a case in point, being a pioneering purpose-built complex devoted to diagnosis, management and prevention of disease in horses. As a result, the country enjoys a high health status in the bloodstock world. In any year, the percentage of live foal births from the previous year's mare coverings is a good indication of the standards of animal health and of the general level of management operating at Irish stud establishments.

Ireland has been a leading Thoroughbred nursery from time immemorial. Whether on the flat or over jumps, Irish-bred horses have achieved success, worldwide, with Irish horses being exported to over 35 countries. Legendary equine "greats" that have graced the Irish turf include the finest steeplechaser of all time, "Arkle"; the Belmont Stakes winner "Go and Go", which was the first European-trained horse to win an American classic; and the Breeders' Cup Mile victor, "Royal Academy". Over time, virtually all the world's top races have been won by Irish horses, including the Melbourne Cup.

Irish mares have featured prominently in the Thoroughbred stud books and on the racetrack from the outset. Early notables include the celebrated eighteenth-century "Paddereen Mare" (said to have run with rosary beads around her neck!). The pre-eminence of the Irish steeplechaser is evident from an analysis of performance at the major UK National Hunt event, Cheltenham, (see Table 6.4).

Table 6.4: Winners at Cheltenham, 1981–1991

Country of Breeding	No. of Winners
Ireland	120
UK	69
US	4
France	3
Canada	1
New Zealand	1
Total	198

Source: Mitchell (1993b).

Development of Irish Racing and the Bloodstock Industry

A betting public had grown up in England in the wake of the Industrial Revolution but did not exist in Ireland until the current century. The huge crowds which thronged to witness the sport of their betters in Ireland generally had no disposable income.

Within the past century there was significant development of Irish racing and disposable income. Consequently, significant illegal betting practices emerged, forcing the Irish Government to act in 1926. Off-course betting was made legal in that year, and further Acts establishing control over it followed in 1928, 1929 and 1931.

Allied to these came the Totaliser Act in 1929 which gave a licence to operate the Tote to the Irish Turf Club and the INHS — Irish National Hunt Steeplechase — committee. In 1930, despite opposition from bookmakers, the Tote came into operation at the Fairyhouse Easter meeting.

In 1945, the Racing Board and Racecourses Bill was passed by the Dáil, bringing into being the Racing Board to provide for the improvement and development of breeding and racing. The bill envisaged that it would do this through better control of racecourses, over which it was given supervisory powers, the operation of the Tote, and the imposition of a levy on on-course betting.

The Racing Board's remit was, however, confined to finance and related matters. Not only were the Turf Club and INHS committee confirmed in their traditional roles, but their powers were strengthened. By virtue of the legislation, bookmakers were required to hold permits from the Board. The effect of the Board's work on the racing industry was immediate and substantial.

A major factor in the growth of the Irish Thoroughbred breeding industry has been the development of large studs of international repute, such as Coolmore and the Airlie-Grangewilliam-Simmonstown conglomerate. The introduction of American-bred horses to studs, such as those at Coolmore and Airlie, has contributed greatly to the Irish breeding industry.

In particular, Arab investment has been significant at Kildangan stud, in Co. Kildare, which was bought in the mid-1980s by a member of the Royal family in Dubai, Sheikh Mohammed, already the owner of the Woodpark and Derrinstown studs.

The result of investments such as these has been that the Thoroughbred horse industry has become an employer on a par with some of the largest industrial sectors in the country. Traditionally, a high proportion of the country's Thoroughbreds has been sold at English sales. Nearly half of the turnover of British sales comes from Irish-bred horses.

Sponsorship

In recent decades, sponsorship has become critical to Irish racing. In all probability, the first instance of commercial sponsorship at an Irish race meeting occurred at Tralee in 1805 when "the Gentlemen of the Profession of the Law of the County of Kerry" gave a prize for a race.

The Irish Hospitals Trust was founded in 1930 by Richard Duggan, a leading bookmaker, following special lottery legislation passed in the Dáil. Duggan's partners in the venture were Joe McGrath and Captain Spencer Freeman. McGrath had been appointed Minister for Labour in the Irish Free State's first government. Subsequently, McGrath was prominently involved in racing, both as an owner and as a breeder. In 1962, the Irish Hospitals Trust contributed £30,000 to the prize money for the "Irish Derby" — Ireland's premier flat-racing classic — run at the Curragh.

This sponsorship had the effect of raising the overall standard of racing in Ireland. Overnight, Ireland was transformed into a country where competition of the highest level was available. In 1986, Budweiser, the giant American beer manufacturer, took over the Derby sponsorship.

Difficulties at Many Irish Racecourses

Despite its success stories, Irish racing, according to the Report of the Commission of Inquiry in the Thoroughbred Horse Breeding Industry (popularly known as the "Killanin report"), was in a "perilous financial state" in 1986. Since then, various aspects of the racing industry have seen growth — for example, sponsorship and the overall level of prize money have increased as a result.

Irish prize money levels rose substantially over a decade, from IR£4 million in 1981 to IR£13 million in 1991. The five Irish classic races consistently lure top-rank international contenders. Minimum race values have likewise been boosted, a doubling of money occurring in one year, 1990–91. Notwithstanding all these developments, many problems loom on the horizon for Irish racing.

Over the past decade spectator facilities at the major racing ventures have been significantly upgraded. In particular, tracks like the Curragh (Irish racing headquarters where the five classic races are contested) and Leopardstown provide sophisticated modern facilities. Festival meetings such as Punchestown and the Galway races draw large crowds to enjoy thrills and spills in a holiday atmosphere. There is even an annual race meeting at Laytown Strand where starting times are governed by the tide!

However, this extra funding has been divided, unevenly, among the country's racecourses. In 1985, it was calculated that 58 per cent of prize money was absorbed by meetings at the Phoenix Park, and the Curragh and Leopardstown.

The result of these developments has been that racecourses, many of which date back to the last century, have insufficient funds to improve amenities and prize money. Consequently, observers fear that the public appeal of a day's racing is in serious jeopardy, and the difficulties have caused one prominent economic consultant to call for rationalisation of the number of racecourses — see Exhibit 2 in the Appendix.

Promotion of Thoroughbred Horse Ownership

The Racing Board, through its new subsidiary, Irish Thoroughbred Marketing (ITM) actively promotes the concept of horse ownership to individuals and groups on the following lines, while highlighting the fact that there is a good support infrastructure, including two international bloodstock auctioning firms — Goff's Bloodstock Sales, Kill, Co. Kildare and Tattersall's (Ireland), Fairyhouse, Co. Meath; a dozen bloodstock agencies, and over 300 trainers in Ireland.

> The dramatic increase in prize money means that horses now represent better value than ever before. Potential new owners should bear in mind, the possible additional costs of agency fees, insurance and VAT, when deciding on their budget which should allow for about £10,000 per annum, on average, for training costs, for both the Flat and National Hunt.
>
> Bloodstock prices, like the asset valuations, have fallen back from the heady heights seen in the late 1980s. The astute investor likes to purchase when there is sound value, so now is a good time to buy into racing. At the present time all the important factors contribute to making horse ownership, in Ireland, more rewarding,

from the initial cost of purchase through to the speed and range of prize money available.

Multiple ownership has become increasingly popular, with horse enthusiasts coming together to share the costs and the rewards. Partnerships, syndicates, corporate ownership and racing-club ownership have all now become integral components of the Irish Thoroughbred racing scene. Estimated annual ownership costs are given in Table 6.5:

Table 6.5: Average Annual Cost of Ownership

Training Fees*	£7,500
Turf Club Fees**	£1,000
Vets'/Farriers' Fees	£750
Travel Costs	£400
Total Cost	£9,650

*   Fees vary, IR£5,000–£10,000 depending on the trainer.
**   Based on an average of four runs under both rules and appropriate Registration and Entry Fees.
Source: Irish Thoroughbred Marketing Brochure, 1992.

In addition to promoting development of the racing industry on the domestic front, ITM is particularly concerned with increasing export sales of Irish Thoroughbreds. As Table F in the Appendix shows, the United Kingdom is the main market, but ITM is attempting to expand its activities to new emergent markets. It is not content to concentrate on "fishing where the (traditional big) fish are", according to ITM's Marketing Director, Matt Mitchell. An indication of the barriers to be faced in the competitive environment is instanced by Japan where up to 65 per cent of races are restricted to horses bred there. The Japanese Racing Association has stated that such restrictions may now be eased.

Responding to current trade barriers, Agence Française has established "Japan Day" when four leading Japanese jockeys ride against their French counterparts at Deauville during sales week. Japanese jockeys are important personalities in their country, enjoying the same status as rock stars, earning high endorsement fees "off track". As a result, Agence Française has been besieged by Japanese film crews wanting to televise the event, and Japanese companies queuing to sponsor the event.

Point-to-Point Racing

One branch of the sport which, more than any other, has thrived is point-to-point racing, originally known as "Redcoat Races". Organised by the hunting community, they were held over natural terrain, and, until the late twentieth century, were free of INHS regulations. Gradually, they have gone much the same way as steeplechasing, becoming subject to increased control from the INHS committee. Prepared fences have tended to take the place of the banks and ditches of former times. Better facilities for spectators have resulted, and the races, which take place mainly on Sundays, have proven very popular.

One of the reasons for the growth of the sport is that it provides a proving ground for steeplechasers, with horses likely to make the grade normally changing to steeplechasing at seven years of age. Despite this "nursery" aspect of point-to-point, and the serious betting activity that it attracts, it still remains a sport for amateurs organised by amateurs. Frequently, the horses, which are required by the regulations to be hunted regularly, are non-Thoroughbred animals, owned and ridden by local farmers at meetings where there is intense local rivalry.

The Thoroughbreds competing point-to-point may go on to better things in the steeplechasing or eventing fields — in top-class three-day eventing, the Thoroughbred hunter-chaser is frequently to the fore. The non-Thoroughbred may become a successful showjumper or show exhibition champion. On the point-to-point field, no distinction is made between breeds. Frequently, the good non-Thoroughbreds provide excellent competition for their more finely bred peers.

It is of interest that there has been a substantial increase in the number of horses participating in point-to-point in recent times, mainly for the following reasons:

- Producers, who were unable to sell their horses as unbroken three and four-year-olds, have kept these horses in the hope of selling once they have been proven in the point-to-point field.

- The cost of running a horse point-to-point race is only a fraction of the cost of running inside the rails, since you can train the horse yourself and entry fees are generally only £5.

Irish Horse Breeds

The non-Thoroughbred sector of the equine industry consists mainly of the "Irish Sport horse". A breeding system originally conceived for the production of horses suitable for working on small farms has been adapted to produce the Irish Sport horse. The Irish Sport horse does not exist as a definable breed as such. It is rather a cross, containing Thoroughbred and Irish Draught blood. Occasionally, it may contain a mixture of other breeds, including the Connemara pony.

The arrival of various horse breeds through the centuries provided Irish breeders with an expanded and varied base from which to exhibit their special skills. In order to appreciate the Irish Sport horse it is necessary to understand the basic breeds which go into its making.

The Irish Draught horse was Ireland's main work animal. It was developed over the centuries into a work horse for use on small farms. As most farms could only afford one or two horses, the need was for a utility animal. A range of specialised horses was found on larger farms and estates only. Accordingly, the Irish Draught was used for all farmwork, to pull the trap, and was saddled up for the hunt. This accounts for the fact that this horse has a variety of qualities and does not fit into the usual categories. It certainly is not a cold-blooded horse in the classical sense, being lighter and much faster than a Shire or Clydesdale, but also more powerful than a Thoroughbred. The Irish Draught possesses qualities of substance, strength, hardiness, stamina and temperament, qualities selected for and evolved over centuries.

While the Irish Draught was generally regarded as a breed in the nineteenth century, the first studbook was not published until 1918. Significant decline in numbers occurred in the years since the Second World War (because of farm mechanisation), until a group of dedicated breeders got together in the 1970s with the aim of preserving and promoting the breed.

The typical Irish Draught can be described as an active short-shinned powerful horse, with a smooth coat. It has an abundance of courage and stamina, with a docile temperament. As three-year-olds, mares stand at 15.2 hands and over (1.57m+), and stallions at 16.0 hands and over (1.62m+). In 1991, there were 676 registered Irish Draught mares at stud.

With the decline in the traditional role of the Irish Draught on many farms, breeders and enthusiasts were forced to seek alternative roles for the breed. In doing so, they discovered that one of the outstanding features of the Irish Draught was that, if crossed with the Thoroughbred, it successfully exploited this cross to produce the sought after sport and leisure horse of today. The basic cross (half-bred) normally produces what is regarded as the heavyweight hunter.

Traditionally, the basic cross was a Thoroughbred stallion on an Irish Draught mare but, more recently, Irish Draught stallions have been used in a "reverse cross" fashion on lighter non-Thoroughbred, and, indeed, some Thoroughbred, mares. Perhaps, the Irish-bred American Olympic team showjumper "Mill Pearl" is the most successful example of this "reverse cross".

While the Irish Draught seems to have the attribute of being technically neat with the use of forelimbs over a fence, it is also true that many horses derived from the Irish Draught do not have sufficient stride ever to make a successful career in equestrian sport.

The consensus of opinion on the most appropriate strategy for producing the best bloodlines in the non-Thoroughbred sector has favoured crossing a half-bred mare with a Thoroughbred stallion, to produce a three-quarters-bred animal. This, it is felt, best combines the honesty and stamina of the Irish Draught horse with the agility of the Thoroughbred.

With so many variables involved in this cross-breeding programme, great skill (or art?) is required in predicting the outcome. Irrespective of the level of Thoroughbred in any particular sport horse, the characteristics of the Irish Draught are almost invariably bound to appear.

Preservation of the Irish Draught Horse

Reports into the horse industry over the years have highlighted the dangers which threaten the Irish Draught. In 1935, a Commission of Inquiry into the horse-breeding industry expressed concern about the quality of such horses. Over time, fewer and fewer Irish Draught mares were being mated with Draught stallions.

Farmers found it more profitable to cross breed with Thoroughbred stallions because the resultant progeny would fetch a better price than that of a mating between two Irish Draughts.

A special survey team, established by the Government in 1965, warned of the danger of the likely extinction of the foundation stock of Irish Draught mares. Five years after the survey team reported, the Irish Government decided to act on its findings and established a semi-state body, Bord na gCapall, (the Horse Board), charged with responsibility for the non-Thoroughbred (half-bred) horse industry.

Bord na gCapall — The Irish Horse Board

From the early 1970s until 1988, when the government abolished it, the body with the greatest resources at its disposal for the education and training of horse and rider was the semi-state body, Bord na gCapall. At an early stage, a farriers' training scheme was established, and riding schools were encouraged to improve the standards of horse management and riding instruction.

Bord na gCapall realised that Irish horses had to be marketed effectively if Ireland were to compete with other countries for the increasing Continental market for horses suitable for leisure riding. The British market, which traditionally had absorbed the vast majority of Irish half-bred horses, had contracted dramatically. In 1972, this number had declined to the 700 mark. The Board devoted much of its resources in its early years to remedying this loss, and established its own sales operation.

Central to the Board's work was the production of the Irish horse register, established in 1974. It became the basis for the identification of all half-bred stock. For ten years, inspections were carried out annually, eligible mares were registered and their progeny recorded. This meant that half-bred horses being sold abroad were equipped with passports which documented their breeding and, if relevant, their competitive performance — information which was of great importance to potential buyers.

A feature of the development of the register since 1979 was the agreement between the Board and the Northern Ireland Department of Agriculture to make it a joint register for horses both from the Republic and from Northern Ireland. The ultimate objective was to have all non-Thoroughbred horses in Ireland registered in the Irish Horse Register, so that each horse would have a "passport" containing a certificate of origin and identification.

The Irish Draught Horse Stud Book is maintained by the Department of Agriculture and Food in Dublin as part of the Irish Horse Register. The Irish Draught Stud Book comprises two parts

— the Register (the main book) and the Appendix. Fillies can gain admission to the main book by being the progeny of a mare, listed in either the main or Appendix sections, and an approved stallion. Stallions must be approved and be the progeny of main-book parents.

Farm Basis for the Industry

Horse breeding in Ireland has remained a farm-based enterprise. Analysis of official data shows that, in 1985, 24,000 farm holdings kept horses (CSO, 1985). Just under 20,000 (10 per cent of all farm holdings) kept non-Thoroughbred horses. While half of these kept only one horse, 1,100 holdings kept five or more non-Thoroughbreds.

In the recent past, financial returns from horses on many farms have been poor. A study carried out in 1979 (O'Neill, Shanahan, Kennedy and McStay, 1979) showed that only 11 per cent of holdings keeping horses cited commercial reasons for doing so. Over 55 per cent said that they "just liked horses" or described the enterprise as "a hobby". However, most did not exclude the hope of making money at some stage. Since this survey was carried out, production quotas and levies have been applied to the main agricultural commodities (especially milk and cereals). Many farmers are now seeking alternative enterprise to supplement their incomes.

Teagasc (the Agricultural and Food Development Authority) has recently shown that a horse enterprise operated under a good management system can achieve returns which compare favourably with a beef enterprise. This analysis of the viability of horse production has been confirmed by the Department of Agriculture and Food which states that "in the case of well-planned and efficiently operated sport-horse enterprises, the returns could exceed the returns from conventional enterprises". Gross margins per hectare of anywhere between IR£100 and IR£1,070 have been predicted. Accordingly, many farmers are now looking on horses from a less traditional perspective.

Development Programme

In the light of the national importance of the horse industry and the increasingly restricted opportunities in the traditional food-producing sector of agriculture, the Minister for Agriculture launched the "National Programme for the Development and Servicing of the non-Thoroughbred Horse Industry".

The programme had three main objectives:

- To maximise output and exports from the industry

- To maximise returns to primary producers

- To develop further the equestrian and leisure side of the industry.

The primary element in the plan concerned the breeding and production package aimed at improving the quality of horses for use across the whole range of equestrian sports, especially showjumping. It was hoped to mould the industry away from the traditional approach, into a more commercially oriented one. While the reputation of the Irish Sport horse derives in the main from its Irish Draught base, every success of such a cross has put the future of the Irish Draught as a pure breed in jeopardy.

Accordingly, commencing in 1990 a grant of IR£400 was paid to the breeder of each pure Irish Draught foal registered in the Horse Register. Additionally, a grant of IR£150 was paid to breeders in respect of foals from approved sires and dams, registered in the Irish Horse Register or the Connemara Stud Book (subject to an annual maximum of five foals). Furthermore, headage payments made on livestock in disadvantaged areas became payable on eligible registered mares in all disadvantaged areas — the rate of grant is IR£70 (see Exhibit 1 in the Appendix).

EU "Leader 1" Programme in Co. Clare

In an attempt to improve the quality of breeding mares in the west of Ireland, the West Clare Breeders Group under the EU "Leader 1" programme gave a £1,000 grant to owners of specially selected quality mares, on production of a live foal by an approved stallion. The aim was to give 25 grants per year for the next two years, and, if enough mares were not found in the area, breeders would be able to buy in mares of the required quality in the knowledge that they would get the £1,000 grant.

It is hoped that this will establish the area, encompassing Lissycassey, Labasheeda, Cooraclare and Miltown Malbay, as one of the top-quality non-Thoroughbred centres, and, in turn, will increase the profit margins of the breeders in the area.

The same group also imported an Italian stallion with proven jumping ability. This stallion will be crossed with mainly Irish Draught mares, and then the filly foals will be kept to form the next generation of breeding mares.

Challenges to the Irish Sport Horse

The image of the Irish horse, internationally, is of a very placid animal, basically sound, with durability and an aptitude for jumping and cross-country. As a consequence, the Irish-bred horse is widely regarded as a most suitable mount for amateur riders.

A very positive image has been created over the years by the success of Irish-bred horses in international competition. But, more recently, the Irish industry has been challenged by horses custom bred in countries with a more sophisticated breeding policy, such as France, the Netherlands and Germany.

There have been, and continue to be, many outstanding individual success stories in the case of the Irish horse. However, at the top level, Irish breeders need to recognise that the marketplace has changed and puts more emphasis, now, on the proven performance of the animal itself and also its ancestors. It is in this sphere that the sophisticated breeding programmes of continental producers are paying off — see Exhibit 3 in the Appendix. One comment often levelled at the Irish horse is that it is successful despite our system, not because of it! Another statement that has challenged the national approach to breeding and production is that "the Irish produce the Rolls Royce of horses — unassembled"!

Most of the non-Thoroughbred sires at stud in Ireland today have had no performance assessment. Therefore (with some notable exceptions) should coverings by these sires continue to climb as a percentage of total coverings, there is the danger of producing plainer, less athletic horses than those demanded by today's international market.

Another problem facing the Irish cross-breeding system is that it depends on the availability of suitable Thoroughbred stallions because, for various reason, such horses have become increasingly difficult to procure at an economic price for the traditional stallion owner in the farming community.

One noticeable fact when reviewing the breeding of successful Irish showjumpers and three-day eventers is that there is no general consistency with regard to the breeding origin, especially in the case of the sires of successful horses. It is very hard to recommend a stallion to a mare owner for a particular trait, and this task is made no easier by the absence of any hard statistical information on stallions and their progeny.

However, the provision of a sum of money by the Government and the European Commission to develop computer systems and set up programmes to facilitate the production of Stallion Genetic Indices is a welcome step in this regard (see Exhibit 1 in the Appendix).

Breeding Support for Sport-Horse Production

The Irish system of physical inspection/performance testing of non-Thoroughbred compares unfavourably with "competitor" countries in Continental Europe where all mares are inspected prior to being granted approval by the breeding authorities — as, for instance, is the practice in the Netherlands, under the control of KWPN. However, the Irish Government, in conjunction with the European Union, provides a range of support measures for the breeders of sport horses (see Exhibit 1 in the Appendix).

New Horse Board Formed

With Dr Noel Cawley of An Bord Bainne (Irish Dairy Board) as its chairman, a new Government-funded "representative body for the non-Thoroughbred horse industry" was established in May 1992. It was assigned the job of promoting the Irish Sport horse as a viable alternative farm enterprise, with the following objectives:

- To improve the quality of the Irish horse
- To identify markets and help define breeding which best serves these markets
- To promote the training of breeders in technical aspects of horse production
- To assist in the promotion of equestrian tourism
- To represent the interests of breeders in relation to other organisations, including Government departments.

Noel Cawley noted that, just like every other commercial enterprise, the horse industry has been led by the marketplace: "We must produce the horses that the market wants and it will be the job of this new body to set up the structures that will help bring that about" (*Irish Farmers Journal*, 16 May 1992).

A member of the new board, John Kennedy, the Irish Farmers Association representative, does not underrate the extent of the task ahead "since replacement of quality mares is a long gradual process but we must begin". He is also concerned that too many young farmers might come into horses without the training needed to deliver the quality demanded by the marketplace. Moreover, he wants to see more concentration on properly developing the Irish Army team as one of the main spearheads in a new strategic approach to marketing strategy (*Irish Farmers Journal*, idem).

Market Potential and Prices for Sport Horses

Traditionally, young Irish horses that show promise have been in keen demand abroad, and the performances of Irish bred horses representing so many nations in international competitions have been well recorded. The outstanding attribute of these horses is their ability to withstand the rigours of international competition over an extended lifespan — with durability and resilience being features of the Irish horse which, with much justification, can be claimed to derive from the dedication of generations of breeders with a passion for hunting, steeplechasing or showjumping.

Although the Irish Sport Horse has made its way around the world, there is considerable uncertainty about the exact level of overseas sales, as the following indicates:

> The official value given for non-Thoroughbred exports in 1991 is IR£3.9 million but this estimate is, in my opinion, seriously under-valued and a more realistic figure would probably be in the region of IR£16 million (Forde, 1991).

Nevertheless, it is clear that exports of non-Thoroughbred horses from Ireland have decreased from over 10,000 in the early 1970s to around a couple of thousand. This decline has taken place against the background of an increasing European market for medium-level horses suitable for sport and leisure. Have Irish horse producers been unable to produce animals to the standard required to cater for this demand, or are they overly handicapped in having to transport their horses across one sea to reach the

British market, and across two seas to reach other European markets? Sea transport is still the norm in the non-Thoroughbred horse industry.

It is significant that countries such as Britain and East European states are currently producing horses at lower costs than Irish breeders. This is particularly important when one considers the cost of shipment of Irish horses to market abroad — for example, approximately IR£1,200 to Italy and IR£3,000 to the Eastern Coast of the United States. However, the potential for increasing exports is considerable.

Sport-Horse breeding, compared with its Thoroughbred counterpart, has fewer market limitations. In the United States, all major horse-breed registration numbers have increased dramatically during the past quarter of a century, reflecting increased prosperity — the recent recession, notwithstanding. In Europe, too, there has been a dramatic growth in interest in equestrian sports, with over 500,000 active riding participants in Germany, and a million people riding in Britain. In Switzerland equestrianism is the third most popular sport, nationally.

New, non-traditional markets such as Libya, Japan, Korea and the Scandinavian countries have also been developing. Interestingly, to judge from an article in a recent edition of the Swedish equestrian magazine *Rid-Sport*, Irish ponies have come to dominate the showjumping section in Sweden, while four of the top ten ponies in eventing have Irish connections.

One of the horses in the US silver medal-winning team at the 1988 Olympic Games in Seoul was "Mill Pearl", one of Ireland's most exciting exports, which had been bred by Noel C. Duggan at his Equestrian Centre in Millstreet, Co. Cork. Duggan, who has been the driving force behind the very successful Millstreet International Show since its inception in the late 1970s, had bought Mill Pearl's mother for £300 in 1979 and crossed her with the Irish Draught stallion "King of Diamonds". The resultant progeny, Mill Pearl, was sold to the US for £60,000 but such was her success that at the time of the Olympics, her value was estimated to be US$2 million.

Top performance horses can be sold for up to US$1 million, while a promising young showjumper at five–six years of age can fetch a price of IR£20,000 or more in Ireland. Such prices refer to top performers with considerable training, while good unbroken three-year-olds, jumping well on the lunge and produced by farmer breeders, make from £5,000–£10,000 on a regular basis.

However, these are horses with outstanding potential.

There is an indication that some major purchasers of such horses in recent years have been disappointed by their prowess under saddle and are not keen to repeat the exercise. Breeders are now more than pleased to receive a prize of £3,000–£3,500 for a three-year-old at Gorebridge Special Sales in September, while foal prices of £1,000–£1,300 and broodmare averages of £2,000–£2,500 are currently considered to be "norm" at the breeding stock sale in October at the same venue.

UK and Continental European sales figures demonstrate that while the market for sport horses is attractive, it is also highly competitive. Of course, horses which do not make the grade at competitive level may still be very suitable for pleasure riding, etc., but it has been said that this avenue is more economically realistic as an escape valve rather than a target in itself.

Yet, there is little doubt that Ireland has the resources to be equally as successful in the leisure riding market, as it has been in the showjumping sphere. However, there are significant differences between the two sectors. For instance, showjumping places a premium on the brilliant horse which every producer dreams of breeding one day, whereas to produce horses for the leisure riding market requires the more mundane commitment to the production and systematic training of the less spectacular, but more numerous, medium-level animal. With better educational opportunities, particularly for young people, in the horse industry, this commitment could be forthcoming.

APPENDICES

EXHIBIT 1: Horse-Breeding Incentive Schemes

Introduction

The Government, in conjunction with the European Community, provides the following support system for breeders of sport horses:

Irish Draught Incentive Scheme

The aim of the scheme is to encourage the breeding of increased numbers of registered pure-bred Irish Draught horses thereby ensuring the future of a high-quality bloodline since the ID breed provides a fundamental base for development of the Irish Sport Horse sector.

A grant of £400 is paid to the breeder of each live pure-bred Irish Draught foal. To be eligible, a foal must be registered in the Irish Horse Register and must be by an approved Irish Draught stallion and out of either a Registered Irish Draught or an Appendix Irish Draught brood mare. Both filly and colt foals are eligible.

Foal Registration Incentive Scheme

The purpose of this aid is to encourage the registration of all foals, bearing in mind EC Directives on zootechnical conditions which govern trace in horses and participation of horses in competitions.

A grant of £150 is paid to the breeder in respect of foals, from approved sires and dams, registered in the Irish Horse Register or Connemara Stud Book, subject to a maximum of five foals per annum per applicant.

Young Connemara Brood Mare Scheme

The aid is aimed at the recovery of the Connemara breed, which is bred mostly in disadvantaged areas and has significantly declined in recent years.

A grant of £500 in disadvantaged areas and £400 elsewhere is paid to the breeder of the first foal registered in the Connemara Stud Book from each young Connemara brood mare.

Quality Stallion Incentive Scheme

This scheme is designed to encourage stallion owners to acquire quality stallions for use in the non-Thoroughbred horse sector. Under the scheme a premium will be paid to selected stallion owners to assist with the purchase of better-quality stallions. The level of

premium will be 50 per cent of purchase price in less-favoured areas and 40 per cent in other areas, subject to an investment ceiling
of £10,000.

In addition, grants are provided, for each of two years, to the
owners of stallions participating in a performance-testing programme.

Grants for Stabling, etc.

In addition to the schemes detailed above, grant aid is also available for housing, fencing and other related facilities. The grant aid
provided will be 50 per cent of the approved cost in less-favoured
areas and 40 per cent in other areas, subject to an investment
ceiling of £10,000.

Scheme of Equine Headage Grants

Headage may be payable on breeding mares registered in the Irish
Horse Register or the Connemara Pony Stud Book in the More Severely Handicapped and Less Severely Handicapped areas.

Other Breeding Initiatives

To provide a scientific database on stallions and their progeny, finance is being provided for the introduction of a pilot blood-typing
scheme, in addition to development of a computer system for the
production of Stallion Genetic Indices.

Source: Dept. of Agriculture, Dublin, Information Bulletin, May 1991.

EXHIBIT 2: "Racecourses Must Go to Save Industry"

Six years ago a Commission chaired by Lord Killanin reported on
the state of the Irish breeding and racing industries. I want to offer
some outsider's comments on the breeding and racing industries....

The main problems in these areas in Ireland have to do with
racing rather than with breeding. While there are difficulties with
the breeding side of the industry, I believe that it is fundamentally
healthy. Sales prices have been falling since 1987, and many
breeders are going through a tough time. But so are breeder's
everywhere. There was a speculative bubble in bloodstock prices in
the mid-80s which has been followed by an inevitable price collapse. But it is universal, and there is no evidence that the relative
position of Irish breeding has worsened in the last few years.

This country has some basic advantages as a centre for Thoroughbred breeding. Principal among these are the simple fact
that Irish people are good at it, plus a sensible tax regime which

has attracted internationally mobile assets (stallions) to Ireland at little or no real cost to the Exchequer....

My main contention is that there are far too many racecourses in Ireland for the 250–260 days' racing that we need to accommodate. Last year, just one million people attended the 262 days' racing in Ireland. With 25 racecourses nationally, this means that the typical Irish racecourse had just 40,000 patrons during the whole year. At £5 a head (and this ignores people getting in for free), gate receipts are around £200,000 a year for the average track. Taking into account whatever can be earned from catering , cars and so on, you are still talking about very small money. The Killanin Commission concluded that only a handful of Irish racecourses were earning sufficient revenue to maintain and review their assets. That situation has not changed since 1986.

How many racecourses do we need to accommodate one million customers per annum? My guess is that 10 or 12 tracks would be plenty. Each track would be guaranteed a minimum of 20 days' racing a year, or more, and that would provide a revenue base which could support better investment in facilities.

There is a popular and attractive National Hunt product. The National Hunt events alone could happily survive without most of Ireland's 25 tracks....

Source: McCarthy, Colum, *Sunday Tribune*, 4 October 1992.

EXHIBIT 3: International Comparative Analysis

In relation to the four countries visited, Germany, France, the Netherlands and Denmark, each is now at a different stage of development in relation to its breeding programme for the non-Thoroughbred horse industry. The riding or saddle horse breeds in all these countries have been developed from their basic draught horses through a programme of crossing, upgrading and selection. At this point in time, the Germans and French appear to be more advanced, particularly in relation to computerisation and data collection of show and competition rules, which can be used to provide progeny information and breeding indexes on all stallions. In order to achieve this stage of development, registration and the breeding identity of all animals in competition was a basic necessity.

The breeding programme in all four countries is very well organised and impressive — all are involved in performance testing of potential riding horse stallions, while progeny test information is now being provided as well.

The situation in this country in relation to performance testing is somewhat different in that our riding horse is basically a first or second cross animal by a Thoroughbred stallion. However, some means should be devised to ensure that potential young sires of our riding horses should be performance tested. In addition, some young Irish Draught and half-breed stallions should also be performance tested.

Preliminary examination of public horse sales confirm the view that we are producing an excessively high proportion of non-Thoroughbred horses of mediocre and poor quality that do not pay for their production. This means that the breeding quality of many of our present brood mares and stallions is low. At the same time, there are, in relation to our total breeding stock, a greater number of high-class Irish-bred showjumpers in international competition than from competing nations. This indicates that there is good inherent performing ability in a proportion of our breeding mares and sires, if it can be identified and propagated.

In Ireland, about two thirds of registered stallions are Thoroughbred. These are nearly all purchased, either at public sales or privately, after flat racing. The most suitable animals both in breeding and conformation are difficult to find. Only those left after the best have been purchased for the more remunerative National Hunt stud duties are available to the non-Thoroughbred industry. And, because of their training, there has been little opportunity and perhaps less attempt made, to test their ability over obstacles. The successful hurdle and steeplechase males are virtually all gelded before they go National Hunt racing. This must result in considerable waste of inherited jumping talent and deprivation within the steeplechasing, showjumping and eventing sports sectors.

There is no reason why an Irish riding horse type or breed of high-performing ability cannot, in time, be evolved from selected existing crossbred (ID x TB) mares and stallions of proved performance derived from known good lines. This should be one of our main objectives. A programme, in consultation with a few uninvolved breeding experts (specially appointed for the purpose), should be devised to encourage and assist the owners of a small select number of such breeding animals to have them propagated, selected and tested to high standards as foundation stock. Such owners should be encouraged to form a breed society to promote the idea. The aim would be to continue breeding within a small number of select groups until type and ability, being adequately reproduced, would be virtually stabilised. This would require ruthless culling of progeny showing undesirable traits.

Source: More O'Ferrall, G. and Brophy, J., "Report on the European non-Thoroughbred Breeding Industry", unpublished paper, 1985.

EXHIBIT 4: The Production of Sport Horses

With overproduction in some of the traditional enterprises, farmers must look to other opportunities to generate a satisfactory income. The production of sport horses is a potential secondary enterprise on many Irish farms. In addition, horses are compatible with grazing animals such as cattle, cows and sheep.

It is essential that farmers who are considering sport horse breeding should start from a well-developed farming base. If sport horse breeding is to become an attractive secondary enterprise on farms, it must be possible to finance it without withdrawing capital from the main enterprise and, when established, it must generate a satisfactory income for the farmer.

To justify the managerial and capital investment required, a minimum size of enterprise based on four good-quality broodmares should be considered. About six to eight acres will be required for this scale of enterprise when allowance is made for the foals and yearlings, and the production of good-quality fodder. This level of commitment will encourage the farmer to master the management skills necessary and to take a deep interest. Attendance at shows and sales is important. This can be quite expensive and time consuming but, if spread over a number of animals, will not be excessive. For four broodmares, elaborate facilities will not be necessary in many cases. Existing hay barns, stables or converted cattle houses may be adequate on most farms.

As expertise and profitability develop, the number of broodmares could be increased. However, before deciding on this type of expansion, a farmer must ensure that

- The present enterprise is profitable;
- Expansion will not result in neglect or interfere with the main farm enterprise, and
- Adequate capital for expansion is available.

Source: *The Production of the Horse*, Alternative Enterprise, Series no. 4, ACOT (now Teagasc), Dublin, August 1987.

EXHIBIT 5: EU Regulations and Directives

The EU has drawn up a number of directives aimed specially at horses. These cover the health conditions governing movement both within the Community and from outside. While the import of horses from outside the Community is subject to strict health conditions, movement between Member States has become quite simple. Horses being transferred from one Member State to another must be inspected by a vet within 48 hours of embarkation.

The European Union allows Ireland to maintain a low VAT rate of 2.3 per cent on bloodstock. This rate gives the Irish bloodstock industry a substantial headstart over competitors in Britain who must pay 17.5 per cent VAT.

The new EU regulations which require that horses now have to state the country in which they were bred, rather than the country where they are resident, should mean that more Irish-bred horses will get international recognition.

Table A: Irish Mares: New Registrations in "Irish Horse Register", 1985–91

County	1985	1986	1987	1988	1989	1990	1991
Carlow	17	10	17	18	42	45	53
Cavan	24	26	16	13	55	69	118
Clare	50	70	45	69	130	143	210
Cork	106	104	101	109	200	201	340
Donegal	16	19	10	19	79	52	132
Dublin	36	29	22	41	30	61	73
Galway	75	76	59	84	188	217	339
Kerry	31	18	19	19	46	88	136
Kildare	24	22	22	19	37	38	48
Kilkenny	28	35	34	26	61	97	125
Laois	27	24	16	16	42	54	63
Leitrim	5	10	14	14	23	33	56
Limerick	47	50	39	32	75	114	110
Longford	10	11	7	9	26	37	76
Louth	22	11	15	7	28	31	60
Mayo	37	18	17	18	60	9	169
Meath	35	26	21	26	35	63	61
Monaghan	28	20	16	23	78	87	103
Offaly	15	32	21	20	27	36	53
Roscommon	20	19	14	22	52	78	120
Sligo	16	17	17	24	51	50	76
Tipperary	76	74	55	42	116	163	244
Waterford	53	32	18	34	64	67	106
Westmeath	31	18	21	18	43	47	74
Wexford	46	59	51	51	101	126	144
Wicklow	34	28	19	31	77	64	144
N. Ireland	45	48	45	65	116	133	187
TOTAL	954	906	751	869	1,882	2,293	3,410

Source: "Approved Stallions", Department of Agriculture, Dublin.

Table B: Number of Mares Covered by Stallions, 1984–91

County	1985	1986	1987	1988	1989	1990	1991
Carlow	120	107	109	99	110	110	144
Cavan	96	113	96	97	124	161	190
Clare	317	296	282	283	267	338	383
Cork	745	687	694	674	693	865	943
Donegal	101	96	87	92	96	116	172
Dublin	78	81	79	77	72	94	127
Galway	385	377	367	398	431	534	631
Kerry	168	144	130	112	103	160	132
Kildare	72	64	65	75	72	93	128
Kilkenny	255	210	194	163	180	202	245
Laois	161	150	128	129	107	167	192
Leitrim	66	62	51	60	64	68	94
Limerick	250	216	240	220	193	229	313
Longford	60	59	42	56	65	70	85
Louth	45	49	46	56	65	81	107
Mayo	148	132	136	118	127	173	215
Meath	86	81	89	111	92	111	138
Monaghan	128	121	120	119	151	229	253
Offaly	119	101	100	90	76	90	119
Roscommon	104	92	100	106	114	151	174
Sligo	72	75	60	74	101	135	159
Tipperary	440	393	395	365	335	379	451
Waterford	208	186	167	178	205	218	257
Westmeath	115	115	104	92	78	112	130
Wexford	408	330	338	293	325	361	462
Wicklow	165	164	154	172	199	194	212
N. Ireland	342	309	304	319	369	418	478
TOTAL	5,254	4,810	4,677	4,628	4,814	5,857	7,034

Source: "Approved Stallions", Department of Agriculture, Dublin.

Table C: Live Foals Registered in the "Irish Horse Register"

County	1985	1986	1987	1988	1989	1990	1991
Carlow	70	65	57	64	74	80	107
Cavan	54	64	41	56	75	116	134
Clare	163	168	131	175	185	249	302
Cork	372	399	368	359	447	543	620
Donegal	42	32	26	35	50	67	116
Dublin	46	48	32	45	45	66	89
Galway	208	221	211	248	303	378	444
Kerry	74	66	51	64	63	116	154
Kildare	40	31	36	48	47	71	100
Kilkenny	122	103	77	97	133	150	183
Laois	59	60	51	67	55	115	143
Leitrim	33	30	19	30	48	44	60
Limerick	140	127	132	122	117	169	226
Longford	25	29	24	31	43	51	71
Louth	28	25	21	27	38	55	82
Mayo	73	62	61	51	65	105	147
Meath	56	49	47	61	63	75	97
Monaghan	73	78	55	74	91	152	180
Offaly	57	44	44	52	48	63	88
Roscommon	49	44	51	63	80	108	121
Sligo	29	33	32	45	71	81	102
Tipperary	233	211	179	211	215	292	342
Waterford	95	109	84	94	126	142	189
Westmeath	59	67	49	53	54	85	101
Wexford	206	194	173	181	225	271	358
Wicklow	80	89	79	102	123	128	135
N. Ireland	160	165	149	171	227	197	344
TOTAL	2,646	2,613	2,280	2,626	3,111	4,069	5,035

Source: "Approved Stallions", Department of Agriculture, Dublin.

Table D: Foals Registered: Detailed Analysis of Data: (Stallion x Mare) 1985–91

Stallion x Mare	1985	1986	1987	1988	1989	1990	1991
TB x ISH/AID	1,669	1,723	1,442	1,505	1,558	1,699	2,096
RID X ISH	558	472	450	562	714	1,046	1,238
ISH X ISH/AID	186	230	168	285	462	656	761
RID X RID	133	127	125	116	165	308	326
RID X AID	24	36	51	44	97	215	251
RID/ISH X TB	17	7	9	18	34	50	120
Unclassified	59	18	35	96	81	95	243
Total	2,646	2,613	2,280	2,626	3,111	4,069	5,035

Note: TB   = Thoroughbred
          ISH   = Irish Sport Horse
          AID   = Appendix Irish Draught
          RID   = Registered Irish Draught

Source: "Irish Horse Register", Department of Agriculture, Dublin.

Table E: New Mare Registrations in "Irish Horse Register": Analysis by Type

	1985	1986	1987	1988	1989	1990	1991
RID Mares	92	70	76	62	86	69	111
AID Mares	122	74	54	186	186	161	266
Pony Mares	76	81	42	73	73	178	583
"Other" ISH	664	681	579	1,537	1,537	1,885	2,450
TOTAL	954	906	751	869	1,882	2,293	3,410

Source: "Approved Stallions", Department of Agriculture, Dublin.

Table F: Horse Exports, 1985–1991

MARKET		1985	1986	1987	1988	1989	1990	1991
Britain	No.	2,946	3,255	3,769	4,265	5,196	4,214	3,128
	IR£m	36.65	32.38	36.63	51.05	52.49	43.51	34.25
N. Ireland	No.	504	421	437	630	257	690	508
	IR£m	0.62	0.42	0.55	1.40	1.52	0.90	1.12
France	No.	111	166	94	103	200	271	290
	IR£m	2.77	4.11	1.40	2.81	3.42	3.76	4.31
Italy	No.	248	297	275	407	271	470	453
	IR£m	2.01	2.21	2.26	3.42	2.44	3.40	3.39
Germany	No.	41	73	—	107	128	145	163
	IR£m	0.08	0.25	—	0.29	1.47	0.37	0.46
Other EC	No.	233	232	281	168	185	147	154
	IR£m	0.70	0.46	0.63	0.44	0.35	0.36	0.33
Sweden	No.	79	96	138	191	217	223	n/a
	IR£m	0.30	0.26	0.37	0.66	0.75	0.79	n/a
Switzerland	No.	217	188	281	212	187	221	n/a
	IR£m	0.42	0.36	0.79	0.63	0.60	0.61	n/a
US	No.	333	368	217	246	115	153	76
	IR£m	13.05	37.81	3.88	3.20	2.23	10.11	1.47
Australia	No.	—	—	—	—	46	19	—
	IR£m	—	—	—	—	2.02	1.80	—
Japan	No.	1	16	—	—	—	14	22
	IR£m	0.01	3.39	—	—	—	0.30	1.70
Other World	No.	172	137	156	148	193	131	564
	IR£m	2.24	1.31	0.86	2.03	1.29	0.88	1.62
TOTAL	No.	4,885	5,231	5,648	6,477	7,995	6,698	5,358
	IR£m	58.98	82.96	47.37	65.93	68.58	66.79	48.65

Source: CSO, Dublin.

Table G: Non-Thoroughbred Horse Exports

MARKET		1985	1986	1987	1988	1989	1990	1991
Britain	No.	567	526	816	863	1,526	813	749
	IR£000	566	663	885	1,150	2,925	1412	1412
N. Ireland	No.	349	241	294	420	586	326	322
	IR£000	304	212	272	528	1,086	392	609
Sweden	No.	69	89	117	159	186	176	177
	IR£000	215	243	318	487	472	459	500
Switzerland	No.	190	141	254	174	172	152	187
	IR£000	333	273	648	441	467	402	403
Italy	No.	66	114	96	77	93	101	114
	IR£000	228	484	368	130	273	322	455
USA	No.	80	97	77	62	43	25	21
	IR£000	638	563	489	259	353	133	183
Germany	No.	26	34	44	72	71	86	63
	IR£000	34	42	68	101	158	133	107
Finland	No.	19	17	9	6	7	11	4
	IR£000	78	78	49	43	55	72	55
Netherlands	No.	15	36	14	11	35	23	19
	IR£000	20	153	28	30	57	36	55
Denmark	No.	50	48	42	6	23	9	21
	IR£000	91	48	42	7	38	15	49
France	No.	6	3	5	11	47	14	5
	IR£000	5	9	23	56	129	31	12
Libya	No.	1	—	—	24	—	16	—
	IR£000	3	—	—	137	—	209	—
Morocco	No.	—	11	—	21	9	8	3
	IR£000	—	43	—	58	203	96	11
Other World	No.	96	74	60	88	74	90	51
	IR£000	208	116	165	133	158	185	72
TOTAL	No.	1,534	1,431	1,828	1,994	2,872	1,852	1,736
	IR£000	2,723	2,927	3,355	3,660	6,374	3,897	3,923

Source: CSO, Dublin.

References

Beecher, J. (1989): unpublished paper, Dublin: Department of Agriculture and Food.

Central Statistics Office (CSO) (1985): Farm Structure Survey, Dublin: CSO.

Department of Agriculture (1991): *Approved Stallions*, Dublin: Department of Agriculture and Food

Fitzgerald, A. (1992): Irish Horses, Just How Many are There?", *The Saddle*, July: 5.

Forde, D. (1991): "Breeding and Marketing the Modern Sport Horse", paper presented at Thomond College/University of Limerick conference "The Horse in Health and Breeding", May.

Horse Racing: Records, Facts and Champions Third ed. (1990): London: Business Books.

Irish Farmers Journal, 16 May 1992.

Irish Thoroughbred (1992): marketing brochure.

Mitchell, M. (1993a): Irish Thoroughbred Marketing, Dublin: private communication, March.

Mitchell, M. (1993b): "Marketing the Irish Thoroughbred", unpublished paper, University of Limerick seminar, February.

Report of the Commission of Equity into the Thoroughbred Horse Breeding Industry ("Killanin Commission") (1987): Dublin: Government Publications Office.

Saddle, The (1992): 11 July.

Questions

1. From whichever viewpoints you consider important, critically analyse the Irish equine sector, indicating whether or not:

    a) it can be classified as "an industry";

    b) it can be viewed as a sector of the Irish economy with significant potential, justifying your answer by referring to points from the case.

2. Describe and comment on organisational and business management features of the Thoroughbred sub-sector that might be applied, successfully, to its non-Thoroughbred counterpart.

3. Assess the effectiveness of Marketing efforts within the Irish equine sector — recommending how a cost-efficient promotional

strategy might be developed to promote Ireland as the "home of the horse".

4. In examining international business strategy, Michael Porter has stressed the importance of factors that can lead to the competitive advantages of nations. Critically assess the position of the Irish equine sector in this regard, justifying your comments by reference to case details, or otherwise.

5. Develop a new strategic approach for the "Irish horse industry", formulating a long-term development plan.

Part 2

The Tourism/Hospitality Sector

7

Castletroy Park Hotel

Introduction

Since opening in 1991, the Castletroy Park Hotel and Conference
Centre has acquired a well-deserved reputation as a first-class
hotel, conference and leisure facility serving the Mid-West region.
Located at the entrance to the National Technological Park, Limerick, the hotel represents a unique investment in the lucrative
corporate-business segment of the Irish hotel market. The development of the hotel came about through a joint-venture arrangement by EGB Management Ltd., an Irish tourism investment
company, and the New-York-based Medallion Hotel Group. The
intention of the proposed venture was to explore the potential
growth opportunities of the tourism and leisure sectors in Ireland,
and to determine the feasibility of investing in a hotel and purpose-
built conference centre. In its evolution to date, the Castletroy
Park Hotel has experienced a number of discrete phases of turbulence and growth.

EGB Management Ltd. and Medallion Hotels Inc.

Believing that the Irish Tourism industry faced a potentially
bright future, EGB Management Ltd. took the initiative and decided to invest in the Irish hotel business. Incorporated as an
Irish company in January 1988, it is part of the international
EGB group of companies. EGB has considerable worldwide experience in the tourism and leisure sectors, and with the potential
for large-scale investment, is sufficiently capable of attracting
new tourism traffic to Ireland. Its worldwide investment to date

[157]

includes the development and management of the Pacific Island Club chain of resorts in the Pacific, and the acquisition and development of a small group of upmarket hotels in the American Mid-West. EGB owns the New York-based tourism-related business in the US, Hawaii, and Pacific region. It has relationships with major airlines and travel agencies in the US and Pacific, and has an international board of hotel and tourism experts.

Medallion Hotels, as joint-investor in the Castletroy Park Hotel, contributes its significant understanding of general hotel management to day-to-day operations. Expertise is provided in food and beverage acquisition, finance, marketing and human resource management. The Medallion mission statement, in articulating the aims of the organisation, seeks to define how best to enhance the personal and professional potential of each individual employee, and the extent to which this contributes to successful organisational performance. Much emphasis is placed on continuous quality improvements, and on the training and development opportunities afforded to facilitate this process.

Why Locate in Castletroy, Ireland?

The hotel is located on the main Dublin road close to the National Technological Park and beside the University of Limerick. The fact that the hotel is on the main link from Dublin to Limerick is considered an advantage that may help gain corporate clients. The close proximity of the university is also perceived as an advantage in attracting conference business. The Mid-West region has long had a need for a quality hotel in the right location offering high standards of food and service, complemented by reasonably competitive price rates. Traditionally, the perception of the Limerick area, from a tour operator's point of view, has been of a marketplace with variable price rates. No one price trend has emerged which could be singularly attributed to the local market. In this context, prices were low in some quarters, while high in others. With no in-between rate to be found in the region, a potential business opportunity existed for those willing to invest. EGB, in recognising this opportunity, decided to fill the gap in the market. The need for a competitive pricing structure was identified, as was the decision not to enter the marketplace with a highly priced product, as it is very difficult to price down without losing reputation and business.

Developing the Castletroy Park Hotel

EGB Management Ltd. first visited Castletroy in 1987 as part of its primary research into investment opportunities in Ireland. In 1988, the company had put together a proposal on an investment in the Great Southern Hotel group, and had developed a hotel scheme for the Castletroy area. By mid-1989, the design had been approved by the local authorities, and in early 1990, construction commenced. At this stage, there was a preliminary construction budget of between £10 and £12 million. The proposal for the Great Southern Hotel did not succeed, but EGB decided to continue with the project and to look for reinvestment/joint venture/marketing opportunities to off-set Castletroy Park Hotel's very high construction costs. In all, the construction programme was a fast-track 14-month project from the breaking of ground to completion, with the hotel and conference centre opening, on target, in May 1991.

Financial Incentives

In terms of grant-aid, the Castletroy Park Hotel availed of an ERDF (European Regional Development Fund) grant for tourism and private-sector expenditure. The purpose of this scheme was to provide financial assistance to private-sector investment in product-related infrastructure work, and to support the development of certain other amenities which are specifically aimed at attracting additional foreign tourism revenue to Ireland. SFADCo (Shannon Free Airport Development Company) is responsible for administering the scheme in the Mid-West region, and to date has allocated a grant to the Castletroy Park Hotel against the £1 million invested in the hotel's leisure centre.

Structure of the Castletroy Park Hotel

In general, the hotel is organic and flat in structural terms, and flexible in its approach to management and organisational development. Management style is characteristically participatory and informal, creating in its approach an environment that is respectful of both customer and employee expectations. Decision-making is decentralised, with each department responsible for the management of its own budget. Employees are encouraged to be flexible in respect of their individual contribution to the organisation, and to be conscious of their participation in a team-based approach to customer service. Because of efforts by senior management to develop a more consistent working environment, standard operating procedures have been put in place, each of which describes the behaviour expected of employees and their required performance levels. Since the hotel and conference centre opened, the operation has experienced much instability in its strategic and structural development, mainly because of changes in its senior management personnel. For example, three general managers were appointed within the first 18 months of business. Leadership, if it existed, could only be described as diffuse and susceptible to variation. Accordingly, harmonisation became difficult to achieve, resulting in a proliferation of operational approaches on how best to run the organisation. Communication was very much an informal affair, with managers and supervisors making decisions for themselves without recourse to any formal hierarchy. Co-ordinating decisions in this environment proved to be an impossibility for the hotel, thus creating the need for strong cohesive leadership.

In January of 1993, Patrick Curran was appointed general manager of the hotel. His appointment marked the emergence of a different approach to management and organisational development. Standardisation and the initiation of formal planning procedures thus became a priority for the hotel. Taking responsibility for its implementation, Curran sought to promote a planned and systematic environment, capable of directing staff in a controlled and co-ordinated manner. Management meetings are now organised on a monthly basis, providing an opportunity for the exchange of financial information; to develop an action plan for the forthcoming month; and to review the previous month's performance. In developing its operating procedures, the hotel follows the guidelines set by the Medallion Hotel Group, modifying them so that they comply with Irish cultural norms and expectations. Customer comment cards, when completed, are returned on a monthly basis for analysis to the Medallion Head Office in Boston. The information is subsequently collated and returned to the Castletroy Park Hotel in the form of bar charts and percentage breakdown. Additionally, an analysis is made of telephone calls within the hotel. A British firm is responsible for conducting this analysis on the speed at which telephone calls are answered, and the knowledge and proficiency levels of the person answering.

Figure 7.1: Castletroy Park Hotel and Conference Centre Organisation Structure

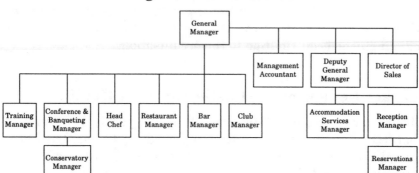

While emphasising the importance of standardisation, enterprising ideas are also invited from staff, and if shown to be feasible, are implemented. For example, one employee identified the need for a beauty salon within the hotel. Having being impressed with her idea, the general manager has made the enterprising employee responsible for the management and development of the hotel's recently established beauty salon. Taken in context, the hotel can be said to have successfully overcome its first turbulent phase of structural development, and has matured into a dynamic, yet robust, organisational form, capable of integrating individualism and teamwork in a way that enhances the overall quality of service.

Organisational Culture

Organisational culture is an elusive concept. Yet every organisation contains a set of underlying beliefs, attitudes and values that collectively guide the behaviour of individuals on a day-to-day basis. It is perpetuated through a system of rights and symbols, but perhaps more significantly, through a pattern of communication that is distinctly unique to the organisation. In terms of culture, the Castletroy Park Hotel is very much task-oriented. Its defining characteristics are its interfunctional expertise, flexibility, problem-solving capability and teamwork. All employees are encouraged to develop a high level of commitment to the organisation's goals, and to participate in efforts to enhance their working environment. For example, employees are encouraged to give feedback to management if they are unhappy about any aspect of their work. Management is willing to listen to employee needs, and will afford them recognition by awarding "Associate of the Month" and "Associate of the Year" to those employees who make a distinguished contribution to the organisation.

Market Review of the Castletroy Park Hotel

The hotel can accommodate from 300 to 350 people in a range of boardrooms, meeting and conference rooms. Each room has natural lighting, complete blackout facilities, screens and audiovisual equipment. Additionally, all ground-floor rooms are air-conditioned and have build-in automatic screens. The conference centre is situated at the east wing of the hotel, far enough away from public areas to ensure that the right environment is created for a successful meeting. Facilities offered include a Business Bureau consisting of secretarial services, fax, photocopying, message-relaying, courier service, and a full-time co-ordinator on hand to assist. The hotel has 107 bedrooms including seven suites, executive and non-smoking rooms. Each room is fitted with an executive-style writing desk with its own telephone, fax-point and computer link. Each room is also fitted with a mini-bar, a tea and coffee maker, hair dryer, trouser press, iron and ironing board. Dining facilities are available in McLoughlin's Restaurant, catering for up to 90 guests and offering the very best of Irish and international cuisine, together with an extensive wine list. The Merry Pedlar Bar is an authentic Irish pub with a great atmosphere offering first-class entertainment throughout the week. The hotel's aqua swim and fitness club comprises a gym that includes both cardiovascular and workout machines. These include computerised treadmills, bicycles and video screens, rowing and skiing units, stair climbers and a complete range of workout stations. There is also a 20-metre deck pool, Jacuzzi, sauna and a Turkish steam room.

The conference centre is available to rent at differing rates depending on the length of the stay and the amount of overnight accommodation required. It is the policy of the hotel to sell meeting and room space with bedrooms. There are various room rates available, all subject to negotiation. The hotel is unique in the Limerick area in so far as it contracts conference facilities and bedrooms to companies. This helps the hotel to plan occupancy levels well in advance, and offers the hotel a degree of certainty in its planning. Price discrimination is used.

The hotel is marketed and sold through its office in Dublin. A marketing and sales manager is responsible for all business dealings in the Dublin area. The parent company of the Castletroy Park Hotel (Medallion Hotels Inc.) has its main reservations office in New York. American business travellers can book accommodation through this office. The hotel is also well connected with 29 tour operators in Ireland and others abroad. Tour groups are brought to the Castletroy Park Hotel through these operators. A very efficient reservations office is in place in the hotel comprising the latest computerised reservations system and two highly motivated and trained personnel. The conference office based in the hotel is on hand to deal with all enquiries.

The hotel engages in relatively little advertising as it spends most of its marketing budget on personal selling. Two people are employed by the hotel on a full-time basis, spending a considerable amount of their time out "in the field" identifying prospects and maintaining contact with existing customers. The hotel has a computerised database of all its past and present customers detailing each company profile and the nature and amount of business received from each company. Promotional responsibilities and activities are further broken down into geographical areas (territories), namely Dublin and the Mid-West. A further two persons are employed by the hotel, forming a support team for sales personnel. The activities of this support team include locating prospects, educating customers, building goodwill and providing after-sales service. As the hotel is mainly business oriented, it places a great deal of emphasis on corporate entertainment. Golf outings for various companies are organised on a regular basis, paid for in full by the hotel. Recently the hotel brought 10 chief executives of locally-based companies to a business seminar in Dublin hosted by Tom Peters, author of *In Search of Excellence*. They were brought to Dublin by train (executive class), attended the seminar and were entertained at the Hotel Conrad Hilton, where they stayed overnight, returning to Limerick the following day. Patrick Curran the general manager, personally accompanied these guests, with the hotel meeting all of the costs involved.

In addition to its regular promotional activities, the hotel offers a facility for those patrons wishing to avail of an exclusive service. The Prestige Club is designed for people who make hotel accommodation arrangements for their company and visitors. Accommodation refers to conference and commercial reservations. The purpose of the club is to reward members for their patronage of the Castletroy Park Hotel, with valuable gifts, travel and entertainment privileges. The club provides special services to ensure that the reservations for members' visitors and VIPs are flawlessly handled. Each member selected by the hotel will receive a card with a reference number and a valid until date. Members quote their reference number when booking accommodation with reservations in order to credit their points. Membership of the club is by invitation from the hotel after booking a minimum of 25 bed nights.

It is the policy of the hotel to give sales management the desired level of control, and to provide sales personnel with acceptable levels of freedom, income and incentive. In general, the hotel is known to pay above average industry wage rates.

Current Market Position

It is difficult to ascertain the current market share of the hotel in respect of the various market segments in the Limerick region, but it is generally felt that it enjoys the lucrative end of the commercial market. Although its rates are higher than those of Jury's (its main competitor in Limerick), the hotel still manages to attract a large portion of the commercial market by offering a superior product and service. Another reason as to why the hotel enjoys a large percentage of the various market segments is that it pursues an aggressive marketing strategy.

The hotel's business mix is spread over various market segments, namely the conference market, commercial business travellers, tour groups and short weekend break market. The percentage share of these markets in the business mix varies with the time of year. For example, in October up to 55 per cent of business comes from the commercial sector. The conference market provides up to 27 per cent of business, while the remaining 18 per cent comes from group and individual business. Because many firms are on holidays during the July/August period, the percentage sales mix of the commercial sector declines. This is offset by the rise in tour groups coming to the hotel as a result of intensified marketing efforts directed at this particular market segment. During these months the hotel capitalises on local wedding business. Throughout the rest of the year, the hotel's mid-week occupancy levels are quite high because of commercial and conference business, yet these markets don't always provide for high occupancy levels at weekends. For this reason, the hotel offers competitive weekend rates to attract the short-break segment of the market. During 1994, average occupancy levels of 73 per cent were recorded, which, given the size of the hotel, compares well with industry averages.

The hotel's markets are basically segmented in three ways. The commercial market accounts for up to 40 per cent of the hotel's business. Another 40 per cent is taken up by the conference market, with weekend groups and tours accounting for the remaining 20 per cent. These three segments share one common characteristic — they all demand a consistently high quality service and value for money. In terms of buying capability, the hotel exerts a considerable influence over its suppliers and has an impeccable record of paying all invoices promptly. As a result, suppliers are willing to sponsor and promote special events and activities organised by the hotel. The hotel's range of exceptional services is communicated by way of personal selling with a designated marketing and sales office in Dublin for this purpose. Product and service planning also feature as part of the hotel's long-term marketing strategy, with a study currently being carried out to determine the feasibility of constructing an additional 50 rooms. The result is expected to be positive. The leisure centre is also being redeveloped. In addition, there is an ongoing test-marketing programme in place with complimentary "thank-you for your custom" meals offered in the restaurant and banquet centre.

The hotel conducts its market research in different ways. Through an effective use of the personal selling process, the hotel can obtain its feedback immediately. The technique of cold calling for information is also employed, as is feedback from questionnaires which are sent to all corporate guests the day after the event. In terms of its social responsibilities, the hotel has a standard respect for the environment, with no specific environmental programme in place.

Human Resource Strategies

From the outset, the Castletroy Park Hotel has sought to promote a planned and integrated approach to its human resource management activities. The hotel's recruitment and selection strategies endeavour to promote, where possible, those candidates currently employed by the organisation. When a position becomes available, the respective departmental manager is required to submit a personnel requisition form to the personnel department. Personnel will then post the job opening in-house for two days prior to advertising the position externally. This process reduces recruitment costs and gives good internal candidates a chance. Managers are then asked how many candidates they would like to interview. Personnel proceeds to screen applicants to obtain the desired number of candidates, and the manager interviews and selects the best candidate for the position. Offers for executive positions require the approval of the managing director. All applicants as part of the recruitment and selection process, are exposed to various aspects of the hotel's operations and are encouraged to present personal ideas for future organisational change and development. This process is designed to test their problem-solving capabilities.

Orientation consists of a five-hour induction programme on the first day, followed by on-the-job training for the probation period of 90 days. The programme will normally detail the history of the hotel and describe the context of relationships between the company, its management, employees and guests. The mission statement and the hotel's organisation structure is explained. Employees are made aware of their benefits and are given a tour of the property. Quality assurance and in-house training programmes are outlined as are fire and safety procedures. The hotel's training and development programmes have previously included its 1994 drive to achieve the international quality standard ISO9002. This was followed by the recently implemented "Personnel Development Programme". The main objectives of this particular programme were to establish job security, to provide for personal development, and to relate future transfer and promotional opportunities. Essentially, the programme encourages employees to develop an interest in their job and to suggest ways of how best to enhance their contribution to the overall success of the hotel. A special fund has been established to help those employees interested in furthering their education, and to promote specialist skill acquisition after the in-house training programme has been completed.

Those employees who best promote the hotel through their efforts and standard of achievement are rewarded through the hotel's performance-management strategy. A key feature of this strategy has been the "Associate of the Month" awards, presented at monthly general associate meetings. Recipients are awarded £25, and are shown on in-house television in formal recognition of their contribution to the hotel. Those employees who receive the distinction of being named "Associate of the Year" are awarded a trip for two to the United States for a week. The hotel does not grant automatic salary increases to its management and staff, but makes its increases on a performance-related basis, thereby creating the incentive for an increased expenditure of effort. In addition, the Personnel Department conducts a twice-yearly salary research study of wage-rate competitiveness within the hotel.

Departmental meetings are held on a weekly and monthly basis, with general associate meetings held on a monthly basis. The hotel's bulletin boards are used to inform associates of employment laws, job opportunities, letters of praise and other miscellaneous information. Associate committees consisting of staff union representatives, the general manager, and the personnel manager are also held. The purpose of these meetings is to encourage associates to express their ideas and concerns in confidence. Interdepartmental memoranda are also distributed to all departments so as to promote consistency and unanimity in communications. Disciplinary procedures are initiated when associates have violated company policy, or if they have failed to perform to expected standards. A verbal warning will be given initially, followed by written warnings and a final written warning before a suspension or other disciplinary action is taken. The hotel conducts its performance appraisals on a six-monthly basis.

Future Growth Strategies

The Castletroy Park Hotel is at a critical juncture in its development. Having successfully overcome its first turbulent phase of growth, the organisation is now in a position to chart its future strategic direction. Strategic growth options should aim to increase overall occupancy levels in the hotel, increase its conversion rates, and develop the leisure-centre facilities, while increasing its membership.

Increasing Occupancy Percentage from 71 per cent to 80 per cent in One Year

For such a young hotel, the Castletroy Park has achieved tremendous growth and has boasted occupancy levels comparable to top hotels in Ireland. Yet the potential for further improvement still exists. In order to increase occupancy levels by nine percentage points, a combination of marketing strategies should be used.

Market Penetration

This is to be achieved by firstly segmenting the markets that the Castletroy targets. The percentage points to be achieved this year will then be divided up and assigned to the different market segments. The commercial market, for example, will have to achieve a 2 per cent increase in its particular market. This same format is also applied to the other markets. All these separate markets are then marketed individually through personal selling. Essentially, personal selling is an important and vital attribute of the hotel, capable of converting seven out of ten enquiries into productive business. Its staff are well coached and trained so that they are competent in their selling of the product to prospective clients. When business arrives such as that of a conference, the hotel staff always provide an excellent service which, naturally enough, helps to sell the hotel and encourage repeat business. There is always a close link between the managers and the co-ordinators of conferences and other commercial guests. Management is constantly selling the hotel as a product to clients. This is achieved through securing close and effective relationships with clients. Personal selling will be combined with a small-scale advertising campaign in selected periodicals. Taken together, this will be the most effective and efficient strategy to increase awareness of the respective markets catered for by the Castletroy Park Hotel.

Addition of 50 Business Guest Rooms with Excellent Facilities

The new guest rooms will offer an in-room computer, printer, and fax where business people can work without leaving the room. This will provide the Castletroy Park Hotel with a unique selling point which differentiates it from other hotels in the Limerick and Shannon region. This expansion also answers the problem of having to turn away business when fully booked.

Communication Strategy

The communication strategy simply involves the increased quality of communication between staff and guests. This will allow information to be gained from customers, which can then be used to improve the quality of service offered by the hotel. Essentially, this strategy creates good word-of-mouth promotion for the hotel, thereby increasing its clientèle.

Increasing the Conversion Rate from 70 per cent to 80 per cent within One Year

The Castletroy Park's present conversion rate is an impressive 70 per cent. This means that seven out of ten telephone enquiries made to the hotel are converted into sales. However, the potential exists for an increased conversion rate of 80 per cent in a year. Through use of a market-penetration strategy, and, more specifically, by employing the concept of internal marketing, it will become possible to increase the hotel's market share. This strategy will focus on the internal customer base, as ultimately the success of the hotel depends not only on the satisfaction of its external customers, but also on its internal customer base. Jobs or positions can be viewed as internal products that satisfy the needs of these employees. Essentially, the strategy will focus on the hotel telephonists, identifying their needs, and treating them as if they were customer needs. The internal marketing programme when applied to the telephonists will include benefits such as retention, empowerment, and a commission scheme. Accordingly, the satisfied employee will positively and effectively translate this into higher productivity and an improved service, which ultimately produces better results. In implementing the strategy, an employee needs analysis will be conducted through use of regular staff surveys and meetings with the rooms division manager. All switchboard telephonists will go through a refresher course in communication and sales skills. An incentive programme will then be introduced wherein a telephonist will be awarded 5 per cent of room-rate per room as commission on each room sold over the phone in excess of the 70 per cent mark. The total commission will be collected along with the telephonist's monthly wage.

In addition, the hotel will conduct retention schemes wherein staff will be offered job security. They will therefore feel safer and more comfortable in their jobs, which will largely contribute to a healthy working environment. Recruitment of potential employees will be tightened, allowing more efficient selection of the "right" person, which will eventually lead to more competent staff. Management will promote and encourage empowerment of staff which means more autonomy in decision-making. This will effectively increase motivation and satisfaction with their duties and department, which will ultimately lead to higher productivity and success.

Developing the Leisure Centre and Increasing its Membership from 500 to 700 People

Here a number of strategies have the potential to be implemented. Examples include the use of an internal promotion strategy — that is, communicating and advertising the club to conference and commercial guests — and the provision of incentives and membership; a product-development strategy which would increase standards and inject more cash into the club; group specials such as accommodating external business leisure clubs; special family offers and rates for membership; newspaper and magazine advertising. Each of these strategies uses alternative and collective methods in achieving higher membership rates and helps to develop further the aqua leisure club as an attractive and prestigious amenity to the hotel, as well as providing an excellent private club to its members.

Investment in the leisure centre has already taken place and it is further planned to inject more in order to increase excellence and maintain standards. Through doing this, present members will experience and appreciate the amenity and will, in effect, advertise to others through word of mouth. It is planned to concentrate mainly on promoting the club to guests. As they check in, guests will be reminded of their entitlement to visit the hotel leisure facilities. It will be specifically advertised to business/ conference clients as they will be enticed to enrol for membership, and will be given special incentives to attract them, with detailed information on the club available in their rooms. There will also be a certain amount of newspaper and magazine advertisements made available in order to attract as wide an audience and interest as possible. However, the Castletroy Park does not normally concentrate on this form of advertising, as it is quite expensive, and does not always target the type of market that the hotel desires which, strictly speaking, is the business market. To this end, the hotel does not rely too much on newspaper advertising. Another possible alternative is to make progress by creating special offers for corporate leisure groups who may use the leisure centre for sporting activity. This strategy may clash with that of offering reduced family rates for those who may desire to join the club.

Recent Developments at Castletroy Park Hotel

By the end of 1995, the Castletroy Park Hotel had a number of notable achievements to its credit. In May of that year it had received the prestigious Egon Ronay "Business Hotel of the Year" award. The presentation of this distinction to the hotel recognises the successful development of first-class business and conference facilities at Castletroy. As far as the conference and banqueting business is concerned, the award will enhance the credibility of the hotel in this particular market, and should attract national and international business to Castletroy. Recent visitors to the hotel include Intel Ireland Ltd., who visited Castletroy for the second year running to hold a five-day conference. In June, the Republic of Ireland soccer squad visited the hotel, utilising the sports facilities of the nearby University of Limerick and the National Coaching and Training Centre. As part of an individual training routine, the players took advantage of the hotel's hi-tech gym, swimming pool and outdoor running trail. Other recent visitors include the Irish Labour Party, and retail and distribution trade union, Mandate. Because visitors are currently beginning to regard conferences as an opportunity to mix business and leisure, the Castletroy Park arranges day trips to Bunratty, the Burren and Killarney. The prestige that accompanies the Ronay award will also benefit the hotel's sales management team in their efforts to promote the hotel as providing the best conference facilities around.

The Castletroy Park Hotel, in providing first-class conference and banqueting facilities, which are complemented by an extensive leisure amenity, is poised to consolidate its position as one of the leading corporate hotels in Ireland. Achieving this position in little under four years illustrates the commitment and dedication of the hotel's staff and management team. Through progressive strategic deliberation, the Castletroy Park Hotel will, in time, significantly enhance and expand the extent of its product portfolio and quality of service, creating in the process a participative and collaborative working environment conducive to generating improved human resource application and commitment. Sustaining this momentum will no doubt serve to stimulate ongoing strategic planning in the immediate future.

Source: Interviews with company personnel.

Questions

1. Assess the existing strengths and weaknesses of the Castletroy Park Hotel.

2. What opportunities are available to the Castletroy Park Hotel to enhance its future growth prospects?

3. Critically evaluate the human resource strategies that are currently generated within the Castletroy Park Hotel.

8

Bunratty Banquet

Introduction

While traffic at Shannon (transit and terminal) had shown a satisfactory growth in the early 1950s, there were dark clouds on the horizon. The development of the Whitney jet engine extended the flying range capability of many airlines, leading to significant overflying of Shannon.

The airport authorities had already seen the need to develop attractions at Shannon which would encourage stop-overs to counteract the above trend. So promotion of duty-free shopping facilities and the *haute cuisine* at the airport restaurant was undertaken. In addition, Ireland's first hotel school, the Shannon College of Hotel Management, was established at the airport in 1951.

The Shannon authorities have always viewed their role within the perspective of the Mid-West region, rather than within the immediate hinterland. This led to the construction during the 1960s of a series of Grade A hotels within the Limerick–Shannon–Ennis triangle to provide a tourism infrastructure to serve the region.

As the troublesome 1950s concluded and a new decade began, losses and redundancies continued to occur at Shannon. A staff member remembers Brendan O'Regan, controller of sales and catering at Shannon, as he watched jet trails of aircraft overhead bypassing the airport, saying of the lost tourism potential: "at least they are on the move, now we must get them to Ireland — all we need is one good trick". Serendipity then took a hand.

Bunratty Castle — Historical Background

In the early 1950s, Lord Gort bought Bunratty Castle for a sum in the region of IR£1,000 as a store for his collection of mediaeval English and European furniture, which he had acquired previously when purchasing the Lough Cultra estate. During the mid-1950s Lord Gort, John Hunt — a professional antiques expert — and Brendan O'Regan met several times to talk about the restoration of Bunratty Castle. As a result of their approaches, the Board of Works undertook restoration of the castle as a national monument, but sources of state finance dried up during a credit squeeze around 1960. The Bunratty renovation "trio", Gort, Hunt and O'Regan, then had a series of discussions with Bord Fáilte (Irish Tourist Board) which agreed to contribute IR£300 on the understanding that local tourist interest did likewise. The Shannon Airport authorities quickly joined Bord Fáilte in this restoration effort. So, with input from both private individuals (Gort and Hunt) and the public sector (Board of Works, Bord Fáilte and Shannon with O'Regan as its head), Bunratty was on the way to being an authentically restored archaeological attraction in the Mid-West region. Not only was the castle of historic architectural interest, but it had the added feature of being a museum containing a valuable collection of period furniture.

Product Search/Research

So by 1961 the genesis of Brendan O'Regan's "one good trick" had begun. It is impossible to pinpoint exactly when the idea arose of using Bunratty for purposes other than those originally intended. However, the idea of providing "period entertainment" at the castle emerged at this time.

Then began the task of formulating a tourist attraction based on the mediaeval practices of the region. In this product search/research phase, the services and opinions of several experts were sought — for example, District Justice Gleeson who had written a history of Bunratty; Ms Nuala O'Faolain who researched the eating habits of the period; and Drs Máire and Liam de Paor, mediaeval historians.

It was quickly decided that it could be self-defeating to attempt to reconstruct the entertainment of the period in its entirety — the popular banquet dishes of the period comprised such items as roast hedgehog and pigeon pie, while most meat dishes were much more highly spiced than modern palates could tolerate. So, on the culinary side at least, poetic licence in the formulation of the product was considered acceptable as long as the style of the period was observed. It was decided that the etiquette of eating with fingers, aided only by a dagger, would be adopted. Consideration was given to the dress to be worn by diners. Provision of period costumes was ruled out on cost grounds and it was agreed that the distinctive feature would be a specially designed serviette ("bib") to be worn by all guests when dining.

A particular problem arose in relation to the form of entertainment to be provided. In marketing research studies on the tourist features most favoured by American visitors generally (the US was the proposed prime target market for the Bunratty banquet), it had been established that both Irish songs and dancing rated highly in the entertainment category. However, it was discovered that because oral traditions had been passed down solely by word of mouth, no Irish songs had been recorded for the period of the fifteenth to the seventeenth century, inclusive. Shannon authorities were equally disappointed to learn that dance, in its traditional Irish form, did not feature at banquets during the period, whereas the harp played a central role.

It was agreed that songs other than from the fifteenth to seventeenth century would be included, as long as they contained the tone and style of the period being recreated. However, it was felt that to include dancing would destroy the authenticity and the credibility of the programme. So it was decided that singing and some story-telling would form the core element, while the harp would figure as an entertainment feature.

Before proceeding further, Brendan O'Regan went to see at least two tourist attractions that might help in the final formulation of Bunratty. He studied an example of Elizabethan entertainment in London — however, it varied from the proposed Irish venture in being set in a modern rather than period setting. He also visited a specially developed Israeli tourism attraction food/wine "'happening'", which, like a German *Bierkeller* evening, derived its success from the sociability, conviviality and atmosphere created, although no attempt was made to construct a definite time period. O'Regan returned, more or less assured that it was possible to develop Bunratty along the lines they had intended, provided that two criteria were observed:

- The offering had to be unique, and

- It had to be acceptable on the domestic market — it must be seen by Irish people to be in good taste.

The latter point was considered highly important. It was quite possible to devise a phoney stage-Irish-type entertainment, which, in the short term at least, might prove an attraction to overseas tourists. But to be credible, any proposed formula had to pass the Irish audience test.

Product Development and Testing

There followed a gestation period of several months from formation of the product idea/concept to prototype development of the banquet at Bunratty.

Considerable attention was then paid to ascertaining the likely acceptability of the "product". A series of trial banquets was held, to which overseas representatives of airlines using Shannon were invited, together with local airport executives. Staff engaged in US market operations for airlines such as Lufthansa, Sabena, Air France, Alitalia, BOAC, Air Canada, TWA, PanAm and Aer Lingus gladly offered their services as "guinea pigs". A consensus emerged that it was an acceptable product, most attractively presented in terms of both entertainment value and period recreation.

But would it sell? It was decided to undertake a series of market tests.

Market Testing

Before recording Shannon's efforts at assessing its likely market acceptability, it is necessary to consider the particular "package" planned around the Bunratty evening and the special circumstances obtaining, which encouraged such a package concept.

Most aircraft coming to Shannon did so for operational reasons such as refuelling, and all flights disembarked passengers. This presented Shannon Airport with two different potential customer types:

- Passengers on transit flights who could avail of the duty-free shopping facilities before re-embarking, and

- Stop-over passengers who could avail of duty-free facilities prior to departure on their outward flights, with the additional possibility of spending time and, it was hoped, some additional discretionary income, in sampling the tourism attractions of the region.

In relation to the latter, the IATA (International Air Transport Association) regulations then in operation provided passengers with the facility of breaking their flight for a limited period, and then proceeding on to their destinations by joining another flight (with the same or any other IATA airline), without incurring a supplementary charge on their air ticket.

Thus, Shannon developed a 24-hour stop-over programme and marketed it in 1962 as a "Free Day in Ireland". The tour incorporated a short tour of Co. Clare and Co. Limerick to give visitors a sufficient glimpse of Ireland to whet their appetites for a longer stay at some future date. The itinerary included an 80-mile luxury coach tour operated by Córas Iompair Éireann (the state-owned transport company) with commentary by a professional courier on areas of interest and on the cultural features of Ireland generally. The programme included a visit to Quin Abbey, a twelfth-century historic building, where the attention of the visitor was drawn to its pre-Columbus-era origins; an intermission at a pub in Sixmilebridge, to quaff Guinness; a visit to the Old Ground Hotel, Ennis, to sample Gaelic Coffee and Irish dancing; and dinner at the airport restaurant. Overnight accommodation and breakfast were included in the cost. The next morning there was to be a sightseeing tour of Limerick incorporating St Mary's Cathedral, St John's Castle, Pery Square and some central city shopping. Prior to departure, visitors would be encouraged to undertake duty-free shopping at Shannon Airport.

The 24-hour mediaeval tour was priced at US$15, including the planned dinner at Shannon Airport. Between the end of August and the end of October 1962, about 500 visitors availed of the offer. Their visits coincided with experimental banquets at Bunratty Castle. The idea evolved therefore that some of the "free-day" tourists might be introduced to the banquet concept instead of the planned dinner in the Shannon restaurant. The results were spectacular. Many visitors thought that the banquet was their most exciting travel experience ever.

Commercialisation

On the basis of the above experience, it was decided to launch the banquet in time for the next tourist season. An extensive consumer advertising campaign and a general marketing communications programme, involving the travel trade and mass media publicity, were undertaken in the US. The promotional budget for 1963 amounted to nearly IR£80,000. The general theme was the airfare feature of "no extra cost" on a stop-over at Shannon.

From its commercial launch, Bunratty was an almost instantaneous success. Word of mouth soon replaced impersonal media as the banquet's main form of marketing communications, so that by the end of 1963, demand was so great that additional alternative sites were being considered. Before this occurred, however, an interesting further development was occurring at Bunratty.

Bunratty Folk Park

At the start of the 1960s, Shannon Airport was preparing itself to cater for larger and faster jet aircraft. This was a brave decision in view of the decline in total traffic at Shannon — see Table 8.1 below. A major new runway was planned, but before seeking government finance for the project, preparation work began on site development. This involved a decision to remove an uninhabited farmhouse.

Before agreeing to the clearance of the site, Brendan O'Regan suggested that it might be a good idea to transfer the cottage to Bunratty to provide an extra tourist attraction there. In discussions with John Hunt in the period 1961–62, this idea was developed further, to encompass the concept of a folk park.

The village of Bunratty had sustained a population of over 2,000 at one time — could they not reconstruct the lifestyle of the old village so that overseas visitors, particularly Americans, could catch a glimpse of rural Ireland recreated? If this proposed tourist amenity should materialise, it could also provide an opportunity for many of the visitors to relate to their ethnic roots.

Again, advice was sought, and gladly given.

- Dr Lucas, Director of the National Museum, outlined for the Shannon authorities proposals that had been made several years previously, by the then Minister for Education, Senator

Table 8.1: Shannon Airport, 1958–93 (000 passengers)

Year	Transatlantic Terminal	Total Terminal	Transit	Total Traffic
1958	54*	90	410	500
1959	50*	83	324	407
1960	56*	103	313	416
1961	65*	118	265	383
1962	70*	118	252	380
1963	76*	138	196	334
1964	97*	173	207	380
1965	125*	215	213	428
1966	150*	257	212	469
1967	185*	317	240	557
1968	220*	367	354	721
1969	257	453	434	887
1970	259	473	360	833
1971	283	513	500	1,013
1972	264	474	489	963
1973	245	452	402	854
1974	242	450	499	949
1975	231	445	587	1,032
1976	254	493	608	1,101
1977	292	551	624	1,175
1978	304	585	556	1,141
1979	313	618	550	1,168
1980	288	559	355	914
1981	289	580	363	943
1982	319	590	453	1,043
1983	306	577	415	992
1984	359	630	458	1,088
1987	381	740	507	1,246
1990	375	934	695	1,629
1992	373	961	704	1,664
1993	392	1002	706	1,709

* Author's Estimate.
Source: Aer Rianta (Irish Airports Authority) and Shannon Development.

Moylan, to develop a national folk park at Kilmainham, Dublin. These plans had come to nought because of an ensuing credit squeeze.

- Mr Kevin Danaher, a senior researcher with the Irish Folklore Commission, recommended a regional folk-park concept for Bunratty which would incorporate dwellings representative of the Mid-West — for example, bothán scóir, Clare farmhouse, West Clare cottage, Golden Vale farmhouses, etc.

While Bunratty Castle was growing as an evening entertainment centre, the folk park emerged as a day-time tourist attraction at the same location — see Table 8.2.

Extensions of the Banquet Programme

From the beginning it was realised that capacity at Bunratty was extremely limited, and even though two, and sometimes three, shift operations had been introduced successfully, the planners at Shannon soon began to seek additional banquet locations.

As part of each 24-hour tour programme, the attitudes of visitors to individual elements of the package were monitored. The courier on each coach distributed copies of a questionnaire for completion by the passengers — the response rate averaged 25 per cent over the season. The result of this continuous survey corroborated existing evidence that the Bunratty banquet was perceived very highly in entertainment terms and, consistently, two other elements of the tour were commended — the visits to Quin Abbey and the Irish dancing interlude that had been included in the visit to Ennis.

So the Shannon authorities studied the possibilities of developing a separate form of banquet entertainment in or near Quin, Co. Clare (about 12 miles from Bunratty).

However, another castle further north, Dún Guaire near Kinvara in Co. Galway, became available before a decision was reached on the Quin location.

Although this castle had considerably less capacity than Bunratty, was located 40 miles from it, and was only available for use between 6 p.m. and midnight each day, it had several advantages that encouraged Shannon to establish a second banquet operation there. The owner, Lady Amtil, was keen to develop the castle as a tourist attraction, and being located less than 17 miles from Galway city, this site offered a new potential stop-over possibility. In fact, Dún Guaire was incorporated in a two-day Galway/Mid-West region package deal. This new offering was aimed at US travellers with more leisure time on their hands, who wished to undertake a Galway Bay/Burren, North Clare tour.

Table 8.2: Historical/Archaeological Attractions, Day Visitors

Year	Folk Park	Knappogue	Dún Guaire	Craggaunowen	Hunt Museum
1963	29,100	—	—	—	—
1964	38,500	—	—	—	—
1965	34,200	—	—	—	—
1966	35,500	—	—	—	—
1967	49,800	—	2,900	—	—
1968	55,800	1,400	2,000	—	—
1969	69,900	1,700	2,400	—	—
1970	72,500	2,800	2,200	—	—
1971	74,800	4,600	4,600	—	—
1972	61,300	2,000	3,800	—	—
1973	71,300	5,000	7,500	—	—
1974	87,100	8,100	14,200	—	—
1975	91,600	10,800	11,400	—	—
1976	96,800	11,300	15,000	11,400	—
1977	113,200	12,400	19,400	23,200	—
1978	133,400	19,500	22,000	35,300	2,700
1979	111,600	16,100	20,000	30,100	1,800
1980	114,300	10,800	19,700	36,900	2,400
1981	123,700	10,300	22,800	43,000	1,900
1982	135,500	9,500	17,900	45,600	1,900
1983	138,700	7,600	19,800	44,100	1,800
1984	154,700	10,200	19,700	47,000	1,900
1987	179,300	8,700	18,000	50,700	1,100
1990	271,900	12,200	24,700	68,300	1,600
1992	274,100	9,700	25,900	67,500	1,600
1993	268,552	9,834	25,970	60,737	2,699

Source: Shannon Development, Annual Report.

The planners were now faced with a product definition problem. Should it be a mirror image of Bunratty, or should they seek to differentiate it from the tried and successful formula already in use? They agreed to adhere closely to the environment and menu provided at Bunratty, but to vary the entertainment. There was to be an orientation towards Anglo-Irish literature, with emphasis on the works of local and regional writers, particularly the Nobel prize-winning poet, W.B. Yeats.

As demand for the banquets continued to grow, the authorities at Shannon were obliged to implement their decision to locate yet another operation near Quin. Knappogue Castle was selected and renovated. Again, it was asked what form the banquet should take here. As at Dún Guaire, the basic Bunratty formula was adopted with a change in the entertainment programme — in this case a "pageant" format was adopted, in which the history and culture of Ireland in general, and the region in particular, were illustrated by means of poetry, verse, mime, song and music.

The Future

In 1968 the Shannon Céilí was initiated at the Folk Park as an alternative form of entertainment for visitors to the Mid-West region. It comprised traditional music, popular eighteenth and nineteenth-century ballads, and Irish dancing. Although product differentiation from "Bunratty" was clearly defined, it was hoped that there might be a significant level of substitution between the Céilí and mediaeval banquets — see Table 8.3.

While Dún Guaire and Knappogue have attracted a growing level of business since their initiation, many times over the intervening years the Shannon authorities have asked themselves whether these two banquets have been successful products in their own right, or whether they have merely contained the overflow from Bunratty.

Perhaps a greater concern to the Shannon planners in their task of developing a total tourism strategy to support Shannon Airport, and in defining the role to be played by mediaeval banquets in particular, is the problem of where to go from here.

Source: Company reports and interviews with company personnel.

Table 8.3: Attendance at Shannon Entertainments

Year	Bunratty Castle	Knappogue Castle	Dún Guaire Castle	Shannon Céilí
1063	6,500	—	—	—
1964	11,100	—	—	—
1965	17,500	—	—	—
1966	17,400	—	—	—
1967	23,600	13,200	—	—
1968	30,300	17,500	5,600	2,600
1969	31,600	26,800	6,900	7,000
1970	37,500	39,600	8,200	8,500
1971	40,800	33,800	7,400	10,000
1972	46,400	22,400	5,300	3,400
1973	50,200	27,800	5,400	3,200
1974	43,400	29,100	5,700	3,600
1975	50,100	30,900	6,100	6,400
1976	56,600	37,000	6,400	5,400
1977	60,500	46,100	8,600	10,800
1978	59,300	47,400	11,300	18,000
1979	61,400	44,700	9,200	14,000
1980	56,200	32,500	7,400	4,700
1981	57,500	35,900	7,900	2,000
1982	57,600	40,900	7,000	1,700
1983	58,000	41,100	7,500	1,200
1984	59,500	47,100	10,000	11,500
1987	62,100	36,700	5,500	13,700
1990	60,100	34,700	6,800	19,100
1992	51,100	31,300	5,100	20,600
1993	56,233	27,992	6,424	18,063

Source: Shannon Development Annual Report.

Questions

1. Analyse the sequence of events by which "Bunratty" and other Shannon entertainment initiatives came into being. From a management viewpoint, critically assess the Innovation/ Product Development process adopted for the introduction of the Bunratty tourist attractions.

   Suggest other potential products/visitor attractions that might be developed to complement the folk park and mediaeval banquets by relating to Irish historical and cultural features, and from which Shannon (and national) tourism could benefit.

2. Describe and comment on any principles and practices of Entrepreneurship that the case may illustrate. Discuss any evidence there may be of the role played in the case by "serendipity" (good fortune) and/or "synergy" (the benefit of combined action). Does the study indicate that Shannon's planning of tourism projects was effective or otherwise?

3. The original "push factor" for developing new tourism products in the Shannon region was the need to take initiatives to offset the downturn in airport traffic. Were "Bunratty" and other Shannon entertainments successful in achieving the aim of redressing Shannon Airport's decline? Justify your answer with reference to data and other information in the case.

   Critically assess the track record of the Shannon authorities in terms of management of the tourism "product range" detailed in the case.

4. International tourism has been a consistent growth sector of the world economy over decades — yet Shannon's share of international tourism has declined proportionally in line with Ireland's market share generally. Suggest factors that could have been responsible for the comparatively poor performance of Irish tourism.

   Discuss the role of tourism in regional development generally, and evaluate the impact of projects such as "Bunratty" in terms of the development of the Shannon region, with reference to particular case points or by implication.

5. The tourism marketplace internationally is becoming increasingly competitive. In examining international business strategy, Michael Porter has stressed the importance of factors that can

lead to the competitive advantages of nations. Critically assess, in this regard, the position of Ireland and, by extension, the competitive status of the Shannon region, in terms of tourism capability. Justify your comments by reference to case details, or otherwise.

9

Jury's Hotel Group plc

Introduction

Jury's is one of the leading hotel groups in Ireland, with a proud tradition for hospitality and first-class service dating back to the last century. It currently operates 11 quality hotels in Dublin, Cork, Limerick, Waterford, Galway, London, Glasgow, Cardiff and Bristol. The hotel caters for a wide market, with the business and tourism sectors as the most important sources of revenue and profit.

Evolution of the Group

The Jury's Hotel Group has a long history in the hotel business in Ireland. As far back as the early part of the nineteenth century, William Jury operated the first commercial boarding house from numbers 6,7 and 8 College Green and from 2 Anglesea St, Dublin. The business was expanded in 1881 when, in association with two other partners, Jury built the Shelbourne Hotel and sold off the other Jury's premises to a cousin, Henry James Jury, who purchased and completely refurbished them, including the now famous ballroom with its balcony which was to be used later for the very popular Jury's Irish Cabaret. Further development was undertaken again in the 1950s when the Jury's Copper Grill was opened. By the beginning of the 1970s, Jury's was a thriving and expanding business with a total of four hotels, two in Dublin, one in Westport, Co. Mayo, and one in Co. Sligo. In 1972, it expanded yet again its Dublin business, purchasing from the Intercontinental Hotel Group, which at the time was moving out of the Irish market. These premises are now known as Jury's Ballsbridge. With this purchase the group also acquired premises in Cork and Limerick. The other hotels were sold off, and the Ballsbridge premises became the flagship of the group's operations.

In April 1986, the ownership of Jury's hotels changed when the group was quoted on the Irish stock exchange, changing its name first to Jury's Hotel Group Ltd. and later to Jury's Hotel Group plc. Up to this time, the group was in the ownership of private shareholders. With the increased funding available from going public, the group embarked on yet another refurbishment programme. In 1987, a new reception area and additional rooms were added to Jury's Dublin. In 1989, The Towers were added, and in 1990 two further premises were added — the Ardee in Waterford and the Pond in Glasgow, Scotland. For the Limerick hotel, new leisure facilities were added. In 1993, the group embarked on its most adventurous strategy to date by opening two new properties — one in Dublin and the other in Galway. Known as the Jury's Inns, these hotels are budget-style properties which the group does not own. Rather, it is leasing them on a long-term basis, a move that has made a significant contribution to the group's continued success in Ireland and abroad. In 1994, a further Jury's Inn was opened in Cork. Jury's also acquired a hotel in Bristol in that same year. In late 1995, the group went on the acquisition trail yet again by purchasing the four-star 143-room Cardiff International Hotel — now being renamed the Jury's Cardiff Hotel, for a modest stg£7 million. This hotel is located in the city centre and is situated directly opposite the Welsh capital's 7,000-seat international conference centre, and is within easy reach of such major visitor attractions as the National Stadium, formerly known as the Cardiff Arms Park. The Cardiff venture is being funded from group resources, which were considerably boosted by the June 1995 rights issue. It brings to four the number of hotels that Jury's now owns in the UK, and particularly complements the 234-room outlet in Bristol, just 50 minutes away from Cardiff. Jury's had been contemplating the Cardiff property for some 18 months previously, when its acquisition intelligence indicated that it was likely to come on the market. The hotel was initially built by the Brent Walker group for stg£10.5 million in 1990, but came under effective control of the banks when the leisure group got into difficulties. The vendors of the property were believed to be keen to dispose of the asset with the minimum of fuss. The consideration thus worked out at £49,000 a room — a figure at the lower end of the average being paid for hotels in provincial UK centres. By comparison, Bristol cost the group some £40,000 per room, but that facility required capital investment to upgrade many of the rooms. One of the key attractions of the Cardiff Hotel is that it is new, and will require little capital upgrading. Overall, the Jury's group now consists of 12 hotels located throughout Ireland and the UK, including Dublin, Cork, Galway, Limerick, Waterford, London, Glasgow, Bristol and Cardiff. Group bedroom capacity therefore now stands at some 18,620, and this figure is set to rise to about 2,100 when the fourth Jury's Inn at the Custom House Dock in Dublin comes on stream in September of 1996. Over the years the hotel group has shown itself to be a consistently successful business in Ireland and this success can be attributed to a number of key factors.

Guest Services

The facilities offered by each of the group's hotels are considered very good. The general layout of each hotel in the group is very similar. For example, Jury's Dublin contains 300 bedrooms, all en suite. The hotel offers a variety of restaurants including the Coffee Dock Restaurant, the Embassy Garden Restaurant, and the Kish Restaurant which specialises in seafood cuisine. Two bars are on offer — the Dubliner pub and the Pavilion Lounge. There are also conference/banqueting facilities available which can cater for up to 850 people. The hotel contains extensive leisure facilities. In addition, Jury's Cabaret, which runs from May to October provides an excellent entertainment amenity.

Along with the hotel, Jury's Dublin has an exclusive five-star wing of 100 super deluxe bedrooms and suites called The Towers. The group is Ireland's leading conference specialist with staff trained to ISO9002 Quality Management Standards available in each hotel to deal with every detail. The group has a deserved reputation for the quality and variety of its services. Meticulous planning is, according to the group, the secret of its success, with close attention paid to all customer requirements. It believes in an extremely high level of personalised service for all of its clientèle.

Highly Trained and Motivated Staff

The Jury's Group advocates continuous investment in its employees, especially in terms of training and development. As far as Jury's is concerned, its greatest asset is its people. Each hotel is operated by teams which have a considerable depth of experience and a culture that has stood the test of time.

Figure 9.1: Organisation Structure

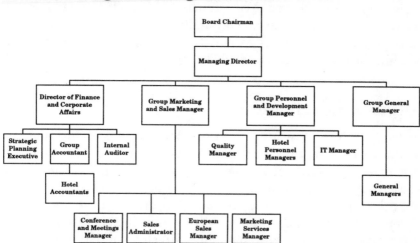

A functional structure is very much in evidence within the group. Tasks are grouped together by function, promoting a characteristically consistent and predictable working environment. For Jury's this form of structure fulfils a number of important objectives. Specifically, it differentiates the organisation into various sub-groups. The main sub-group consists of finance and corporate affairs, group marketing and sales, group personnel and development, and group general management. All of these various functions report to the managing director of the group, Mr Peter Malone, who in turn reports to the Board of Directors, which represents the interests of the shareholders. This board is under the chairmanship of Mr Walter Beatty.

A functional structure also helps to ensure effective co-ordination and good communications across all levels within the organisation. The structure enables the organisation to interact with the external environment, and thereby influence the extent to which the external environment affects the operation and success of the group's business. By grouping people together on the basis of their expertise, Jury's can both utilise and co-ordinate its resources in a way that contributes to successful organisational performance. In this context, the benefits of a functional structure become apparent. Strictly speaking, it promotes the specialisation of labour. Efficiency is encouraged, and the need for an elaborate system of control is minimised. Rapid decision-making is facilitated, and better opportunities for staff promotion and career development are afforded. Yet a functional structure does have its drawbacks. It can force accountability to the top. Line-staff conflict may become obvious, as may the growth of sectional interests within the organisation as a whole.

Organisational Culture

Several factors have influenced the development of Jury's organisational culture. Specifically these factors include the history of the hotel, the values of key members within the group, the organisation's growth pattern to date and notable events in its history. Of these, the values of key members have exerted the greatest influence on the organisation's culture. Key members include the executive committee, the managing director, the Group's personnel manager, the quality manager and line managers within the different hotels. Seemingly, the group's commitment to quality has also influenced the formation of its culture, as has its commitment to customer care and staff satisfaction. In this context, the group's mission statement seeks to articulate the essence of the culture by promising a total dedication to customer care through provision of outstanding service levels, by respecting the dignity of other team members, and by conducting its business in an ethical and professional way.

The organisational culture is formal and task oriented. A culture of this type is characteristically attributable to an organisation with a tall hierarchical structure. A top-down approach to management is evident, with all tasks clearly defined in well-documented job descriptions. The culture does not encourage employees to reflect critically on higher-level decisions. Efficiency, as opposed to effectiveness, in task implementation is very much the standard condition of performance. For Jury's, the presence of a strong culture has a number of strategic benefits. Specifically, it allows the group to identify what is important in the external environment — that is, what the organisation should attend to and monitor. For senior management, this may be group performance, competitor activity, market share, etc. For staff it may be customer focus, suppliers, etc. The organisational culture can also be used to illustrate the responsiveness of the group to change. In addition, it can indicate, in a more subjective way, issues of importance to the group, such as goals, work methods and behaviour. Moreover, it provides the group with a medium through which friendships can develop, which ultimately will affect the successful functioning of the organisation.

Maintaining Organisational Culture

Jury's, like most organisations, has a number of tools which it uses to reinforce and maintain its organisational culture. For example, the group places a great deal of emphasis on recruiting and selecting the right people, a process which requires careful consideration as the future well-being of relationships within the organisation is at stake. The group has a comprehensive induction programme for its new employees. Issues covered include the history of the organisation, various personnel issues, an address from the group's managing director, and a tour of the hotel. In addition, the group has its own official staff magazine and has a social club in each hotel. Another area of significance in its contribution to maintaining culture is that of training and development. Essentially, if staff are to provide a level of quality service, they need to be properly trained to begin with. Jury's also endeavours to provide ongoing development opportunities for its supervisory and senior management staff. All staff are afforded every opportunity to put their training to good use, with internal promotion prospects providing an added incentive.

The decision-making process within Jury's has been described as complex at group level, mainly because it involves a considerable number of people. As a publicly-quoted company, any decision taken has to be first and foremost of benefit to the shareholders. The hotel's executive committee meets every Monday to formulate both operational and long-term strategic objectives and to propose ideas of how best to achieve these. The general managers also hold a monthly meeting to discuss issues of concern to specific hotels in the group.

Strategies for Success

Investment in Infrastructure

The group believes that its policy of infrastructure investment has contributed enormously to its success over the years. In the past three years alone, the group has invested a considerable amount in its hotels. Examples include the £18.5 million investment in the three Jury's Inns at Christchurch, Galway and Cork. The Jury's hotel in Kensington, London cost the group £10 million. Each of these investments has been achieved through a strong balance-sheet position and by way of cost-effective financing. This latter point is reflected in the development package used to finance the three Jury's Inns. By way of third-party investment, the group was in a position to negotiate a long-term lease arrangement with the investors, while the £7.5 million used to purchase the London hotel was raised through a rights issue. In 1990, the group purchased the Waterford Jury's for £2 million and the Ponds Hotel in Glasgow for £10 million. Expansion of this order would not have been possible were it not for a strong profit base, one that the group has steadily built up over the years by offering attractive levels of customer service. The group, however, has not only spent money on acquiring new hotels, it has also invested in the refurbishment of existing hotels. Room refurbishments are currently being carried out in both the Ballsbridge and Cork hotels.

Investment in People

Jury's has invested not only in infrastructure development — considerable time and money are also expended on human resource development. All of the group's 1,000 employees, plus its 500 part-time staff, participate in ongoing training programmes consisting of operational and supervisory development. In addition, the group affords management-development opportunities to up-and-coming trainees. When recruiting new staff in 1994, Jury's extended its commitment to training when a rather unique training programme was initiated. Essentially, the group sought to source employees for its Christchurch Inn from the local unemployment pool. In association with CERT and the Community Development Association, a third of the staff required were recruited from this programme. The group also offers risk management, health and welfare programmes.

The aim of these training programmes is to enable staff to realise their full potential, and to develop strong teams to assist in expanding future operations. In addition, the attention paid to employee development may have in some way contributed to the group's present low level of employee turnover, a figure which for some years now has been running at 2–3 per cent. Another reason for the low level of employee turnover may be the group's recent expansion programme, which has created many new employee promotion opportunities.

Strategy for Total Quality Management

One of the most recent changes that has taken place is the corporate drive for total quality and achievement of ISO9002 accreditation. The drive for ISO accreditation was primarily an internal exercise in providing Jury's with a consistent and workable quality management system. For more than two years, all 1,000 employees worked towards the ISO objective. Traditionally, many organisations, in seeking to implement a change in management strategy, face functional difficulties as they attempt to reformulate existing structural and cultural formations. Yet for Jury's the change process was one of common sense.

A time-scale of one year was set for achieving ISO9002 accreditation (the International Quality Standard which is awarded by the International Standards Organisation and administered in this country by the National Standards Authority). But before Jury's could aim for this standard they needed to modify ISO requirements in such a way as to make them relevant in their application to the hotel sector. Accordingly, some 18 clauses were altered and modified. To achieve this, a working group was set up consisting of hotel and catering industry representatives. This ensured that the necessary levels of credibility, expertise and commitment were on hand to facilitate the process. Because ISO9002 is very much based on the notion of internal customer care, organisations must align functional activities so that each department becomes a sub-unit in a chain of activities that are critically dependent on each other for resource and informational support. In other words, each organisational sub-unit becomes both a client of a service provided to it, and a producer of a service to other departments, before, ultimately, external customer satisfaction is achieved. With this internal customer orientation in mind, the working group, headed by Personnel and Development Manager Simon Murphy, began the process of implementing the programme. In its implementation, the group has sought to promote organisation-wide participation through the formulation of various project-specific teams. In facilitating this process, a number of consultative committees were established, focusing their efforts on directing and coaching employees to become more autonomous, yet mutually dependent in their work. If properly directed, such an approach can help to build a more participatory and collaborative working environment.

Strictly speaking, a well-developed quality management programme can help an organisation to become more focused in its provision of customer service. By specifying the standards to be achieved, a programme can guarantee an assured quality level, which, through an ongoing audit and review process, can facilitate long-term workability and effectiveness in achieving strategic objectives.

Awarded the ISO9002 Quality Management Standard

Jury's hotel became the first hotel group in Europe to achieve the ISO9002 certification for Quality Management in its hotel. In 1993, the National Standards Authority of Ireland (NSAI) awarded Jury's Waterford the honour of becoming the first Irish hotel to be certified to ISO9002 standards.

Up until quite recently, ISO standards have been predominantly achieved by large multinational organisations operating in the manufacturing sector. However, this trend is beginning to change, with sectors such as printing and transport getting in on the act. It has long been the policy of Jury's to offer the highest quality service to its customers. Because ISO can offer standards of consistency and quality in a way that affords customer recognition, it became a perfectly sensible business decision for Jury's to apply for accreditation. Yet before the hotel embarked on a group-wide quality programme, it initiated a pilot scheme in its Cork hotel. Having learned from this experience, the group was then in a more forthright position to formulate a comprehensive certification strategy.

The success of any quality programme depends very much on top management support and employee commitment. For this reason, the Jury's board of directors gave the programme its full backing by developing a quality statement setting out the group's philosophy on customer service. Meetings with employees were held to explain programme objectives, with performance manuals compiled to give them appropriate expression and substance. In monitoring programme execution, an internal audit committee was established to co-ordinate the various departments in their implementation of the programme, and to make necessary adjustments for any area that did not meet with specified requirements.

Because the drive for total quality was a group-wide effort, all of the group's hotels were involved from the start in the formulation of performance manuals. Yet, individual hotels were afforded the opportunity to focus on issues of specific importance to their day-to-day operations. With the quality programme in place, the next step was to apply for ISO accreditation. Before NSAI began the audit process, a quality officer was appointed in each hotel to co-ordinate the programme, and to liaise with the NSI auditors. In 1993, following the certification of the Waterford hotel, Ann T. O'Carroll was appointed group quality manager with specific responsibility for attaining ISO9002 standards for the whole group. In January 1994, all of the group's mainstream hotels had achieved accreditation, with the final certificate awarded to Jury's Ballsbridge. Objectives for the future include accreditation for the group's most recent ventures, the Jury's Inns at Christchurch, Cork and Galway. It also intends applying for ISO accreditation in its London and Glasgow hotels.

Hotel Industry Overview

The defining characteristic of the Irish hotel industry can be very much described in terms of a fragmented infrastructural base. Economic units are small, affording an exceptionally low level of return on capital investment. The industry is seasonalised and is highly dependent on food, drink and ancillary services for its profits. It derives the bulk of its room business from non-corporate sources. There is also a critical dependence on packaged business generated by wholesale tour operators, which can diminish the industry's ability to command reasonable prices. Far from being over-priced, many top-grade Irish hotels charge well below their international counterparts.

The industry does have its positive features in that it is now better equipped and more professional than was the case a few years ago. With Bord Fáilte projecting a more scientific approach in its marketing and product development, various new tourism products aimed at niche markets have emerged. Taken in this context, the problem facing Irish hotels is not so much the sustained contraction of the marketplace, but rather the extent to which the various hotel groups can maintain and increase their share in a growing market. In the past decade, more beds have been empty on any single night than have been occupied, resulting in a much lower share of the total bedroom market. Seasonality has also been a contributing factor to lower room-occupancy levels — it is extremely difficult to attract guests to resort hotels during the "'shoulder" and "low" seasons. Low occupancy levels can have a depressing influence on the profitability of Irish hotels and are a prime reason why hotels represent a poor asset investment. Generally speaking, pre-tax profits average at 7.7 per cent of sales, with a 5.1 per cent return on capital investment. Higher room occupancies would certainly improve these ratios.

The industry also exhibits varying customer characteristics. For example, the American customer is keen to stay in hotels, resulting in Irish hoteliers becoming increasingly dependent on US business. Research has shown that Irish hotels have a greater dependency on American room sales than they have on those in any other country. Germans, French and Scandinavians prefer to cruise on the Shannon, tour the guesthouse circuit, dwell on farms and go camping near lakes and woods. Nevertheless, the excess reliance on the US market is not a sufficiently useful strategy because of its volatility. During the 1980s, higher air fares, Middle Eastern terrorism, a weak US dollar and a presidential election contrived to produce dramatic downturns in the number of US tourists coming to Ireland. And even when the Gulf War ended, it was a considerable length of time before US tourist numbers picked up again. It is for reasons such as these that Ireland desperately needs to develop new markets.

Hotel Characteristics

In Europe, the "hotel" has a very different image from its counterpart in Ireland. European hotels tend to be on a "grand, formal" level, and they can charge a fortune for a bed. The Europeans go to hotels on business, but spend their holidays in cabins or caravans, as hotels are generally perceived as expensive. Also, in Irish hotels, a very different operational set-up is in place, with management emphasis very much on ground-floor operations. The typical Irish hotel today is a curious mix of disco, function room, lounge bar and swimming pool, with the Irish hotel relying very heavily for its profits on these ground-floor activities. This is in sharp contrast to hotels in most other countries where room sales account for more than 50 per cent of total revenue. However, there are exceptions to the rule, and it must be noted that some hotels are full, or nearly so, all year round. There is also a greater awareness of marketing, with emphasis placed on the value of hotel accommodation in the home market, of employing such concepts as Yield Management to introduce the flexible pricing aimed at eliminating the waste of an empty room, and of providing all-weather facilities which will attract guests in low and shoulder seasons. Moreover, a strong effort is being made to identify and develop niche markets such as senior citizens, young people, families and special interest groups. Hoteliers are joining marketing groups, are travelling abroad to meet tour operators and travel agents, and have sales teams on the road to promote their product. At national level, the Irish Hotels Federation has established a marketing function and has upgraded the annual hotels guide. The signs of enterprise and commitment are to be seen everywhere in the industry, but there is a long road ahead before Irish hoteliers like Jury's can achieve the business ratios which are the norm.

Market Outlook

In the past, Jury's has not been able to attract budget-conscious guests to its hotels because ratings in its various hotels vary between four and five star properties. But management has not failed to recognise that the budget segment of the market represents an area of growth and profit, hence the development of the Jury's Inns which are aimed at the budget guest looking for low room rates. The group has also furthered its objective of expansion into the UK market, with the recent purchase of a hotel in Kensington, adding to is recently purchased Glasgow property. The group in the future can be seen making further developments in the UK market, and eventually in the European market with possible property opportunities available in Brussels and Amsterdam.

Financial Overview

The years 1992 and 1993 were two of the most difficult experienced in the hotel industry for many years. Particularly so for Jury's which had to manage a hotel business in the depth of a recession and steer a publicly quoted group through an interest rate and currency crisis. At the end of April 1993, the group reported a pre-tax profit of £2.32 million, a fall of 7.7 per cent on the previous year. Yet the group had staged a recovery in profits on the back of improved demand and a larger operating base. In fact, the earnings per share of 11.1p recorded in fiscal year 1994 are only 5 per cent off peak earnings in 1990. With a currency price of 153p Jury's shares are trading at a 30 per cent discount to the net asset value, and offer a prospective yield of 4.7 per cent. Capitalised at IR£52.4 million, its enterprise value (market capitalisation and net debt) of IR£83 million is significantly below the cost of a newly built four or five-star hotel.

Table 9.1: Trading Record of Jury's Inn, Christchurch

Y/E IR£ m	April 90	April 91	April 92	April 93	April 94	5-yr. avg. growth
Sales	22.0	27.0	26.1	26.3	33.6	12%
Operating Profits	3.9	5.0	4.1	3.9	5.1	16%
Net Int. (Paid)/Recd.	(0.7)	(1.8)	(1.6)	(1.6)	(1.4)	15%
Pre-tax Profits	3.2	3.2	2.5	2.3	3.7	10%
Tax	(0.4)	(0.4)	(0.3)	(0.3)	(0.4)	
After Tax	2.8	2.8	2.2	2.0	3.3	12%
Attributable						
Profits	2.8	2.8	2.2	2.0	3.3	12%
FRS3 EPS (p)	7.1	10.6	7.9	7.2	11.1	9%
Adj EPA (p)	11.8	10.6	7.9	7.2	11.1	-1%
Dividends per share (p)	4.6	4.7	4.7	4.7	5.2	5%
Cash flow per share (p)	13.7	12.5	9.9	9.3	13.5	6%
Interest Cover	5.6	2.8	2.6	2.4	3.6	
Dividend Cover	2.6	2.3	1.7	1.7	2.2	

Jury's Irish portfolio, including the Inns, currently generates in excess of 85 per cent of Jury's Group operating profits, with its flagship Dublin hotel accounting for 33 per cent of its domestic roomstock and for close to 48 per cent of group operating profits. Of the 400 rooms in the Dublin hotel, 100 are from the group's luxury extension, The Towers. Jury's has almost 20 per cent of the top end of the Irish hotel market, primarily targets the business traveller — 60 per cent of Jury's sales are business and event related — and is increasingly tapping into the lucrative incentive travel and conference business.

Table 9.2: Jury's Group Five-Year Trading Record

	1990 IR£000	1991 IR£000	1992 IR£000	1993 IR£000	1994 IR£000
Turnover	22,048	29,996	26,006	26,277	33,635
Operating Profit	3,874	5,051	4,119	3,968	5,127
Interest payable and similar charges	(742)	(1,795)	(1,606)	(1,648)	(1,406)
Profit on ordinary activities before taxation	3,132	3,256	2,513	2,320	3,721
Taxation	(411)	(366)	(315)	(315)	(448)
Profit on ordinary activities after taxation	2,721	2,890	2,198	2,005	3,273
Earnings per share* (p)	11.8	10.5	7.9	7.2	11.1
Total shareholders' equity	56,404	63,847	64,740	64,469	73,872
Total bank loans and overdrafts	10,025	15,320	15,389	14,829	16,568
Debt/equity ration (per cent)	18	24	24	23	22

*   Earnings per share is calculated by adjusting historical earnings per share for the bonus element of the rights issues in May 1990 and November 1993 as appropriate.

Sales increased 28 per cent in the year to April 1994. The group's Irish hotels, which account for over 55 per cent of the total room-stock, enjoyed the benefits of a stronger domestic economy. Despite the seasonal bias of the new Inns, the second six months with pre-tax profits of IR£.9 million were the best ever by the group. The gross and operating margin remained unchanged — operating margins are currently around 15 per cent — reflecting the lower-margin Inns business and the fact that the London hotel only contributed in the winter months. In the first year of operation for the Inns, an increased sales and marketing spend of between

IR£.6 million and IR£.8 million contributed an estimated IR£.2 million to operating profits. To generate trading profits of IR£.2 million, the Inns averaged occupancies of 62 per cent at yields of IR£30 per night.

Jury's interest bill was lower than anticipated, reflecting the benefits of the November 1993 rights issue which raised a net IR£7.5 million. A lower average cost of funds for the year of around 9 per cent, as opposed to 11 per cent the pervious year, was also a factor. Even including the IR£7.75 million option on Christchurch, gearing did not exceed 34 per cent, while interest charges were covered a comfortable 3.7 times.

Turnover for 1990 was IR£22.048 million with profit before tax at IR£3.874 million. The earnings per share were 12.4p and total borrowing amounted to IR£10.025 million, with the debt to equity ratio at 18 per cent. For 1991, pre-tax profit was IR£3.256 million, up from IR£3.132 for the previous year. Turnover also increased on the previous year's figure to IR£26.96 million. Retained profit was IR£9.013 million up from IR£7.444 million in 1990 and earnings per share were 11.1p, down from 12.4p a year earlier. Total numbers employed were 944, up from 754 a year earlier. Of those employed, 894 were operational and 50 administrative staff. The total wage bill was IR£8.967 million.

For 1992, pre-tax profit stood at IR£2.51 million, which was down from the 1991 figure of IR£3.26 million, with group turnover standing at IR£26.12 million, down from IR£27 million in 1991. These profits and turnover were achieved during a very difficult year of adverse market conditions. A number of factors contributed to the end-of-year results. The crisis in the Gulf had a considerable impact on international travel. The number of overseas visitors to Ireland for the year showed a decline of 2.6 per cent. Also the continued recession in the UK and in the Irish business market tightened during the second half of the year. Earnings per share were 8.3p, down from 11.1p. A final dividend of £3 per share was paid with an interim dividend of £2 per share which was the same as last year. Jury's room occupancy rate for the year fell by 3 per cent to 55 per cent. Jury's turnover easily outstripped Ryan which had a turnover of IR£19.3 million. However, the Ryan group sold more rooms; Jury's sold 225,000 rooms, a drop of 6,000 on the previous year, Ryan group sold about 240,000, a decline of about 10,000.

The disappointing turnover and profit figures pinpoint the fundamental problems facing both Jury's and Ryan:

- Both hotels suffered from a lack of scale, and the limitations of the Irish market will make it very difficult for either to reach a size which would attract renewed institutional interest.

- Both were trying to carve out a niche for themselves in a market that is changing from the traditional middle-class US and UK visitors to a market which is divided between up-market international and budget-conscious holiday-makers from Europe and the US.

For the six months to 31 October 1993, a pre-tax profit of IR£2.803 million was recorded which was an increase of 30 per cent on the corresponding period in 1992 (IR£2.155 million). Turnover was IR£17.57 million, an increase of 21.3 per cent on the 1992 figure of IR£14.49 million. Earnings per share amounted to IR£10.1, compared to the 1992 figure of IR£7.6. This relatively strong performance was aided considerably by the trading of the new Inns at Christchurch and Galway. The Irish economy, while continuing to show some recovery, was very much aided by the lower interest-rate levels of that particular year. In order to maintain its strong occupancy levels, the group intensified its marketing initiatives, and despite some unfavourable conditions, the group managed to increase the combined overall bedroom occupancy levels of its hotels. In October 1993, the group completed the purchase of the Onslow Hotel in Queensgate, London, and renamed it Jury's Kensington Hotel. Costing Stg£9.8 million, the hotel contains 171 bedrooms. The purchase of the hotel was funded by a Rights Issue which raised IR£7.59 million net of expenses. The balance of the prices was paid by way of borrowings. In all, the investment programme since 1986 has resulted in a total investment in excess of IR£24 million by the group. In addition, the group has spent a substantial sum in upgrading existing hotels, including IR£5.5 million on building the exclusive Towers building at Jury's hotel, Dublin. Recently, the group has acquired the 245-bedroom hotel, the Unicorn in Bristol and another in Cardiff. Costing Stg£6 million, the Bristol hotel, which has been acquired from the Rank Organisation, has been renamed Jury's Bristol Hotel. The acquisition will be financed through debt. As with the London hotel, Jury's Bristol enjoys an excellent city-centre location and will add considerably to the group's UK product portfolio.

The Future

The Jury's Hotel Group will continue to examine potential acquisitions which have a good location, fit in with the group's existing hotel structure, which possess the potential to improve operational performance further under Jury's management expertise. The group has taken a reasonably conservative approach to its gearing over the years, enabling it to move quickly when availing of the right opportunities. This strategy will probably be continued, with the group adopting a prudent gearing policy, maintaining a strong financial position, and retaining the capacity to develop its group operations.

Source: Interviews with company personnel.

Questions

1. Critically evaluate the growth and development of the Jury's Hotel Group since its small beginnings.

2. What present strengths and weaknesses exist within the Jury's Hotel Group?

3. Evaluate Jury's Hotel Group's recent expansion activities and comment on the contribution that the "inn" concept has made to the group.

4. What opportunities exist for future growth?

10

Campbell-Bewley Group

Introduction

In 1986, Patrick Campbell, then 42, retired from Campbell Catering, the company he had set up with his wife almost 20 years previously. When he set up the business, he was no stranger to the hotel and catering industry, having been born into a family which ran a city-centre Bed and Breakfast business. On finishing school, he enrolled for a three-year hotel management course at the College of Catering in Cathal Brugha Street. On completing the course, he worked first at Ashford Castle before moving to London and then on to Sweden. When he came home he joined the family business, but found it frustrating and lacking in sufficient challenge. At the time, outdoor catering was in its infancy, with a few professional operators. Patrick Campbell saw the opportunity to start a business which had the potential to grow, and decided to set up an outdoor catering company with his wife Veronica, who had also trained in Cathal Brugha Street College, Dublin.

Their first tender as Campbell Catering was for a contract to provide Dublin Corporation with 25,000 sandwiches for daily distribution to 120 schools in disadvantaged areas. New and full of enthusiasm, the company was glad to get the business, but it turned out to be a salutary lesson in how not to do business — because of a lack of business experience, it was a financial disaster. The company lost heavily on the contract, and for the next five years the spectre of the debt hung heavily. To cap things, the company lost the contract at the end of the year. However, Patrick Campbell believed that this was actually a blessing in disguise, because it forced the company to start looking at other and more profitable types of business. The real turning point for Campbell

Catering came in 1971 when it won two major contracts — one for
Sun Alliance, and the other for Nett in Arklow. This was effectively the company's first step on the road to growth, and a decision was taken by the company to aim for long-term contracts se-
curable by a strong commitment to constant top-class customer
service. The catering division now has in the region of 100 contracts. Total employment in the group stands at 2,000 people, the
majority of whom are full-time staff. Group turnover by 1991 had
reached £40 million, and after the acquisition of Bewley's in 1986,
the business was split roughly 50/50 between catering services
and the products division, which includes Bewley's tea, coffee and
bakery and the Campbell International Catering House.

As the business began to grow, Campbell Catering, then operating from Patrick Campbell's parents' hotel in Gardiner Street in
Dublin, was forced to find new premises. But while it moved from
the city centre to North County Dublin, it retained the family
connection, as the new premises in Swords were owned by the
family. The head office is still there, but senior management now
operates from Dublin city centre. Also many of the company's
employees are local and have stayed with the company from its
inception, thus providing a firm foundation for the organisation.
In the late 1970s, when Campbell Catering was rapidly expanding
and looking for new opportunities, Marathon was in the process of
finishing the construction of its two gas platforms off Kinsale.
Campbell won a contract to supply food and janitorial services to
the rigs, and its long association with the off-shore industry, which
continues to this day, began.

However, in 1984 the company became embroiled in a long-
running industrial relations battle with local union representatives over the right to select those who would work on the rigs.
With strike action lasting for three months, the company's Cork
offices were put under a militant, and at times volatile, siege. Yet
it did give Campbell invaluable industrial relations experience
which stood the company in good stead when it came to dealing
with the complex web of union representation at Bewley's. Campbell saw this period as the culmination of a build-up that had
been coming on for years because the drilling exploration companies, anxious to get in and out of sites as quickly as possible,
agreed to union demands, which in the longer run could not be
sustained. It got to the stage where the unions were trying to dictate on issues such as who should be employed on the rigs, who

should be promoted and so on. In this context, Campbell had little choice but to fight or else lose control of the situation.

Having learned from its experiences, the company began tendering for other off-shore work, both in Ireland and overseas. A joint-venture with an Indonesian company followed, which worked well until oil prices began to fall in the mid-1980s resulting in the level of activity at the rigs declining. This led to the catering company pulling out. However, the Indonesian contract gave Campbell invaluable overseas experience which has allowed it to make a lot of good business contacts. From Indonesia, the company's international arm extended to Libya where it has served a US company drilling in the desert. From there the company moved into Egypt. In all, these contracts were very lucrative for the company, but over the past 14 years the competition in the industry has intensified, and so profit margins have been cut considerably.

Catering continues to be the main activity of the group's business, with ongoing contracts to supply companies such as Guinness, Nixdorf, Fujitsu, Motorola, Marathon and Irish Distillers, and institutions such as the University of Limerick, University College Cork and the Blackrock Clinic. While catering gained the company its first national exposure, it was the acquisition of Bewley's that commanded widespread attention, and Patrick Campbell was not slow to make full use of the business opportunities afforded by the Bewley name. When Campbell Catering acquired Bewley's, the café chain already had three franchised outlets. It now has 15, including one in Belfast. Since acquiring Bewley's, Campbell has also taken steps to make the name known internationally. Grants of Ireland has been licensed to manufacture a coffee-flavoured liqueur which sells under the brand name Thomas Bewley, and a joint venture has been entered into to make a Bewley's Irish ground coffee. With Bewley's firmly integrated into the group, Patrick Campbell became interested in overseas acquisition. In 1989, Campbell Catering and a UK property company undertook such a move when they bought the UK-based Cranks wholefoods restaurant chain from Guinness — an acquisition which seemed to be a good fit, but in retrospect proved to be an expensive diversification.

The Bewley's Acquisition — 1986

By 1986, the café chain, formerly owned by the Quaker Bewley family, was facing major problems — it was losing customers to the fast-food industry, losing money at a rate of £400,000 a year, and was heading for closure because of a pension scheme funded by the company's cash-flow. The Bewley's premises were in a very bad state, there were too many unions, and there were more pensioners on the payroll than staff. The outlook for the future was bleak. The connection between Dublin and Bewley's coffee goes back as far as 1835 when Samuel Bewley started exporting tea. Two generations later, in 1894, the family, under the direction of Earnest Bewley, opened the first Bewley's Oriental Café in George's Street in Dublin. He gave coffee-making demonstrations, while his wife served scones to attract customers.

The Grafton Street café, which has always been the flagship of the Bewley's operation, opened in 1927 after an investment of £69,000. When the chain came on the market, Campbell was not the only group interested in making a purchase. However, other interested prospects were deterred by the complex union structure present in the company — there are six different unions representing about 400 people — and the unusual structure of the company. Campbell, hardened by its own big industrial relations battles, saw the intricacies of Bewley's as a challenge. Nevertheless, sorting out the troubled company was not a straightforward exercise, and Patrick Campbell estimates that it took him three years to put Bewley's firmly back on a profitable footing. He was fortunate in that he had time to do so.

Ownership of Bewley's had been vested in the staff in 1972, but this transfer of ownership of the company to the staff had been done in such a way as to make it virtually impossible to sell the company, and while the intentions behind the strategy were honourable, it did have a negative long-term impact on the business, as it meant that no one specific person had ultimate responsibility for how the company was being run. At the time it was very much a progressive and liberal concept, but the downside was that it prevented the company from sourcing adequate capital to fund the modernisation of its facilities. The sale of Bewley's to Campbell Catering was finally achieved after much negotiation, and before the revenue commissioners came looking for payment of a £1 million bill. Campbell Catering spent about £5.5 million on the acquisition. This included a £1 million figure to settle the company's tax bill, £1 million to set up an independent pension fund, and £3.5 million to pay creditors and meet other liabilities.

The acquisition was funded from three sources, namely, bank borrowings, retained earnings, and Campbell's own funds. Having purchased Bewley's, Patrick Campbell then set about putting a major investment package together to refurbish the Grafton and Westmoreland Street outlets. The Grafton Street café was completely refurbished at a cost of £1.5 million. Funds were also needed for the development of a new Bewley's café in Mary Street, and for the upgrading of production facilities at the company's tea, coffee and bakery subsidiaries. In total, almost £6 million was spent, using the proceeds of a sale and leaseback deal on the company's Grafton Street premises, to inject much needed capital into the business. Campbell felt that this level of investment was necessary in order to turn Bewley's into a profitable company.

Organisation Structure

The acquisition of Bewley's was a major step for Campbell Catering, and one that has since prompted Patrick Campbell to design a more appropriate structural form, reflecting the now consolidated organisation. Since late 1990, a new holding company has been established to bring the various businesses of Bewley's and Campbell Catering together. Patrick Campbell, who is the majority shareholder in what is now called the Campbell-Bewley Group, is chairman and chief executive. The group's business has been split into two operating divisions — services and products — each of which is headed by a divisional chief executive. Although the group has been reorganised into two separate divisions, in reality there is no distinct demarcation line, as both divisions work closely together on a day-to-day basis. All senior management is based in the same building above the Bewley's café on Dublin's Westmoreland Street. There is a lot of inter-group trading, with the retail houses providing the best custom for the products division.

Overseeing all operations is Patrick Campbell. As chairman, his main function is to act as chief executive of the product division. He also acts as advisory executive to the catering and food group of which he is the major shareholder. Campbell also plays much the role of an intermediary, representing the staff, customers and management in any conflict that may arise. Each division operates on a stand-alone basis under the direction of its own team of managers. By means of a family trust, Patrick Campbell and his wife own 80 per cent of the group, while the remaining 20 per cent is held by the group's senior management. The sales division is under the direction of Gerry Fagan, who came to the group in

1975, reaching the position of financial director three years later. In 1986, he became managing director of the group's international interests, including the catering contracts with the oil and gas exploration companies in the Middle East. The group has also developed extensive sales contracts in the German supermarket sector and provides a mail-order business supplying teas, coffee, shortbread and preserves to the German market.

Figure 10.1: Campbell-Bewley Group Organisation Structure

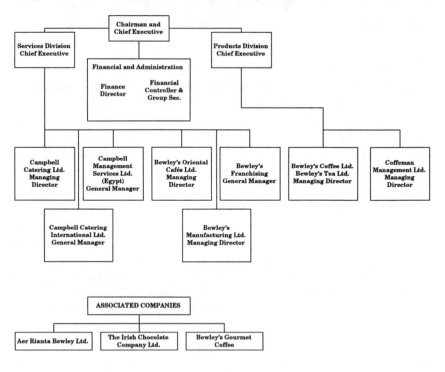

The product division is run by Patrick Bewley who is credited with the considerable improvements made to the distribution of Bewley's coffee, and with the development of a franchise business in Britain, a move made possible through the group's acquisition of the Coffeeman company. The financial director of the group is Michael O'Sullivan. By broadening the Bewley's base, and through an increased expenditure programme, the company is now in a profitable position, with a more equitable balance between the contract-catering retail restaurant and the beverage business. Group turnover expanded significantly over the period

1988–93, from £29 million to an estimated £50 million. Margins continue to be tight, with the return on equity averaging 22 per cent. In 1994, the group spent up to £1 million promoting its Bewley's tea brand, but in doing so had to contend with tough competition from Unilever, which is spending in the region of £2 million to relaunch the Lipton brand. Both companies are aiming to cut into the market share of the big players in the tea market in Ireland, namely Barry's and Lyons.

At present, the Bewley's share of the tea market is about 4 per cent, yet the group is hoping to more than double this figure over the next three years through the expansion of its supermarket sales. When Campbell Catering took over Bewley's, its image was somewhat tarnished. What was bought was an old reputation which had a lot going for it, including the uniqueness of its brand, while its new purchaser was a strong believer in the effectiveness of branding and the importance of a corporate identity in establishing and maintaining brands. The first step was to get the company on a sound business footing. It then set about drawing up a new corporate identity manual, detailing every aspect of the company's identity from its logo to its application on all the packaging, advertising, etc. At the centre of the corporate identity is the value of the brand, and the Bewley's brand, because of its success, is able to command a premium price.

Joint Ventures

The group has entered into three joint ventures so far. The first was a 50/50 partnership entered into with Aer Rianta in 1992, a year in which the company was awarded the catering contract for Cork Airport. Since then, the group has expanded to Southampton Airport and Stansted Airport. The partnership also affords the group opportunities for expansion into Eastern Europe.

The group has a 30 per cent holding in the Irish Chocolate Company with the Sorensen family who produce Butler's Irish Chocolates. This joint venture has launched a Bewley's brand of butter chocolate and handmade sweets. The third joint venture is a 50/50 partnership with Fairwinds Coffee Inc. to market Bewley's Irish Cream flavoured coffees in the American market.

Company Acquisitions

Having successfully acquired Bewley's in 1986, Campbell felt that an acquisition strategy was the best approach when, in 1992, it purchased a UK coffee distribution company for £1.4 million. The company, Coffeeman Management Ltd., operates as a manufacturer and distributor of coffee and tea through a network of 70 franchised distributors to some 7,000 outlets throughout the UK. The company's warehousing and distribution will be based in Birmingham, and it will be supplying coffee and tea from its existing production facility in Dublin. The group sees great potential for growth in the UK market where it had a small coffee shop and tasting room on The Strand, opposite the Savoy in London. Unfortunately this café had to be closed in 1993 because of poor trading conditions.

At present Bewley's holds 61 per cent of the Irish market for ground coffee supplies to catering outlets, and while it could not expect the same level of penetration to the UK, a small percentage of that particular market would significantly add to its revenue. In 1993, Campbell-Bewley acquired two more UK specialist distributors, Countryside and New City Drinks, and these operations were integrated into the group's business, with their brand names being gradually phased out. The group has also plans to expand its current chain of 15 franchise-owned cafés from Ireland to the UK where it hopes to have several dozen franchised cafés operating within the next five years. For the moment, Irish expansion will be by way of franchise. However, in Britain the initial cafés opened will be operated by the group directly. The group already has two in operation in Britain — one at Stansted and the other in Edinburgh. The reason for the expansion into the British market is that Bewley's coffee already has a 60 per cent controlling share of the home market, so that room for growth is limited for the future — hence the need to look to other markets for future growth.

Franchising Activities

Franchising has recently become an important expansion strategy for the group. There are currently 22 Bewley cafés, five of which are owned and operated by the group. The others, including the Bewley's café in Tokyo, are franchised out, each selling the group's products and recreating the traditional coffee house ambience.

The Tokyo venture came about in May 1993 when the company signed a franchise agreement with Sanyu, a restaurant based in the Harajuka district of Tokyo. The food offered to the Japanese is very different from that served to the Irish customer, as is the packaging of Bewley's products sold in Japan. Instead of sticky buns, the Japanese palate prefers subtlety and sophistication in its confectionery tastes. A Tokyo confectioner was found to develop a range of confectionery products to suit this particular market.

In order to attract discerning Japanese consumers, the packaging of tea, coffee and other products was appropriately modified. Through research the company has found that the Japanese reaction to the original packaging was that it was nice and homely but that it would not sell. Again, something more sophisticated was required. Accordingly, the new packaging features plain bold colours, decorated only with Bewley's signature. The group has introduced the same concept for the Bewley's products on sale in Ireland and the UK.

The group may be expanding, but the core of the business is still very much in the catering sector, with over 800 staff employed, providing up to 60,000 meals a day in Ireland. The group dominates the home market, and with the exit of John D. Carroll and National Catering, Campbell Catering is the only remaining Irish-owned major player. With the entry into the market of some British players such as Gardner Merchant, the group is seeking to grow through entry into other markets, principally Britain, with the recently acquired Eurotunnel contract providing a major boost to the group's aspirations. The group is also looking at opportunities in the US, with Chicago in mind as a specific target.

The Channel-Tunnel Deal

In January 1994, the company won the contract to construct and operate the restaurant in Calais at the French entrance to the Eurotunnel. The group is also running the Eurotunnel restaurant at the British end in Folkstone. The group had initially been providing catering services for 300 people during the construction of the tunnel, but was not guaranteed the passenger service contract. Apparently, senior Eurotunnel executives had paid a visit to Ireland and were said to be suitably impressed with the relaxed, informal style of restaurant that Bewley's provided. A European flavour was what they were looking for, and Bewley's met their requirements. Another determinant for the group was the quality image associated with the Bewley name, and because the group had previously operated in different countries, it was well equipped to manage a cross-cultural situation.

The tunnel restaurants — one in England and one in France — cost the group up to £1 million to be fitted out, with turnover for the first year approximating £3.5 million. The contract serves about 3,000 customers an hour at the two terminals, with Bewley's providing the restaurant service and Aer Rianta running the duty-free shops. The Channel Tunnel development involves four operations, including two staff canteens all run exclusively by Campbell Catering, creating up to 130 jobs in total. In recruiting for these vacancies, the group sourced many of the employees internally, offering French classes to those wishing to enhance their linguistic competence. The tunnel contract has some added benefits, in that Bewley's tea and coffee products are now sold in all four outlets. The outlets could prove to be a very useful vehicle for any future plans by the group to move into the European market.

Campbell-Bewley Group Financial Performance

The year 1993 was a successful one for the group. Group turnover was £45 million with pre-tax profits standing at £1.91 million and profits amounting to £1.44 million. The services division, encompassing the retail and catering contracts, accounted for approximately £40 million of group turnover, with the products division, consisting of wholesale coffee and tea, making up the remainder. At the start of the year, the group had long-term borrowings of £1.62 million, an overdraft of £1.13 million, and shareholder funds of £6.27 million. The group's debt to equity ratio fell from 83 per cent to 56 per cent, and with the integration of the 1994 Granville acquisition into the consolidated group accounts, the balance sheet has been cleared to put Campbell-Bewley in a net cash position. The group managed to raise up to £1 million through a Riada Business Expansion Scheme (BES), which is to be directed at building the group's share of the tea market. Because the group is committed to a programme of overseas expansion, it is estimated that the successful implementation of any such programme in the longer term will require an annual turnover of up to £100 million. As for the future, many of the group's expansion plans will be focused on the British market, and in this context, the Granville alliance will afford Campbell-Bewley the necessary expertise for success in this particular market.

Table 10.1: Campbell-Bewley Group Financial Performance*

| | 1990 | 1991 | 1992 | 1993 |
	£m	£m	£m	£m
Turnover	30.8	34.8	42.4	45.7
Pre-tax Profits	1.0	1.4	1.93	1.91
Profits	—	—	1.53	1.44
Borrowings	5.0	5.6	5.09	4.47
Shareholders' Funds	2.6	7.28	6.27	6.32

* 1994 figures unavailable at time of publication.

Total Quality Management Initiative

One of the founding fathers of the Bewley enterprise focused much attention on the notion of quality, an attribute which he believed would become the defining characteristic of the organisation. His philosophy on quality still applies to this day. When Campbell acquired Bewley's in 1986, a refurbishment programme was initiated in the café chain, but perhaps more significantly, an expensive training and development programme was embarked upon with the sole objective of achieving the ISO9000 quality standard. Bewley's coffee was initially earmarked for registration. In August 1992, the improvement process began at the coffee-manufacturing facilities in Hanover Street in Dublin, and within 15 months the facility and its 40 employees were awarded the quality standard. It was the first coffee company to achieve ISO9000 accreditation in the country. Bewley's coffee offers a 24 hour service to its customers and also blends coffee for a number of important clients who require a specific blend for their customers. The Campbell-Bewley Group is currently in the process of implementing a full-blown Total Quality Management (TQM) programme, with the ISO9000 award viewed as a tentative first step in this ongoing process.

One of the benefits of the ISO award is that the group is able to confirm, in a manifest way, its commitment to quality and customer service. It has helped the group to focus on a longer-term strategy of continuous improvement. The quality assurance manager is Helen O'Riordan, who is assisted in her work by the production manager, Ben O'Connor. All the staff were involved in drawing up the manuals and operating procedures, generating in their efforts a commitment to the successful implementation of the quality programme. In this context, the ISO award is in recognition of the staff contribution to the process, and has helped to forge stronger links between management and staff. This quality team is now putting its experience to good use by helping the tea division, which has recently applied for ISO accreditation. With its slogan "Who is responsible for quality? I am", the group is poised to harness the energy and abilities of its staff in a way that will ultimately make them responsible for a superior quality of service.

Recent Strategic Alliances

In 1994, the group had to bring in a British company as a minority shareholder in order to finance its expansion plans. One of Britain's biggest venture-capital companies, Granville Private Equity Managers, announced in May 1994 that it had acquired a 14 per cent stake in Campbell-Bewley in a deal which put the value of the group at £21 million. Granville paid some £3 million for its stake. The move adds considerably to the group's ability to continue in its expansion programme. Campbell-Bewley had engaged in discussions with various institutional investors both in Ireland and in the UK, looking specifically for someone who would take a long-term perspective. The group is very interested in increasing its presence in the UK. Because Granville have already a strong presence in this particular market, they will contribute their expertise to the Campbell-Bewley group. Along with an acquisition strategy, the group is also interested in an expansion policy focusing on new restaurants and cafés in Ireland and the UK, as well as a franchising strategy for the home market, the US and Japan. The group has plans to expand in the contract-catering market in the UK, and to extend its Coffeeman business there too.

The most immediate impact of the group-investment programme is that it has allowed the group to clear its debt and put it in a net cash position. The investment impacted considerably on the ownership of Campbell-Bewley, which, up to quite recently, was very much a privately owned enterprise. For a start, the stake of the Campbells was reduced from 80 per cent to 69 per cent. Staff and management had a further 17 per cent, with Granville holding 14 per cent. The group has pointed out that this move is not a future indication of plans to go public.

Source: Interviews with company personnel and company reports and other documents.

Questions

1. Critically evaluate the Bewley acquisition by Campbells in 1986. What type of growth strategy was Campbells pursuing?

2. What strengths and weaknesses currently exist within the Campbell-Bewley group?

3. Evaluate the benefits and limitations of purchasing as it applies to the Campbell-Bewley Group.

4. What strategic options are available to the Campbell-Bewley Group in the future?

11

Berkeley Court Hotel

Introduction

The Berkeley Court is a member of the Doyle Hotel Group, an organisation that has been in operation for over 30 years. In that relatively short period of time the Doyle Group has become Ireland's largest hotel group. It is a privately owned company with seven hotels in Dublin, accounting for over 40 per cent of the capital's hotel bedrooms. The hotel group has also expanded overseas with the Clifton Ford in London and the Washington Courtyard and Normandy Inn in Washington DC. The success of the hotel group can be attributed to its ability to offer an executive product that meets the highest international standards, in prime locations, and at value for money prices.

Background

The Berkeley Court is a member of the Leading Hotels of the World Group, an organisation established in 1928 and now comprising a number of hotels. According to the 1994 Annual Report for the Doyle Group, the hotels in the group share a common goal: to offer their guests the highest possible standard of luxury, service and attention, to provide a quality of food and accommodation that will meet the demands of the most discerning traveller.

The Berkeley Court is the flagship of the Doyle Group. Originally, the hotel was fitted with an indoor swimming pool, a small conference centre, sauna, two restaurants, a bar, ladies' and gents' hairdressing salons and boutiques. Situated in the Embassy district of Ballsbridge in Dublin, the Berkeley is within walking distance of the Royal Dublin Society. The hotel is also five minutes away from the Financial Services Centre and provides free parking for patrons. Set on the former Botanical Gardens of Trinity College, the location was chosen for its suburban residential appeal. The hotel also happens to be located beside Jury's Hotel. Although this may be viewed as a disadvantage, it is of mutual benefit to the two hotels as it enables both to feed off each other, creating a shared synergy in the process. A feature on entering the hotel is the splendid lobby furnished with valuable antiques and paintings. The bedrooms are fitted in elegant fashion with a combination of soft colours, oak furnishings, fine lighting and colour television. The suites of the Berkeley Court are regularly the choice of royalty and heads of state when they visit Dublin.

The Berkeley room restaurant is well known for its excellent cuisine, while the Grosvenor and Herbert Suites provide banqueting facilities for 20–250 guests.

Development

In 1989, the hotel added on a new penthouse wing with executive rooms aimed at the corporate market. The penthouse offers total privacy with 7,500 square feet of room. The penthouse is also equipped with a study which has all the modern office conveniences to hand, for example, fax machines and other facilities required to carry out any business from your own room. The hotel was originally equipped with a swimming pool, yet a feasibility study conducted by the Doyle group found that it was rarely used. It was replaced with a modern gym open to guests 24 hours a day.

In 1994, all 180 bedrooms, eight suites, and the 12 spacious executive suites were redecorated. All the rooms are complemented by classic furnishings and many extra finishing touches. All rooms are equipped with private bath and shower, colour television, radio and direct-dial telephone.

In April 1994, the Berkeley Court opened its new conference centre. The new Berkeley Court Conference Centre reflects a new era in conferencing. The main conference area is the Grosvenor Suite, with a capacity for 350 people dining banquet style, or in the case of conferencing, 400. It is a fully integrated banqueting facility capable of dealing with a wide range of functions, and incorporates a separate pre-function reception room, conference bar and lounge independent of the rest of the hotel, as well as containing washroom and restroom facilities.

High-tech, state-of-the-art conference facilities include the following:

- Back projection and video facilities
- Remote-control dimming facilities
- Remote-control retractable screens
- Remote-control black-out facilities
- Central control room
- Full sound system
- Telephone, fax and TV points
- Uni-struts installed in ceiling for display mounting, special lighting effects, etc.
- Full air conditioning.

The entire facility has been conceived of as being totally independent of the main hotel. The Berkeley Court's second function room is the Herbert Suite which is as suited to a conference or meeting as it is to a dinner party or cocktail party. It is fitted with state-of-the-art technology, furniture and finishing which create a feeling of comfort and intimacy.

One of the most important features of the Doyle Hotel Group, and especially the Berkeley Court, is the calibre of its staff. They are a hand-picked group of men and women, carefully trained to make sure that a client's stay is as pleasurable as possible.

The hotel currently employs 180 full-time staff and 30 casual staff. On a ration of staff to bedrooms the Berkeley Court works out at 1:1, which is very acceptable for a five-star operation.

The hotel places tremendous emphasis on training. Eighty-five per cent of its full-time staff have attended Cathal Brugha Street College of Catering. Staff members train in their specific areas by attending day release courses of between two and three years' duration. They attend these courses on a day-per-week basis, and all costs are covered by the hotel. As well as receiving tuition, staff have access to the libraries in CERT and Cathal Brugha Street. Emphasis is also placed on on-the-job training where many staff members who have been with the hotel since 1978 act as mentors to younger members.

Figure 11.1 presents the basic organisation of the hotel.

Figure 11.1: Organisational Structure of Berkeley Court

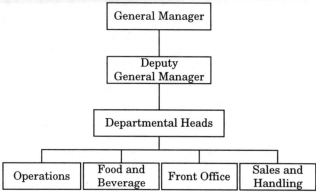

Hotel Market Review

Those in the hotel business tend to talk not so much about new hotels coming on the market, as about the number of new bedrooms available. Such discussion allows for the fact that hotels vary in size, and gives a much better measure of the state of the market. At the moment, hotels equivalent to more than 3,500 bedrooms are being built or proposed in Dublin. To put the number in perspective, more than a million visitors would each have to stay one night in any one year to fill the new hotels. However, many of the hotels for which planning permission is sought, and a lot of those which are announced as going ahead, never get off the ground. According to Bord Fáilte, market needs show that Dublin can accommodate about 250 new bedrooms a year for the next five years. It is in Bord Fáilte's interest to encourage new hotels, as a shortage of accommodation acts as a disincentive to visitors, but new hotels seem to be popping up all around Dublin, implying that the developers agree with the tourist board's assessment.

Hotel development in Dublin was at a standstill until a few years ago. The economic downturn which followed the Gulf War was accompanied by a reluctance by US tourists to visit Europe. Then there was a currency crisis, accompanied in turn by phenomenally high interest rates. But things have improved. According to the latest Bord Fáilte figures, tourist numbers grew by 75 per cent between 1988 and 1993, in spite of the Gulf War. Since then, according to Bord Fáilte's manager of tourism services, Bob Bowman, this pattern of growth has continued. But while the growth in Dublin could be described as frantic, hotel development outside Dublin is, at best, sluggish. The Irish Hotel Federation (IHF) does not have any easy explanations for the particular growth being experienced in Dublin. It suggests, however, that one contributing factor may be the trend towards short breaks. According to the chief executive of the federation, John Horan, people tend to have more disposable income and more leisure time than previously. Free to supplement their normal holidays with short breaks, they tend to opt for cities.

While the removal of the Shannon stopover did not lead to the predicted devastation of tourism in the west, it did seem to add to the numbers visiting Dublin. The pick-up in the economy has also been a contributing factor to the increase in tourist numbers. The buoyant market, which has facilitated the development of more hotels, has also encouraged business generally, leading to more business people staying in hotels. That buoyancy was in part helped by the onset of peace in Northern Ireland, a factor that has had a direct and positive effect on the number of people travelling to Dublin. The pick-up in business traffic is welcomed by the IHF, which says that it brings Ireland more in line with European countries. In Ireland, two out of three hotel guests are tourists, but in the rest of Europe, tourists account for only two out of every five guests. According to Mr Horan, more than half the revenue for an average European hotel comes from the overnight charges, whereas in Ireland they account for only one third of a hotel's turnover.

Some hotels have introduced a pay-per-room rate, a pricing strategy that has been popular outside Ireland for some time. It is particularly popular with families. With an average of 1.63 people staying in Irish hotel rooms, some hoteliers will find themselves offering a discount to unaccompanied guests. Many of the new hotels in Dublin operate this pricing policy and, in time, some existing hotels will undoubtedly find themselves following suit. But this is not to say that the traditional Dublin hotel, with a vibrant bar and restaurant, will disappear to make way for the higher-margin European model. According to Mr Horan, it is not unusual for the Irish to socialise in their local hotel, but in Europe the idea of going to a hotel restaurant or bar, if you are not a guest, is not as common. This, according to Mr Horan, is one of the selling points of Irish hotels: "A visitor can get involved in an Irish hotel, which is a strong marketing point, even if it is a weak financial point". It would be viewed as a weak financial point because the margins on room sales are higher than on the ground-floor activities such as bar and restaurants. Mr Bowman points to rates of £20–£30 per night in budget French hotels, and believes that more budget-type hotels are needed in Dublin. The Irish hotel market is experiencing organic growth with more of the new developments being pursued by Irish hoteliers. The return on investment from an Irish hotel is not sufficient to attract foreign investors since it is only two-thirds of the European average.

The good news for hoteliers is that the future looks bright. The 75 per cent growth in tourism numbers between 1988 and 1993 was as the government had projected. More significantly, revenue over the same period increased by about 100 per cent. There were not only more tourists, but those that came were spending more. The IHF said that it was revenue, rather than numbers, which were important when it came to making market projections. The government is projecting that revenue from tourism in the five years from 1994 will grow from £1.25 billion a year to £3.35 billion a year. For the IHF, straightforward growth, no matter how dramatic, is not enough. One of its targets is to spread the season. IHF philosophy is simple — the longer the season, the higher the margins, allowing more profit to be gained from the same turnover. So if things go well for Dublin, its hoteliers will benefit from increased visitor numbers who will spend more, and allow the hotels to make a greater percentage profit.

Competition in the Dublin Five-Star Market

There are four key five-star competitors.

The Conrad Hotel

The Conrad Hotel is Dublin's newest five-star hotel having opened in late 1989. Situated at the heart of the Earlsfort Business Centre opposite the National Concert Hall, the hotel is a subsidiary of the Hilton Corporation USA. The Conrad is 85 per cent Irish-owned with six major investors. The remaining 15 per cent of the equity and management contract is owned by the Conrad Chain. The hotel has 191 rooms, including eight executive suites and one presidential. Targeting the corporate business segment, the hotel was built with the business traveller in mind, yet it will take small reservations for tour groups.

The Towers

In February 1989, the Towers at Jury's Hotel in Ballsbridge was opened. The management at Jury's recommended to the board of directors that the rear of the hotel should be developed into a five-star property, to compete with the opening of the Conrad during the same year. Construction began in late 1987, and the Towers was opened in February 1989 at a cost of £5.5 million. During early 1995, a complete renovation and refurbishment programme began on The Towers and recommendations were made to build a totally separate entrance at Lansdowne Road to overcome the guests' disappointing initial impression once they arrived at the main hotel block. The hotel has 104 bedrooms including two presidential and two executive suites. There is also a boardroom situated off the Towers lobby, which will be available to the Towers resident at a reasonable rate. The bedrooms in the Towers are the largest guest rooms in Dublin. The hotel's marketing strategy is based on a number of principles, chiefly to attract a broader client base and to achieve increased occupancy levels. The levels of service and quality must be considerably higher than those of the main hotel, and consistency must be maintained. The product and service must be seen to be the best, to ensure that the Towers becomes a leader in the five-star marketplace.

The Westbury Hotel

The Westbury Hotel is one of several hotels owned by the Doyle family. A sister hotel of the Berkeley Court, this five-star property was opened in 1978. Located in the heart of cosmopolitan Grafton Street, the hotel has a total of 203 rooms including executive, standard and luxury suites. It also has a presidential suite and penthouse. The hotel offers a fitness room as part of its leisure facility to guests. The Westbury's main competitor is the Conrad Hotel in terms of location and clientèle.

The Shelbourne Hotel

The Shelbourne Hotel is Dublin's oldest hotel, and is a landmark and property with a lot of history attached to it. Situated directly opposite St Stephen's Green, it is a three-minute walk from

Grafton Street. The hotel, which opened its doors in 1824, sells itself not as a hotel but as a legend: the Irish Constitution was drafted in one of the hotel's function rooms back in 1922, and the hotel's logo is "the most distinguished address in Dublin". Part of the worldwide Forte chain of hotels, the Shelbourne has 164 rooms including five suites. It contains two bars, one of which is the renowned Horseshoe Bar, which has never been redecorated as the locals appreciate its history, originality and charm. The Shelbourne, like the Conrad and the Berkeley Court, does not market itself as a tours hotel. It does take bookings for incentive groups, but rack-rates are charged. In terms of services and location, the Shelbourne sees its main competitor as being the Conrad Hotel. Before the Conrad opened in 1989, the Berkeley Court was its main rival.

The Berkeley Court Package

The Berkeley Court is a high-class, deluxe hotel, and this is the market they are aiming for. With the addition of the Grosvenor Suite and the Herbert Suite, a main part of the hotel's market is the corporate market. There has been a worldwide growth in the corporate market of about 5 per cent. This has seen a large increase in competition as more hotels are adding facilities to try and get a piece of the market. The amount of accommodation available in Dublin alone has risen sharply over the past few years to meet this market. Not only does the Berkeley Court have to compete with other hotels in Dublin, but also with hotels internationally, as the corporate market is destination driven — it is necessary to sell the surrounding area as well as the hotel. Fortunately, Dublin has become increasingly popular as a destination point, which is an advantage in attracting potential customers. The main reason why the corporate market is so viable is that a lot of large corporations give their employees sizeable incentives, and when going to conferences, they are rarely constrained to a budget. The hotel is also targeting the more affluent tourists, especially the Americans who are renowned for their high spending. The increase of the "short-breaks" and "second holidays" in Europe is a huge business opportunity for the Berkeley Court to exploit and to take full advantage of, which they are currently doing.

With other hotels in Dublin and in the rest of Ireland, the most significant market trend is that of cost-cutting. Cost-cutting also applies in order for Irish hotels to compete with their European neighbours who are offering good quality accommodation for as little as £20–£30 per night. Also, the spreading of the season is something that will gradually happen as Ireland tries to capture a share of the second holidays market. The Berkeley Court is not interested in cost-cutting, as it feels that its customers are not interested in the price of the product, but rather in the quality of the service provided.

The Berkeley Court Hotel is not price sensitive, as the market at which it is aiming is more interested in luxury and quality of product than in the actual price. The hotel is aimed at the deluxe end of both the business and the travel/leisure segments, and operates a premium pricing structure, offering a two-tier price rate. The rack rate, which is not advertised, is the top rate for corporations given at a discount based on the volume of the corporation's business to the hotel. Weekend and promotional rates are the more common prices which appear in the hotel's advertisements. For example, the Berkeley Court Hotel's rates for 1995 are as follows:

- For one night in the penthouse — £1,500

- For one night in a standard suite or executive room — £215–£225

- For one night in a twin/double room — £155

- For one night in a single room — £139.

The hotel offers high-quality services and facilities. All bedrooms were refurbished last year and the new conference rooms are the most modern and up-to-date in Ireland. The provision of services in the conference rooms has been a prime selling point for the hotel, and this has resulted in the Berkeley Court hosting a number of important diplomatic conferences, as well as a host of important business conferences for large corporations. The introduction of the penthouse and executive suites has meant that the hotel has regularly played host to important heads of state and royalty. Situated in a prime location with ample parking space, the hotel is close to the city centre, a feature which has proven to be a strong selling point. Because of its location, the Berkeley Court also takes advantage of any promotions, shows or concerts in both the Point Depot and the RDS.

The Berkeley Court offers a number of promotions including

"Weekend Business" specials. These rates are advertised in the national media and in the *Belfast Telegraph*. The hotel also produces special weekend brochures aimed at this vast and growing market. Christmas flyers are given out along with Christmas cards to regular guests. In general, all of the hotel's Christmas season brochures include vouchers offering discounts in the hotel and its facilities, such as the restaurant and hair salon. The hotel also offers special rates during racing festivals such as, for example, the Christmas racing festival at Leopardstown, where the rate is £44 per person sharing a twin room, and includes a full Irish breakfast, with service charges and tickets to the reserved enclosure at the racetrack. The Berkeley Court also runs a Viennese Ball on New Year's Eve, and offers a special discount to guests who wish to stay the night afterwards. The hotel offers golf packages where guests can spend a weekend in the hotel, and also get to play on one of the more prestigious golf courses in Dublin, such as Portmarnock. This has proven to have been very popular with both the tourist market and the corporate market. Brown Thomas discounts are also offered to guests who are holders of the Brown Thomas card. Special prices are offered to Visa and American Express card holders, as are special rates offered to holders of the Bank of Ireland gold card, aimed at the corporate market. It also offers discounts to those over the age of 55. The Berkeley Court regularly participates in trade shows both in Ireland and in the rest of the world. The hotel is involved in the CPP (Corporate Partners Programme) dealing with Virgin Atlantic and British Midlands, giving customers air miles based on the number of nights that they spend in the hotel. Commissions of 9 per cent are also offered to travel agents.

Berkeley Court Marketing Strategies

The main aim of the hotel's marketing strategy is to achieve higher-growth figures through use of various mechanisms. Essentially, the hotel is seeking to bring about a greater penetration of divisions and departments within potential client companies by increasing its communication on the hotel's improvements and the promotions that are currently on offer. The Berkeley Court recognises the volume of business that the corporate market provides, and has designed its own corporate brochures outlining the discounts available to companies based on their volume of business to the hotel.

The hotel also seeks to increase its customer base by attracting more business from existing companies, and by attracting new client companies through its corporate market programme. It is currently attracting business moving into the new industrial estates and business parks, and is inviting business from the IFSC Development which is viewed as having enormous potential for the Berkeley Court. To do this, the hotel recognises that with the increased competition it will have to formulate a strong and aggressive advertising campaign. It will be necessary to make greater use of personal selling in order to build hotel awareness. In addition, building a strong corporate identity is of strategic importance to the hotel. Because the Berkeley Court is part of the Doyle Hotel Group, any corporate promotion and development programme carried out will be under the umbrella of the group.

The bulk of the Berkeley Court's advertising is done through Bord Fáilte's brochures and through regular features in a number of leading Irish tourism magazines. Direct mail/marketing also forms a major part of the hotel's advertising strategy. In essence, this approach is aimed at the corporate market where a database is kept by the group, and where companies are regularly informed of rates and special incentives. Under the corporate heading, direct marketing is aimed at financial services companies; ITM (Irish Travel Managers) Association; executive secretaries, as they are the people who book the hotel for the executives; embassies; chambers of commerce; Leadership of the World Hotels through Lhell and LRI which are both reservation systems. The main exhibition companies at the RDS and Point Depot are also afforded this direct-mail/marketing service. Leisure interests including the Irish Racing Board, previous clientèle of the Berkeley Court, and the DGOS — Dublin Grand Opera Society — are extended the service as well. Also covered by the service are regional tourist offices, Bord Fáilte international offices, airlines, car-hire companies and shipping companies. As for conference and incentives, the hotel mails directly to companies using Bord Fáilte Listings, Doyle Group Listings, Trade and Professional Organisations and SITE (Society of Incentive Travel Executives) members.

The Berkeley Court Hotel is marketed as part of the Doyle Group by the group marketing/promotions manager, based at the Burlington Hotel. Major strategy decisions are obviously made at group level, but each hotel has a sales/marketing manager responsible for tactical marketing decisions. The group has a public relations manager also based at the Burlington, responsible for co-ordinating activities affecting each hotel.

It is the responsibility of the sales manager of the Berkeley Court to interface with the clientèle, to perform an appraisal of current business and to investigate any occurrence of customer dissatisfaction. The sales manager's job also includes seeking new business.

The Berkeley Court Conference Centre

The Conference Centre is marketed separately from the hotel and is targeted at both the UK and European Conference market as well as at the Irish market. It advertises through its literature which is both mailed to potential companies by using the Doyle Group's database and presented at the Leading Hotels of the World conference showcases in both the US and the UK. A large amount of personal selling is used to attract major US and UK corporations to hold conferences in the Berkeley Court. The thrust of the advertising campaign is through specialised publications distributed through relevant tour operators, accompanied by a video of the facilities that are on offer.

Berkeley Court Corporate Mission

The Doyle Group mission statement is "Total Quality Management". The Berkeley Court Hotel does not have a specific mission statement, rather it views itself as being a hotel in the hotel business. Its aim is to keep its market leadership in terms of room nights, and in the quality of the service that it provides. It believes in setting the standard for others to follow.

Unique Problems Facing the Five-Star Market

According to Mr Tony Rooney, general manager of the Berkeley Court, the most important challenge facing the hotel is creating and maintaining an environment where "attention to detail" is at the forefront of every staff member's mind. He believes that getting to know the customers and their specific requirements is a crucial part of the role of each staff member who works at the interface. He stresses the importance of establishing a rapport with the customer and in particularly listening to what the customer has to say.

> This business is very much a communications business — finding out if what we provide is different from what the customer expects and finally implementing action based on the feedback we receive from customers.

The Berkeley Court records comments made by regular clients, such as whether they have a favourite room. Customers need to feel that they are receiving individual attention.

Linked to the "attention to detail" ethos is learning to be constantly critical. The secret to success, according to Mr Rooney, is "never taking anything for granted".

Future of the Five-Star Market

Tony Rooney is extremely optimistic about the future of the five-star market.

> There will always be a place in the market for this type of product. People are constantly looking for a quality product and Ireland, in particular Dublin, is fast becoming a very attractive, cosmopolitan destination for foreign visitors.

This is an important point considering that 70 per cent of current business at the Berkeley Court consists of foreign visitors.

He does not consider the five-star market to be oversupplied. The only possible environmental trend which could pose a threat to the five-star market would be a downturn in the world economy — a recessionary period in the future would have obvious implications for this market.

Source: Interviews with the General Manager.

Questions

1. How would you assess the competition that faces the Berkeley Court in the five-star market in Dublin?

2. How has the Berkeley Court geared up to meet the needs of its market segment?

3. What types of marketing and promotion strategies could the Berkeley Court use to remain competitive in the future?

12

Mosney Holiday Centre

Introduction

Mosney is a holiday centre situated in Co. Meath, 26 miles north of Dublin, on the main Dublin to Belfast road. It comprises accommodation facilities and numerous fun attractions. Mosney caters for day visitors and residential holiday-makers. The centre covers an area of 350 acres (250 of which are woodland) and has 450 accommodation units on site. It is opened mainly during the summer months — May to September. A public limited company, in 1993 it had a turnover of £3,795 million from a total of just over 200,000 visitors.

Mosney opened in 1948 as the first Butlins holiday camp not in Great Britain. It was built to cash in on the post-war "eating holidays" taken by the British public in Ireland, and was successful because of the rationing experienced in the UK. Crossing the Irish Sea was relatively cheap. Butlins was purchased by the Rank organisation in 1967, but because this centre was away from Britain there was a major disinterest in the camp and it went through a period of disinvestment.

In 1981, Phelim McCloskey bough the centre and changed its name to Mosney. Since this date, over £10 million has been invested in upgrading the facilities — for example, £3.5 million was spent on the Waterworld swimming pool and £1.5 million was spent on new accommodation. As a result of these developments Mosney has experienced consistent growth in sales since 1981.

Target Market

Mosney's market is the whole island of Ireland. This is primarily because Ireland has such a small population. The holiday camp traditionally attracts a C2, D and E category of residential visitor. Largely as a result of investment in new attractions and accommodation, Mosney now attracts more C1 visitors. This group is welcomed as it has more disposable income per capita In 1995, more emphasis was being placed on attracting visitors from Northern Ireland, because of the opportunities provided by the peace

Table 12.1: Visitors to Mosney Holiday Centre

	1992	1993	1994	93/92	94/93	% +/–
Antrim	4,923	6,404	5,295	1,481	-1,109	9.71
Armagh	833	954	709	121	-245	1.64
Carlow	372	326	274	-46	-52	.73
Cavan	178	176	198	-2	22	.35
Clare	497	504	252	4	-249	.98
Cork	4,820	4,919	4,161	99	-758	9.51
Derry	2,424	3,069	3,292	645	223	4.78
Donegal	1091	1,154	1,151	63	-3	2.15
Down	1535	1,906	1,828	371	-78	3.03
Dublin	20,602	16,402	16,409	-4,200	7	40.63
Fermanagh	194	254	251	60	-3	0.38
Galway	1180	1,198	808	18	-390	2.33
Kerry	390	344	359	-46	15	0.77
Kildare	712	770	712	58	-58	1.40
Kilkenny	438	493	368	55	-125	0.86
Laois	369	275	258	-94	-17	0.73
Leitrim	149	193	127	44	-66	0.29
Limerick	765	958	656	193	-302	1.51
Longford	126	183	124	57	-59	0.25
Louth	837	813	1,669	-24	856	1.65
Mayo	591	566	484	-25	-82	1.17
Meath	601	547	843	-54	296	1.19
Monaghan	290	361	354	71	-7	0.57
Offaly	339	292	303	-47	11	.67
Roscommon	175	140	149	-35	9	.35
Sligo	324	371	265	-7	-52	.64
Tipperary	946	758	790	-188	32	1.87
Tyrone	778	806	665	28	-141	1.53
Waterford	886	920	630	34	-290	1.75
Westmeath	464	403	350	-61	-53	.92
Wexford	611	575	690	-36	115	1.20
Wicklow	881	769	579	-112	-190	1.74
Others	1,389	2,328	539	939	-1,789	2.74
Total	50,710	50,074	45,524	-636	-4,532	

process. A second distinct market consists of day visitors. The target groups here are families, school tours, special groups and individuals.

The main areas from which customers come are Dublin, Antrim and Cork. Table 12.1 above represents a breakdown of the counties from which visitors come.

The reason why holiday-makers come to Mosney is primarily that the holiday is well packaged, and once they get there everything is laid on for them. Table 12.2 presents a breakdown of residential and day visitors.

Table 12.2: Residential and Day Visitors

Year	Res	% +/–	Day	% +/–	TOTAL	% +/–
1987	29,472		110,352		139,824	
1988	35,021	18.83	140,000	26.87	175,021	25.17
1989	40,000	14.22	151,000	7.86	191,000	9.13
1990	49,000	22.50	162,000	7.28	211,000	10.47
1991	54,000	10.20	168,000	3.70	222,000	5.21
1992	56,600	4.81	169,600	0.95	226,200	1.89
1993	55,607	-1.75	144,562	-14.76	200,169	-11.51
1994	53,808	-3.24	161,836	11.95	215,644	7.73
1995	56,500	5.00	175,000	8.13	231,500	7.35

Mosney segments its market in a number of ways:

- Lifestyle

- Geography

- Volume usage.

A number of strategies are in operation. One product is targeted to one specific segment — for example, the children's rides for the youngsters or the bars for the adults — and another product may be targeted to several segments — for example, the promotion of Funtropica Waterworld or a chance to visit the centre for a day or to stay there overnight for mini-breaks or full weeks. The main products on offer are accommodation, entertainment, bars, restaurants and funfairs.

Buyer Behaviour

Mosney's various types of customers go through the decision-making process differently. For example, a family deciding to go on a residential holiday may progress through all the stages of the buying process. Other customers, such as individuals on a school tour, may skip stages such as the information search, alternative evaluation etc., because the trip is organised for them. From market analysis of their residential booking forms, Mosney estimates that 70 per cent of residential visitors return again within three years.

Mosney's Product Mix

Figure 12.1 presents Mosney's product mix.

Figure 12.1: Mosney's Product Mix

←	Accommodation	Entertainment	Bars	Restaurants	Facilities
Product Line Length	* Caravans * Camping * Self-Catering Flatlets * Suites * Woodlands	* Bingo * Race Nights * Family Shows * Talent Contests * Discos * Cabaret	* Dan Lowrey's * The Theatre * The Harp Bar * The Wine Bar * Ballroom * The Showbar	* The Garden Pool Grill * The Kosy Kitchen * Chinese Takeaway * American Parlour Forest	* Funtropica * Star Trek * Go-Karts * Mini Golf * Bumperboats * Boating Lake

(Header spanning table: "Product Mix Width" ← → across top)

A problem that Mosney has encountered is that a number of products it offers have distinct types of product life cycles, and the rate the products flow through these life cycles varies dramatically. In the case of holiday camps, sales pass through a succession of life cycles, based on the introduction of new products, discovery of new segments/users etc. — for example, the development of the fun fair in the 1970s and Funtropica Waterworld. Mosney has continually had to develop new attractions for the centre to keep drawing customers, otherwise interest would drop and sales decline. Hence the introduction in 1995 of the Star Trek Experience.

Some products have simply gone through a normal life cycle — for example, the use of snooker tables. The 20 snooker tables are in the decline stage of their life cycle. Management has decided to halve the number of tables and use the space saved to add a sauna and gym. Other products have been fads, such as the karaoke competitions, which are no longer popular. Mosney realises that it must continually develop new products, as people will not return for the same products. Market research is used to identify problem areas or weak products that should be dropped.

Pricing of Products

Mosney operates the following pricing system:

- *Day Visitors* are charged £4.90 each for a day visit to the centre.

- *Residential Visitors*: A varying price structure is in operation for residential visitors. Prices start from as little as £50/60 for campers, and rise to £658 for a week's stay in the woodlands accommodation at peak times.

The objectives behind Mosney's prices vary considerably. These include the following:

- The objective behind the day-visitor price of £4.90 is to maximise sales growth — Mosney wants to maximise the number of day visitors to reach levels of capacity. It is believed that this price will facilitate higher sales volume, which will lead to lower costs per visitor and higher long-run products.

- In the case of the high pricing of Woodlands accommodation, Mosney estimates that the customer who wants that type of accommodation will be prepared to pay that price for it. Thus, Mosney hopes to skim the maximum amount of revenue from the wealthier market segment.

Mr Charles O'Brien, the managing director, believes that the pricing of food and drink in the camp are price inelastic in that these meals/ drinks, although priced higher than they would be in a normal environment, do not lead to a decline in sales volume, because customers are willing to splash out to have a good holiday.

The week-to-week price changes are decided by the market. A higher price reflects greater demand for that accommodation than the same week in the previous year. The following are examples of pricing methods. They take account of prices charged by Mosney's competitors.

- Those organising a group tour of 30 people or more are only charged £3.75 each at the gate (as opposed to £4.49).

- Those booking their holiday out of season get a discount. In 1995, those booking before 31 March could get 10 per cent off their holiday.

- Mosney used one tactic last year in response to low visitor numbers because of the World Cup. It offered two people entry to the centre for the price of one. The success of this strategy is evident from the fact that, of 150,000 vouchers issued nation-wide, 22,000 were used.

- If it has spare capacity, for example, for the following week, Mosney drops the price of its accommodation by 50–100 per cent. It will advertise these vacancies on local radio. No money is made on the accommodation (in fact it costs Mosney money to provide accommodation services). However, the logic of selling at this rate is that a good deal of money will be made on the sale of food, drink, souvenirs, etc.

- Mosney prices different categories of its accommodation at different levels. For the day and residential prices charged, visitors have access to all of the facilities, plus access to all the bars, restaurants shops, etc. There are, however, additional charges for some of the facilities, such as video games.

- Senior citizens can get 10 per cent off all holidays at any time in the season. Families get special rates, as do school tours.

- If potential customers are fortunate to live within a distance of the Dublin–Belfast railway line, they can get a day pass to Mosney, and their rail travel is only £7.50.

Promotion

Mosney has used a range of promotion techniques at one time or another. Publicity is designed to promote Mosney's image. The company has used photo shoots with celebrities such as Sue Pollard from *Hi de Hi*, who opened Funtropica Waterworld. Every year Mosney receives free publicity from RTE when it televises the annual community games. In the 1995 season, Mosney launched its Star Trek Experience on the *Late Late Show* on 26 May, and as part of its deal with Paramount Studios, Patrick Stewart, who plays Captain Jean Luc Picard in the series, opened it on 27 May.

Recently, all the papers of the Independent newspaper group carried a free Star Trek/Mosney poster. This deal was negotiated by Charles O'Brien. The newspaper group is willing to distribute the free poster because it realises that having these posters in the papers will increase sales — people will buy the papers to get the souvenir posters. On the 1995 June bank holiday weekend Mosney had a photo-shoot with John Bruton in Mosney. Another form of publicity used by Mosney is the yearly release of its annual report.

Every year Mosney holds a draw for a chance to win a free holiday. The real purpose behind this is to get names and addresses of those who entered the draw, who obviously had some interest in the product. This will be followed up on, and brochures sent to all entrants at a later date. Mosney takes part in holiday fairs in Ireland — in the RDS, for example. It gives gifts to visitors — in 1995, a star fleet wallet was issued in which younger clients could display their pass. Coca-Cola printed 150,000 Mosney/Star Trek labels for their 2-litre Coke bottles with special coupons on them. Each year, Mosney holds an art competition for younger children, the prize for which is a family day pass to the holiday centre.

Mosney engages in personal selling at holiday fairs in Ireland each year. On the second week each January, two sales teams go nationwide to supermarkets, shopping centres, etc. to talk to potential clients and give out draw tickets. Mosney advertises in *The Irish Independent, The Herald, The Star* and *The Sunday Independent*. It runs advertising campaigns on local radio and on 2FM.

Advantage is also taken of the relative cheapness of television advertising in Ireland. Charles O'Brien states that a similar type of operation in the UK would not be able to afford television advertising. Mosney ran a £120,000 television campaign on RTE in summer 1995, which started on 15 May.

In 1995, 175,000 residential and 350,000 day-visitor brochures were printed, thereby making the product more tangible for new purchasers — allowing them to see what they were buying.

Billboards are used on the approach roads to Mosney, and in 1995, thousands of posters were distributed, which doubled as brochures to credit unions through the country.

Elements of Mosney's Success

Staff

Staff constitute a very important element of Mosney's success. Employees are trained to be courteous, polite and co-operative. They, as well as the facilities, help to make the holiday. Off season, 200 are employed at the holiday centre, with up to 300 at peak times. There is a deliberate policy to recruit from all parts of the country, because customers come from all over, and they feel more comfortable if they hear a familiar accent among the staff. Also, there is a resistance by some rural people to what they see as an extension of Dublin. This happened in Butlins in the early 1970s, when most employees would have been local. Figure 12.2 presents the structure.

Figure 12.2: Organisational Structure of Mosney

Physical Layout

The layout of Mosney does not follow the standard design of Butlins camps in Britain. It differs in that vast areas of greenery were left, which appeals to urban consumers. The colour scheme tries to incorporate red and yellow as much as possible. This is a deliberate strategy, says Charles O'Brien, as red and yellow are perceived as vibrant, happy colours. Staff uniforms are red and white. The grounds are maintained by 27 maintenance staff, and £25 million has been invested in this area since 1981.

Customer Satisfaction

If a visitor has a problem — with the accommodation, for example — Mosney has procedures to follow. There is a customer-care team of 10 employees around the site who have a hierarchy of recompenses to offer depending on their assessment of the situation. These range from a free meal to a free pass for another day. The policy is not to let customers go away unhappy.

Mosney also has a policy of catering for people with disabilities. Two permanent staff can use sign language, and there is improved access to all buildings for those with disability. There are several first-aid offices within the camp.

Group Marketing

Mosney works in conjunction with Irish Rail and Northern Rail, with whom it meets every November to set a rate for the following season. Block selling is done in advance, which means that it is then up to each rail company to promote the tickets. This works successfully as Mosney is the only facility of its kind in the country to have its own private stop on a railway line.

Marketing is also done through Bord Fáilte, which carries Mosney's literature at some exhibitions and Mosney is listed in some of Bord Fáilte's brochures. In 1995, Mosney gained access to the Irish credit union network — posters which doubled as price brochures were distributed in each branch.

Competition

Mosney identifies its main competitors as Trabolgan, Aquadome in Tralee and Dublin Zoo (day visitors). In 1993, Dublin Zoo launched Dino Live, and as Mosney had no such attraction to compete with this, it had a dramatic impact on Mosney's sales. In 1995, Mosney hoped to reverse the tables and scoop all the sales with the launch of its Star Trek experience. It was felt that there would be no new entrants into this type of activity for some time as the barriers to entry are high, and a large capital investment and favourable location are needed.

The Future

For Mosney, 1995 was the second year of a five-year plan. The 1995 season's highlight was the Star Trek experience, which will be followed by some spectacular event in 1996. Mosney will therefore be concentrating in the future on providing attractions that will give the holiday centre national publicity and credibility.

Mosney has come a long way since its Butlins days. It now provides a sophisticated range of products for an increasingly demanding market. It has improved its image in the past through continued efforts and investments in its facilities. It has also met significant challenges and looks likely to become a significant force in the Irish holiday market in the future.

Source: Interviews with company personnel.

Questions

1. Evaluate the growth and development of Mosney Holiday Centre since its inception.

2. Assess the marketing strategies adopted by Mosney Holiday Centre and comment on their effectiveness.

3. What are the main sources of competition for Mosney Holiday Centre and how can they be counteracted?

13

CIE Tours International

A Brief History

Tourism, as distinct from travel, began with the introduction of the railway over 160 years ago. For the first time, a large number of people could travel in comfort from place to place. In general, the first tourists travelled from major cities to the countryside or seaside resorts.

At the end of the 1920s, transport in Ireland was provided by a wide range of railway companies. One of these, Great Southern Railways, which also owned a series of hotels in prime resorts, decided to commence the operation of coach tours. These early tours were designed mainly for Irish people and, as far as possible, used the facilities available to them in its hotels. However, as time moved on, overseas tourists began to avail of these services. Great Southern Railways made a significant decision in 1935 when it decided to appoint a full time representative in New York, whose function was to sell the services of Great Southern Railways to Irish Americans planning to visit Ireland.

At the end of the Second World War, it became obvious, as competitors fought for passengers, that there was not enough business for everyone. Therefore the government of the day decided to rationalise transport on a national basis. It purchased most of the railway and bus companies and started what is now known as Córas Iompair Éireann (CIE). Included in this organisation was a department within Great Southern Railways, which had operated coach tours since 1929 and now became known as CIE Tours.

In the period 1920–50 tourism from overseas was virtually non-existent. The early visitors, and they were small in number, came mainly from the US. The small numbers, and the relative affluence of those who did come, required a very high standard of personalised service. CIE Tours met this demand with a number of deluxe and expensive tours, and thus their reputation as a deluxe operator was established.

The addition of the word "International" to the name CIE Tours signified a major development in the growth of the company. Tourism from overseas markets began to increase in the early and mid-1950s. It was then that two major decisions were made. The first of these was the appointment of a representative in London, and the second was an agreement made with Thomas Cooke and Son Ltd. in New York to provide a marketing service for the company in the US.

As a result of these decisions, there was again an increase in the volume of passenger flow, and in due course the arrangement in the US was superseded by the formation of a new company called British and Irish Railways Incorporated. With offices in New York, Los Angeles and Toronto, the company was created to provide a marketing and reservations service for both British Rail and CIE Tours. This, in turn, led to a further expansion in traffic until finally, in 1967, CIE tours decided to establish its own marketing organisation within the US, known as CIE Tours International. This marked the beginning of the modern history of the company.

Further significant diversification took place with the opening of offices in Germany in 1981 and France in 1983 to generate tourist business for Ireland. CIE Tours International now has offices in four countries — Ireland (head office), USA, Germany and France, with a staff of nearly 100 employees.

Mission of CIE Tours International

CIE Tours International's mission is to provide inward tourism services, marketing Irish holiday products throughout Europe, North America, Australia and New Zealand, and is Ireland's only significant tour operator.

The company provides coach tours and other holiday products, including special interest holidays, self-catering holidays, car hire and accommodation services to 60,000 tourists annually. Sales offices are operated in all main markets and active marketing programmes are undertaken.

CIE Tours Conference Service Division provides a fully integrated management service for conference organisers, including planning, budgeting, accommodation control, registration and conference operation.

The Organisation Structure

During the mid-1980s, CIE was reorganised and now consists of a holding company and three separate and independent subsidiary companies. These are:

- Iarnród Éireann (Irish Rail)

- Bus Éireann (Irish Bus)

- Bus Átha Cliath (Dublin Bus).

Each of these companies has a separate board of directors and operates independently of, and in some ways in competition with, the others. The holding company controls the subsidiary companies and provides many services — such as human resource, computing, legal, and secretarial — to the subsidiaries. In addition, the holding company controls related activities which do not easily fit within the areas of responsibility of the subsidiary companies. These include:

- CAN — the sale of advertising on CIE property throughout Ireland

- Rosslare Harbour — operation of this major port in the southeast of Ireland, which is owned by CIE

- CIE Consult — a company which manages consultative and aid programmes throughout the world

- CIE Tours International — Ireland's national tour operator, and the subject of this case study.

CIE Tours International is responsible directly to the holding company. It has four offices — New York, Paris, London and its main office, located at Abbey Street, Dublin. Figure 13.1 presents the structure.

Figure 13.1: Structure of CIE Tours International

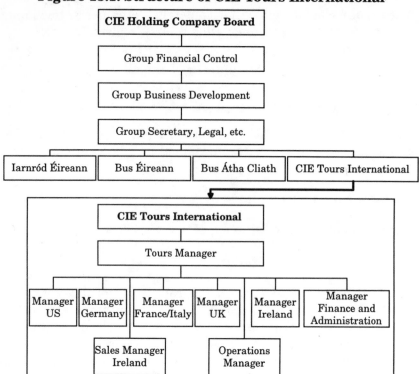

Marketing CIE Tours International

Market segmentation is crucial to CIE Tours International as there are very few companies willing to woo the entire population. The likelihood is that not all people will be interested in, or want to purchase, its products. The total market for tourism-related products therefore tends to be segmented into sub-groups which become far more achievable targets. Companies like CIE Tours International have to decide what segment of the market they are aiming for.

In terms of tourism, CIE Tours International tends to segment according to age, gender, and socioeconomic grouping. Once a segment can be identified and data exist about a group of customers, it is possible to target accordingly. Many tourism businesses segment their market successfully into a variety of potential customer segments. Different marketing mixes appeal to each segment accordingly.

Traditionally, CIE Tours has gone for the middle-aged to elderly groups. This focus was because younger people tended to go for sun holidays or activity-based holidays. Older age groups also tend to have more disposable income, and are more inclined to take coach tours than younger people. However, CIE Tours has decided to aim for a wider market and have therefore introduced products and services aimed at younger people, such as car hire and accommodation packages. Up to now, the company's main type of segmentation has been demographic. In recent years, it has experienced a large increase in younger people availing of its services. However, over 75 per cent of its passengers are still aged 45 or over.

In 1994, the company decided that for different products they would target different age groups — for example, car and accommodation packs for 21–35 age group; coach tours for middle-aged people and older (no infants are allowed on coach tours).

Table 13.1 presents a breakdown of competitors' prices for two tours.

Table 13.1: Gardens of Ireland v. Northern Heritage Tour

Gardens of Ireland Tour		Northern Heritage Tour	
CIE Tours	£419	CIE Tours	£300
Abbey Tours	£404	Abbey Tours	£299
Brendan Tours	£390	Brendan Tours	£315
Pabb Tours	£399	Pabb Tours	£299

These figures illustrate that CIE is the most expensive on the market, but CIE argues that it gives the best customer service.

CIE Tours International Products

CIE Tours International is generally viewed to be the front runner in the "tours industry". The management is always looking to see if it can improve the quality and range of products. At present the company has an impressive list of services and products.

Coach Tours

The company's main area of operation is coach tours. This was the first service that the company provided, and to this day it is the most profitable activity. At present, CIE Tours operates coach tours to Ireland, Europe and the US. These tours are between one and two weeks in duration. The price of the tour includes sightseeing throughout the country by luxury coach tour, hotel accommodation, and a professional guide. In Ireland, CIE Tours has a substantial coach and tour market, and it has expanded this by adding tours and centre holidays in Britain and Europe. The company has also taken advantage of its dominance in the Irish market by using it to fill any shortfall on tours sold in overseas markets.

Charter Flights

In the 1970s, air fares were substantially higher than they are today and the company decided to tackle this problem by operating charters from various American cities to Ireland. This was a brilliant innovation on the part of CIE Tours. To this day, charter flights are run to Germany and the US. The prices offered are very competitive, yet make CIE Tours a handsome profit.

Conference and Incentive Groups

CIE Tours management realised that during the off-season its products would not sell so well, and thus profits would decline. A product/service was needed that would sell profitably during the off-season. The company decided to market Ireland as a destination for conferences and for incentive groups. The attraction of this type of traffic is that, in general, it tends to travel in low-season, and, in addition, it offers a high return to the business. A significant number of conference and incentive groups visit Ireland each year.

Weekend Breaks

These breaks are shorter versions of the coach tours and typically last three or four nights. The price charged includes sightseeing by coach, hotel accommodation, breakfast and all government taxes. In 1995, CIE Tours offered weekend breaks to Cork, Donegal and Clare.

Special Tours

One other area in which CIE Tours provides a service is in special interest tours. CIE Tours offers a range of products to groups in

Britain and Ireland. Such groups include clubs and societies, educational organisations, and common-interest groups. The company provides all of the services that these groups may need, including air travel, hotel accommodation, meals and visits. As a result, CIE Tours has developed a substantial amount of traffic, which is particularly useful in selling excess coach capacity.

Car and Accommodation Packages

CIE Tours offers a range of packages involving car and accommodation. When tourists arrive at the airport of their destination, a car and hotel/bed and breakfast await them. With accommodation vouchers issued by the company, they can travel anywhere and stay at a range of hotels throughout the country. This type of holiday is very profitable and particularly popular with continental Europeans.

Figure 13.2 presents a breakdown of tourists travelling with CIE Tours during the period 1991–93.

Figure 13.2: Tourists Travelling with CIE Tours, 1991–93

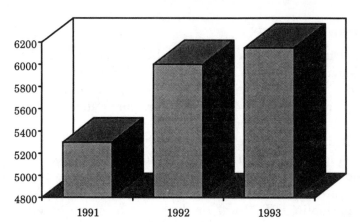

Figure 2 shows that the number of tourists travelling with CIE Tours International is steadily increasing. The figures for 1994 are not officially available, but the general trend in 1994 was one of increased growth. Management predicts that by the year 2000 CIE Tours International will have 100,000 tourists availing of its services.

CIE Tours International Strategies

North America

CIE Tours is positioned as a wholesaler in the US market. Its tours and independent packages are sold through travel agents. Group tours are sold through group organisers who may also be travel agents. The company receives business from about 16 per cent of travel agents in the US each year. About 20 per cent of the passengers on scheduled tours and independent packages are repeat customers. In the group tour market there is also a high degree of repeat business. CIE Tours' US strategy employs the following elements:

- Efficient brochure distribution

- Personal sales calls to nearly 3,000 travel agents

- Presentations at sales seminars

- Advertising to the retail travel trade

- Press and public relations activities

- A limited amount of advertising to the consumer.

Great Britain

The coach tours sold in Great Britain are also sold in other markets, such as Ireland, Australia and North America. In Britain, 13 per cent of sales originate through wholesalers, 47 per cent through retailers, and 40 per cent are made directly by passengers in the London office.

In Britain, there are approximately 6,000 retail travel agents — of which one-third are branch offices of multiples. The multiples demand an over-riding commission, and will sell the products of appointed operators only. According to Paul O'Neill, sales manager in Dublin, CIE Tours' products are favoured by all of these multiples. The concentration of CIE Tours' brochure distribution and personal sales is therefore to the multiples, together with a selected number of independent agents. Advertising is planned in conjunction with Bord Fáilte. CIE also participates at a number of holiday shows nationwide.

Continental Europe

CIE's main European offices are located in Düsseldorf and Paris. The prime responsibilities are for Germany and France, but the

French office also has responsibility for Spain and Portugal, whilst the office in Germany has responsibility for Austria, Holland and Switzerland. In these countries CIE Tours has marketing agreements with major wholesalers.

Ireland's Sales Strategy

In Ireland, coach tours are sold by brochure distribution, solicitation of past customers, advertising and, to a small extent, the use of travel agents. Group travel bookings are received from local Irish group organisers.

Table 13.2 presents a summary of key products provided by CIE Tours.

Table 13.2: Key CIE Tours Products

MARKET	Coach Package	Independent Travel & Car Package	Groups & Incentive Travel	Conference
US to Ireland	X	X	X	X
US to UK	X	X		X
US to Europe			X	
UK to Ireland	X	X	X	X
Germany to Ireland	X	X	X	X
France to Ireland	X	X	X	X
Ireland to UK	X	X	X	
Ireland to Europe	X	X		X

X = Presence in Market.

Irish Tourism and CIE Tours International's Markets

Ireland's major source of markets for tourists are the UK, the US, Germany and France. This represents four of the five countries with the highest spending on export tourism. They are also the major source markets for CIE Tours International, which maintains representation in each of them. Table 3 below shows the importance of each of these markets both for Irish tourism and for CIE Tours International.

Home holidays by Irish residents accounted for a further 4.3 million tourists. The Irish market contributed a further 14,500 passengers to CIE Tours.

Table 13.3: Principal Sources of Overseas Tourism for Ireland and for CIE Tours International in Volume (number of visitors) and Value for 1992

Source Market	Volume %		Value %	
	Ireland	**CIE**	**Ireland**	**CIE**
US	22	62	41	70
UK	58	16	37	9
Continental Europe	17	18	17	17
Others	3	4	4	9
Total (100 per cent)	1.9m	0.4m	£462	£12.9m

CIE Tours International Revenue Situation

Figure 13.2 presents a summary of revenue for the period 1991–93.

Figure 13.2: Revenue, 1991–93

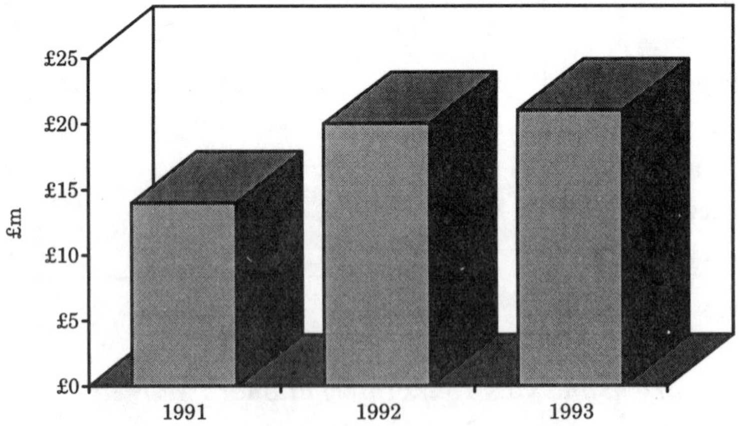

In 1991, CIE Tours International's revenue was £14 million, which was actually up on the previous year. However, the company just about broke even with a profit of £14,000. It was decided that expansion and innovation were required. This was accomplished in the European market, and in the following year revenue increased to £20.4 million — a very significant increase of 50 per cent. Things were starting really to look up for the company, and this trend was reinforced in 1993 when the company reported a record revenue of £20.7 million. The recent growth in the revenue of CIE Tours is primarily a result of the targeting of a younger clientèle, which has opened up the market and increased sales of coach tours, car hire and accommodation packages.

Figure 13.3 presents a summary of profit for the period 1991–93.

Figure 13.3: CIE Tours International Profit, 1991–93

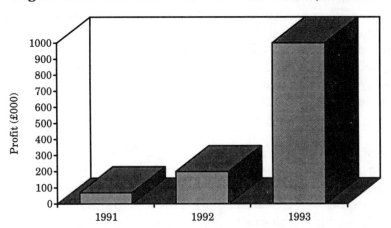

In 1990, CIE Tours International was in real financial trouble, making major losses. In early 1991, the board decided to restructure the company, and new management was brought in. In 1991, CIE Tours International made a profit for the first time. Even though a profit of only £18,000 was recorded, it meant that the company was on a sounder footing. With this foundation, expansion into Europe was accelerated, which resulted in profits of £197,000 in 1992. With this boost to the company's finances, management knew that CIE Tours could become a very profitable organisation if appropriate strategies were adopted.

The company generated gross revenue of £20.7 million in 1993 and achieved a profit of £1 million, compared to £4 million in 1992. Payments to hotels, coach companies and airlines amounted to £17.1 million. The results, which included significant gains in currency management, were ahead of internal budget forecasts.

CIE Tours spent £2.8 million on overseas marketing in 1993, including the distribution of 1.5 million brochures printed in six languages. The cost of promotion was decreased in 1994 because of a joint marketing programme with Waterford Crystal, which included television advertising in the US.

The Future

The company strategy for the future is to build its business through innovation and in a way that allows it to adapt to the changing commercial environment. Innovation lays the seeds for the future growth, but this must be accompanied by a willingness on the part of the organisation to accept change as an inevitable part of business life.

The CIE group has benefited in recent years from an effective government approach towards the development of transport and tourism. At present, CIE Tours International is in a position to expand, and management should take full advantage of its position by increasing market share in the future.

Progressive national policies are now being actively supported through EU-funding programmes for the development of CIE Tours assets and operations. Over the past three years, CIE Tours International has changed from being a loss-making company to being a profit-making one. CIE Tours' management aims in the immediate future to consolidate the company's position as the front-runners of the Irish tours industry and as travel professionals, and then to focus on strengthening its position abroad.

Source: Interviews with company personnel.

Questions

1. Evaluate the contribution that market segmentation has made to the success of CIE Tours International.

2. Using an appropriate model, evaluate the product/service range of CIE Tours International.

3. What risks/threats does CIE Tours International face in the foreign marketplace?

4. What additional future options are available to CIE Tours International given its present level of profitability?

Part 3
The Semi-State Sector

14

Aer Lingus

Introduction

Aer Lingus and its sister company, Aerlínte, operate the national airline, and as both are government owned, they effectively belong to the Irish people. Aer Lingus has not only provided and developed an air transport system in Ireland, but the company is also committed to such policies as helping tourism and economic growth.

Evolution of the Group

Aer Lingus began operations in 1936 with one five-seater aircraft on a route from Dublin to Bristol. Within a matter of months the service was extended to London, and seasonal services to Liverpool and the Isle of Man were developed within three years. After the Second World War, an agreement was drawn up between the governments of Britain and Ireland giving the company responsibility for developing an airline service between the two countries. On renegotiation of the contract in 1956, British European Airways (BEA) had entered into these routes. During the 1950s, the company's service was greatly expanded and developed, adding many Continental routes. In 1958, the now controversial routes of Dublin through Shannon to New York and Boston were added using leased aircraft, and within two years the company had its own planes on these routes. The 1960s were a period of great growth for the company, with more people and businesses travelling by air. By 1966, new transatlantic routes had been introduced to include Montreal and Chicago, with the company investing in two new

Boeing 747 "Jumbo" planes, specifically for its North Atlantic routes. In line with this, there was a changeover from the airline's short-haul fleet to jet aircraft to meet the new demands, with the result that a much extended service was being provided by 1970.

However, Aer Lingus faired poorly after 1970 owing to a decline in traffic on the North Atlantic routes, and new competitors entering the market offering a cheaper and better service. The airline really suffered as a result of the oil crises of 1973 and 1979, which resulted in the price of fuel going through the roof. Aer Lingus, like most airlines, is unable to control some 70 per cent of its costs, costs which include interest rates and the cost of fuel. Moreover, Aer Lingus was not helped by the fact that there was little growth occurring in its major markets during the 1970s. In the face of a serious crisis, the company underwent a change in management strategy, including the implementation of a diversification programme. In 1970, it diversified into the hotel business with the acquisition in the UK of the London Tara Hotel. In 1976, it moved into the US market with the acquisition of the Dunfey Corporation, a US hotel chain.

Smaller developments at this time included the acquisition of a leisure centre in Surrey in 1973, followed in 1974 by a holiday property development in Tenerife. In 1973, the company in a joint venture with Guinness Peat Aviation became involved in aircraft brokerage. Other diversifications since the 1970s have seen the airline getting involved in the provision of services for other airlines, such as aircraft maintenance and passenger handling. The airline also contracts out services, with various departments selling their services externally. In line with this, some of the subsidiaries created by the company include Cara Data Processing, PARC, Devtec and Airmotive.

Business Activities of Aer Lingus

The activities of Aer Lingus can be divided into four main business groupings:

- Air Transportation
- Airline-related services or ancillary activities
- Hotels, food and leisure
- Financial and commercial services.

The latter two are non-ancillary activities in that they are external to the company and non-airline-related.

Air Transportation

This constitutes the core business of the airline, and is divided into Atlantic operations and Intra-European operations. This sector of business is marked by low profit margins. Other market characteristics include diseconomies of scale and extreme seasonality. Moreover, the segment of the market targeted by Aer Lingus is more leisure oriented than those in which major international carriers succeed. As a result, the potential for growth is constrained, putting excessive pressure on Aer Lingus to be responsive to market needs. The factors contributing to the low air transport profit margins up to 1987 included adverse currency fluctuations with a strengthening US dollar, a slackness in demand for air transport, and intensified competition. Aer Lingus had to respond to these pressures by initiating a range of strategies which included a more aggressive approach to marketing in terms of pricing, presentation, promotion, and quality of product. The company also developed a more systematic approach to its cost-reduction programme. Furthermore, it made an inventive exploration of new sources of ancillary profit activities, and re-appraised its route structure in respect of return on capital.

Because of the revitalised approach adopted by the airline, an operating profit of £6.5 million was achieved in 1987 — the first operating profit since 1972. This profit was derived from an increase in traffic resulting from stronger promotion, better service and a stronger emphasis on the customer. Steps to improve the quality of service offered by Aer Lingus had been undertaken at various stages in the company's history, but it was not until 1984 that the company drew up a specific strategy aimed at improving quality. A programme called "Quality Quest" was a more complete approach in that it considered not only the product package, but all aspects of the organisation's culture. The results were encouraging, with passenger compliments beginning to outnumber complaints. This programme was viewed by Aer Lingus as a continuous improvement process, and was relaunched in 1990 as a programme called "Quality Focus", with the objective of making quality a way of life for Aer Lingus.

Primarily because of this quality strategy, 1988 was another good year for the company. The airline was now focusing on three related factors — lower unit costs, lower unit revenue and increased traffic flow, with the latter reaching its highest level in over 20 years. There was a drop in profits in 1989 because of a significant decrease in fares, with fewer North American visitors to Europe because of the Chernobyl disaster and terrorist incidents in Europe. Another loss in 1990/91 resulted mainly from declining numbers on Atlantic and European routes. The war in the Gulf also had an adverse effect on traffic movement. In 1991/1992, air transportation experienced losses similar to those in 1990/91. The economic recession triggered by the invasion of Kuwait in August 1990 continued to create adverse conditions for the travel market. While the airline achieved substantial cost savings in pay-roll and other operational costs, increases in fuel and navigational charges offset these savings. There was also an adverse effect from the strengthening of the US dollar. The year 1992/93 was another loss-making one for air transportation. A reduced level of Aer Lingus operations produced savings in flying costs despite increased depreciation charges, principally related to the airline's newer fleet. In 1993/94, the group implemented a group-wide restructuring programme, resulting in the recording of a sizeable profit before tax and exceptional items for the 21 months to end of December 1994.

One of the major problem areas for Aer Lingus over the years had been the transatlantic route. Because large airlines use long-haul routes to offset the economic disadvantage of short-haul operations, Aer Lingus had been constrained it its ability to generate sustainable market penetration on the route, principally because it entered this market relatively late — its first commercial flight to North America was not until 1958, 10 years after the originally planned flight. The delay meant that some competitive advantage had been lost, as overall traffic on the route had grown an incredible 600 per cent during the 10-year period. Thus, it is not surprising that by 1982 a deficit in the region of £13 million was being recorded by the group. Government support was forthcoming, however, offsetting the non-commercial costs incurred on the route, but variations in the frequency of payments did not help the airline's situation.

Airline-Related Services or Ancillary Activities

A recession hit the airline industry in the 1970s, and it was not helped by spiralling oil costs in 1973 and 1979. To support its core air transportation activities, and to supplement its loss-making North Atlantic routes, Aer Lingus decided to diversify into other money-making activities. The thrust of this diversification programme was twofold:

- To develop businesses directly related or complementary to the air transport industry

- To establish departments within the airline as profit centres selling services to third parties in the industry.

During the 1960s, a strategy of backward integration into areas such as aircraft maintenance, ground handling, air-crew training, airline computer systems, and catering provided the opportunity for diversification into related service activities. The strategy was reinforced through a series of acquisitions which extended the range of markets served and services offered by Aer Lingus. In line with this diversification strategy, a subsidiary called Airmotive, an engine overhaul facility, was established in 1981. The whole area of aircraft maintenance, jet engine overhaul, repairs and sales culminated in 1991 with the establishment of TEAM Aer Lingus, a wholly owned subsidiary of the company, focusing specifically on this high-technology market. TEAM combines the specialist expertise of the various Aer Lingus companies to provide an all-inclusive package.

Hotel, Food and Leisure — Non-Airline-Related Activities

Aer Lingus has had a long involvement in the hotel industry in Ireland. This move was a forward integration on a minor level to cater for more of its passengers' needs. The later expansion into hotel interests abroad put an emphasis on the purchase of four-star hotels in key European locations, which offered high accommodation and modern conference and leisure facilities, as for example, the purchase of the Copthorne hotel chain of 11 hotels from the British Caledonian Group.

Financial and Commercial Services

The main ventures here include:

- GPA, where effective use is made of the core skills of the company, i.e. their aircraft leasing expertise

- CARA, where time on the company's mainframe computer is sold

- PARC, where general business recruitment as well as aviation-crew placement take place.

The acquisitions in this group are all progressive businesses contributing significantly to the overall profits of the Aer Lingus group. In fact, such profits have been a feature for many years, providing the financial mainstay of the group as a whole.

TEAM (The Experts in Aircraft Maintenance)

Maintenance and overhaul of other airline aircraft, engines and components had in the past been carried out at the Aer Lingus maintenance facilities at Dublin Airport and by its subsidiaries, Airmotive Ireland, SRS Aviation at Shannon, and Aviation Traders at Stansted airport in England (the latter was eventually sold because of unsatisfactory profit and performance). This area of work has been consistently profitable for Aer Lingus, yet it has been dogged by a series of industrial disputes, with the airline having to fight off competition while at the same time dealing with internal wrangles. Nevertheless, while the industrial relations problems mounted, the airline's management did manage to win many contracts with some of the major leading airlines, such as Pan Am and Nigeria Airways. These contracts added considerably to the scale of airline business, as did manufacturer and regulatory approvals received in 1987, including those of the UK Civil Authority and Shorts for the maintenance of Shorts aircraft. It was because of these developments that Aer Lingus decided in 1988 to combine the maintenance and engineering facilities at Dublin Airport with those of its subsidiaries, Airmotive Ireland and SRS Shannon, to offer a comprehensive service of overhaul and repair for aircraft, engineering and components. Traditionally, 35 per cent of maintenance work done by the airline was for other airlines. But as a result of recent changes in strategy, with the introduction of a policy to replace the shortfall fleet, capacity for customer work was expected to increase to 60 per cent.

With "Targeting for Excellence in Aircraft Maintenance" as its motto, TEAM was initiated to provide a high-quality, quick turn-over and cost-effective maintenance for customers, involving the further development of engineering facilities at Dublin Airport. During 1990, several customers were found, including Saudi Airways, Virgin Atlantic and Qantas. With no profit expected in the core flying business, the TEAM venture was scheduled for operation by early 1991. The TEAM facility at Dublin Airport was planned to have six hangars and 40 workshops, and was expected to generate turnover of approximately £25 million per annum. The main hangar, when constructed, was to accommodate six passenger aircraft at any one time, including two Boeing 747-400s, the largest commercial aircraft available.

In order to attract business, TEAM Aer Lingus researched the long-term opportunities in the market, segmented its products to suit customer needs and developed modern systems for market analysis, planning and control. Along with aircraft overhaul, TEAM also handles mechanical and avionics components overhaul. TEAM's product is of the highest standard, on a par with high-quality airlines such as Lufthansa, Swissair and KLM (Dutch). Pricing structures are constantly reviewed in line with competition in the marketplace. TEAM promotes its services through a selective and structured advertising campaign, and through a marketing system that gives TEAM staff up-to-the-minute data on international airlines, their fleet, overhaul requirements and capabilities.

Aer Lingus in the 1990s

In the early 1990s, Aer Lingus was a company facing severe difficulties. Effectively it had become a loss-making enterprise, kept afloat by exchequer money. The airline's losses on its transatlantic route, for instance, almost doubled to an estimated £228 million in the year to the end of March 1992. The following highlight the extent of the problems facing the airline mid-way through 1993:

- Group profits of £28 million in 1989/1990 had been transformed into a loss of £116 million by 1993.
- Shareholder funds had fallen over the same period, down from £443 to £104 million.
- The group was losing over £1 million a week.
- Group debt stood in excess of £500 million.
- Committed cash facilities were exhausted by the end of August 1993.

- Uncommitted facilities had been reduced from £173 to £78 million.

- The air transport division had recorded losses of £22.9 million in 1993. In the previous year, the corresponding figure was £16.2 million.

In early 1992, the airline informed the government that it would lose a further £11 million on the transatlantic route in the following financial year, unless the 48-year mandatory Shannon stopover was amended. Aer Lingus believed that pressure from the US authorities for direct access to Dublin and other Irish airports in line with its "open skies policy" couldn't be resisted indefinitely. The company felt that its loss of market share in the US was attributable to access difficulties, and that the trend had to be reversed. It stated that its ranking on North American travel agents' computer screens would improve if fares were lower and if travel time to Dublin were reduced. It was also pointed out that the European Commission was not sympathetic to the Shannon stopover.

Up to 1992, it had been generally assumed that the airline's poor performance was the result of cyclical factors. However, it had been shown that the poor performance resulted from structural changes in the industry, and that unless these issues were addressed, the airline would be forced out of business. The profit performance of other divisions of the group had also deteriorated and could no longer support losses in the core airline business.

The Rescue Plan

The first step taken in the process of turning the airline around had resulted in a rescue package being drawn up by the Aer Lingus board under the chairmanship of Bernie Cahill. Throughout his career, Cahill has shown that he is not a soft touch. He has managed to hold onto his position as chairman of Greencore and subsequently Aer Lingus while the chief executives of both, Chris Comerford and Cathal Mullen, were forced to depart. In August 1991, the then Taoiseach, Charles Haughey, appointed Cahill to the Aer Lingus chairmanship. By March 1993, Cahill's position had been upgraded to executive chairman, on foot of a government decision that he should take over the day-to-day running of the group. This appointment rendered insignificant the position held by Cathal Mullan, then group chief executive. Mullan accordingly resigned his position. Assuming the executive chairmanship of the group, Cahill was given absolute responsibility to take whatever action was necessary to restore the company to commercial viability. His role was to continue until such time as the right structures were in place to allow his rescue strategies to be fully implemented.

Cahill's appointment to Aer Lingus in 1991 came one month before the Greencore controversy erupted. When Chris Comerford resigned from that company amid claims that he privately profited from a pre-flotation sugar-company deal, Cahill, like Comerford, came under intense pressure to resign his position as chairman of Greencore. However, he did not succumb in the end. Cahill's position in that company has since been considerably strengthened. Once things had settled down at Greencore, Cahill was able to give his full attention to the grave financial difficulties that the airline was facing. He assembled a team of experts to undertake an extensive study of Aer Lingus's operations, following this review with the formulation of a number of key strategies. Essentially, the core airline business was to remain the focus of concentration, with the group to be restructured into a number of strategic business units. The financial situation of the group required extensive asset disposal and an equity injection, while to realise the group's potential as a commercially viable business, any artificial constraints, such as the Shannon stopover, needed to be amended, if not removed.

The Cahill rescue plan, "Strategy for the Future", when endorsed by the government in 1993, proposed the following course of action:

- The group to reduce its cost base by £50 million at a minimum. This would involve 1,200 redundancies at the airline proper, and 250 redundancies at TEAM Aer Lingus. All redundancies were to be voluntary as far as possible.

- Possible pay-cuts or a pay freeze for remaining Aer Lingus staff.

- The government to provide an equity injection of £175 million over the following three years.

- The transatlantic Boeing 747 fleet to be based at Shannon and a low-cost operation geared mainly to tourist traffic to be based there too.

- Some flights to fly directly from Dublin to New York, ending the Shannon stopover.

- Disposal of non-core assets such as the Copthorne Hotel chain and Cara Computers.

- An equity partner for TEAM Aer Lingus to be brought in when the company's fortunes improved.

- Strategic alliances to be forged, where appropriate, with other carriers.

The principal focus of the company's strategy was to return the core business of airline transport to profitability. Specifically, this involved a restructuring of business operations, amending the Shannon stopover policy, and a group cost-reduction programme.

Restructuring of Operational Divisions

This was implemented in the following way:

- Aer Lingus to serve Ireland, the UK, and Continental Europe on existing routes

- Aer Lingus Shannon, based at Shannon, to provide direct services to the US from Shannon and from Dublin on current routes with three existing B747 aircraft

- Aer Lingus Express, a low-fare/low-cost carrier, to compete mainly in the UK market

- Subsidiary and support companies within the Aer Lingus group to become independent profit centres responsible for their own cost structures.

Amending Shannon Stopover Policy

This required an amendment of existing policy, allowing for services to operate directly between Dublin and New York, and Dublin and Boston. The strategy also aimed at a higher level of transatlantic service than was then the case. This was to be achieved through a general growth in leisure traffic because of more competitive fares arising from a lower cost base. The strategy also sought to reverse the adverse trend of indirect travel to Ireland over London, Manchester, etc., enhancing the group's ability to generate valuable new traffic from the UK by feeding from existing UK provincial services to transatlantic services. Essentially, the strategy was designed to improve the financial viability of the route to a point where replacement aircraft for the 747s could be justified.

Reducing the Group's Base

An essential element of the strategy was a £50 million cost-reduction programme. This was specially designed to bring the core activity, air transportation, back into profit. Because some 80 per cent of the controllable costs were payroll related, cost cutting fell into the area of work practices, productivity and employment. A separate cost-reduction programme was prepared for TEAM, with cuts designed in such a way as to maintain the competitiveness of the facility in the event of an improvement in the international maintenance business. Other problems suffered by TEAM in 1993 included losses of £1 million a month, borrowings of some £47 million and ineffective and inappropriate work practices. The directors of the subsidiary had written down the value of TEAM assets by £16.3 million, with the result that its balance sheet showed net assets at £18.2 million, less than half the £40.6 million called-up share capital. In the year to end-March 1993, TEAM increased its aircraft maintenance work by 26 per cent to £64.5 million, but suffered a 3 per cent decline in engine and components business to £25.1 million, and a one-third decline in aircraft-part sales to £7.9 million. Overall, turnover grew 4 per cent to £111.5 million in 1993, and, of this, £54.5 million was work for Aer Lingus or sister companies. For 1993, TEAM managed to improve its operating margins to 6.6 per cent, bringing in an operating profit of £7.4 million. However, this was totally cancelled out by an exceptional item of £27.7 million. Also, there was an increase in trade creditors, up from £1.1 million to £4.4 million, while the Revenue Commissioners were owed £5.8 million, compared to only £1.3 million in 1992. Bank overdrafts were reduced from £8.7 million to £2.1 million, but debts to other Aer Lingus companies were up by £7 million to £27.4 million. Moreover, the £25 million share of the government's £175 million bail-out contribution, which had been allocated to TEAM, was not to be released by the parent company until such time as major changes were successfully implemented in the maintenance facility. Thus, three years after its inception, TEAM was very much linked to its parent company, which was exercising financial control over its operational performance.

TEAM was intended as an independent operation, but its 1993 accounts revealed that it had an arrangement with Aer Lingus to provide £9.6 million worth of management administration and personnel services. This figure was double the £4.9 million recorded for 1992. Of TEAM's total borrowings of £47 million, £27 million was owed to Aer Lingus, which had also helped TEAM out on its leasing commitments to the tune of £10 million. TEAM owed the banks £12 million in 1993.

Despite its difficulties, 1993 was the first year when TEAM did not show an operating profit — it lost £6.5 million, of which £4.5 million went towards financing charges. However, these figures were questionable as, up to this time, Aer Lingus had been subsidising TEAM. Once these subsidies stopped, TEAM was very much exposed to the rapidly declining demand for third-party (i.e. non-Aer Lingus) maintenance. In 1993, Aer Lingus accounted for 35 per cent of TEAM's business, with TEAM capacity for Aer Lingus restricted to 20 per cent. Aircraft maintenance companies such as TEAM hire out their services on a cost-per-hour basis. With increased competition, the net result meant that TEAM had to reduce maintenance prices by a third. In 1991/92, the price charged was £57/60 per hour. This figure had fallen in 1993 to as low as £25/£30 per hour.

One of the major problems for TEAM was the high cost of its salary payments — the average salary was £23,000. Some of its competitors were paying approximately half this figure. Workers at the British Airways subsidiary in Cardiff, for instance, were on around 60 per cent of the TEAM rate. This British Airways subsidiary was particularly damaging for TEAM because it competed with TEAM directly on 747 aircraft, which formed the core of TEAM's business. Before TEAM was set up, the average labour cost in the maintenance division of Aer Lingus was £24,700, some 22 per cent higher than British Airways, 51 per cent higher than British Midland and 64 per cent higher than Air UK. The number of staff employed on any one particular job was 60, while British Midland could get the job done with only 17 people. When TEAM was formed, it inherited these inefficiencies, putting it in a position where it was never able to compete for business globally. Moreover, none of its rivals had to contend with another legacy that TEAM inherited — an agreement that its workers, former Aer Lingus staff, would not lose the salary and other benefits enjoyed while working at the parent company.

In May 1994, TEAM Aer Lingus acquired a new chief executive, Donnacha Hurley. Hurley was originally based in Paris as vice-president (operations) with Sterling Health Europe, the pharmaceutical multinational. Before joining Sterling Health in 1986, Hurley worked for MF Kent. He had also previously been a project director at the Aughinish Alumina plant in Co. Limerick. On his appointment to Aer Lingus, Hurley asserted that TEAM could be made more profitable with a more competitive cost base, flexible work structures and a stronger marketing drive. His appointment came a week after the recruitment of former Gilbey's chief, Garry McCann. An accountant, McCann was to work alongside Bernie Cahill with whom he had previously worked in Grand Metropolitan's Irish operations. In 1993, Cahill brought in John Behan, a tough industrial relations negotiator, to face down the trade unions. The craft unions at TEAM represented the greatest obstacles to winning agreement with the 1,600-strong workforce. TEAM workers in general were not too happy with previous management decisions, and were particularly perturbed by the fact that TEAM customers, at the time, knew more about the affairs of the subsidiary than they did themselves.

The Cahill rescue plan, at the time of its formulation and proposed implementation in 1993, was contingent upon an equity injection of £175 million by the government. The stipulation attached by the government was that it would not be provided unless the Aer Lingus group of unions complied fully with the implementation of the Cahill proposals. The full implications of the Cahill rescue package were, in the longer term, to have returned the airline to a level of profitability which would be the very minimum necessary to maintain the viability of the group.

Impact of the Changes

In 1993, Aer Lingus management was of the opinion that Aer Lingus could return a group profit by 1997 if its restructuring proposals were fully implemented. The airline losses up to March 1993 amounted to £116 million, which contrasted considerably with the £11.8 million loss reported for the previous year. The loss of the air transport business alone amounted to £64 million. Only services from Cork/Shannon to Heathrow, services to Continental Europe and charters had been making money for the airlines. Flying the Atlantic route cost the airline £26 million for 1994, with £6 million lost on domestic routes.

Aer Lingus's return to profitability in the core air-transport division rested on planned cost savings of £50 million annually, with almost all of this amount to be achieved through staff reduction. By seeking a total of 1,200 redundancies, Aer Lingus hoped to have remaining staff work fewer hours, so that a total of about 1,500 "man years" could be taken off costs. The redundancy package offered was six weeks' pay per year of service, costing the airline about £45 million. Of the £175 million injection from the government, £45 million was to be spent on the restructuring programme. The remaining £130 million was used to improve the Aer Lingus balance sheet before disposals. The company's borrowings in March 1993 were £555 million, a figure which was reduced to £365 million by December 1994. A major factor in the £190 million reduction in the debt was the receipt of £25 million of fresh equity from the government. Gearing over the same period declined from 688 per cent to 353 per cent.

Job cuts ran wide and deep at Aer Lingus, beginning at the top. The group's chief executive Cathal Mullen resigned in March of 1993. He was followed by Kyrl Acton, chief executive of passenger services. John Hartnett, chief executive of cargo, took early retirement, while another senior figure, Donal Downing, also stepped down. The extent of the job cuts was necessary for the airline to reduce costs by at least £50 million per annum. Yet 70 per cent of the group's costs were externally imposed and therefore uncontrollable. Of those costs that were controllable, some 90 per cent were payroll related, thus legitimating group-wide workforce redundancies. Aer Lingus transatlantic operations were another contentious example of the group's payroll inefficiency. In 1993, the group had approximately 350 permanent staff in the US, servicing one flight a day in the winter months. By contrast, British Airways in New York had fewer staff looking after more daily flights.

The proposed divisionalisation of the core air transportation activity into three operating units meant that an express service was now to operate low-fare, separately-branded services between Ireland and the UK. The Aer Lingus Express service was to be based in Dublin, providing direct competition for the perkless Ryan Air service to the UK, which had considerably increased its market share on the Dublin–London route. Yet getting the new service off the group was difficult to achieve as the European Commission, in endorsing the government's £175 million equity injection, stipulated that the airline's growth capacity on the key Ireland–UK route be limited to 7 per cent, subject to the airline's achievement of annual £50 million cost-reduction targets, as proposed in the Cahill rescue plan. This 7 per cent was imposed after considerable lobbying from both Ryan Air and British Midland. Also, under the divisionalisation arrangement, a separate company to be known as Aer Lingus Shannon was to be set up, operating direct flights to the United States from both Shannon and Dublin, using existing Boeing 737s.

Non-Core-Asset Disposal

Aer Turas and Shannon Repair Services

In March 1994, Aer Lingus announced the sale of two more of its subsidiaries, Aer Turas and Shannon Repair Services (SRS) in deals worth close to £14 million. Aer Turas was sold to the company's management team for £18 million. However, in reality, this sale meant a £6 million loss for Aer Lingus because part of the condition of the sale was that the airline would take responsibility for two Bank of Ireland loans that the company had on its books, totalling £25 million. Aer Lingus took on the expense in order to rid itself of the loss-making freighter airline which was expected to continue making losses in 1995 and 1996.

The other deal concerned the sale for £450,000 of SRS, the Shannon-based maintenance company, to Omega Aviation Services Ltd., a private company owned by brothers Des and Ulick McEvaddy. The sale, however, was not without its problems. It was alleged that the airline did not consult the 80-strong workforce on the sale, nor their union representatives, SIPTU. Nevertheless, the SRS divestment was a clean break from the parent company, resulting in few or no job losses. Moreover, Omega arranged to subcontract the SRS handling business to Aer Lingus until 1997, thus reducing the opportunities for another handling company to compete with Aer Lingus at Shannon.

Irish Helicopters

In line with the group restructuring programme of non-core asset disposal, Irish Helicopters, a subsidiary of Aer Lingus, was sold in July 1994 to a joint venture between the Louisiana-based Petroleum Helicopters Inc. (PHI) and the English company Bristow

Helicopters, for £4.9 million. Irish Helicopters, which employs 54 people, has a fleet of five helicopters which operate from bases in Cork, Shannon and Dublin. The company operates the air-sea rescue service on contract to the Department of the Marine. It also provides a range of other services to public and private-sector organisations.

Cara Data Processing

In July 1994, a £6.3 million management buyout was agreed at Cara Data Processing, the computer services subsidiary. Aer Lingus had been trying to sell Cara since the middle of 1993. In 1992, the last year for which figures are available, Cara made profits of £600,000 on a turnover of roughly £30 million. While its performance was not broken down in the 1993 result, Aer Lingus did say that profitability and turnover in its commercial holdings division — which includes Cara — were both down by about one-third. The company, which is best known for payroll management systems, is based in Dublin and has offices in Cork and Limerick, as well as in Germany, Belgium and Britain.

PARC

In April 1995, the senior management of PARC Group, the personnel and management services subsidiary, bought the company for a price in excess of £11.5 million. Again the sale was part of the airline's strategy to dispose of non-core businesses. PARC was founded in 1975 to provide recruitment and manpower leasing of aviation, medical and engineering staff around the world. The management buyout was backed by Mercury Development Capital, part of the London merchant bank, SG Warburg.

Hotels

Although Aer Lingus had been reluctant to sell the hotel sections of its business, not least because this section had contributed enormously to the airline's profit in the past, the government in 1993 insisted on a sale as part of the group's overall restructuring package — this despite the fact that selling conditions in the UK, where the bulk of the group's hotel assets are located, were recessionary, making it difficult to realise the net book value of the hotels, estimated in 1992 to be worth £235 million. In normal market conditions, the group's most saleable asset would have been its Copthorne hotel chain. In 1993, the Copthorne hotel chain consisted of 15 hotels — 11 in Britain, two in Paris, and one each in Brussels and in the Gambia. Selling the hotels at this time in Britain would have realised significantly less than the 1992 net book value. In 1993, there were hundreds of British hotels in receivership or in the control of the banks, waiting to come to the market when the recession ended. Aer Lingus, if it were to sell, could have expected reasonable prices for its central London hotel, the Copthorne Tara, and for its two hotels close to Gatwick Airport, although reasonable prices for the other UK hotels were unlikely. The Paris hotels, if sold at this time, would have suffered from the depressed state of the property market in that city. Profits for the Copthorne Hotels in 1993 were £7.9 million on a turnover of £66 million. In this recessionary context, Aer Lingus withdrew the chain from sale in 1994 in anticipation of a recovery in the hotel property market.

In September 1995, the Aer Lingus board agreed to sell the Copthorne chain to the Singapore group, CDL, for £219 million. In the 12 months to the end of March 1995, Copthorne made profits before tax, interest and exceptional items of £11 million sterling. On the basis of Copthorne's 3,963 rooms, CDL paid Aer Lingus an exceptional £55,000 per room for the hotel chain, suggesting that Aer Lingus was correct in deferring a sale of the chain at a price below its true worth.

Airmotive

In May 1994, Airmotive, the jet-engine overhaul subsidiary, was considered for sale if the right buyer could be found. Employing 610 people, Airmotive was previously regarded as a core activity of the airline, and therefore unsaleable. However, its status had been subsequently amended to that of a non-core activity, making it a saleable asset. Other strategic options considered by Aer Lingus for the subsidiary included a joint venture with an appropriate strategic partner. Accordingly, the airline was in negotiations with a number of possible partnership companies. The Swedish car manufacturer, Volvo, which also has a jet overhaul business, is an example of one such company.

Chronology of Recent Developments at Aer Lingus

European Commission Approval

In December 1993, the Commission of the European Union (EU) approved the government's application to be allowed to invest £175 million in Aer Lingus. The Commission approval was sought because the EU prohibits state investments that may distort competition — this restriction applies equally to state-owned and private enterprises. The Commission approved the investment subject to the imposition of a 7 per cent cap on Aer Lingus's growth capacity on Ireland–UK routes. Moreover, the Commission insisted that Aer Lingus operate as a commercial business without any other financial subventions for support. The Commission also restricted the manner in which the government was to inject the £175 million equity capital into the group. The restriction meant that the equity would be injected on a phased basis, subject to the achievement of annual £50 million cost-reduction targets.

Replacement of Boeing 747 Fleet

Also in December 1993, Aer Lingus replaced its 20-year-old Boeing 747 fleet with new Airbus A330 aircraft. The new aircraft were acquired by way of a leasing arrangement, and were to be used to compete profitably on the highly competitive transatlantic route. The 747s, while perfectly serviceable, were increasingly expensive to maintain, making it an attractive option to secure the new aircraft.

Proposed Strategic Alliance

In March 1994, discussions took place between Aer Lingus and the US global airline, Delta, on a proposed strategic alliance on the transatlantic route. The discussions centred on the possibility of opening up a new shared route to Los Angeles and other US cities. The alliance proposed to target the leakage of US–Ireland traffic to rival British and American carriers flying into London. Nearly 60 per cent of all visitors to Ireland in 1993, flew to London first.

The proposed alliance sought to develop significant operational and marketing co-operation between the two airlines. Specifically, it would include the sharing of seat capacity, crews, marketing facilities, and the matching of flight schedules. The question of Delta taking an equity stake in Aer Lingus did not emerge in the negotiations, but both sides suggested that the matter might arise at a later stage, if the relationship were to develop. Other gains for Aer Lingus from such an alliance would include increased business-fare yields, resulting from greater penetration of the US domestic market. The alliance would also improve Aer Lingus ratings on the international computer reservations system, affording access to new US gateways beyond Boston and New York. For Delta, the alliance would help promote its image in the US as a friendly Irish US carrier among the country's 40 million strong Irish-American constituency. It would also increase Delta load factors and business-fare yield, while increasing its access to European cities by feeding into Aer Lingus's extensive European network. Complications for any proposed deal included the release of both airlines from early lease agreements on aircraft and terminals, the matching of Delta and Aer Lingus flight schedules, and making room for Aer Lingus at Delta's expanded facility at New York's JFK Airport.

After American Airlines and United Airlines, Delta is the third largest airline in the world. Based in Atlanta, it has an annual revenue of approximately $12 billion and a global fleet of 500 aircraft, transporting some 6 million passengers monthly. Delta serves 259 cities in the US, and has up to 58 international destinations in North America, Europe, the Middle East and Asia. In 1989, Delta joined marketing forces with Swissair (5 per cent stake), Singapore Airlines and Varig of Brazil.

The Developing Problems of TEAM

When proposed in May 1993, the Cahill rescue plan sought a £50 million reduction in the Aer Lingus group cost base. Of this figure, a £14 million reduction was required at TEAM, the maintenance subsidiary. This was to be achieved through a programme of voluntary redundancy, involving some 250 workers. The rescue plan also proposed a £25 million equity injection into the subsidiary from the parent company. This injection was conditional on the subsidiary's implementation of key amendments to work practices and other productivity arrangements. By late October 1993, Aer Lingus staff and management, after a period of protracted negotiations, came close to the £50 million savings envisaged in the plan. However, negotiations at TEAM did not achieve the same level of progress. Having formally rejected the Cahill cuts agenda, unions at TEAM were in dispute with management over a number of issues exclusive of the Cahill proposals. One such issue was the decision to hire 100 temporary workers to cater for an unanticipated supply of business during the second half of 1993. This decision, taken at a time when management was pressing for redundancies, made the industrial relations environment at TEAM all the more intense. Compounding issues further was the compensation claim by TEAM craft unions for the temporary lay-off of 300 of their members during the summer of 1993, a time when TEAM hangars were empty.

In January 1994, management at TEAM set a deadline of 28 February for conclusion of negotiations centred on key issues such as the proposed new 13-hour shift, the use of part-time workers; various changes in work practices, and a two-year wage freeze, as was agreed in the parent company. At this time, almost 550 workers had applied for the voluntary redundancy package, and of these some 150 had already left the company. While TEAM management originally sought 250 volunteer redundancies, it was now prepared to let 350 go. This followed an announcement that losses for 1993 would amount to £6.5 million. These additional redundancies represented a change to the original Cahill "rescue plan". TEAM required these redundancies because the airline had made changes to its aircraft fleet, replacing the older planes with newer models, resulting in a lower maintenance requirement. The original Cahill plan was based on old fleet requirements. Of the £14 million cost-reduction target, the 350 redundancies would have achieved some £11 million, leaving £3 million to be negotiated in the context of the aforementioned key issues. Contentious among these was the proposed 13-hour shift. The unions insisted that it was not essential, but management felt it necessary as a system that would replace the expense of current overtime payments. The use of part-time workers would also complement such a new working arrangement.

As the end of February deadline approached, the Director of Aer Lingus Group Personnel, John Behan, issued a letter to all TEAM employees cautioning that unless changes were agreed, job losses could reach 650, including 200 management and support staff. The letter went on to highlight that while in 1991/92, the company could command £57/60 per hour of maintenance work, in 1994 they were faced with competitors quoting £25 for the same work. These lower prices were quoted because of the huge overcapacity in the marketplace, resulting in a number of major maintenance companies going out of business in 1993. While talks were continuing right up to the deadline, a factor which further complicated issues was that each employee who transferred to TEAM in 1990 from the old maintenance and engineering division in the airline was still actually employed by the parent company. In 1990, all employees were offered legally binding employment contracts, a device which was seen as necessary to get trade union agreement for the setting up of TEAM. Another issue of consideration, and one that was squarely placed at management's door, was its inefficient invoicing and recovery of some £17 million outstanding from bad debtors. This figure in 1993 was £4.4 million, up from £1.1 million in the previous year.

When the February deadline finally arrived, a tentative agreement was reached between management and craft unions (agreement with SIPTU members working at the subsidiary had earlier been reached). A number of concessions were offered by the craft unions, notably a proposed "extraordinary" shift instead of the company's 13-hour shift. This proposal would have given the company the degree of flexibility it originally sought under the 13-hour system, thereby allowing it to meet specific overhaul requirements whenever they might arise. Yet despite the tentative agreement of the craft unions, a key question remained unanswered — whether there would be a two-year pay pause, or a pay freeze, as was accepted by SIPTU members at the subsidiary. The craft workers took the view that it was a pay pause, implying that there would be a back payment at a later date. This interpretation did not satisfy management, so that by early May a new set of changes was being sought by the subsidiary, with an early-June deadline set for agreement. The proposed new package was to have two key arrangements — a new annualised hours system and changed non-union status for front-line supervisors. The annualised hour system was proposed so as to develop a new pattern of seasonal working. This would mean that a craft worker could be laid off in the summer months, but would be paid a basic wage, and would work as required during the winter on the same remuneration. The second proposal, involving supervisory staff, sought to augment the level of management responsibility taken on by these workers, thereby charging them with implementing change on the ground. These supervisors, who were also trade union members, were to relinquish their union membership, and be paid executive salaries.

By mid-May 1994, the craft unions, in rejecting the new proposals, balloted their members for industrial action. The unions' position was quite clear — after a period of protracted negotiations, agreement on the restructuring had been reached, but within a week, management, which had pronounced itself happy with the agreement, had sought further concessions. Management, in response, wanted to refer the craft workers' dispute to the Labour Relations Commission (LRC). By the end of May, the LRC, at the instigation of the Minister for Enterprise and Employment, had set up an investigation into the crisis at TEAM. Submissions were heard from both sides without any direct face-to-face negotiations. The prescription offered by the LRC proposed 250 redundancies, a pay-freeze and a maximum-hours agreement. The maximum-hours agreement would involve employees working 48 hours in peak periods without overtime, and an average of 30 hours during slack periods.

The LRC proposals, despite considerable political pressure, were rejected by the unions, leaving TEAM management in a precarious situation, which led to its issuing of protective notice to all TEAM employees. Management subsequently proceeded to lay off some 850 workers. Given this scenario, many of the workers felt that the hidden agenda of both government and management was to pre-empt a situation that would make privatisation of the subsidiary an attractive strategic option.

The failure of the LRC to resolve the impasse prompted an expectation that the Labour Court might intervene. Meanwhile, the Irish Congress of Trade Unions (ICTU) became involved, mainly because of craft union pressure. However, its efforts resulted in very little substantial progress, and finally in the intervention of the Labour Court. The Court's recommendations, when issued in August 1994, proposed the application of a 10 per cent cut in basic pay as was initially mooted by the company. Also recommended under basic pay was a pay-freeze, including increments due, to July 1996. In respect of shift rates, the Court recommended that existing rates remain unchanged and that certain qualifications be applied for night-duty payments. Overtime, the Court proposed, should be paid for at the existing premium. On seasonality, the Court's recommendations recognised the need for the introduction of flexible working patterns to meet existing business demands. The subsidiary's existing productivity scheme should, according to the Court, cease immediately. It also suggested that when TEAM returned to viability, discussions should be held with the unions on a future scheme based on company performance. Moreover, the Court believed that front-line management would form an essential part of the new management team, and therefore must be proactive in the development and utilisation of systems and controls necessary to improve the performance and effectiveness of the company.

While initially rejected, the Court's recommendations were subsequently accepted by the unions after some clarification of issues, enabling the company finally to implement its restructuring programme in full. However, the delayed implementation of the restructuring meant that some of TEAM's ongoing contracts were lost, and because of the decline in the prices quoted by TEAM competitors, the improvements agreed in the Labour Court were insufficient to enable TEAM to win profitable business in 1994.

By 1995, TEAM Aer Lingus had much yet to achieve in terms of cost-reduction if it were to become a viable commercial enterprise. A new five-year development plan was prepared by the parent company, detailing cost savings in the order of £8 million a year, involving a further workforce reduction of 250 employees. The plan also called for substantial investment in TEAM to establish the company's finances on a viable basis. The need to find a strategic and compatible partner was also addressed by the plan, suggesting that such a partner was necessary to secure the medium-term future of the subsidiary.

Financial Performance of Aer Lingus

In 1989, net profit increased on the previous year to £39.7 million, with turnover also improving to £604.1 million. Profit after tax was £36.09 million, up from £32.3 million in 1988. Air transport produced an operating profit of £2.8 million but after interest payment, a net loss of £1.1 million resulted. Other areas fared much better with airline-related services producing a net profit of £14.7 million and ancillary activities a very satisfactory £26.1 million.

In 1990, net profit was down on the previous year to £37 million. Airline-related services reported a very impressive 61 per cent increase in profit to £23.7 million, while external ancillary activities showed a 27 per cent increase in net profits to £33 million. In contrast, air transport incurred an operating loss of £10.5 million which included £3.5 million loss arising from AL Holdings. All this compares badly with the previous year's profits of £2.8 million. After interest charges of £9.3 million, the net loss from air transport amounted to £19.8 million, showing a serious deterioration in core business results. Ancillary activities earned £33 million, a 27 per cent growth on the previous year. Earnings per share were down on the previous year to 45.9p, return on capital employed stood at 11.9 per cent from 13.7 per cent the previous year. Debt as a percentage of total assets was 29 per cent from 27 per cent a year earlier.

Table 14.1: Financial Performance, 1989–94

	1989 £m	1990 £m	1991 £m	1992 £m	1993 £m	1994* £m
Operating Revenue	604	716	786	849	817	1,480
Group Operating Profits	22.7	118.9	27.3	15.6	.762	34.8
Operating Profit earned from:						
— Air Transport	(1.01)	(19.7)	(42.5)	(37.9)	(22.9)	—
— Airline-related Services	15.2	14.7	23.7	20.7	13.3	—
— Extra Ancillary Services	22.5	26.1	33.0	28.0	10.4	—
Net Profit Before Tax	37.8	39.6	37	6.2	(190.7)	(128.8)
Net Profit After Tax	32.2	36	31.5	7.9	(188.0)	(129.1)
Debt per cent of Total Assets	38	27	29	52	—	—
Total Passengers	2.6	3.5	4.0	4.2	—	—

*   Figures for 1994 are for extended 21-month accounting period to end December 1994.

For 1991, group profits for the year were £7.9 million despite very poor results from air transport. The air transport division incurred an operating loss of £19.6 million and a net loss after interest of £42.5 million. The airline industry worldwide produced losses of $5.1 billion in 1990. Airline services contributed a net profit of £20.7 million, while construction work began on a £35 million hangar for TEAM Aer Lingus at Dublin Airport. Hotels produced a net profit of £12 million, with commercial holdings contributing net earnings of £16 million. Return on capital employed was 1.3 per cent, down from a year earlier, while net debt as a percentage of total assets was 52 per cent, up from 29 per cent in 1990.

In 1992 the group incurred an after-tax loss of £11.8 million, the first in 10 years. The air transport divisions pre-tax loss was £37.9 million, a £4.6 million improvement on the previous year. Airline services reported a £14.6 million profit which was down 29 per cent on 1991. Hotels showed a pre-tax profit of £12 million, almost the same as 1991. Commercial holdings showed an overall pre-tax profit of £8.2 million, down by 49 per cent. Group turnover increased by 8 per cent to a total of £849 million. Non-air-transport activities generated a turnover of £350 million, producing profits before interest of £45.4 million. Air transport, which generated turnover of £449 million (58 per cent of total), produced losses before interest of £8.8 million. Group profits before interest and tax amounted to £36.6 million including net exceptional credits of £17.9 million. Total interest charges increased to £39.7 million, up from £14.7 million in 1991. The resultant loss before taxation was £3.1 million compared to profit of £6.6 million in 1991. Taxation increased to £8.6 million up from £7 million in 1991, while group capital expenditure amounted to £169 million which was £67 million less than the previous year. The debt/ equity ratio as a percentage of shareholders' funds and minority interests increased to 132.8 per cent.

The year 1993 saw losses of up to £188 million and much of this was a result of the costs of restructuring the airline, as well as write-offs of the group's investment in GPA, and losses in the air transport division and in its subsidiaries. The interest cost on the group's debt of £500 million was also included in the operating loss figure. Compounding matters further was the difficulty experienced by the group in leasing the two Boeing 767 aircraft it had previously acquired for the now abandoned Dublin–Los Angeles route.

The year 1994 was the first in many when the airline made money out of flying. The core air-transport division turned in an operating profit of £28.826 million, a considerable figure in light of the loss made in this area in the previous two years. This positive result was derived from a refocused marketing strategy, emphasising quality of fare yields as opposed to passenger volumes. However, this operating profit was turned into a loss of some £30.9 million after interest charges and exceptional costs associated with the Cahill plan. The group's subsidiaries performed dismally, turning in a loss of £25 million compared to the £22 million profit recorded in 1993. TEAM produced a loss of £32.5 million. Included in this figure was a provision for bad debts of £6.7 million. Airmotive also put in a below-par performance, encouraging the parent company to review strategic options for the subsidiary. The only positive non-core performance was derived from the hotels division, with the Copthorne hotel group producing a profit of stg£2.4 million. Copthorne was sold in 1995 for £219 million.

The Future

The crisis faced by Aer Lingus in the 1990s has taken place within a context of global turbulence in the air transport business. In 1992, for example, members of the International Air Transport Association lost a cumulative $5 billion. Specific international examples include Aer France, losing some £400 million in 1993. By 1995, after some years of recessional business conditions, many European airlines finally began to generate profitability, albeit in conditions that resulted from large-scale rationalisation and restructuring. Moreover, once bitter rivals were now collaborating, forming strategic alliances with one another in a bid to generate mutual and sustainable synergistic benefits. Investment in the upgrading of higher-margin premium services was also taking place so as to support profit margins that have fallen, even in the face of currently increasing passenger numbers. Aer Lingus, in responding to the business environment, has managed to stave off many of the problems afflicting it in the recent past. Through a process of radical change, the airline has secured its immediate survival, developing concurrently a commercially viable and customer-focused future. Nevertheless, the nature and extent of Aer Lingus business is structurally dependent on a number of factors derived generally from the global economics of air-transportation. The key economic factors affecting Aer Lingus include:

- *Small Size:* The population of Ireland is a consistent 3.5 million people. This figure in itself serves to limit the scope of potential domestic growth for Aer Lingus.

- *Short Average Flight Length*: The key to long-term commercial aviation success is determined by the extent of an airline's long-haul routes. Aer Lingus has only two such routes — Ireland–NewYork and Ireland–Boston. Because Aer Lingus has not sufficiently developed long-distance air routes to other parts of the world, it remains a niche company, ideally as the preferred carrier into and out of Ireland. In any event, the current (1994) Aer Lingus balance sheet is simply not strong enough to pursue development strategies on a global scale.

- In 1997, within the single market of the EU, a full deregulation of Europe's skies will permit Aer Lingus full access to Continental markets. However, deregulation could also spell trouble for higher-cost carriers such as Aer Lingus, as a new generation of low-cost start-ups may undercut their fares.

Concluding Remarks

In 1995, Aer Lingus conducted a strategic review of its business. The review has directed Aer Lingus to invest in new technology, and to formulate a new advertising and marketing strategy, including a redesign of its corporate logo. The group has redefined its mission statement, asserting the need to achieve sustained profitability through commercially viable products and practices, and a keen customer focus delivered by committed and well-motivated staff. The statement also seeks to position the group so that its subsidiaries are profitable and viable within themselves, and are strategic in their support of the core airline business. Operationally, Aer Lingus is to develop twin hubs out of Dublin and New York on transatlantic routes. Discussions are also ongoing with Delta and, more recently, TWA, with a view to increasing traffic out of New York. The Dublin hub will feed from the recently revamped British provincial services.

Aer Lingus has undergone radical transformational change. As of 1996, the group is considering its strategic options, assessing in the process the business structural and contextual factors likely to affect its future performance.

Source: Company reports and interviews with company personnel.

Questions

1. Evaluate the way in which Aer Lingus has diversified since it began operation in 1936.

2. What factors have prevented TEAM from being the success which was predicted?

3. Evaluate the way in which the rescue plan was initiated and managed. What lessons does it teach us about business retrenchment and turnover?

4. What type of competitive forces does Aer Lingus face in the airline business in the future?

15

The Electricity Supply Board

Overview

The ESB was established under the Electricity Act, 1927, and its primary function is to control, co-ordinate and improve the supply, distribution and sale of electricity in Ireland. The ESB is a large, complex company and one of Ireland's major industrial concerns. It is a publicly owned company. The company operates in the semi-state sector of industry and is the largest engineering company in the state in terms of assets, employees, and revenue. It is the sole electricity utility for Ireland and so has a monopoly of electricity generation, transmission, distribution and supply. The core electricity business serves 1.3 million customers with 10,000 employees, and a payroll of over £200 million. Another 1,000 people work in ESB's ancillary businesses which include international consultancy, fish farming and various joint ventures in manufacturing.

The ESB is headed by a board, chairperson, deputy chairperson and 10 other members. All are part-time members and are appointed by the Minister for Transport, Energy and Communications for a period of five years (except worker directors). This board ultimately takes its directions from the Minister for Transport, Energy and Communications. The membership of the board of ESB is widely based to represent the totality of interests, including those of the customers, and of employees of the company. The day-to-day management of the organisation rests with department managers/generation managers. The generation side of the organisation operates under the heading "Generation Transmission and Operations" (GTO), and is headed by an executive director. This area employs about 2,500 employees out of the total permanent staff.

The size of the company can be gauged by its turnover of £800 million per annum operating on a non-profit basis. The vast majority of the turnover is related directly to the sale of electricity, which amounts to approximately 13,000 million units per annum. The performance of the company is very much judged by its ability to be self-sufficient.

The Evolution of the ESB

1927–1944

The ESB was set up under Section 2 of the Electricity Supply Act, 1927. Its first chairman was John J. Murphy who held the post from 1927 to 1930. Staff numbers for the first year were 829, with a customer base of 47,000. By the end of 1930, staff had increased to 1,602, double the previous year. The difficulties facing the company in the first years of operation were primarily issues like organisation structures, recruitment, sales and supply of electricity, the latter especially in periods of severe drought. In 1930, F.R. Browne became chairman and held the post for the next 30 years. He only took the post on the promise of government support, and the internal freedom that he required to manage the company effectively. Initially the ESB experienced many boardroom and revenue problems. Demand was not meeting overhead costs, with the result that losses of £250,000 were reported for the period 1931–34. The number of customers did, however, rise during the 1930s, so that by the end of 1938, the ESB had over 145,230 customers.

The general path of longer-term development of the company was going to show less reliance on hydroelectric power and more on thermal power. The period of war, 1939–45, was an extremely difficult time for the company, with some restrictions and shortages taxing the company's resources. There was the added problem of steeply rising prices for coal and materials. In 1944, a prolonged dry spell made matters worse. The end of the war marked the end of very difficult times and the start of a more energetic period of rural electrification and major expansion. Turf started to make an important contribution to electricity generation and would do so especially during the oil crisis in the 1970s. Between the early 1950s and late 1960s the ESB installed a total of 407.5mw generating capacity based on turf. Although the absolute size of turf-fuelled generating capacity was subsequently increased during the 1970s, the importance of turf as a percentage of total capacity peaked in the early 1960s to under 40 per cent. This happened at a time when oil prices were low and falling. When oil prices rose sharply in the early and middle 1970s, turf had fallen back to 25 per cent and so was not able to cushion generation costs against rising fuel prices. Furthermore, turf could be an unreliable source, depending as it did on good weather conditions.

1945–1960

The post-war period was taken up with rural electrification. The ESB faced a new set of technical and administrative problems for which existing machinery and procedures were inadequate. Post-war conditions were not favourable with shortages of material and rising prices. The peak years of the rural development scheme were 1948–51 and it finally wound up in 1975. In the 30 years since the scheme had started, 420,000 houses had been connected at a cost of £80 million, of which the state provided £27 million and ESB £53 million. This represented about 98 per cent of rural households; the remainder were connected by 1980. The scheme was one of the major factors contributing to the modernisation of rural Ireland and constituted one of the great social revolutions of the century. It did, however, cost more to supply electricity to rural areas than to urban areas. After the war, demand increased largely in the domestic sector and the ESB moved quickly to achieve an improvement in its capacity, with new power stations being built. However, a recession in the mid-1950s resulted in considerable overcapacity. By 1966, however, things had levelled out, and the ESB's development of turf power was completed.

1960–1973

The period 1960–73 was marked by significant change and re-evaluation. Rural turf schemes were now completed, some of the company structures had become obsolete, and the ESB began to experience serious industrial relations problems. The Irish economic base began to change from 1960 onwards. Many of the people who guided the company from its initiation had retired, including chairman R.F. Browne. Dr T.F. Murray took over, and he was a determined defender of the ESB's independence. He remained chairman until 1975. This period was marked by sustained growth in output and employment, a rise in income and an increase in industrial output. At this stage in its development the company opted for oil in its newer power stations.

The 1960s, however, were not solely a period of painless expansion and boom for the company; industrial relations problems were also significant. It appears that the company's machinery for managing industrial relations did not change to meet the changing circumstances of the organisation. Between 1927 and 1960, the ESB experienced a mere eight strikes. Between 1961 and 1968, this had increased to 38 strikes. The rapid economic and social changes of the 1960s put severe strain on industrial relations structures and this was even greater in the ESB given its size, and the fact that any strike in the company was a threat to the country as a whole. The company failed to predict such trends and/or devise new industrial relations structures to keep pace with the overall growth of the organisation. Things were not helped by the fact that there was a fragmented union membership: 27 unions were present in the company in 1962, for example. To help matters, a Joint Industrial Council was set up in the late 1960s, and new personnel policies were developed and implemented. As part of the 1970s restructuring, the company got its first personnel director, P.J. Moriarty, the present chairman of the company, and by the mid-1970s these strategies were bearing fruit as relationships between management and employees had improved considerably.

World Recession, 1974–1978

At the end of the oil crisis in 1973, the company was over 60 per cent dependent on oil, but it was more the degree of uncertainty together with the collapse of the economy and a dramatic shift in fuel prices which changed the environment within which the ESB had to operate. However, by the late 1970s things were beginning to pick up again. By 1978 a number of trends had become evident:

- There had been a huge development in the scale of the company's activities and a continued trend towards increased efficiency.

- The company operated under constraints imposed by the government, resulting at certain times in a system of capacity higher than what the company would have chosen. The overcapacity was mainly the result of forecasts of demand being significantly off target.

For a long time ESB was overstaffed, with a significant absence of flexibility in the utilisation of manpower. For the first 30 years of its existence it was very much influenced by the need for maximum employment. This led to an emphasis on job creation and job retention which became an integral feature of the organisation and union expectations within the company. Steps had been taken to reduce overstaffing, and the company had also looked at its problem of low productivity. However, there was a general unwillingness to deal with the problem.

The 1980s Onwards and Organisation Reform

The period of the 1980s was marked by difficult trading conditions, especially in the early 1980s, and the company's performance for this period reflected these difficulties. For instance, in 1984 a deficit of £23 million was recorded, one of the worst ever experienced by the company. Much of the company's performance can be attributed to the inadequacies of price levels for the previous decade to sustain the financial health of the company. Furthermore, price increases had not been adequate to cover costs. In fact, since 1986 a policy of no price increase has been in force, with the result that the company has had to pay the cost of no increase, in some instances up to £10 million per annum.

In the mid-1980s changes in structure were deemed necessary. A major restructuring of ESB was carried out as a result of the Millar report between 1984 and 1987. Up to this, the country was divided into 12 districts. It then changed to 6 distribution regions.

There was a major strike for one week in May 1991. It disrupted electricity supply in most parts of the country. Arising from this strike, the ESB and ESB group of unions agreed to establish a joint steering committee to carry out a comprehensive review of relationships in the company. The chairman of the committee was Mr Peter Cassels, General Secretary of the Irish Congress of Trade Unions. The parties agreed to approach the review jointly and openly. Their objective was to make a significant contribution to the achievement of a peaceful working environment in ESB, reliability of supply to customers, commercial efficiency, a fair deal for employees and the establishment of a genuine partnership. They decided to undertake the review in two phases: firstly, to identify the issues at the root of relationships; and secondly, having gained general acceptance of these issues, to make recommendations which would address them. In the course of their investigations, the working groups reviewed current practice in the ESB and examined relevant external developments. This led to the identification of eight key issues which the committee saw as central to the achievement of quality working relationships in the ESB:

1. The need to develop shared objectives

2. The need to build trust

3. The need to recognise and foster the aspirations and contributions of individuals

4. The need to make the industrial relations process more effective

5. The need to develop a framework for participation for ongoing involvement in change

6. The need to improve communications

7. The need to develop the roles of both management and trade unions

8. The need to discover how to build on their strengths.

The commitment to the success of ESB of staff and management at all levels impressed the Joint Steering Committee. The pride of people in their location and their category, and their desire to contribute to the provision of excellent service in every part of the company, gave confidence to the committee in bringing forward its recommendations. The committee believed that this quality of relationships in ESB must be built on a commitment to the achievement of shared objectives, mutual respect and high levels of trust between management, staff and unions throughout the company. In particular it would require a significant change in how they both defined and discharged their roles. The committee believed that the recommendations would benefit not only the management, unions and staff, but also customers and the national interest, by providing a framework which would ensure peace and progress in ESB and enable it to adapt to the challenge of the future.

It was finally recommended that any major changes in the future of ESB should be undertaken in the context of the content and spirit of the report. It should be implemented on a phased basis, allowing for trust and experience between each stage, and should be subject to regular review by the Corporate Forum.

Restructuring, 1991

The EU Commission wanted to create a new European common market in electricity, open to international competition. The Commission hoped that this would lead to a more efficient electricity system and provide the community with cheaper power. The ESB believed that the correct response was to face up to the challenge, reorganise itself to take on competition and make the most of the opportunities. It appointed international consultants McKinsey and Company, Inc. to work with senior management on a dynamic blueprint for the future. The Minister for Energy appointed Coopers and Lybrand to carry out a detailed review of the options for a new structure for the electricity industry. McKinsey considered many alternative ways in which the ESB might be organised. The one they recommended involved a radical reshaping of the organisation, dividing the ESB into a power and supply company. They recommended a radical restructuring of ESB into independent business units, in conjunction with a fundamental change to the management approach within the company. This should take place within the context of a single, semi-state company but should be accompanied by the creation of an independent industry regulator. The regulator should agree clear targets for ESB performance and for the development of a competitive market in Ireland, in order to promote this requisite change. Their key reasons for recommending this approach were:

- A restructuring of the ESB into business units would allow all of the original objectives for the Irish electricity industry to be fully achieved

- A less radical approach which might meet some of the key external objectives — such as introducing competition or private capital —would fail to realise much of the potential for internal improvement

- A more radical approach to breaking ESB up would offer limited additional benefits — mostly in the form of some increase in transparency and the making of profit measures more real unless it was accompanied by privatisation.

Table 15.1 presents the main objectives and the means of achieving them.

The McKinsey blueprint was adopted in 1992. Five business units were set up, each having responsibility for one of the present company's major functions. Each unit was to function as an independent business in its own right, with full responsibility for its own activities. Each unit has its own general manager responsible for the unit's success as a competitive commercial enterprise.

Table 15.1: Achievement of Main Objectives

Objective	Mechanism for Achieving Objective
To create full transparency in generation, transmission, distribution and supply	• Creation of independent business units • Establishment of formal contracts between business units
To support competition in generation	• Creation of a power procurer at the corporation centre distanced from generation business unit • Use of open, competitive bidding process • Oversight by industry regulator
To facilitate private-sector investment	• Publishing of fair and transparent transmission and distribution "use of system" changes • Establishment of a competitive bidding process for new contracts • Establishment of industry stability thorough an industry regulator: distanced from political pressures and taking a long-term view.
To give customers a greater say	• Provision of a choice of supplier for large customers • Establishment of an industry regulator to be a guardian of small customers' interests
To encourage greater efficiency through a more profit-oriented approach	• Creation of profit-oriented business units • Introduction of significant competition • Establishment of tough external and internal profit and price regulations
To achieve a major change in the approach to the management of ESB	• Redesign of core processes • Devolution of business decision-making • Refinement of the company vision and setting tough new corporate targets • Linkage of personal performance goals and rewards of business goals

Each is free to develop its own policies, management style and culture. However, all of the units come under the co-ordinated leadership of the Corporate Centre. The McKinsey blueprint sees this corporate centre as a compact team which will concentrate on overall strategy under the direction of the chief executive, who in turn is answerable to the board of the company and all its business units. The chief executive has four specialist corporate directors to provide assistance: commercial, engineering, finance and personnel. Between them, they co-ordinate policies and strategies for the organisation as a whole. They set business targets for the five units and monitor their individual performance.

Cost and Competitive Review

The Cost and Competitive Review (CCR) was launched in February 1994. This is a tripartite committee involving the group of unions, the Government and ESB management. It was a significant initiative designed to build upon the strength of the ESB and to bring about major change in a spirit of co-operation and trust. The results would form an important input to the Government's consideration of the ESB's application for a price increase.

The purpose of the CCR was to reach agreement between the three parties on a programme of changes which would enable the ESB to compete effectively in the new market.

The early stages of the review involved a detailed analysis of costs and an in-depth examination of performance and results compared to companies in both the US and Europe, which had similar characteristics to the ESB. Teams consisting of management and union representatives visited these companies and studied how they organised their activities, the work methods they employed, the resources used and the results achieved. This work provided the basis for a comparison with ESB, which identified gaps in performance. McKinsey and Company made presentations to teams of management and trade union representatives for discussions over a period of time. Presentations set out the detail of the changes in work practices, methods, organisation etc., which in their view were possible for ESB and were necessary to bring performance up to best international standards. They also set out the expected impact of such changes on organisation arrangements, employment and cost savings, across all business units. McKinsey identified many areas where

ESB performance was up to a high standard: fuel purchasing and management, the customer service ethic and its international consulting business.

McKinsey and Company identified a surplus of 2,900 staff in ESB and £120 million potential savings per year. They proposed the following ways of achieving these changes:

- Extensive flexibility in working practices

- Extensive use of technology to improve productivity

- Centralisation of activities supported by use of modern communications technology

- Systematic budget-driven prioritisation of construction and maintenance projects

- De-layering of management

- Demarcation.

The chief executive gave a firm commitment that the company's existing policy of no compulsory redundancy would continue.

A new voluntary severance scheme would be launched at the conclusion of the CCR process, or earlier if agreed between management and the group of unions. A key principle was that the scheme was voluntary on both sides. A decision to apply for severance was a mater for the individual. ESB had the option of declining a request for severance. The company was conscious of the need to retain key skills and this was to be a factor in the application of the voluntary severance scheme. The package would be a comprehensive one, embracing a set of support services which would enable people to consider the issue fully. These services included career counselling and advisory services, training services (including job-seeking skills), job-search services and pre-retirement modules. Full details of the total package would be announced at the time of its launch and would be comprehensively communicated to all staff.

The Financial Performance of the ESB

The financial performance of the ESB for the years 1988–94 is presented in Table 15.2. Appendices 1 and 2 to the chapter present a detailed breakdown of the ESB's financial position.

Table 15.2: Financial Performance, 1988–94

	1988 £m	1989 £m	1990 £m	1991 £m	1992 £m	1993 £m	1994 £m
Income	756	789	819	860	915	943	977
Expenditure	751	777	818	856	913	964	996
Surplus	5	12	1	4	2	(21)	(19)
Cumulative (Deficit)	66	54	53	49	47	68	87
Sales (Million Units)	10,616	11,169	11,768	12,370	13,104	13,439	14,025
Capital Expenditure	87	85	92	116	140	170	156
Borrowings	77	58	101	108	117	161	220
Debt Liabilities	1,103	1,004	1,007	976	916	938	1,009

The year 1985/86 was a good one for the company with sales increasing by 5.5 per cent and achieving a near breakeven result — deficit of £7.7 million on a total income of £790 million. The accumulated deficit stood at £72 million which had been allowed to build up mainly through a reluctance on the company's part to increase electricity prices in times of rapidly rising costs and increasing fuel prices in the 1970s and 1980s. The ESB considered 1986 as a watershed year: a year in which the company achieved certain goals and laid the foundations for future strategies designed to bring about greater efficiency within the company and to improve its service to customers. It was the first year that the company was able to introduce price reductions. This happened twice in 1986. The overall financial result for the latter nine months of 1986 saw a surplus of £6.369 million. In 1986 sales increased by 4 per cent on the previous year partly as a result of greater promotion and marketing efforts. Consultancy turnover was £7.3 million but only a breakeven result was achieved, compared to the late 1970s, when an £80 million turnover was attained, producing a net profit of £5 million.

In 1987, the company achieved yet another deficit, this time of £5 million with the accumulated deficit to date standing at £177 million. For the first time in almost 20 years the ESB's overall level of debt fell, partly because of the completion of major construction work, increased efficiency, and favourable exchange rates. Yet debt of £1.21 billion remained a major financial burden for the company. The year 1988 was a good one for the company with prices falling by 4.7 per cent making it the fourth year in a row for price reductions. These price reductions, however, did reduce income by £28 million, but this was offset by a fall in fuel prices and interest rates, a weak US dollar and an internal cost-reduction programme. This yielded a modest surplus of £5.4 million. Industrial demand stood at 4 per cent, with a 2.5 per cent increase in the commercial sector. There was only a 1.5 per cent increase in domestic demand mainly because electrical appliances were more efficient, and there was less house building and more intense competition. Turnover stood at £756 million.

In 1989, a modest surplus of £11.5 million was achieved — a large insurance claim settlement contributed £2.5 million to this surplus. However, despite a turnover of £787 million, the outcome for 1989 was no more than breakeven. The company had to absorb the 5 per cent increase in VAT on electricity, and had to use the year's surplus to apply a special discount to domestic electricity prices from 1 March 1990. Over the previous five years an average of breakeven results had been achieved, but the average over the previous 10 years was a deficit of £3.5 million, which generally reflected the very difficult trading conditions under which the company had to operate. The accumulated deficit for 1989 stood at £54 million with total debt at £1,025 million. This represented 21 per cent of the cost of a unit of electricity.

In 1990, prudent management policies ensured another satisfactory year for the company. Prices were kept stable, costs contained, and there was a surplus in trading. The buoyancy of the economy was reflected in the demand for electricity, which increased to 5.4 per cent in 1990, compared to 4.7 per cent in 1989. Growth occurred in all sectors but the most significant growth was in the commercial sector, with a 7.5 per cent rate compared to 5.6 per cent in the residential sector and 3.9 per cent in the industrial sector. There was a downside to this increased growth because excessive major borrowing was necessary to finance the construction of new facilities. The surplus for the year was £1.6 million from a turnover of £800 million. A major factor influencing finances was the special discount given to residential customers, which cost the company £12 million. This discounting policy was adopted to offset the impact of an extra 5 per cent in VAT put on electricity in the budget. The company continued the policy in 1991, costing them a further £16 million, and added to this a further £16 million absorbed in prices from an earlier 5 per cent VAT applied in 1988.

Profit for 1991 was just £3.7 million on an £859 million turn-over. However, the company's true profit was much higher. The ESB provided £30.8 million for repayment of borrowings; it made a £20 million provision for liabilities and charges and an £8.8 million depreciation charge. Its net assets increased from £700 million to £745 million during a year in which it repaid £27.5 million of borrowings. For 1992 the company was able to report a surplus of £1.9 million on total income of £915 million. Total sales had increased on the 1991 figure to 13,110 million units and the cumulative deficit for the company stood at £47 million.

The results for 1993 were not good, with the ESB losing £20 million after taxation and loan repayments. The board sought a 3.5 per cent increase. Over the previous years, the price of electricity had dropped by 34 per cent in real terms — a trend which could not continue indefinitely if the company were to become a profitable enterprise again. It was now cheaper to buy electricity than ever before. The company maintained that if it got the price increase it was looking for it would not have made a loss in 1993.

Between 1991 and 1992, the wage bill increased by £23 million. In 1991, the average number employed at the company was 10,676, at a total wage cost of £206.6 million or total pay-roll cost of £258 million — this latter figure includes pensions and PRSI. In 1992, total numbers employed had increased to 19,946. The results for 1993 show that after January devaluation of the Irish pound added more than £40 million to the company's debts. Even before this devaluation, by December 1992 the company had borrowings of close to £1 billion. This figure was to be reduced in 1993 by paying off £176 million and a further reduction of £7,752 million in 1994.

Financial performance for the financial years 1993 and 1994 was overall poor. An operating deficit was recorded for both years, with the cumulative deficit in 1994 standing at £87 million. Customer numbers and sales continued to increase. By 1994, this figure stood at £1,375,975. Payroll costs continued to increase and currently stand at £308 million.

Business Activities of the ESB

The ESB is a diversified organisation with many ancillary activities. The main ones are listed below.

ESB International

The ESB has been engaged in international consultancy work since the mid-1970s. The impact of the recession of the 1970s was a major spur to the ESB's involvement in the consultancy area. However, it only received the legal authority to establish subsidiary limited companies in 1988. The company earns approximately $15 million plus per annum and employs around 250 people. It has three operating subsidiaries: ESBI-US, ESBI-UK and ESBI-Computing, a software, sales and support company. With the privatisation of electricity in Britain, the company has found a ready market for its consultancy services among investors seeking technical and economic evaluations. Similar work is undertaken in the United States.

FTI

FTI is a subsidiary of ESB Financial Services Limited and comprises much of the former treasury division of the ESB. The origins of the company go back to the late 1970s when treasury management became vital for the ESB largely because of major borrowings for capital investment. The main services provided by FTI fall into three categories:

- Client consultancy, which focuses on the strategic management of foreign exchange and interest-rate risk

- Client portfolio management, which provides cost-effective management of foreign currency and interest-rate exposure portfolios

- Treasury, which provides clients with services such as market analysis and technical analysis, and training programmes designed to develop treasury skills throughout an organisation.

Salmara Fisheries Ltd.

Salmara Fisheries Ltd. is a new company with a long pedigree. Incorporated in 1988, Salmara continues the work of the fisheries division of the ESB. The importance of the company to the ESB is not only that it is a profitable operation, but it has also pioneered joint ventures with the private sector, including local interests, and a development co-operative.

Top-Tech

Top-Tech is a new joint venture with Aer Lingus to make sophisticated computer cabinets.

The success of the ESB's diversification strategy is open to question. Cumulatively, the subsidiaries have lost a considerable amount of money in the past. In 1994, a breakeven result was managed, compared to a $5 million profit in the late 1970s. Appendix 1 provides a full list of business activities.

External Environment of the ESB

There are many external environmental factors which influence ESB operations.

The Product Market

The ESB operates in a monopoly market in electricity terms, but not in terms of supply of fuel substitutes, because of competitors such as Bord na Móna, Bord Gáis, CDL. The ESB has to be efficient in electricity production, since, while having a captive market for domestic electricity sales, a different situation exists in the commercial industrial electricity market. Here it has to compete for its share of the market with Bord na Móna, etc. In the near future, the ESB will have its position of monopoly electricity production diluted for the first time by the introduction of direct interconnector schemes across the Irish Sea, and through the advent of independent power producers. Bord na Móna has indicated an intention to build an independent turf-burning power station in the midlands.

The Labour Market

The staff of the ESB come mainly from an engineering background, with ancillary support drawn from clerical accounting areas. When recruiting engineers, universities are the first choice. Staffing levels have remained constant as growth is maintained through current capacity. Any replacement of skills, necessary because of retirement, etc., usually draws from the top end of the labour market. Employment in the ESB is seen as very attractive because of the level of job security guaranteed and the remuneration package.

Fuel Prices / Market Conditions

Fuel prices and market conditions have a major impact on the ESB's activities. The volatility of the oil/fuel market can affect fuel prices. Approximately a third of the operating costs of the ESB are attributed to the cost of fuel. The currency crisis in 1992–93 added almost £60 million to the ESB's costs overnight through its effect on fuel and other costs and on level of debt in foreign currencies. The current wage cost of the GTO area alone amounts to £17 million in overtime costs or 22 per cent, or 40 per cent of the total ESB payroll costs for only 25 per cent of the staff.

Public Policy

The government's policy on ESB prices is currently restraining the organisation. Unit cost has remained constant since 1984 because of a pledge by the company of no further price increase for three years. This pledge in effect continued until 1995. However, during this time, the Government has increased VAT on electricity from 0 per cent in 1989 to a current level of 16.5 per cent. Along with this, the effect of cumulative consumer price indices from 1989 at 3–4 per cent each year has meant that the ESB has absorbed inflationary costs of 25 per cent, making its prices among the most competitive in Europe.

Human Resource Management within the ESB

Management Values and Culture

The ESB is essentially a bureaucracy displaying many characteristics of inflexibility, strong discipline, rules and procedures, slowness to change, and ineffective decision-making. Such a culture is difficult to change. However, in the mid-1980s the company attempted a culture shift towards greater emphasis on customer service. It spelt out this message in clear unambiguous terms and spent two years travelling the country selling the message and winning commitment to it from staff. This initiative was by and large successful.

The current chief executive is highly supportive of cultural change and of the need to win staff commitment to such a change, and to develop staff. He has stated: "we can buy the technology, we can build the systems, but developing our people is the competitive edge in the 1990s."

People Management Philosophy

Human resource management within the ESB has as its principal aim the task of ensuring the optimum use of human resources to the benefit of the company, community, etc. The company values its employees by nurturing them in an organisation that has relatively high salaries, high job-security levels and recognises many trade unions. In practice, however, the following characteristics are in evidence.

- There is heavy reliance on comprehensive agreements between unions and management.

- There is considerable confrontation with unions and the interaction has been reactive rather than proactive.

- Promotions tend to be internal, based on length of service.

- There is an inflexible single-skilled workforce.

- Participation councils have proven to be an ineffective mechanism for improving communications.

- The tradition of trade unionism in the ESB is one of looking after the aspirations of its members even to the detriment of the company, and taking an adversarial stance towards management.

Training and Development

The ESB has a large well-established training and development department employing 120 staff. It is divided into electrical training; mechanical training; IT; management/supervisory/personal skills training; strategy section; and design section. The strategy and design sections were set up in 1991 to improve needs identification, design, and quality assurance systems, working closely with the line.

In looking at the evolution of training within the ESB it is useful to divide its progress into three stages. Stage one occurred in the 1970s. Training was seen in terms of direct training. It was not linked strategically to the ESB goals and objectives. In 1973–74 training was largely suspended.

Stage two came about in the mid-1980s. Training became more professional. It started to support corporate strategy. In this era, programmes such as Customer Service Phases 1 and 2 were run involving 3,800 staff. This was the first ESB-wide, corporate programme where training was seen to support the ESB business needs strategically.

Programmes for senior managers were also run in the late 1980s. During these programmes all managers attended a three-week modular programme, with substantial supporting projects. The training was supported by a faculty comprising members from University College Dublin and senior ESB managers who also lectured on the programme. The thrust of the programmes was strategy formulation and strategy implementation. The seeds for a training and development function linked to corporate strategy and line involvement were sown.

Stage three came about in 1992 when a task force on training and development was initiated. The Task Force Group consisted of representatives drawn from ESB management and Anderson Consulting (US). The group interviewed 360 staff from all areas of the business, spoke to senior managers, directors, chief executive, unions, etc. Its brief was to see how training and development could meet the current and future needs of the company, how it could be delivered more efficiently, and how equality of opportunity might be promoted. Five key issues were identified:

- Insufficient line-management ownership and involvement in training and development

- Non-recognition of the strategic importance of training and development

- Lack of (internal) consistency in the design and development of training programmes

- Need to further equality, remove career barriers, etc.

- Need to meet the large demands for training in ESB.

The strategies agreed by the directors to address the first three issues in the report were to gain greater line involvement in training and development, promote greater top management support for training and development, commence a new partnership between trainers and line managers in the design and delivery of training and development, and refocus the training and development function on improving performance in the company.

The status of this report within the ESB is significant. It got full board and chief executive approval, and a committee of directors was set up to guide its implementation. The framework for managing training in the company was developed directly from the Task Force Report. The range of staff consulted, the top management support, and the quality of the task force team all lent weight to its findings.

The need for individual development plans has been recognised by both managers and staff within the organisation. Such a system was put into effect in 1992. The plan is drawn up by the manager or supervisor and the individual, and addresses training and development from three perspectives: the business needs, the day-to-day operational needs and the individual needs. The plan is action-oriented, setting out how and when identified training and development needs will be addressed.

Succession Planning and Promotion Patterns

Traditionally, succession planning was carried out on an informal basis, with no formal record of succession candidates for management positions, or the skills profile necessary to undertake specific roles. As a result, no long-term view was taken of future management requirements, or of the individual requirements of candidates. In terms of promotion policies, positions are generally filled internally. Jobs are advertised internally, specifying the basic requirements. Such requirements generally preclude staff who are more than two grades below the grade being advertised from applying. This has the effect of producing promotions patterns which result in individuals serving many years in the same position.

Workforce Characteristics

These are very varied: on the one hand, the organisation has considerable expertise, skills, etc. The average age of the workforce in the ESB is 43 years, with only 15 per cent having third-level qualifications. With an older workforce, staff are conditioned in a certain way, which may not be very conducive to flexibility, retraining, etc. Such characteristics pose significant challenges in the future in terms of planning change. There are many primary and secondary labour markets within the organisation.

The Reward System

The reward system in the ESB has traditionally been a set wage or salary for a given position independent of performance. The Gleeson Report recommended the introduction of a bonus scheme for senior managers, based on performance. This was implemented in 1986. The ESB Charter introduced in 1991 indicates that pay and conditions will be fair and equitable and designed to attract the best people and retain the million. It stresses intrinsic and extrinsic rewards. Extrinsic rewards include generous annual leave, sick leave, promotion, staff welfare, etc. It centres around high levels of pay, but not linked to performance. The ESB has had more success here than with the management of intrinsic rewards. Job satisfaction is low because of the company's rules, procedures and red tape. The culture of overtime is slowly being changed, with a gradual reduction in overtime levels being managed towards an eventual target of zero.

The Future of the ESB

According to management, the ESB is in good shape and can face the next ten years and the single market with confidence. The company is competitive in terms of average European electricity prices. Up to 1986 the company was very much out of line with the rest of Europe. However in the past ten years it has made considerable reductions in price for both the industrial and private users. There is a strong corporate commitment to contain prices and keep the company competitive. A number of challenges are however presented:

- To remain competitive the company has had to tackle internal costs. One step was the reduction in staff from 13,000 to 10,000. Previously, the company had not seen any real change along staff lines since 1931.

- Debt is being monitored more closely. It is a costly business financing £1.3 billion in loans and so, to this end, in 1993 the company restructured its whole portfolio and now has 96 per cent of total debt in fixed-interest pound borrowings which were bought when interest rates were at their lowest.

- The company has closed off foreign currency risk. It now has a very attractive treasury operation but it needs careful monitoring.

Confidence and a switch in priorities are the key elements to the ESB's new external investment strategy. Greater emphasis is being put on the profit involved, in a belief that social good will ensue.

- A deficit of £.5 million for 1987 was turned into a surplus of £4.5 million by 1990. Total indebtedness also continues to fall and is now at £1.3 billion or 65 per cent of net assets.

- A sub-sea electricity interconnector between Britain and Ireland linked internationally with the European grid is now feasible. While it could cost the ESB £150 million, it would give the country the ability to sell as well as to buy electricity.

- As an alternative to privatisation, any new power stations being built, will be built by Irish construction companies, with the result that the ESB will just be a buyer of units of electricity. Commercially, the ESB remains a formidable cash generator, with net funds in 1992 of £101.4 million.

The company has potential for large profits. However, its does face some daunting problems. Over the next 10 years, while servicing its massive debt of over £1 billion, it will also have to invest heavily in new plant. The scale will depend on demand requirement which is at present increasing at a rate of 6 per cent per year. The total capital requirement estimate is said to be around £2.2 billion, £600 million of which will be needed purely for environmental requirements. With nearly a 6 per cent growth level at present, debt could increase to £2.4 billion. This could be exacerbated by adverse interest and currency rate movements. If the company could manage to keep the demand growth rate down to 3 per cent, no significant investment would be required by the year 2000, and debt would not exceed the present £1.3 billion. The challenge for the company in the next 10 years will be to keep growth down to about 3 per cent without hindering national economic prosperity. The company believes that this rate will be maintained through better work practices, better equipment in factories, and a campaign to promote efficient use of energy by all customers.

Demand management is only one feature of the ESB's future strategy. The company is looking at the range of fuels available. Coal represents 42 per cent of the company's energy requirements, gas 34 per cent, and oil represents 10 per cent, down from 70 per cent in the early 1970s. The ESB has to buy its gas from Bord Gáis and has no say in either the price or the quality, so the company firmly believes in the idea of building a commercial pipeline to the UK to tap into North Sea gas. Another restriction on the ESB is that it is obliged to buy its peat from Bord na Móna at prices determined by the Department of Energy, so electricity interconnection with the UK is being actively pursued.

The "Station Performance Incentive Programme", introduced in 1991, was designed to get current utilisation of plants up from 78 per cent to 82 per cent through cutting maintenance times and streamlining production. With a five-year lead time for building new stations, the aim is to get more output across the national generation grid, while at the same time managing growth through customer initiatives in the energy-saving area. Incentives of 6 per cent of income in lump sum are being offered to employees for improving output.

The ESB's network is getting old, and there has been very little investment in new power stations or plants for the past decade. Of the £1.3 billion needed up to 1997, half will go toward replacing and upgrading the supply network. About £300 million will go to the refurbishment of old plants, and some peat stations are near the end of their lives. Instead of borrowing, the company hopes that a price increase will raise 30 per cent of the bill.

Management and union negotiators faced an uphill battle to secure a final workable agreement on the implementation of the proposals arising from the autumn ESB Cost and Competitiveness Review in time for the 31 May deadline set by the Government. The trade unions remained highly sceptical about the detailed proposals for changes in work practices identified by McKinsey Consultants in the run up to the unveiling of the CCR proposals. Final agreement had not been reached by December 1995.

"What McKinsey is proposing is an amalgam of all the best practices in all the utilities. This is fine in theory but totally different in practice", according to Denis Rowan, ATGWU Assistant branch secretary. Many savings in the area of labour costs, he argues, could result in costs elsewhere. "In America, they run plants until they stop. In the ESB, however, much preventative maintenance work is carried out with the aim of extending the life of the plants."

According to Rowan, whose union represents 3,700 ESB employees and is easily the largest in the ESB group of unions: "We would not agree that a reduction by 2,900 in the ESB work force is realistic". However, he refuses to tie himself to a figure which he would consider to be realistic from his union's point of view.

It may be difficult to put together an appropriate redundancy package. It is generally accepted that the value of the pay-off will work out at £80,000–£90,000 per departing staff member.

The Government will be looking carefully at the severance package on offer in an effort to ensure that there are no knock-on effects for employees elsewhere in the public sector. However, the employees will no doubt be keen to see that their pay-offs match those available in Telecom Éireann. Telecom has been offering people nine weeks per year of service. This will be difficult to match as ESB union sources concede. In fact, the unions are less likely to go to the wire on the question of severance pay. Here, their interests do not coincide exactly with those of their members. After all, a highly generous package, leading to a huge take up by their members would work against their interest in maintaining their membership base.

The real issue as far at the unions are concerned relates to the work practices to be enjoyed, or endured, by those remaining behind. Apart from the added production burdens placed on a diminished complement of workers, the unions fear that a downgrading in craft skills would result from the introduction of the new ESB craft apprenticeship which is based on the US model. Unions such as the TEEU, which represents craft workers throughout the organisation, are particularly fearful about the erosion of the skills of their members.

Clearly the idea of a competitive internal market within the ESB as a means of equipping the company to survive in a more competitive external world has yet to be taken fully on board by many on the union side.

Yet management must press for reforms including the elimination of demarcation lines, and it has made the idea of the multi-skilled utility worker one of the cornerstones of the CCR reform proposals. Management insists that the retraining will be to a high standard, with issues in respect of certification and recognition of skills having already been threshed out. The unions, however, will be pressing for a properly funded retraining package as a condition for agreement on the restructuring sought. Union officials also sound a warning note about the political consequences of full implementation of the McKinsey proposals in respect of manpower levels. Even without complete closure of power stations, there will be a major loss of employment in areas completely dependent economically on the ESB. Implementing the Cost and Competitiveness Review proposals will have the same impact as a major hospital closure programme.

The issue of the replacement of outdated power plants could prove a thorn in the side of the parties to the ESB restructuring talks. Should an outside consortium win the contract to operate the proposed new £100 million peat-fired station in the midlands, this would create added problems on the industrial relations side for the ESB.

In some union circles, it is assumed that the ESB will eventually operate this station, in which case the plant would be expected to take in staff from near-by power plants coming to the end of their life. However, the EU, as a condition for providing grant aid for the plant, will insist on an open tendering process. The unions claim that it is incongruous to be embarking on a major electricity expansion plan while, at the same time, shedding thousands of workers.

Management sources claim that time is not on anyone's side, with both a price increase and the go-ahead to phases two and three of the Poolbeg project now urgently required. The Department of Energy counters that the ESB has little time to get its house in order before the Irish electricity market opens up. Each side in the process is in a position to do grave damage to the other. The clout of the ESB unions was apparent for all to see back in 1991. At local level, ESB workers also possess considerable political clout. The Government too has its share of cards to play. It can go on withholding the price increase sought by the ESB and defer a decision on Poolbeg while paving the way to outside competition. Little wonder that ESB management is desperate for a positive outcome to the talks and for implementation of the restructuring proposals to begin in earnest.

If the ESB can bring it off against the odds, then it will indeed have achieved a milestone in the history of Irish industrial relations, while proving that there is life, yet, in the Irish state sector.

APPENDIX

Figure A: Customer Numbers, 1990–94

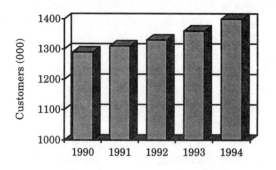

Figure B: Peak Load Trends, 1990–94

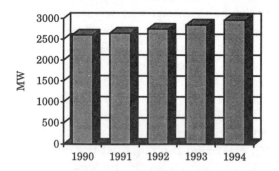

Figure C: System Demand Trends, 1990–94

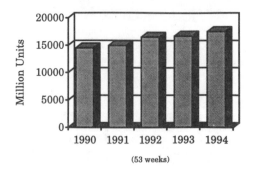

(53 weeks)

Figure D: Structure of ESB's Subsidiary Companies

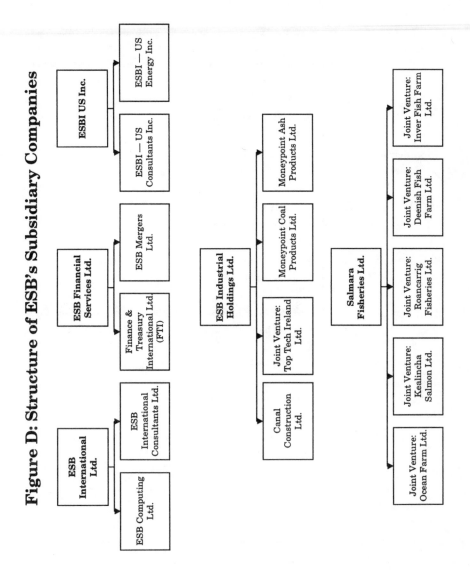

Subsidiary and Associated Undertakings

Subsidiary Under- takings	Registered Office	Group Share %	Nature of Business
ESB International Ltd.	Stephen's Court 18–21 St Stephen's Green Dublin 2	100	International Engi- neering, Consultancy & Computing Services
ESB Engineering Ltd.	Stephen's Court 18–21 St Stephen's Green Dublin 2	100	Engineering
ESB Engineering (Overseas) Ltd.	Stephen's Court 18–21 St Stephen's Green Dublin 2	100	Engineering
ESBI Contracting Ltd.	Stephen's Court 18–21 St Stephen's Green Dublin 2	100	Contracting
ESBI Consultants Ltd.	Stephen's Court 18–21 St Stephen's Green Dublin 2	100	Consultancy
ESBI Engineering UK Ltd.	122 London Road King- ston on Thames Surrey KP2 6QJ Great Britain	100	Engineering and Gen- eral Consultancy
EPIN European Pro- curement Information Network Ltd.	Stephen's Court 18–21 St Stephen's Green Dublin 2	100	Marketing Software
ESBI Computing Ltd.	Stephen's Court 18–21 St Stephen's Green Dublin 2	95	Computer Services
Civil, Environmental and Construction En- gineering Ltd.	16–18 St Stephen's Green Dublin 2	100	Civil Engineering
Computer Plus Ltd.	27 Lower Fitzwilliam St Dublin 2	100	Software Development
Salmara Holdings Ltd.	39 Merrion Square Dublin 2	100	Commercial Fisheries
Salmara Fisheries Ltd.	39 Merrion Square Dublin 2	100	Commercial Fisheries

Subsidiary Under-takings	Registered Office	Group Share %	Nature of Business
Kealincha Salmon Ltd.	39 Merrion Square Dublin 2	100	Fish Farming
Fleet Fish Farm Ltd.	39 Merrion Square Dublin 2	100	Fish Farming
ESB International Services Ltd.	37 Upper Fitzwilliam St Dublin 2	100	Financial Consultancy and Computer Services
FTI Finance	Russell Court St Stephen's Green Dublin 2	82	Financial Management Consultancy
ESB Fund Managers Ltd.	37 Upper Fitzwilliam St Dublin 2	100	Funds Management
Finance Electric Ltd.	37 Upper Fitzwilliam St Dublin 2	100	Customer Credit
ESB Industrial Hold-ings Ltd.	27 Lower Fitzwilliam St Dublin 2	100	Industrial and Com-mercial Projects
Power Generation Technology Snd Bhd	Wisma Cyclecarri 288 Jalan Raja Laut 50350 Kuala Lumpur Malaysia	100	Power Generation Contracting

Associated Under-takings	Registered Office	Group Share %	Nature of Business
Irish Salmon Produc-ers Group Ltd.	Kilkieran Connemara Co. Galway	37	Salmon Marketing
Top Tech Ireland Ltd.	Poppintree Ind. Estate Finglas Dublin 11	50	Supply of special proc-esses to Computer Industry
Sevent Industries Ltd.	27 Lower Fitzwilliam St Dublin 2	49	Electrical Distribution Material Manufacture
ESBI Energy Company	2800 Post Oak Road Houston Texas 77056 USA	50	Engineering Consul-tancy

Associated Undertakings	Registered Office	Group Share %	Nature of Business
Transpower Ltd.	Stephen's Court 18–21 St Stephen's Green Dublin 2	50	Development of Independent Power Projects
Seeboard International Ltd.	Grand Avenue, Hove East Sussex BN3 2LS Great Britain	49	Consultancy
ESB/ETV Ltd.	Szecheny 1 RKP 3 H 1054 Budapest V Hungary	50	Engineering Consultancy Services
Hoermann Security System Ltd.	Mahon Industrial Estate Blackrock Cork	21.6	Electronics Manufacturing
Corby Power Ltd.	Mitchell Road Phoenix Parkway Corby Northants. NN17 IQ7 Great Britain	20	Power Generation

Source: Company reports and interviews with company personnel.

Questions

1. Critically evaluate the current strengths and weaknesses of the Electricity Supply Board.

2. What factors triggered the restructuring that started in the late 1980s?

3. Evaluate the human resource policies and practices within the ESB. How have they facilitated and/or inhibited organisational change?

4. What strategic implications would arise from a decision to privatise the ESB?

16

Telecom Éireann

Evolution of the Organisation

Despite huge improvements in its structures and services, the Irish public has become accustomed to complaining about Telecom Éireann. Stories of delays in installing lines and excessively high telephone bills were very much part of our national culture during the 1970s and early 1980s, and it will take some time for the company to shake of this image. Regardless of this, the national telecommunications service is now a fundamentally different operation from what it was a decade ago. Telecom has become a much less bureaucratic organisation in the eight years since its split from the Department of Communications; it has better management structures; it has put a greater emphasis on training and development; and, most noticeably, it has made a huge investment in the national telecommunications infrastructure. But the complaints still come, a frequent one being that city dwellers get a better deal than their rural counterparts. However, as the company is quick to point out, it costs much more to connect a remote location, yet the customer involved pays the same annual rent and installation cost as everyone else. Telecom maintains a network of 6,000 pay phones throughout the country, half of which do not pay their way.

The former Telecom chief executive, Fergus McGovern, is known to be a man who thinks carefully before he speaks, and does not waste words. Born in Co. Cavan, he joined Radio Éireann in 1953 as a balance and control engineer. From there he went to the Department of Post and Telegraphs as an engineer assistant. Visits to stations around the country gave him a grounding in the practical operation of the network. Next, he went to Waterford where he was given his first managerial responsibility with 100 staff and substantial assets under his supervision. Fergus McGovern had risen through the ranks to the position of engineer-in-chief by the time Telecom was established in 1984. When its first chief executive, Tom Byrne, resigned in 1986, Fergus McGovern was an obvious successor. He held that position until 1994.

In March 1994 the company announced that the new chief executive to replace the retiring Fergus McGovern was the former British Telecom executive Alfie Kane. He joined the company on a five-year contract with his remuneration well in excess of £70,000. Mr Kane — whose parents are from Donegal — was born in Limavady Co. Derry, in 1944. He is a graduate of Queen's University where he studied electrical engineering. He joined British Telecom over 20 years ago, where he worked in a variety of posts, including marketing, sales and systems development. He was chief executive of British Telecom Northern Ireland from 1984 to 1988. From 1991 to 1994 he was director of BT Operations, Worldwide network, managing 25 million lines. It is this experience and these achievements that will be of greatest benefit to Telecom, as he joined the company at a critical stage.

The decade leading up to Telecom's formation was a period characterised by industrial relations conflicts, underinvestment in the infrastructure and poor morale. The strikes in the late 1970s changed the organisation fundamentally in the following ways:

- They inspired the breakaway, along with An Post, from the Department of Post and Telegraphs. They also brought about a change in the way that the organisation was to be run.

- There was an acceptance that the authoritarian style of management would have to go and a more participatory style introduced.

- There would have to be a rationalisation of the grading structures in order to make the organisation work as a team.

Figure 16.1 outlines the organisation structure of Telecom Éireann.

Figure 16.1: Organisation Structure of Telecom Éireann

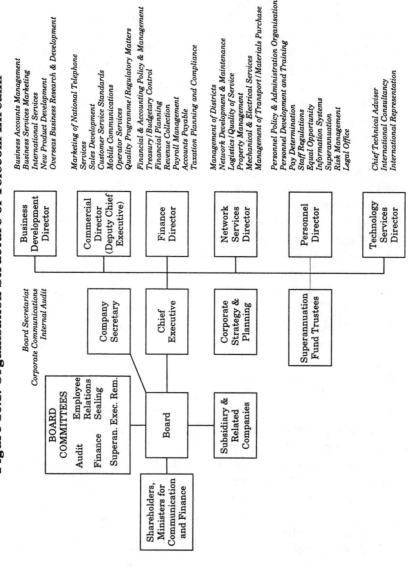

Strategy for Future Survival — Seeking a Partner

Overstaffed and burdened with £1 billion in debt, the company is desperate for investment in an industry where technology is rapidly changing. Owing to deregulations in Europe, the company has to face the prospect of competing with some of the world's largest telecommunication companies. Recent figures show that Telecom Éireann is one of the least efficient telecommunications companies in Europe, despite reducing its staff numbers considerably over the past 10 years, and increasing productivity. In Europe the average operator has 70 employees per 10,000 lines, Telecom has over 100. The level of telephones per member of the population is the tenth lowest in Europe at just over 30 per cent. Two factors in its favour are that it has the fourth lowest waiting list for new customers and it has the third most modern telephone network in Europe.

However, in order to maintain this network, the company will have to invest up to £800 million over the next five years to keep the system updated, which works out at between £160 million and £180 million annually on investment in new technology. Telecom Éireann's customers pay on average £704 per year for the telephone line, 28 per cent more than BT's bill of £550 and 30 per cent more than European users' average cost per year of £543. It is the intention of Telecom over the next few years to shed another 2,000 of a current workforce of 12,000. The company is also aiming to increase productivity by up to 50 per cent and to improve its efficiency ratios. Telecom Éireann has 78 telephone lines per employee, compared to British Telecom and Bell's regional companies in the US, which have a ratio of 216 and 258 per employee. Telecom is not making sufficient progress fast enough. The ratio of operating costs to turnover has been static at 57 per cent for four fiscal years, and the debt/equity ratio is very high at 250 per cent. The wage bill reached £263 million in the year to April 1993, compared to £232 million four years earlier, despite the ongoing rationalisation process to reduce costs.

At present, there is strong competition for international and long-distance calls, even though the domestic telephone service is not scheduled to be open to outsiders until 2003. In November 1993, the government informed Telecom that it would no longer have a monopoly on mobile phones, and issued a licence to a rival operator, with Independent Newspapers and 98FM chief executive Denis O'Brien expressing an interest. The most likely contenders are said to include the international telecommunications company Cable and Wireless, an Irish operator ESAT Cellular, UK mobile operator Vodaphone, and Independent Groups 50-per-cent-owned cable company Prince's Holdings. At the beginning of 1994, the go-ahead was given to ESAT Telecom, headed by 98FM boss Denis O'Brien, to lease lines from Telecom Éireann and to operate its own telephone service offering cheaper rates.

Many of Telecom's competitors — AT&T in the US, British Telecom, Cable and Wireless — are offering a low-cost high-technology international service, and most of the European operators are privatised or considering the idea. Telecom needs cheap access to international telephone lines, and it is therefore under immense pressure to keep updated on the rapidly evolving tele-communications technology. Although the company will not face the full glare of competition until 2003, the pace of change in the industry is such that for Telecom to compete and survive it needs a strong partner. The company is under pressure at the moment because of its high debt and high-cost base. Alliances, privatisa-tion and competition are currently characteristics of the industry throughout Europe. Ireland and Telecom cannot afford to be left behind, especially as Telecom Éireann is one of the small players in the field. Telecom maintains its monopoly on transmission and switching facilities, but companies such as ESAT and others can lease lines and provide external communications to companies at much lower prices. Telecom stands to lose considerable amounts of money with greater competition from companies outside the state because the EU intends to allow for an alternative to Tele-com's main transmission system, so companies such as the ESB, which maintains its own telecommunications network, will be able to compete directly with Telecom.

Telecom has, over the years, used its profitable international revenues to subsidise cheap local calls, but with the deregula-tion strategy now taking place in Europe, this could not continue and the company has had to restructure its charges radically. In September 1993, the company introduced time charges for local calls, which led to much dissatisfaction, but in fact these price-rebalancing changes have worked to the benefit of the consumer and the community in general. As predicted, customers have re-arranged their phoning patterns, making less calls during the day and more during the cheaper off-peak times and at the weekend. The company's revenue has not suffered either, be-cause of the increased international calls at a cheaper rate — in fact, the international traffic is now growing at 28 per cent over-all. The company, as a result of the changes, is winning back market share on international routes, and there are indications that Telecom's market share has increased considerably. This was one of the key objectives of the change to prices in September 1994. The company's competitiveness has been enhanced by the recent introduction of a volume discount of as much as 30 per cent for international calls. The net result of these price changes is that the company is on target with its budget and, more importantly, the company's considerable debt could be reduced by some £50 million.

Having got its pricing strategy right, the next step is to find a suitable partner. This has been a focus for the company for some time, with Cable and Wireless making an initial approach in the past few years. Taking the lead from this, Telecom sought the assistance of Monitor Consultants, Boston, to advise on a possible alliance. Many contenders are said to be interested — not only Cable and Wireless, but AT&T is also being mentioned as a suitable contender. The latter is the world's largest international telephone company and is considered the best for Telecom. AT&T's advanced technology and global network, like Cable and Wireless, would be of immeasurable benefit to Telecom. But like Cable and Wireless, if AT&T were going to link up with Telecom, certain conditions would be attached to the deal, including board representation; the placing of personnel in key operational positions within Telecom; and some financial stake, such as an equity interest in Telecom.

The International Competition — Potential Partners

AT&T

AT&T (American Telephone & Telegraph) has annual revenues exceeding £114 billion, and like many companies these days, recently announced a reduction in staff by 15,000 over the next two years from its present figure of 95,000 — a move that will save the company a yearly sum of £643 million. The company's presence in Europe is not extensive, and in order to strengthen its position, it is seeking alliances with some of the main European operators such as Deutsche Telekom, and also the Dutch and French equivalents. Last year it launched its "Worldsource" programme, which is a set of customised international business services. The corporation's goal is to provide a "one-stop-shop" to the global operations of large companies — offering them such services as the latest in data and voice facilities and a single point of contact — and ultimately to manage and integrate its customers' networks.

Cable and Wireless

Cable and Wireless has been discussing taking a stake in Telecom Éireann for some time. It could also be a case of Telecom seeking a suitable partner before it is exposed to the full force of EU telecommunications liberalisation. Talks have been taking place about the possibility of a joint venture or a strategic alliance. Cable and Wireless is the fifth largest telecommunications company in the world and first began a detailed study of Telecom to see what could be gained from some from of alliance for both parties. Telecom was not unknown to it because Cable and Wireless has a factory in Tallaght and entered into a deal in 1989 with Telecom whereby Telecom could feed telephone calls into Cable and Wireless's transatlantic cable. It had delayed its presentation of a proposal to Telecom for a number of reasons, the main one being the arrival of Telecom's new chief executive, Alfie Kane. Meanwhile, Telecom was undertaking its own homework, with Monitor Consultants reporting that the preferred partner was AT&T, the world's largest telecommunications company

Cable and Wireless is in a much stronger position than Telecom. For the tax year to March 1994, the company had a £4 billion turnover and £100 million pre-tax profits. It is the third largest company in Europe, worth about £12 billion on the stock market. It operates in over 50 countries worldwide and employs up to 39,000 people. In some of the countries in which it has operations, it operates in partnership with the local telephone operators, usually the government. In other countries, it operates other services such as providing links. The company's main business is its 57 per cent Hong Kong Telecommunications, which has a monopoly in this British colony until 1997, as regards domestic calls, and this is extended to 2003 for international calls. The company was set up in the UK over 120 years ago and is at present under the executive chairmanship of Lord Young, the former secretary of State for the Thatcher government.

In addition to the above, the company owns 80 per cent of the BT rival company, Mercury, 25 per cent of an Australian telecom-

munications company, as well as monopolies in Jamaica and Bar-
bados. It also operates similar projects in Eastern Europe and
Moscow, and has a strategic link with Bell Canada which owns
the other 20 per cent of Mercury. Cable and Wireless owns 20 per
cent of Bell Canada's UK cable interests. In contrast to Telecom,
Cable and Wireless's gearing is running at just 13 per cent; its
pre-tax profits in 1994 stand at £918 million; its net assets are
just over £4 billion and the company intends to spend more than
£3 billion between 1994 and 1996. Of this, £1.3 billion will be
spent on the further expansion of Mercury Communications,
£0.99 billion in Hong Kong and £0.2 billion in Jamaica. However,
the company's real strength is its Global Digital Highway. This is
a multinational communications system, and Cable and Wireless
is the only company in the world to have its own in-house international telecommunications network.

For Telecom, the important thing is to gain access to the Cable
and Wireless network. Telecom is thinking in terms of technology,
and if it did get access to such a network it would be saving a lot
of capital investment. The company would also be provided with
cheaper international links. Cable and Wireless is thought to be
in the process of finalising a proposal which would offer Telecom
£400 million to acquire 25 per cent of the company. This option
may also involve a joint-venture management company being established by both parties to operate the telephone network here.

British Telecom and MCI

British Telecom and MCI are also said to be possible contenders.
BT is the world's fourth largest telecommunications company,
with a turnover of £13.6 billion and a £2 billion pre-tax profit for
the year ended to March. This company has also been utilising a
staff-reduction strategy since its privatisation in the mid-1980s. It
currently has 165,000 staff worldwide and this is to be reduced to
142,000 by 1995. Last year, BT entered a deal with the world's
sixth largest telecommunications company, MCI, by purchasing a
20 per cent interest.

Because Cable and Wireless is not the only interested party, it is
believed that Telecom is talking to at least four other companies
about a possible alliance. However, it is believed that the burden
that the £1.6 billion valuation and the £400 million offer would
place on the 11,370 employee company may be inappropriate. At

present, the company is in the process of linking up its various operations throughout the world through the use of fibre optic lines, placed underground and under the sea. The great benefit of this linking process is that telephone calls, computer data, television pictures and many other signals can be sent at the same time, without the need for regular boosters to maintain the linking process, as required with conventional telephone wires. AT&T, MCI and British Telecom are also focusing on a global network strategy.

A Strategic Alliance

AT&T's size alone would put off many contenders in the race for an alliance with Telecom. AT&T already handles 60 per cent of Telecom's US business and it has a manufacturing plant in Co. Wicklow. More importantly, AT&T was already in the process of negotiations with Deutsche Telekom, and with French Telecom about a possible alliance. If this came to fruition, it would result in the alliance of the world's three largest telecommunications companies. These talks have since faltered and from a competitive point of view, the European Commission would not look favourably on such a formidable alliance. However, if Telecom had become part of this group, it would have strengthened its base considerably.

For Telecom, the benefits of a strategic alliance would include the following:

- From Telecom's viewpoint such an arrangement would be very beneficial if only to relieve the company of the £50 million bill that it has to meet annually in order to upgrade its network, while at the same time not adding to the already not inconsiderable debt of £1 billion.

- It would put Telecom in a position to compete more effectively, especially in the high-yield business traffic area, and also with the issuing of a second mobile-phone licence.

- Cable and Wireless's global operations could make better use of the expertise among Telecom's 12,700 staff. Four out of five people in the world are not within access of a telephone, which offers other companies like Cable and Wireless great potential for growth.

From Telecom's point of view, it is not going to be rushed into a deal with anyone. The decision will ultimately be made by the government and the shareholders, but the recommendation from Telecom's board will be the vital factor. If Telecom were to form an alliance with Cable and Wireless, the trade unions would not be very pleased. Cable and Wireless only formally recognises unions or staff groups in half of its 60 companies. Telecom is the largest state employer and is overstaffed owing to the less labour-intensive equipment it is installing. The company has tried to reduce the number of layoffs required, by setting up spin-off joint-venture subsidiaries like Minitel and Eirpage, but this strategy has not worked and Telecom is seeking 2,000 voluntary redundancies over the next few years. Cable and Wireless has also been reducing staff numbers to minimise costs.

It is also worth noting that Telecom has expressed some dissatisfaction over the role of the Department of Communications and its wish for the setting up of an independent regulatory body to oversee the operations of Telecom and other such operators. It appears that Telecom is unhappy with the dual role that the department plays — that of owner and regulator — and would prefer the separation of these two roles, which would allow the company greater flexibility and freedom to run its business on a more commercial basis. Like most companies, Telecom would like to be able to exercise more control over its pricing policy, and a more effective employment policy which would allow it to offer workers an attractive redundancy package to entice sufficient numbers of the right type of employees to leave the company. It appears that the government is considering such a possibility, and from Telecom's point of view the sooner an independent body is set up to regulate the industry impartially, the better.

Telecom's Diversification Strategy

Irish Telecommunications Investment plc (ITI)

This is a wholly-owned treasury and investment financing subsidiary of Telecom, whose purpose is to raise finance both on the domestic, and foreign markets and to provide for Telecom treasury and debt-management services. Recently, this company has moved into international finance by establishing a wholly-owned subsidiary ITI — International Finance, to provide treasury consultancy services to clients overseas. ITI has a shareholding interest in Investel, and entered a joint venture arrangement with MATAV (the Hungarian telecommunications company), in 1991.

Telecom Éireann Information Systems Ltd (TÉIS)

TÉIS is another wholly-owned subsidiary, with responsibility for the marketing and sales of voice and data telecommunications customer equipment. Among the products sold include modern multiplexing and networking equipment.

Eirecable Ltd. / Cablelink Ltd.

Eirecable is the wholly-owned subsidiary established for the purpose of holding the 60 per cent share that Telecom has in Cablelink, which was acquired in late 1990 — the other 40 per cent is held by RTE. Cablelink is involved in the distribution of multichannel television and radio services through cable systems in many parts of the country. Recently, the company entered discussions on the future of this subsidiary with Time Warner (TW) of the US, one of the largest communications companies in the world. The discussions focused on the exchange of information about engineering and programming. Telecom invested in Cablelink in June 1990 by paying a total of £40 million to RTE, which then reduced its shareholding from 80 per cent to 40 per cent, and to AIB-subsidiary Allied Combined Trust, which sold its entire 20 per cent. Telecom has an option to purchase a further 15 per cent from RTE for £13 million.

Telecom Éireann (US) Ltd.

This subsidiary is responsible for the marketing of Telecom in North America.

Eirtrade Ltd.

Eirtrade Ltd. has responsibility for the development, delivery and support of electronic trading services. Its services include data interchange and Eirmail 400 electronic mail.

Golden Pages Ltd.

Telecom has a 49 per cent share in this company, which produces the classified telephone directories under licence, and it also has responsibility for the production of the alphabetical telephone directories and the fax directory.

Broadcom Éireann Research Ltd.

Telecom has a 45 per cent share in Broadcom Éireann Research Ltd., which is jointly owned by L.M. Ericsson (45 per cent) and

Trinity College (19 per cent). It was established for the purpose of undertaking research into communications, in particular under the European Community RACE (Research for Advanced Communications in Europe) programme.

Eirpage Ltd.

This is a joint venture with Motorola Ireland Ltd., with Telecom holding a 51 per cent interest. It was established for the purpose of marketing a paging service nationwide.

Telecom Phone Watch Ltd.

Telecom Phone Watch Ltd. is a 50/50 joint venture with the NYNEX Corporation of New York to provide advanced home security and home management services in Ireland.

Minitel Communications Ltd.

Telecom has a 30 per cent share in Minitel Communications Ltd., an Irish–French joint venture set up in 1990 with AIB plc (20 per cent), Credit Lyonnais (20 per cent) and Intelmatique, a subsidiary of French Telecom (30 per cent). It was set up to provide videotext services to the business and domestic consumer and also to distribute low-cost Minitel sets.

INET Ltd.

INET Ltd. is a joint venture with PostGEM (an An Post subsidiary in which Telecom holds a 50 per cent share). It was established to provide electronic access for the clearance of customs documentation through the Revenue Commissioners Automated Entry Processing System.

The Appendix provides details of Telecom's business activities.

The past 10 years have shown changing financial fortunes for Telecom. In 1986, a loss of £24.3 million was made, representing over 5 per cent of income. This compared with a loss in the previous 15 months of £82.7 million or 17 per cent of income. This improvement resulted from growth of business, an emphasis on cost containment and price increases, favourable interest and currency movements. Major cost reductions were undertaken, with staff numbers being reduced by 1,400 or 8 per cent. The telecommunications business grew by 10 per cent, resulting in a substantial reduction in unit costs. Total debt for the company was a major burden standing at £1,100 million, giving an unfavourable debt/equity ration of 4.7 per cent, compared to 3.8 per cent for the previous year. The price increase at the end of the period averaged 3.5 per cent, well below the inflation rate. It is worth noting that since 1983, telecommunication charges have increased by 11 per cent, compared with a 20 per cent inflation. A total of £120 million was spent on capital investment.

Table 16.1: Financial Performance of Telecom

	1986	1987	1988	1989	1990	1991	1992	1993	1994	1995
	£m	£m	£m	£m	£m	£m	£m	£m	£m	£m
Turnover	467	516	553	621	704	782	788	814	871	979
Operating costs incl. depreciation	392	399	415	463	525	577	599	465	521	572
Operating Profit	75	117	138	158	179	205	189	196	173	152
Profit (loss)	(24)	(8)	17	53	79	94	91	50	80	74
Capital Expenditure	129	138	122	136	162	174	156	161	164	172
R.O.C. %	5.20	7.71	8.8	9.9	11.1	12.1	11.2	10.6		
Debt/Equity Ratio %	4.68	5.26	5.0	4.0	3.0	2.9	3.0	2.5	2.2	1.9
Total Debt	1,069	1,158	1,184	1,143	1,056	1,053	988	996	986	862
Number of Employees	15,850	15,080	14,560	14,270	14,215	13,544	13,325	13,099	13,069	12,662

In 1987, the company made a loss of £8.2 million, representing about 1.5 per cent of turnover. This compared to a loss of £24.3 million a year earlier, or over 5 per cent of turnover. If profits and losses caused by currency movements were excluded, the improvement (£41.6 million in 1986 to £4.8 million in 1987) would be more significant. Turnover was £516 million, an increase of 10 per cent. Most of this growth in business volume amounted to nearly 7 per cent, which was considered satisfactory given the economic climate at the time. Operating costs continued to fall relative to turnover from 69 per cent in the previous year to 63 per cent. There was an improvement in the utilisation of fixed assets, and the return on capital increased from 5.2 per cent to 7.7 per cent. The staff reduction programme continued, with numbers decreasing from 15,800 to 15,000. There was a major increase in the self-financing ratio and the company financed internally 50 per cent of the year's capital investment. Additional net borrowings amounted to £88 million, bringing total debt to £1,1588 million, which was too great a burden on the company, leaving it excessively exposed to interest and exchange-rate movements. Capital investment for the year amounted to £138 million.

In 1988, the company achieved a net profit of £17 million. This improvement was achieved through a combination of business growth and cost containment. Turnover for the year was £553 million, an increase of 7 per cent. There was no change in telephone charges so the increase was the result of growth in call traffic and in the customer base. Operating costs relative to turnover decreased from 63 per cent in 1987 to 59 per cent,. There was an increase in the utilisation of fixed assets and the return on capital increased from 7.7 per cent to 8.8 per cent. Staff numbers continued to be reduced falling from 15,100 to 14,600, with good productivity gains made. The self-financing ratio improved to 85 per cent up from 50 per cent for the previous year. Capital expenditure for the year was £122 million. The growth in net borrowings was down from £88 million to £26 million and total debt stood at £1,184 million.

In 1989, the company made a net profit of £53 million for the year or 9 per cent of turnover, which was edging closer to their target of 10 per cent. The improvement was caused by strong business growth and cost containment. Turnover was at £621 million, which represented an increase of 12 per cent, reflecting strong demand for telecommunications services and an improvement in the economic environment. Operating costs as a percentage of turnover were 59 per cent, remaining stable. Capital expenditure on network development and extensions amounted to £136 million, and was fully met from internally-generated funds, plus EU funding. The year saw an improvement in the utilisation of fixed assets and the return on capital increased from 8.8 per cent to 9.9 per cent. Staff numbers fell by 2 per cent to 14,270.

The year 1990 was an excellent one for the company, with net profit increasing by 50 per cent on the previous year to £79 million. Company debt was reduced by £88 million, and the company was able to finance a capital investment programme of £160 million almost entirely from internal resources. Turnover increased by 13 per cent to £704 million, and net profit at £79 million was over 11 per cent of turnover — the increase in turnover reflecting increased growth. Operating costs as a percentage of turnover fell to 57 per cent and 59 per cent the previous year. Capital investment was £162 million or 23 per cent of turnover, and there was considerable improvement in the utilisation of fixed assets, with the return on capital increasing to 11 per cent from 9.9 per cent. Staff were reduced to 14,215, and outstanding debt still stood at over £2 billion, with interest payments at almost £100 million per year. Demand for telephone services increased by 7 per cent over the previous year.

The following year, 1991, was also good for the company, with net profits increasing by 19 per cent to £94 million, representing 12 per cent of turnover, which increased by 11 per cent to £782 million, and capital investment totalled £174 million. A total dividend to the state of £35 million was declared. Financial costs were higher because of less favourable interest and currency movements, but the effect was limited by effective debt management. The return of capital improved was still low at 12.1 per cent — between 17 and 20 per cent is required. Capital expenditure of £174 million, or 22 per cent of turnover, was undertaken and financed entirely from internal resources. Staff numbers were reduced considerably from 14,215 to 13,544. Customers increased by 7 per cent to 893,000, and telephone traffic grew by 11 per cent.

The net profit for 1992 was £91 million, down £3 million on the previous year. This was considered satisfactory, having regard to the pricing package implemented in January when telephone charges were reduced by 8 per cent, a move which cost the company £50 million, and the impact of increased VAT. The increase in operating costs to £599 million was contained at 2 per cent and was the result of an effective debt-management policy. Financial debt charges fell by £13 million. Debt was reduced by £55 million and was now below the £1 billion figure. Capital expenditure was £156 million, and turnover for the year was £788 million, up from £782 in 1991. Operating profit was £189 million, down from £205 million a year earlier. Growth in traffic was 6 per cent, down from 11 per cent, and staff reductions continued to be made from 13,544 to 13,425.

In 1993, despite less favourable economic and financial conditions, the company had a record performance. Turnover increased by £26 million to £814 million, and operating profit was up 4 per cent to £196 million. However, net profit fell to £50 million as a result of the January 1993 currency realignment, which cost the company £44 million — otherwise, net profit would have stood at £94 million. Demand from new customers grew by 6.7 per cent, and growth in traffic was up to 10 per cent from the previous year's figure of 6 per cent. Operating costs were up on 1992 to £465 million, and the company's capital expenditure amounted to £161 million, up from £156 million in 1992.

Financial performance in the years 1994 and 1995 was satisfactory. Turnover continues to increase and now stands at £979 million. Overall profits were down in 1995 by some £6 million. However, capital expenditure in 1995 increased by £8 million. Eighty-eight per cent of turnover was generated domestically, the balance of 12 per cent being revenue from international telecommunications transfer and from staff working abroad. During the period 1993–95, group debt was reduced by £107 million, and the existing debt equity ratio has been achieved through a reduction in debt as well as growth in shareholders' funds.

Telecom's Management Strategies

Worker Involvement

Telecom Éireann has been one of the more innovative organisations in developing worker participation in management. Even before the establishment of the organisation, national and district monitoring committees had been set up as part of a productivity agreement. Subcommittees of these examined specific organisational topics, allowing employees their first taste of decision-making. Telecom's joint technology committee was largely responsible for the smooth introduction of digital equipment in the 1980s — a process that allowed cuts of up to 50 per cent on some exchanges.

A shared learning experience has been in operation since 1985 whereby management and staff consider projects that would be of benefit to the organisation. This has resulted in the formulation of customer-service teams, which carry out seminars and set up job-creation and presentation groups; and the completion of staff attitude surveys.

Promotion

Traditionally, the organisation has been composed of general civil servants, professional civil servants, engineers and telephonists/

supervisors. It was virtually unknown for any cross-over to take place between these grades. These essentially artificial boundaries made promotional opportunities difficult. This has now changed — provided that people have the competencies to do the job involved, they can move anywhere within the organisation. Promotion is now based on merit.

Management Development

Management Development has had a key role in changing the organisation over the past decade. During 1984–85 the organisation had to take a long, hard look at itself, and the outcome of this was the drawing up of four key aims for the organisation:

- The development of a capable and innovative management team

- The creation, through leadership skills, of a confident workforce

- The placing of emphasis on customer orientation at every level within the organisation

- The achievement of commercial viability.

The Irish Management Institute has been heavily involved in the management-development process at the company, focusing on both junior and senior management. Between 1988 and 1990 the IMI was jointly involved with the company in devising a senior management-development programme for the top 250 managers in the company. This covered such areas as leadership, communications, working with people, customer service, employee relations and financial and strategic management.

At the other end of the scale, the organisation, since the Post and Telegraphs days, always had good technical training. Traditionally, staff were recruited after Group and Inter Cert and trained through programmes in Kevin Street College of Technology. The result was the development of top-class technicians who were able to deal with organisation technology that would be put in place during their lifetime. Now this process has been extended, and technical staff have been offered scholarships to allow them to make the transition from technicians to engineers. The management development strategy of the company has recently been redefined, and in the future the emphasis will be on identifying individual competencies, matching those competencies with jobs, developing individuals within those jobs, and then evaluating their performance. The issue of performance-related pay is currently been examined within the company.

Infrastructure

As well as investing in its managers, the company has put considerable investment into its infrastructure in recent times. The total investment in the infrastructure in the period 1985–94 amounted to £2 billion, despite the fact that the company is servicing a dept of £12 billion, which amounts to £100 per line. The result of all this investment is that the company's telecommunications network is now very advanced by international standards, and it is Telecom's belief that having such a good infrastructure will play a major role in helping the economy to develop in coming years.

The company does not believe that telephone charges are too expensive in Ireland. It maintains that if competition were introduced to the Irish national telecommunications network, not alone would prices not drop, but they would rise even higher. Telecom points to the UK experience to bear this out. Because the company is state-owned, it is obliged by law to meet business needs and social needs, but it also has to pay its way and keep prices competitive. The difficulty is in striking a balance between these potentially conflicting objectives. As the country's largest employer, the organisation has a role to play in the creation of jobs. The company is confident that it can create more jobs over the coming decade, and within certain specialist areas there has been a growth in numbers. In 1984, there were two accountants, ten years later there were 14. There were 156 marketing staff nine years ago, now there are 236.

It will take time before a full assessment can be made of the way in which Telecom Éireann has gone about transforming the telecommunications system in Ireland. But it is worth noting that many of the benefits that have been achieved so far have been accomplished not under an authoritarian top-down approach to management, but from spreading power and accountability right down through the organisation.

A Questionable Decision

Telecom's decision to purchase the former Johnston Mooney and O'Brien site for £9.4 million — less than a year after another company, UPH, paid just £4 million for it — has to rank as one of the worst property deals ever made by an Irish company. At the time Telecom was under the chairmanship of Dr Michael Smurfit who had been appointed to the post of chairman of the company in 1984, and had helped transform the company from a loss-maker to a highly profitable enterprise. He used the same hard business acumen that has built Smurfit into an international corporation. For instance, he cut staff levels by 35 per cent, with the result that the dividends to the state have been increasing steadily each year as a consequence. He had ambitious plans for Telecom, including privatisation and flotation on the stock market, going so far as to commission feasibility studies by National City Brokers (NCB) among others. Another of the chairman's aspirations for the company was that corporate headquarters should be found so that board members and senior management staff could be located in the one building. It is the methods used and their subsequent repercussions which have led to what has become known as the "Telecom Affair".

Initial Negotiations

In May 1989, the chairman wrote to Finnegan Menton & P.E. Hassett for ideas on suitable sites, while at the same time failing to inform the board of Telecom, which did not hear about the matter until a month later. By October of that year, a number of sites were recommended, including the 5.5 acre former Johnston Mooney and O'Brien (JM&OB) site, which was being sold by John Finnegan of Finnegan Menton, who later requested a finder's fee from Telecom even though he was acting for the vendor of the property. Dr Smurfit was informed that Dermot Desmond of NCB stockbrokers, through a company, United Property Holdings (UPH), had sold it to the present vendor for £6 million. It transpired later that Dermot Desmond owned 25 per cent of UPH and that UPH had in fact originally purchased the site from the liquidator for JM&OB for £4.4 million. At this stage, an idea for building new headquarters was considered but not taken up.

A month later, Michael Smurfit offered Dermot Desmond £7.5 million for the site, subject to board approval. At this point only two Telecom directors had visited the site, and professional appraisal had yet to be undertaken. By December, the board was informed of the situation, and management got authorisation to enter into negotiations for the site. Mr Fergus McGovern (CEO) had talks with Dermot Desmond on possible purchase of the site, and on 21 December, Dermot Desmond, following discussions with the vendors, put forward three options:

1. Owners develop the site and let it to Telecom

2. Sale of site to Telecom for £10 million

3. Sale of four acres for £7.5 million.

In January 1990, senior Telecom executives met with Dublin Corporation chief planning officer and got a favourable response. But estate agents acting for rival developers claimed that Dublin Corporation put the maximum office space allowed at 11,000 square feet, while Telecom's plan was believed to be for 67,000 square feet.

Agreement of Terms

Dermot Desmond offered Fergus McGovern the entire site for £9.4 million, with the condition that the sellers retain an option to purchase the residential element, if such units were to be developed. The board decided on terms and Dermot Desmond was informed. By February, Telecom's solicitors had received the draft documents including the purchase agreement for the shares of Chestvale Properties Ltd., a conveyancing vehicle, with the completion date set for 11 April. Telecom's property manager, Dr O'Neill, advised company management that the option agreement was in favour of the properties vendors, Hoddle Investments, because Telecom was obliged to secure its architects' input prior to application for planning permission. The sellers had the option of not taking up the residential portion if they so chose. At this stage, allegations were circulating concerning the involvement of Michael Smurfit and Dermot Desmond in the company that was selling the property to Telecom, but nobody could substantiate on what exactly their involvement was, and all parties denied any involvement publicly.

A statement on all matters was circulated to the board for clarification. On 20 February, Mr Desmond suggested that Telecom protect itself from any further publicity by incorporating a number of conditions into the agreement including:

- Telecom would have an option to purchase or lease the property, on receipt of planning permission.

- Telecom could reject the deal if no planning permission was received.

With these conditions, Telecom had the option of not going ahead with the deal if it was not financially viable from Telecom's point of view.

In March 1990, Mr Smyth, solicitor for the vendors of the property, Chestvale, agreed to sell for £9.4 million, "subject to planning permission". Fergus McGovern told the Telecom board that agreement had been reached to purchase the site for £9.4 million without planning permission, but added that he felt that there was some doubt as to whether planning permission could be obtained. It was pointed out that failure to carry this risk, i.e. subject to planning permission, would mean paying dearly to the vendor because contracting to buy subject to planning permission meant incurring bank interest charges. On 12 March, Mr O'Halloran was appointed architect to design models of the scheme and to ensure that the market value of the completed job would exceed the purchase price, thus preventing any public criticism. He was paid £317,000 for his services. In April, Telecom's property manager, Dr O'Neill, put the completed property value at £27 million, inclusive of construction costs of between £15.99 million and £18.3 million. A month later, Telecom signed the contract and made a deposit of £0.94 million. At this point, Michael Smurfit received a letter from John Finnegan of Finnegan Menton seeking £150,000 finder's fees, and to back up his letter he referred to some site visits he had made on Telecom's behalf. The board was informed of the letter and it emerged that board members were not aware of the visits mentioned. However, Dr Smurfit informed the board that such information was correct, and the fee was negotiated down to £40,000. The sale was closed on 29 June with the remainder of the price handed over.

A Formal Inquiry

The government decided that a number of questions arising from these transactions needed to be answered, the most important being:

- How did the property price increase from £4.4 million to £9.4 million in a very short period of time? The valuation office in October 1991 had placed a price of between £6.5 and 7 million. Some claim that the site was never worth more than £3–£4 million.

- Was Michael Smurfit a shareholder in UPH despite denying it when it first came to light?

- What was the exact role of Dermot Desmond in the transactions?

- Did John Finnegan act for both buyer and seller of the property?

- Who were the beneficial owners of Chestvale, Hoddle and Delion? Delion, a property company registered in Cyprus, bought Chestvale in order to complete the purchase from UPH and then used Hoddle as a vehicle for sale to Telecom.

It was because of these controversial issues that a formal inquiry was undertaken on the instruction of the Minister for Transport Tourism and Communications, Mr Séamus Brennan. An interim report published on 2 October 1991 made the following recommendations:

- That mandatory procedures for all land purchases be introduced by Telecom.

- That the company adhere to the highest possible standard as regards its disclosure policy. Michael Smurfit's assurance that he was not aware of the UPH connection was noted.

- That when purchasing land from non-Irish companies, Telecom should insist that the vendors disclose who the ultimate beneficial owners were.

- That the Minister for Industry and Commerce has the power to appoint an inspector to look into company matters if it is in the public's interest to do so.

- That an inspector be appointed to investigate Chestvale, Hoddle and their transactions with UPH, Delion and Telecom. Delion was involved in both the purchase and sale of the site but because it was not an Irish company the investigator could only have limited powers.

Because of the recommendations, Mr Lawrence Shields, solicitor, was appointed by the Minister for Industry and Commerce to investigate Hoddle Investments and Chestvale Ltd. and the persons who had a beneficial interest in them. A second inspector had to be appointed on 9 October when Mr Shields stepped aside after disclosing that he had acted for Mr Desmond. Mr John Glackin was the new appointee

In his investigations, Mr Glackin discovered that another company — Freezone — was involved, and was owned by a foreign resident, Mr Colin Probets, and registered in the Isle of Man. The company provided finance for Delion in its purchase of UPH and made a profit of £11.3 million on the transaction. Dermot Desmond has close associations with the company and acted on behalf of Mr Probets in this instance. In response, Mr Desmond stated that he had made no profit from this particular deal, and his legal advisors argued that because the company was registered in the Isle of Man, the investigator had no jurisdiction over it. He also claimed that the inspector was straying from his brief by asking about private dealings including Freezone.

Mr Desmond applied to the High Court to restrict Mr Glackin's brief and to hold the Minister for Industry and Commerce in contempt of court after he spoke out on the issue on radio. In a judgment of 9 January 1992, the latter's actions were held to be "indiscreet", but the court rejected the request to limit the inspector's brief, and said that Mr Desmond was architect of the deal and that the inspector was entitled to ask any questions, Mr Desmond hoped to appeal on this point to the Supreme Court. At this stage, planning permission for the site had not been granted and a decision on the issue was not to be taken until 5 May 1992. City planners pointed out that such a site might be in contravention of the 1980 Dublin Development Plan which states that corporate headquarters must be built in the inner city.

Outcome of the Investigation

Twenty months on and more than £1 million later, Telecom inspector John Glackin delivered his final report, with Dermot Desmond coming out the worst. The report concluded that Mr Desmond was the beneficial owner of Freezone and that he "misrepresented" to the banks that certain people were UPH shareholders. He misrepresented his status by not telling Michael

Smurfit that he, Mr Desmond, was financially interested in the success or failure of Chestvale, and that he effectively controlled it. He also failed to disclose the following to Telecom chief executive Fergus McGovern:

- His personal financial interest in the success or failure of the company that owned the site

- The fact that he effectively controlled the company

- The fact that only a few weeks earlier he had tried to sell the same property for £6.3 million.

The inspector contended that:

- Mr Desmond was financially interested in and controlled two companies, Chestvale and Hoddle, which owned the site for most of the period during which its value increased from £5.8 million which UPH received for Chestvale to the time it was sold to Telecom for £9.4 million.

- Mr Desmond owned the offshore company Freezone which supposedly helped finance the purchase of the site by Pat Doherty.

However, Mr Desmond claimed that Colin Probets was the beneficial owner. According to him, he merely acted as agent for Mr Doherty, and he was in a position to organise the finance from Colin Probets and Freezone, i.e. he acted as an intermediary. It was handled in such a way that it was hard to distinguish it from the personal business of Mr Desmond. He represented himself to Freezone bankers as the owner of Freezone and they advanced an £8 million loan on the understanding that this was the case. Mr Desmond still maintains that he is not guilty of anything, nor has he done anything wrong. As for Michael Smurfit, the investigation shows that his only interest in the site was through his shareholding in UPH. However, there are still questions to be answered about Telecom's boardroom procedures in its purchase of the site.

Conclusion

Telecom Éireann has a clear need for international partnerships to help it to accelerate its change process. It is having difficulty in getting the right purchasers who will need to give it access to a global network, assist it in strengthening its balance sheet and improve its marketing capabilities.

Telecom is in ongoing discussions with the Government to identify ways in which it can move strategically. It has established a joint strategic consultative group which brings together Telecom management and unions to establish how it can make significant changes in the way it operates.

APPENDIX
Subsidiary and Related Companies

Subsidiary Company	Interest in Ordinary Shares at 30 March 1995 %	Business
Irish Telecommunications Investments plc (ITI plc)	100	Telecommunications Financing and Treasury Management
Telecom Éireann Information Systems Ltd.	100	Marketing and Installation of Telecommunications Customer Equipment
Eircable Ltd.	100	Investment Holding Company
Telecom Ireland (US) Ltd.	100	Marketing of Telecom Services in USA
Eirtrade Ltd.	100	Provision of Electronic Trading Services
ITI International Finance Ltd, (Subsidiary of ITI plc)	100	Provision of Treasury Management and Consultancy Services
ITI International Finance Europe SPRL (Subsidiary of ITI plc)	100	Provision of Treasury Management and Consultancy Services
ITI Hungary Consulting KFT (Subsidiary of ITI plc)	100	Provision of Treasury Management and Consultancy Services
Minitel Communications Ltd.	100	Provision of Videotext Services and Terminals
Telecom PhoneWatch Ltd.	100	Installation, Monitoring and Maintenance of Residential Security Systems
Cablelink Ltd. (Subsidiary of Eircable Ltd.)	60	Construction and Operation of Cable and MMDS Television Systems
Cablelink Galway Ltd. (Subsidiary of Cablelink Ltd.)	60	Cable and MMDS Television Systems
Cablelink Waterford Ltd. (Subsidiary of Cablelink Ltd.)	60	Cable and MMDS Television Systems
Little Bird Ventures Seven Ltd. (Subsidiary of Cablelink Ltd.)	60	Dormant
Eirpage Ltd.	51	Marketing of Radio Paging Service

Related Company	Interest in Ordinary Shares at 30 March 1995 %	Business
INET Ltd.	50	Managed Network Provider
Golden Pages Ltd.	49	Directory Publishing
Broadcom Éireann Research Ltd.	45	Broadband Telecommunications Research and Development

Source: Company reports; *Chestvale Properties Ltd., Hoddle Investments Ltd., Investigation under Section 14(1), Companies Act, 1990* (Glackin Report); interviews with company personnel.

Questions

1. Why does Telecom Éireann need some form of strategic alliance in order to survive in the next century? What form of alliance should it be?

2. How has Telecom Éireann grown in external terms? Categorise the different types of diversification it has engaged in.

3. What trends are evident in the financial performance of Telecom Éireann in the past seven years?

4. What types of ethical issues, if any, are raised by Telecom's decision to purchase the Johnson, Mooney and O'Brien site?

17

Shannon Airport: The Aeroflot Connection

Shannon, the most westerly airport in Europe (currently under seven flying hours from New York), was originally selected in 1936 by US and European aviation experts as the prime and strategic location on the Eastern Atlantic seaboard to meet the technical transit (refuelling) requirements of all North Atlantic carriers.

In 1945, scheduled transatlantic services through Shannon commenced, and as an up shot of the jet age, over 50 per cent of all North Atlantic traffic, westbound and eastbound, transited Shannon. Even with the introduction of longer-range jet aircraft, Shannon dominated the transatlantic technical transit market. This was not only because of its strategic location, but also because of its operational appeal, enhanced by progressive development and competitive pricing.

Fuel Crises

The fuel crises of the early 1970s when the price of all fuels rocketed, and of the late 1970s when a fuel shortage developed because of the Middle East war, forced radical changes in the pattern of civil aviation developments generally, but, even more specifically, the changes that occurred in the North Atlantic area had a very negative effect on the economics of Shannon. There were three main areas of adjustment which had adverse effects on the Shannon operation:

1. Because of the increase in fuel costs in the late 1970s, the airlines began to ground the bulk of their fuel-inefficient narrow-body fleets, replacing them with larger wide-body aircraft,

which were more efficient in the use of fuel. These narrow-body aircraft were the lifeblood of Shannon's technical transit traffic prior to this change.

2. In 1979, when the fuel shortage became critical, multinational oil companies introduced a non-transferable fuel quota system for transit airline customers, the effect of which was to deny an adequate supply of fuel at Shannon.

3. A fuel-pricing policy by the multinational fuel companies at Shannon made fuel costs there significantly more expensive than those at other airports in north-west Europe (such as London, Brussels, etc.) which were competitors for technical transit traffic.

Decline in Transit Traffic at Shannon

The combination of the above factors — all involving fuel — led to a decline in technical transit traffic operating through Shannon from 1976 to 1981. The level of transit traffic at Shannon has always had a direct bearing on the profitability of the airport, since it traditionally formed a high proportion of total traffic. The net result was that, from 1977 onwards, Shannon's profitability went into a nose dive, with a decline from a profit of IR£1.51 million in 1977 to a loss of IR£1.57 million in 1980.

In 1977–78, when all the normal local corrective actions (such as making representations to the multinational oil companies on fuel price) had failed to yield a positive response, it became clear that some dramatic and innovative action would need to be taken to reverse the tide of decline in Shannon's technical traffic.

Aeroflot/Soviet Airline Transatlantic Operation

The change in pattern of North Atlantic operations of Aeroflot/ Soviet Airline in the second half of the 1970s was symptomatic of the general trend in the industry.

Aeroflot commenced operating through Shannon on a technical transit basis in September 1975 on its flights from Moscow to Havana to the US to Canada. However, in the late 1977, because of fuel costs at Shannon, the Soviet airline decided to change its operation to Moscow/Gander/US/Canada. The logic of this change was that it would be more economical to operate on the longest possible leg of the trip out of Moscow using home produced fuel. Again, Shannon lost the business because of fuel costs.

The Innovation

At this time, Mr Michael Guerin, Aviation Division Manager of Aer Rianta at Shannon, conceived the innovative idea of Aer Rianta offering to construct at Shannon a completely new fuel farm for Aeroflot (see Appendix 1). Together with related facilities this would permit servicing and storage of Aeroflot aircraft consignments of fuel tankered from the USSR. The carrier could then use consignments of home-produced fuel all the way through to Havana (its main transatlantic terminal) when operating flights Moscow/Shannon/Havana in both directions. An outline of the proposal was formally put to the Aeroflot authorities in February 1978. The Soviets responded favourably. This idea was quite revolutionary in that not only was it unheard of for an airport authority to become involved in the aviation fuel business, but, at this time, the multinational oil companies held a vice-like grip on all facets of the oil industry, worldwide.

Project Planning

The planning of this project involved extended negotiations in several areas, leading to an agreement in principle, dated May 1979, and subsequently to formal contracts as follows:

- Bilateral agreements between the governments of the USSR and Ireland covering the operation of flights between the USSR and countries in the western hemisphere, with technical landings at Shannon Airport (July 1980)

- A technical Transit Servicing agreement between Aer Rianta and the General Department of International Air Services Aeroflot (6 July 1979)

- Fuelling Facilities Services agreement between Aer Rianta and Aeroflot (6 July 1979)

- Agreement between Aer Rianta and Aer Lingus covering ground handling services for Aeroflot flights at Shannon, (6 July 1979)

- Agreement between Aer Rianta and Tedcastle Aviation Fuels Ltd. covering the operation of Aer Rianta's fuelling facilities at Shannon (May 1980).

The initial agreement covered a five-year period with the right to renew at the end of that contract (see Appendix 2).

Cost of Fuel-Farm Project

Apart from the formal agreements concluded, the planning involved financial approval for an expenditure of £1.2 million for the construction of fuelling facilities. These facilities included adaptation of Dernish Island to accept fuel from Russian tankers, pipeline to fuel farm, construction of four 1-million gallon tanks and pipelines from fuel farm to aircraft apron where a new hydrant refuelling system was installed.

Operational and Financial Benefits

The project was completed and the first Aeroflot flight was fuelled with Soviet fuel on 3 July 1980. The evidence of the success of the venture can be gauged from operating statistics summarised for the five-year period 1980–85 (Table 17.1).

Table 17.1: Development of Shannon-Aeroflot Business, 1980–85

Details of Service Outputs	
Number of Aeroflot Flights through Shannon	4,799
Number of Passengers in Transit	560,900
Fuel Throughput (gallons)	74.81 million
Details of Income	
	Revenues Generated
Aer Rianta	10.37 million
Aer Lingus	1.97 million
Tedcastle	2.09 million
Miscellaneous	3.10 million
TOTAL	17.53 million

Barter Fuel Agreement

As an outgrowth of the above agreement covering the technical transit of Aeroflot's North Atlantic flights, a further agreement was finalised with Aeroflot in March 1983. This permits Aer Rianta to draw down a limited quantity of Aeroflot fuel supply at Shannon for sale to Western customers who might be attracted to make any required technical landings at Shannon. This agreement is worked on a barter arrangement whereby the revenues earned by Aeroflot for fuel supplied are set against charges incurred by them for services at Shannon, such as landing fees, inflight food services, etc. In the first year, a total of 2.2 million gallons of Aeroflot fuel was dispensed to other carriers, and in the second year, this figure increased to 4.2 million gallons. The sale of this fuel has resulted in substantial revenues for Shannon in landing fees, duty-free shop sales, etc. The project has proven very profitable in its own right and has been the means of attracting additional traffic to Shannon, which would otherwise have gone to other airports.

Subsequent to negotiations with Aeroflot, the project involved the following aspects:

- A separate agreement covering the term of supply and barter arrangements

- Aer Rianta establishing an independent company to market and handle the fuel product (This wholly owned subsidiary company, Shannon Aviation Fuels Limited, commenced trading in April 1983.)

- Special banking and accounting facilities, including the opening of a bank account in New York.

- Agreements with Tedcastle Aviation Fuels resulting in the appointment of that company for aircraft refuelling

- Financial approval for expenditure of £0.5 million for the construction of an additional 2-million gallon storage tank and an extension of the hydrant fuelling system on the apron.

Commercial Operations

From the initial co-operative venture of providing fuelling facilities for technical transit landings, it became apparent that several commercial enterprises could be developed and built around the Shannon experience. Already, significant progress has been made in developing Shannon as a connecting point for American tourists destined for the USSR by operating flights on the Shannon–Moscow and Shannon–Leningrad routes to tie in with services bringing these passengers from New York.

Also, a new bilateral agreement between Ireland and the USSR was concluded, which gave Aeroflot commercial rights from Shannon to the western hemisphere, excluding the US and Canada. This offered the prospect for development of commercial services to such destinations as Havana, Mexico and Lima.

APPENDIX 1

Our ref. AM 172/112   Aer Rianta, Shannon

Mr Vladimir Marassanov   8 February 1978
Manager
Aeroflot
Shannon Airport

Dear Mr Marassanov

I refer to our several recent conversations relative to your company's decision to switch their North Atlantic technical transit operation from Shannon to Gander. My company, as you know, has responsibility for the promotion of technical transit traffic at Shannon and are, naturally, concerned at the not inconsiderable loss of Aeroflot's business, In this context LOT — the Polish Airline — made a similar switch over 12 months ago and both companies are, we believe, motivated in this decision by the economics of flying the longer over-ocean leg with low cost home source fuel.

If the switch of transit location had been motivated by other than economic considerations we would refer you to Shannon's unparalleled operational attractions for an operation such as yours. Our year round open weather history, our accessibility, excellent facilities and services including the quite unique passenger attraction provided by our world famous duty free shop, are transit amenities that are quite unmatched. These, together with our competitive transit costs are the ingredients that motivate the major international airlines to designate Shannon as their primary North Atlantic transit airport, as, no doubt, they were the factors that similarly influenced Aeroflot in 1975.

As a solution to the financial constraint imposed on Aeroflot at Shannon by the non-availability here of Russian origin fuel, we ask you to propose to your management in Moscow that they examine the possibility of importing Russian origin aviation fuel to Shannon. Already Russian origin oils are imported directly to this country and we are unaware of any Departmental constraint to the similar importation of Russian aviation fuel. We feel that your fuel vendor could handle the commodity through their depot in Limerick docks and service your aircraft thereafter on a handling charge basis. The implementation of this proposal would enable Aeroflot to fly the entire route from Moscow to the US via Shannon with low cost fuel and would further make practical economics of a Shannon landing on the return flight.

We would welcome an opportunity of elaborating on this proposal with your management and would be available at any time for discussion with them in Moscow or London. Perhaps, in due course, you would kindly let me know your company's reaction to the proposal.

On a personal note I want to express may appreciation of your never failing courtesy and co-operation with me during your all too short stay at Shannon.

I look forward to hearing from you.

Personal regards.

Yours sincerely,

Michael Guerin
Deputy General Manager

APPENDIX 2

PRESS RELEASE 1

From the Press Office   <u>FOR IMMEDIATE RELEASE</u>
Aer Rianta Irish Airports, Dublin Airport
Phone 01-379900   9 July 1987
Contact: Flan Clune or John Gallagher

100 MILLION GALLONS OF SOVIET FUEL AT SHANNON

On Wednesday, 11 June, 1980, the Soviet tanker, Ardatov unloaded a one and a quarter million gallon cargo of aviation fuel at the Dernish Island jetty in the Shannon Estuary. The fuel was then pumped through more than a mile of pipeline to tanks built by Aer Rianta at the airport. The cargo came from the Baltic port of Ventspills to Shannon for use by Aeroflot.

Today, 9 June, 1987, Shannon celebrates the pumping of the 100 millionth gallon of Soviet fuel into a Soviet airplane and the significant contribution which this activity has made to Shannon.

When the contract was first negotiated it was anticipated that 3,000,000 gallons would supply 300 flights a year. However, shortly afterwards 17,000,000 gallons were pumped into 1,200 Soviet flights annually.

Arrangements to use Shannon as a refuelling stop by the USSR airline on its Moscow-South & Central American routes were completed between Aer Rianta and Aeroflot in July 1979. The benefits of the Aeroflot deal for Shannon are quite significant. Aeroflot flights into the airport commenced on 3 July, 1980, with six refuelling stops per week. By the end of 1981 Aeroflot was sending 20 transit flights through Shannon per week.

The agreement between Aer Rianta and Aeroflot is protected by a bilateral agreement between the Irish and Soviet governments. The extension of air travel from Eastern Europe restores Shannon's position as a primary re-fuelling stop and now makes it again the crossroads of the Atlantic. Aeroflot are rapidly expanding their scheduled services from the USSR to the western hemisphere and Shannon will play a vital role in their operations in years to come.

In June 1985, Aer Rianta management at Shannon secured a five year extension of the agreement which is expected to bring four times the business of the initial contract into the region.

Spinoffs from the Soviet agreement include the initiation of a barter arrangement allowing Aer Rianta to set up its own fuel agency and provide economical fuel for technical transit flights. It includes a valuable programme of transferring North American passengers to Aeroflot flights from Aer Lingus transatlantic flights bringing them on to the USSR: and it also created additional business for airport catering, duty free shops and for restaurants, shops and hotels throughout the Shannon region, worth in all approximately £60 million.

At present up to 26 flights a week pass through Shannon between Moscow and destinations in South and Central America

ENDS
090787

Source: Interviews with company personnel.

Questions

1. Environmental scanning is a recognised prerequisite for market planning. Suggest the environmental factors to which the success/failure of the Aer Rianta/Aeroflot relationship can be attributed. Attempt to isolate the "controllable" and "uncontrollable" elements in your analysis.

2.   "Entrepreneurship, founded as it is on exploiting business opportunities and being driven by the profit motive, properly resides in the private sector. Any resemblance to it in the public sector is purely coincidental".

   Comment in relation to the case.

3. According to Igor Ansoff, three possible strategies of a company seeking growth are Market Penetration, Market Development and Product Development.

   Discuss Ansoff's approach in relation to Aer Rianta and how the airports authority might pursue growth through each of these strategic options.

   Which in particular do you suggest might most recommend itself to Aer Rianta and why?

Part 4

Multinational Companies and Manufacturing

18

Waterford/Wedgwood

Overview

Glass-making in Waterford dates as far back as 1785, with a cessation in 1825 because of excise duty pressure. In 1947, the tradition was revived by Bernard Fitzpatrick and Charles Bacile, a native of then Czechoslovakia. The Irish Glass Bottle Company, which was run by Joe McGrath and Joe Griffin, was very much interested in this related industry, and in 1950 they joined forces, with Waterford Glass as a subsidiary of the Irish Glass Bottle Company. A year later, a new factor was established in Johnstown, Co. Waterford. Skilled workers, not available in Ireland because of emigration and a scarcity of the necessary skills, were brought in from Europe from 1952, to work on a "piecework" basis. This latter arrangement was not to become an issue within the company until many years later. From 1954, the company began to support itself as a result of an increased volume of sales, while at about this time, markets were developing, especially in the US, where increased affluence was leading to a demand for such things as *objects d'art* — a trend which did not escape the attentions of Waterford Glass's management.

As a result of the influence of the McGrath family, a productive culture was very much in evidence in Waterford Glass. The decision-making process changed from being centred around the owners to a simple line and staff structure which had existed in the bottle company. This became bureaucratic through company growth, with centralised power, definite rules and procedures, top-down communication, clear job descriptions, and high differentiation between areas. Yet the influence of the McGrath family also had a positive impact because it ensured a strong policy on close working relationships, with high trust between management and employees — something that changed with the arrival of new management in later years.

Evolution of Waterford/Wedgwood

Specific strategic expansion periods can be identified in the group's development:

- 1960–72: expansion of the production facilities and forward integration
- 1972: concentric diversification
- 1974: the group was emerging as a conglomerate
- 1980s: a focus on retrenchment and divestment
- 1990s: consolidation.

During the 1960s and 1970s, the company underwent major expansion of its production facilities. Originally, it was planned over the period 1968–84, but because of the high demand for the group's products, the work had to be completed by 1972. In order to finance this expansion, Waterford Glass shares were placed on the stock exchange in 1966, raising £300,000. Three years later, a further issue was necessary, raising £400,000. In the early 1960s, with huge demand, price constraints were not an issue. With the US as a market of endless demand, and this accounting for 80 per cent of the group's sales, the company set up some marketing subsidiaries there in 1961, to promote and distribute its products. In this market, the company's goods had a prestigious image, with many people looking upon them as family heirlooms, and some becoming treasured possessions — this despite the fact that the company's existence spanned a mere 30 years. The goods sold in the US were distributed exclusively to large department stores with established prestige, thus allowing for direct access to retail customers. This selective distribution process enhanced the product's exclusivity tag.

At this time also, the company purchased distributors EG Wiundantd in the UK. This policy continued into the 1970s. The following are some of the acquisitions and joint ventures entered into as part of the company's concentric diversification strategy in the 1970s:

- 1972: Aynsley China — manufacturers of high-quality bone china, which represented related diversification

- 1973: John Hinde — an 81 per cent acquisition of a printing company, which was bought to enhance Waterford's image

- 1973: Switzers — retailers bought in partnership with the House of Frazer, providing assets for the balance sheet

- 1973: Joint venture with Norco of Connecticut — a precision engineering company to bring more highly skilled employment to Waterford

- 1974: The Smith Group — in the automotive industry and un-related to Waterford's primary activities, yet taken on without much regard for corporate strategy.

Overall the group had become a conglomerate, something which would cause problems for management in the future. The group was also beginning to exhibit certain characteristics which would go some way towards explaining the problems encountered in the 1980s.

With very little technical change within the group over this period, the industry was thus characterised by high labour intensity, highlighted by the fact that 78 per cent of costs were labour related, while management rewards were substantial, hence little turnover. The policy on training was to make use of such bodies as AnCo, with no use whatsoever made of universities, thus showing the company to be inconsistent with the times. The 1970s were a period when no restraint was placed on wages because of the seemingly buoyant nature of the market, and with management exercising little or no control. To highlight this, it is worth noting that in 1979, as a result of increased taxation, the McGrath family was willing to step in and offer to suspend payment of wages where PRSI was due, and instead gave loans equivalent to gross wage, a move that was stopped by the government. At this time, current profits were able to absorb any cost increase, so, between 1976 and 1984, labour costs rose by an incredible 150 per cent. But all good things must come to end, and eventually cost-cutting strategies with moderate wage agreements became necessary. It was not until 1980 that the group saw a slip in profits for the first time in 25 years because of increased costs, taxation, and the recession. By 1982, sales volume had declined as many dealers were operating a destocking policy, while the recession began to hit hard. The good times for the group were at an end, and it started on the slippery slope to decline and almost ruination.

Between 1980 and 1984, the McGrath family disposed of 50 per cent of its interest in Waterford Glass, hinting at changes in the future, and in 1984 the family's remaining 20 per cent was sold to Globe Investments. The McGraths left behind a wage agreement with pay rises, benefits, and a shareholding equal to a 44 per cent increase, while inflation at this time was only 3 per cent. These factors eventually led to the restructuring of the company under new management whose policies caused major unrest among workers. From this point on, Waterford Glass was to become a more managerial enterprise.

Recent History 1984–94: Wedgwood Acquisition

In 1985, Globe Investments appointed Paddy Hayes as chairman of Waterford Glass to oversee the redirection of the company and to redefine the core business as that of china and crystal. The specific objective was to increase return on investment — thus a strategy of divestment was undertaken with the sale of Switzers for £6.4 million, which went some way towards reducing borrowings which had accumulated as a result of poor practices, even though demand was greater than supply. The new management focus was making Waterford Glass a market-driven company in the top-table and giftware industry, and in line with this move, a gallery at the company's headquarters was opened in 1986. The year 1985 saw the end of an era with the resignation from the board of Dr Paddy McGrath.

A slump in the US market in 1986 made it a bad year for the group as up to then it had been was highly dependent upon that market. To help remedy the situation, the loss-making Smith Group was sold and a new marketing strategy of increased investment in research and development was embarked upon in order to have new designs available more frequently. The most important event in the group's recent history was Waterford Glass's purchase of the Wedgwood Group in November 1986 for £253 million. Wedgwood, a related business, supplied different markets to which Waterford wished to gain easy access. In essence, the move gave synergistic benefits to both companies. By 1987, the situation in the group had reached crisis point, and so the principal aim for management was the restructuring of Waterford. Central to this plan were major redundancies in both Waterford and Wedgwood — 986 in the latter, and 1,005 in the former. This restructuring plan encountered many problems — it was not planned properly, and key craftsmen were allowed to take redundancies, leaving the manufacturing process vulnerable. The cost of restructuring was put at £18 million initially, but the actual cost was closer to £50 million. Along with these problems, things were not helped by a slump in the US market caused by the fall in value of the US dollar. Wedgwood, by contrast, improved because of the restructuring, and returned profits of £25.1 million for the year.

After the sale of the Smith Group, the divestment strategy continued with the sale of Aynsley China in 1987, in order to concentrate on the top-table and giftware markets. At Waterford, the infrastructure was improved with continuous melting tanks and diamond-cutting wheels installed in order to improve productivity and quality in the future. The year 1988 did not see any ease up in the restructuring problems, and things were further exacerbated by poor quality and productivity, leading to high wastage levels and increased costs. On top of this, the half-yearly accounts were misleading and inaccurate. An independent investigation was undertaken by consultants Peat Marwick McClintock, which brought to light the true costs of the group's restructuring plan, and, more fundamentally, the inadequate company controls in existence at the time. From this investigation, major changes in management were made, one being the appointment of Paddy Galvin as head of the crystal division. He had previously worked for Guinness carrying out a similar cost-cutting exercise there. But in order to return fully to profitability, it was necessary for management to secure workforce support and commitment.

Despite the group's difficulties, demand for its product remained high, and in order to meet this demand, former craft workers were sub-contracted back to Waterford. However, the US market was still a cause for concern and this was intensified by the emergence of imitation glass in the market. Whatever Waterford's difficulties, Wedgwood still continued to produce a profit, and to mark its consistent success, the company's name was changed to Waterford/Wedgwood plc. In 1989, Paddy Hayes, resigned, and as a result of the accounting errors, he was not alone. A new management team was introduced:

> Howard Kilroy — Chairman
> Bob Darvis   — Chief Finance Officer
> Paddy Byrnes   — Group Chief Executive Officer

The year 1989 saw the group's performance continue to cause concern with pre-tax losses of £20 million as against profits of £2.8 million in 1988. Wedgwood, on the other hand, continued to perform favourably with profits of £16.3 million. With debt continuing to rise, management efforts were focused on its immediate reduction. In 1990, the group sought an injection of equity capital of £10.2 million through the issue of 212 million shares to Shuttleway, (50 per cent Fitzwilton and 50 per cent Morgan Stanley), and also a one-in-five rights issue of 82 million new stock units at 25.5p per unit. As a result of the new injection of equity, the gearing ratio was reduced from 183 per cent to 26 per cent. Along with this equity injection, a financing agreement for £105 million over three years was agreed with a syndicate of banks in order to secure the future growth of the company. Also around this time, a major strike lasting 14 weeks occurred at Waterford Glass, leading to a new wage agreement being drawn up which was necessary for future company success. In December, the group was reorganised into two separate business units, Waterford and Wedgwood, each with its own board, management, capital investment programme and resources. It was felt that the future development of the business would be best achieved in this way.

In 1991, Dan Brennan of Morgan Stanley, which was in partnership with the Fitzwilton Group, was appointed chairman. He expressed concern over the amount of management energy expended on the area of industrial relations, and the fact that while on the one hand the group's workers complained about management's lack of ability to sell the crystal, they on the other hand made such a job impossible by making the production of the product so expensive that Waterford Crystal was driven out of sections of the market. In order to reduce costs, short-time was introduced, and to help competitiveness, the new Marquis range, aimed at the middle price market, was introduced. The Gulf War did not help matters by reducing the number of US tourists visiting Europe — affecting sales of both Waterford and Wedgwood products.

It has been touch and go at Waterford Crystal since 1987. The acquisition of Wedgwood had hardly been completed when things began to go badly wrong. The combination of a failing dollar, and soaring production costs almost proved fatal for the company. The company had to go to the very edge of the precipice before its traditionally militant workforce could be persuaded of the need for radical change. In 1987, losses were £18.7 million and in 1988 they increased to £20.5 million. By 1989, by they had reached £21.3 million. The situation could not continue, so in April 1989, Paddy Galvin came to Waterford. He had a reputation for being a "hard man", and his new position required that he use all of his toughness. For a labour force traditionally regarded as being among the "aristocrats" of Irish industry, Paddy Galvin's pill was a bitter one to swallow — management threatened to close the three crystal factories in Waterford if its plan to restore competitiveness was voted down by workers. The main features of the plan included a seven-year pay freeze, a 25 per cent pay cut, reduced benefits and revised work practices. Despite its militant reputation, the workforce, when faced with a choice of accepting the plan or oblivion, voted overwhelmingly to accept the deal. The company had to reduce the cost base and to capture market share from its competitors. The achievement of these aims was going to be difficult — particularly so at the current exchange rate. Essentially, the company faced two major problems:

- *It was dependent on the US market for 85 per cent of its sales*: The pound/dollar had fluctuated violently and these fluctuations proved to be very expensive for Waterford Crystal, particularly because of the potential to increase or decrease profits by as much as £2.5 million or £3 million. The strong dollar of the early to mid-1980s led directly to many of the company's problems, notably its now infamous 1985 agreement.

- *The nature of the crystal industry itself*: The crystal industry is labour- rather than capital-intensive. In 1987, labour numbers peaked at 3,300, a figure that was down to 1,570 in 1994. Increased labour costs were reflected in retail prices, and these price increases put Waterford well beyond the reach of many of its traditional customers. However, the introduction of the Marquis range of crystals made Waterford less traditional and more affordable to a wider customer base. Marquis is moderately priced, contemporary in outlook, and has emerged from nowhere to became the sixth best-selling brand in the world, with sales of $13 million in 1992. Total crystal losses amounted to a horrific £137 million between 1987 and 1990. At the end of June 1993, the company had net debts of £72.6 million, while overall group gearing stood at 65 per cent. As the company points out, it needs to become more profitable in order to be capable of further investment. The group can achieve this by focusing on its core business — crystal — and by improving gross margins and manufacturing competitiveness. Until these improvements are achieved, the company will not be able to rest. It does not help matters that the company operates in a high-cost country like Ireland — a factor which will ensure that Waterford will always have to work hard at being competitive.

Operating Strategy at Waterford

Waterford Crystal's principal manufacturing plant is located on the outskirts of Waterford, with two other plants located in Co. Waterford.

Industrial Relations

A hierarchic system on the shop floor is very much in evidence. On having obtained a noteworthy skill the hard way, a master craft worker is not likely to relinquish the status gained, nor to accept easily any changes in the status quo. The resulting effect is an inflexibility and change-resistant workforce, making it an ideal breeding ground for an all-powerful union. It has been suggested that the company has one of the most radical left-wing union branches in the country — a factor which has made management reluctant to interfere with the workforce. The McGrath family became involved in the company in 1950, three years after the re-establishment of Waterford Glass. Without any financial assistance, the family supported the company up to 1958. Because of skill shortages, resulting in part from emigration, the apprentices had to be trained by craft workers from Europe. By the time that the company had made its first profit in 1955, considerable losses had accumulated despite the McGraths' financial assistance in the form of loans from the Irish Glass Bottle Company. A managerial power culture consistent with single-family ownership developed in those very difficult early years, establishing a paternalistic bond between the craft workers and the McGrath family.

At times up to 3,000 people were employed by the company, with the McGrath family on a first-name basis with most of the master cutters and blowers. Because of the shortage of skills in the early years, the family's benevolence towards the workforce became legendary. Accordingly, the emerging success of the company led to a lack of restraint in the face of union demands for huge increases in pay and benefits. As market demand far exceeded supply during the 1960s and 1970s, the McGraths feared provoking any industrial action, and because each union demand met with little resistance, the union's power base grew very much out of control. When the family departed the company in 1984, a three-year deal by the unions had been negotiated, giving employees a 44 per cent increase (wages, benefits, pensions). Yet there was no evidence to suggest that in return for these concessions, productivity was increased or that any of the restrictive practices were eliminated.

Complacency had set in at all levels because of continuously high levels of growth. Industrial relations became so bad that Waterford Glass and the county in general were perceived as an industrial relations black spot. Paddy Hayes' aim was to reduce the cost of manufacturing drastically, and in order to do this he had to contemplate redundancies, a move previously unknown to Waterford, but nevertheless crucial for the company's future survival. The cost of the proposed rationalisation was exceptional — a figure of £50 million, £31 million of which went directly on redundancy payments. In fact, the terms were so generous that an extra 255 workers accepted, 35 per cent above the originally required figure of 750. Management was only too glad to oblige these workers as long as industrial action was avoided. It was not until 1990 that management finally took on the unions — there was no other choice as the company was insolvent. A stringent cost-management programme was put in place, its first target being to abolish the "bonanza payments" for wedge cutters, an award that cost the company £750,000 per annum. When the union heard of this move, strike action was called for. The resultant strike lasted 14 weeks and was often bitter and acrimonious, with the unions eventually realising that after six weeks of negotiation they must in some way yield to management demands. Accordingly, the unions conceded defeat, thus ending 35 years of excess, with the balance of power shifting back to management.

Process Improvement

It was not until the oil crisis in the early 1970s, that the need to convert from oil furnaces to gas-operated ones was properly investigated. The resulting conversion saw the introduction of a continuous supply of better-quality molten crystal. Yet changes in general to the group's infrastructure have been slow, and have very much lagged behind industry requirements.

Productivity

With the implementation of the rationalisation programme, productivity has been improved by the introduction of diamond cutting wheels. Also introduced were automated conveyor systems for materials handling. It is only recently that Waterford Glass has become receptive to top-class manufacturing techniques, which depend heavily on workforce flexibility — a feature that the group did not previously have.

Quality

This is one of the company's vital attributes, yet the group relies solely on in-line inspections to determine the source and quality of workmanship. As a result of this particular strategy, Waterford ran into serious difficulties in maintaining its standards of excellence following the restructuring programme in 1987. With many senior craft workers taking redundancy, there was a break-up in work teams with detrimental results, as much work-in-progress had to be written off, a move which cost the company some £14.8 million. For Waterford, quality is very much built into the production process. Yet quality was not the group's only concern as its poor delivery performance also provided headaches in that it gave competitors an opportunity to erode Waterford's market share by getting finished products more quickly to the market. With advances in manufacturing technology, Waterford has been able to produce a range of goods in many European locations at a much lower cost. Currently, a range of giftware is being made in Germany, Bosnia and Portugal. For Waterford, this manufacturing process is more technology-intensive, in that goods are machine blown and cut. Accordingly, a less skilled workforce is required. It allows Waterford to set up plants closer to their markets, thus reducing distraction costs.

Operating Strategy at Wedgwood

The Wedgwood plant is located in the heart of the potteries region in Stoke-on-Trent, Staffordshire, England.

Infrastructure

With an unbroken tradition stretching back hundreds of years, Wedgwood is one of the dominant companies in the area, and is surrounded by many china manufacturers. There is a ready supply of skilled labour on hand, with suitable training provided by the local polytechnic. Because of the skill supply, employees were never in a position to demand excessive pay and benefits. As a result, the cost base is very much in line with the industry norm. Relations between employees and management are said to be good.

Restructuring

After the takeover by Waterford in 1986, the company was operating at full capacity, but sales nevertheless were low, resulting in a build-up of stock amounting to £48 million. Paddy Byrnes was appointed chief executive and set about tackling the problem by reducing stock by 25 per cent and the workforce by 986. The product line was also rationalised, with approximately one third of the lines becoming discontinued. All of this took place with little fuss, and resulted in increased productivity.

Technology

The increased productivity in the company a result of the introduction of top-of-the-range technology. For example, six new dry-dust presses speeded up operations and new fast-fire kilns cut firing time from six hours to 25 minutes. This new technology has allowed Wedgwood to buy pre-mixed china and turn out huge volumes at high speed.

Quality

Like Waterford, Wedgwood has always paid attention to quality. With the new technology in place, the company has been able to increase yields by 6.8 per cent. And with a rejection rate of 14 per cent, the company has managed to reduce its work-in-progress levels substantially. Under its new management, Wedgwood hopes to add £20 million to the bottom line by aiming for "zero-defect" production. The organisation has responded well to initiatives on quality.

Workforce

New management in Wedgwood has been moulding a group of "flexible" and "receptive-to-change" individuals. The company was the first to introduce Quality Circles to Britain in 1981, and has a tradition of continuous improvement. Yet Wedgwood was producing goods which had diminished returns and has as a result discontinued various lines, allowing the company to become more profitable and efficient.

Marketing Strategy for Waterford/Wedgwood

Both Waterford and Wedgwood are prestigious luxury brand names. Waterford produces premium stemware, giftware, and creative tableware products. All are hand-crafted by highly skilled people with reputations for excellence. During the period 1972–82, Waterford Crystal did not add a single new product to its market, but through policy changes which have emphasised research and development, the company has been able to introduce over 200 new crystal designs in the areas of lighting wares, chandeliers and sporting trophies.

Wedgwood, at the time of its takeover, was a complete contrast to Waterford, with excessive lines, some of which were not profitable. Yet through the brand management and development of Waterford, Wedgwood managed to rationalise its product range and consolidate its manufacturing by dropping some of its poorer product lines. It discontinued its sale of seconds and stopped distributing through discount stores. The company also acquired professional marketing expertise and design advice. Wedgwood's fine bone china and figures compete in the premium market, while its creative tableware and earthenware have found a niche in the lower market. These moves have saved the prestige and brand name of the company. The new range from Waterford, Marquis, is machine-made glass of contemporary design, and is aimed at the lower market, a market which Waterford had not contemplated up until quite recently.

In 1990, 66 per cent of Waterford's sales were to the US. The company had targeted the Irish-American ethnic group, "over forties", and the bridal market, with total sales estimated at $17 million. Much of the sales at home are to visiting American tourists, thus highlighting perhaps an over-dependence on the US market. Wedgwood is better balanced, with a strong home base and a wider global spread of markets. The creative tableware and earthenware lines are dependent on the home and UK market. The company has a solid market in Japan and the Far East, which Waterford has yet to establish. Following the merger of the two companies, they jointly distributed their products from their own distribution subsidiaries, in many cases selling their products side-by-side in the same retail outlets. However, on establishing two separate businesses in 1991, the distribution channels had to be disbanded, and now the products are distributed separately. One exception to this is that Wedgwood continues to distribute goods in the Far East where they are long established.

Both Waterford and Wedgwood are currently involved in a forward integration strategy, with each company having its own distribution subsidiaries. Both are now expanding their own "shop-in-shops" and "brand-exclusive" retail outlets to ensure better promotion and a more competitive edge. The distribution costs in the US were reduced considerably recently because of rationalisation of retail outlets and cost-cutting, with the result that the product now goes directly from the factory to the wholly owned distributor and directly onto the retailer. Both companies use highly prestigious outlets such as Bloomingdales and Harrods, and "High Street" locations for affluent tourists. Also, the larger duty-free shops at airports are used. The Waterford Crystal gallery has proved to be highly successful since its opening in 1986, with over 100,000 visitors each year. Wedgwood has over 150 "shop-in-shops" and "own-brand shops" in the UK. Both companies are highly dependent on the Christmas market.

Waterford crystal goods, such as single goblets, can be priced as high as $150, with a very small segment of the market requiring customised items. The French crystal company, Baccaret, also sells in this market. Waterford targets the premium market with prices ranging from $30 to $120. It is the leader in this particular market, with a 65 per cent share — the nearest competitor only sells 10 per cent. In the medium market, $29–$50, Waterford has only entered recently. This market is twice as large as the premium market but is highly competitive, and dominated by Lennox of the US. The new machine-made Marquis range, is targeted at this market. Waterford also produces a lighting-ware range of products with prices ranging from $250 to $2,500. The giftware products are more expensive than those of competitors, resulting in the company losing some market share both to other crystal makers, and indirectly to giftware products like silver and jewellery.

Because of excessive demand during the 1960s and 1970s, price was not an issue for Waterford. But the present pricing levels of such products in recessional times is fast becoming unacceptable. There is too high a dependence on the US market, and the dollar fluctuations are affecting the company greatly. In a competitive market with increasing competition, discounting is becoming a threat for Waterford as its prices are some 40 per cent higher than those of its competitors. Wedgwood, on the other hand, which manufactures more closely to its main rivals has remained efficient and competitive because of better balanced geographical markets, less susceptible to exchange-rate fluctuations.

Both companies advertise in exclusive magazines and the media, thus reaching the premium-market customer. To emphasise their premium products, the advertising focuses on a "hand-crafted by highly skilled people to the highest quality" strategy. By being selective in their advertising strategy, a certain "snob appeal" is given to the products. In the US, Waterford Glass was promoted and perceived as being traditionally and essentially Irish, an heirloom passed on down through family generations. It was promoted as the chief adornment of American sideboards, particularly those of people of Irish descent; as a necessity in a bridal trousseau; and as a potential wedding present.

As the goods are hand-crafted, supply cannot be increased to any great extent because craft workers, to be properly trained, can take up to five years to complete an apprenticeship. As a result, long delays with deliveries can at times prove inevitable. Yet Waterford had managed to capitalise on this prospect through use of its very successful ad slogan: "Waterford Crystal — worth waiting for". This slogan was used to project Waterford Glass as a much sought-after product, one that customers should feel privileged to receive. However, this slogan would not work today as delays are seen to be unacceptable and costly in terms of the company losing market share to competitors. In the home crystal market alone, Waterford has only a 25 per cent share, a figure that is now declining. Contributing to this decline has been the fact that many former Waterford employees are now competing against the company by supplying similar quality products at a price that is some 30 per cent lower, and with shorter lead times. In the Irish market alone, there are such companies as Galway Crystal, Tipperary Crystal — former employees of Waterford Crystal — and Cavan Crystal, among others competing directly with Waterford.

At the time of restructuring, Waterford Crystal changed advertising agencies in order to revitalise promotion efforts, resulting in advertising being extended to magazines not previously targeted. $3.5 million alone was spent in the US on promotional efforts. Waterford also make many exhibition pieces to be displayed in prominent New York stores as a publicity ploy, and also to maintain its high-profile image over its competitors. Many of the company's finest chandeliers are installed in such prominent public places as the National Concert Hall in Dublin, and the London and Dublin stock exchanges. The company also produces many custom-made commissioned pieces for special awards which bring great publicity. Waterford Crystal's lighting-ware products are being successfully promoted in the Middle East, while the company has become involved once again in the sporting trophy business, producing some exquisite pieces for many major international and Irish events in golf and tennis. Market research has shown that the vast majority of customers have no idea where the product is made. The benefit of this finding for Waterford is that it can source lower-cost foreign manufacturers to produce its lowest pitched Marquis range, a move which has ultimately increased profits. But in order to protect the prestigious image of Waterford Crystal in the premium market, the Marquis range has its own brand identity, logo and packaging, with a more contemporary design and lighter cut. It is hoped that this move will not take from existing Waterford sales, but from those of competitors. Accordingly, Marquis has its own advertising and in-store merchandising. Its only visible link to the renowned Waterford name is the logo — "Marquis by Waterford, made in Germany".

Financial Success of Waterford/Wedgwood

The last good year of results at Waterford was 1984. In August of that year, UK-based Globe Investments Trust plc bought out the remaining 20 per cent stake held by the McGraths for £17.2 million. In May 1985, the former chairman of Ford Ireland, Paddy Hayes, was appointed executive chairman of Waterford. The aim in that particular year was to increase return on investment, while Paddy Hayes was convinced that more profit could be squeezed out of the company through expanding sales and eliminating profit drains. A major disposal programme was undertaken in that year, starting with the sale of the 60 per cent holding of Switzers Group to House of Frazer for £6.43 million. It was not a profit drain, but Waterford was no expert in the retail business and it felt that it should put its money where its knowledge was. In retrospect, 1985 was a good year for the company with:

- Borrowings reduced by some 52 per cent to £22 million, compared to 1984's £45 million

- Group turnover increasing 4 per cent to £255 million

- Earning per share increasing by 21 per cent to 6.73p

- Crystal inventories down, bringing stock levels down to 23 per cent.

However, with a weakening US dollar things turned for the worst, and this weakening effect continued until the US elections in November 1988. In 1986, Waterford purchased Wedgwood, funded in part by a share issue for £253 million — a purchase which saved Waterford from virtual extinction. The Smith Group was disposed of later in the year because it had been losing money since 1982. A pre-tax loss of £750,000 was recorded. However, the sale succeeded in reducing Waterford's net debt by over £17 million as the banks took over the Smith debts. Sales in 1986 dropped 49 per cent to £130.8 million because of the sale of Switzers and the Smith Group, and the decline in the number of US tourists visiting Ireland. Pre-tax profits increased 26 per cent to £23.3 million, compared to £18.5 million in 1985. Earnings per share rose 28 per cent to 8.62p which represented compounded growth of 23 per cent since 1982. Operating margins doubled from 8.5 to 17.4 per cent, and pre-tax margins increased from 7.2 to 17.8 per cent. The latter half of the year was affected by a slump in the number of US tourists to Ireland. Borrowings increased on the previous years figure of £21.863 million to £67.255 million, and the debt/equity ratio was 65.8 per cent, up from 28.0 per cent in 1985.

By 1987, because of the three-year wage agreement, labour-related costs had risen 44 per cent even though inflation was only 3 per cent. The company's wage costs were 50 per cent greater than those of their main competitor, the French crystal company Baccaret. At the same time, the company's main US competitor, Lennox, was benefiting from the weakening US dollar. To make matters worse, instead of tackling the cost structure, the company increased prices in the US by 21 per cent between 1984 and 1987, with predictable disastrous results — sales fell back and stock piled up. Something had to be done — hence the rationalisation programme initiated in 1987. Management hoped to save £16.5

million per annum by reducing the workforce by 750. The programme ended up costing some £50 million, with the company showing a loss of £47.8 million, which at the time was the biggest loss ever recorded by an Irish-quoted company. The company still paid out £1.9 million in dividends, but the loss to the shareholders was £597 million. A total of 1,005 workers took voluntary redundancy, cutting wage costs by £20 million, but disruption to production resulted in £14.8 million worth of inventory being written off. In December 1987, Aynsley China was sold for £19.7 million. It was sold mainly because one of its products was competing directly with Wedgwood. The total assets disposed of in 1987 amounted to £51.4 million. In 1987, turnover of £282.4 million was achieved, compared to £130.8 million in 1986. However, as a result of restructuring after the Wedgwood acquisition in 1986, net profits before tax were only £4.5 million. Net borrowing for

Table 18.1: Finances of Waterford/Wedgwood, 1990–94

	1990 (£m)	1991 (£m)	1992 (£m)	1993 (£m)	1994 (£m)
Wedgwood Group	231.2	219.1	197.3	217.1	216.2
Waterford Crystal	76.7	73.0	76.3	102.1	108.8
Waterford/Wedgwood plc	307.8	292.1	273.6	319.2	325.0
Operating Profit (Loss)	9.9	9.1	9.1	16.5	28.3
Profit/(Loss) before Tax	(22.50)	(2.90)	(17.03)	10.1	22.6
Taxation	(5.69)	(2.53)	(2.00)	(1.10)	(2.00)
Profit/(Loss) after Tax	(28.19	(5.40)	(19.0)	9.0	20.6
Profit/(Loss) Retained	(28.19)	(5.40)	(19.0)	9.0	14.9
Capital Expenditure	7.9	6.9	6.5	12.0	17.2
Net Debt at 31 December	38.0	50.2	54.6	50.4	36.4
Gearing at 31 December	26%	36%	54%	41%	28%
Dividends	—	—	—	—	(5.4)
Earnings per Share (p)	-.43	-.07	-2.7	1.3	2.9
Share Price at 31 Dec (p)	21p	34p	22p	47p	58p
Average Employee Numbers	1,0161	9,546	8,325	7,668	7,415

year-end stood at £84.3 million, while shareholders' funds stood at £92.1 million, and the debt/equity ratio was 91.5 per cent. Wedgwood performed strongly with profits of £25.1 million on sales of £168 million.

The year 1988 saw some improvement in sales, with total group sales increasing by 8 per cent to £304.4 million, up from £282.4 million in 1987. Later in the year, John Hinde Ltd. was sold for £4.3 million because of its poor performance in latter years. Total disposal of assets realised some £45 million, and this disposal policy, aimed at reducing borrowings, continued until 1989. Yet 1988 saw borrowings increase by 33 per cent to £109.5 million. Peat Marwick was appointed to review operations of the internal control systems. Profit before tax was £2.7 million, compared to losses of £10.3 million in 1987. Taxation amounted to £7.9 million, which arose primarily on Wedgwood operations. The loss per ordinary shares was 1.27p, compared to a 1987 figure of 4.33p. An interim dividend of 1.2p was paid and debt at year end was £109.5 million, up from £84.3 million in 1987. Operating profit fell from £10.9 million in 1987 to £6.7 million because of the poor performance of the crystal business, while interest expenditure of £11 million was up from a 1987 figure of £6.4 million. Operating profit fell from £10.9 million in 1987 to £6.7 million because of the poor performance of the crystal business, while interest expenditure of £11 million was up from 1987 with £6.4 million, reflecting an increase in the group's net debt to £109.5 million, up some £25 million on 1987. Wedgwood represented over 60 per cent of group sales at £190.4 million in 1988, a 12 per cent increase on 1987, while operating profits increased to a record £27.5 million and capital expenditure to £10.7 million. Ireland represented only 4 per cent of group sales.

In 1989, there was a further increase in group sales to £349 million. The results showed a second-half operating profit of £300,000, with a full-year operating loss of £1.1 million. Interest costs were £19.5 million, contributing to a pre-tax loss of £20.6 million. Taxation equalled £8.4 million, and the loss after tax was £29 million, up from £5.2 million in 1988. At year end, net debt was £125 million, down from £145.3 million at half year, but £15.5 million higher than at the end of 1988. Wedgwood produced profits of £16.3 million, down from £21.8 million in 1988, and sales of china increased to £164.7 million, from £140.5 million in 1988, with all of the growth in the early part of the year. Waterford's crystal division incurred a loss of £21.3 million, compared to a 1988 figure of £20.5 million. The result of all this was that the stability of the Waterford/Wedgwood Group was now in serious doubt and desperately in need of funds, and to this end no dividends were paid out in 1989.

Turnover in 1990 was £307.8 million, and operating profit was £9.9 million. In 1990, the funds arrived with Dr Tony O'Reilly and Fitzwilton injecting £96.2 million of new equity, with the result that net borrowing fell by 70 per cent to £38 million, and working capital was increased. A 14-week strike reduced stock piles, and the debt/equity ratio was reduced from 183 per cent to 26 per cent, all of which gave the company breathing space. The 14-week strike also saw management gain more concessions on work practices and productivity. The latter improved after the strike, but Waterford Crystal's performance had cancelled out the good financial returns of Wedgwood. The directors decided to split the two companies to protect Wedgwood and place more emphasis and urgency on the need for recovery at Waterford.

In 1991, there were difficult trading conditions yet again for the company, with sales at £292.1 million, and operating profit at £9.1 million, lower than in 1990. However, financial costs at £6.5 million were down from 1990 with £12.9 million. Taxation at £2.5 million was also down from the 1990 figure of £5.7 million. Net borrowings at year end stood at £50.2 million, up on the 1990 figure of £38 million. This was a major improvement on the half-year figure of £59.6 million. Gearing at year end stood at 36 per cent.

For 1992, the group operating profit was £9.1 million, the same as 1991. Sales revenue fell to £273.6 million on the 1991 figure of £292.1 million, but overall volume held up. Financial costs were £7.7 million, reflecting higher average debt over the period, and the taxation charge was £2 million lower than pervious years. With the restructuring, resulting exceptional costs were £18.4 million and resulting losses were £19.0 million, while net borrowing stood at £54.6 million, leading to a gearing ratio of 54 per cent, reflecting the significant cash impact of the £7.7 million restructuring and capital investment at the company. There was good news too with the crystal division producing an operating profit of £0.5 million which was the first profit for the division since 1986. Sales also increased to £76.3 million. Wedgwood had a bad year with sales down on the previous year's figure to £197.3 million (1991 was £219.1 million). Operating profits also fell to £8.6

million from £10.3 million in 1991.

The recession during the years 1991 and 1992 reduced the demand for luxury products including crystal and china. The Gulf War caused a fall off in the number of US tourists on whom Waterford depended heavily, with the significantly weakened dollar exacerbating things even further. Waterford's uncompetitive high prices and long lead times added to the problems, and resulted in short-time working being introduced at Waterford, with some workers only working two weeks in the year. A week-on/week-off system has been the policy for some time. Wedgwood, despite strong competition, has managed to keep its market share, but the overall industry has suffered reduced demand. Wedgwood currently operates a four-day week.

In 1993, the group returned to the black with pre-tax profits of £10 million, compared to a loss of £17 million in 1992, and a loss of £2.63 million in 1991. Operating profit rose 81.5 per cent to £16.5 million, compared to £9.07 million in the previous year. Group sales increased by 17 per cent, totalling £319 million, compared to £173.6 million in 1992. Waterford crystal sales increased 33.8 per cent to £102 million — a year earlier they stood at £76.3 million. The division had operating profits of £7.8 million, compared to just £457,000 in 1992, giving an operating margin of 7.64 per cent. An operating loss of £1.22 million was recorded in 1991. The results of the Wedgwood Group were also very good with sales increasing by 10.04 per cent at £217.1 million — this figure is still below the 1991 figure, £138.6 million. The gearing for the company — which is the ratio of borrowing to shareholders' funds — fell to 41 per cent from 54 per cent a year earlier. No dividend was paid, and the earnings per share were 1.27 per cent, compared to a loss per share of 2.69p in 1992.

Waterford Wedgwood's impressive recovery was taken a stage further in 1994 when earnings per share more than doubled, and the first dividend since 1988 was declared. The results show a 71.5 per cent increase in operating profits from £16.5 million to £28.3 million on a sale increase of just 1.8 per cent, from £319 million to £325 million. Even taking into account the fact that £6 million worth of less profitable lines at Wedgwood were eliminated, underlying sales growth was less than 4 per cent. However, a combination of favourable exchange-rate movements, cost savings and efficiencies, and an improved sales mix saw operating margins improve from 5.2 per cent to 8.7 per cent.

The group's balance sheet was strengthened significantly during 1994. Net debt at year end was reduced to £36.4 million, £14 million below the 1993 figure despite capital spending of some £17.2 million (the highest since 1988). Gearing had improved to a very acceptable 27.5 per cent, while earnings per share at 2.9p were the best since 1986. A dividend of 0.8p per share was declared, setting a base for future earnings growth. Interest charges, down from £6.4 million to £5.7 million were covered a healthy five times by profits. Thus, 1994 was a year when the group returned to healthy operating profitability. It managed to reduce its debt substantially, and to improve its gearing significantly, while recommending the payment of a dividend for the first time in seven years.

The Future

The main aim for the future of Waterford/Wedgwood is again to become a competitive company. In order to achieve this, the group believes that employment numbers will need to be reduced to 1,400. The company also needs to be able to reduce its level of short time, a policy which has been in practice since 1990. Waterford manufacturing needs to become more viable and secure, a move which will only come about through capital investment in the latest technology. The company also needs to develop new markets, thus lessening its reliance on the US market, and it must do this through the development of competitive products. These strategies should allow the company to be better able to cope with the uncertainties of the 1990s, and restore shareholder confidence in it. Internally, company-wide improvements that need to be made include:

- Greater control of the product in terms of quality, cost and material usage through investment in the most up-to-date information systems

- Investment in research and development

- The development of new products

- The development of a more participatory style of management

- Maintaining the company status as being one of the best employers in the country.

Waterford/Wedgwood is aiming to be a company committed to:

- Achieving and remaining competitive in its markets
- Achieving a satisfactory level of profits, thus ensuring an adequate return for its shareholders and funding for investment in new technology
- Encouraging the development of a culture in which management and employees participate at all levels
- Paying workers a fair wage with regard to the overall requirement to remain competitive
- Maintaining its status as a top-class producer of quality goods, but doing so in a manner that allows it to be a competitive in its various markets
- The fair and equitable treatment of all employees.

As the results for 1994 show, the group's restructuring programme is beginning to show results. This turnaround has come about because of a greatly improved performance from both the company's crystal and Wedgwood divisions. Operating profits in the crystal division increased by £5.2 million on the 1993 figure of £7.8 million, to £13 million, while profits in the Wedgwood division increased by 76 per cent, up from £8.7 million to a year-end figure of £15.3 million. This substantial increase in profitability was matched by an improvement in the group's finances. Despite capital expenditure of £17 million, significantly ahead of depreciation (£12 million), net debt fell by £14 million to £36 million, while gearing improved from 41 per cent to 27.5 per cent. The company in 1993 spent in the region of £18 million on promoting its products, up £3 million on the previous year, with most of this budget spent in the US market. On the capital side, the most immediate requirement is the installation of new furnaces, which will cost the company about £8 million. Along with this, the company hopes to bring in new technology, something that could potentially lead to more redundancies in the future.

In April 1994, Waterford Crystal announced that it was seeking a further reduction in employees, with a plan for 300 job cuts over a three-year period. In tandem with these job cuts, the division also wants to impose wage restraints and changes in work practices as part of its overall restructuring plan, which has recently managed to return the company to profitability. The money saved from these changes will help to pay for a new £10 million furnace for the Kilbarry plant. Discussions with the employees will cover the issue of a voluntary redundancy package, the first for the company's workers. In 1993, with the announcement of a £7.8 million profit, the workers received a profit-share bonus of £110. If profits are improved upon in the future, the bonuses of the workers will reflect this, with workers receiving some £1,000 if profits hit the £20 million mark. This incentive, it is hoped, will gain the backing of the workers. Another major incentive for the workers is the possibility that a number of crystal products made outside Ireland might be brought back to Waterford. Also, if the company is successful at reducing outsourcing, it could affect the number of jobs lost in Ireland.

While good progress has been made at Waterford, at Wedgwood the pace of growth and level of profitability are not as yet satisfactory. Wedgwood problems are different from Waterford's because it has a wider range of products, higher levels of stock inventories and a wider range of markets to serve. The strategies at present being implemented at Wedgwood are aimed at reducing the fixed cost base and at introducing more production efficiency, and to this end, there would be an increase in capital expenditure. There is no doubt that the company has managed to get back on the profitability trail. The only question that hangs over it now is how long it will take to get margins up to the 15 per cent target.

Source: Company reports and interviews with company personnel.

Questions

1. Analyse the external strategic decisions Waterford/Wedgwood has made since the late 1960s. What messages emerge from their success or failure?

2. What factors contributed to the Wedgwood acquisition and how successful has it been in your view?

3. Evaluate some of the internal problems that Waterford/Wedgwood has faced in the human resource area.

4. What implications does the present financial health of Waterford/Wedgwood have for it future growth?

19

Guinness Peat Aviation

Introduction

Superlatives come easily when writing about the phenomenal success of Guinness Peat Aviation (GPA), the Shannon-based aircraft leasing and finance group, the dominant player in its field. GPA, latterly GPA/GE, is the world's largest operating leaser of modern commercial aircraft and is a major participant in the global civil aviation industry. At the end of 1992, GPA had two principal lines of business:

- Leasing aircraft to a wide range of airlines throughout the world. As part of this activity it buys and sells aircraft as operating assets, and provides a wide range of management and technical support services to investors and airlines. As a result GPA is in a position to offer a full range of leasing options to its customers, from "dry" leases where the operation simply leases the aircraft with no technological support, to "wet" leases whereby GPA provides the aircraft, pilot, and maintenance support necessary.

- Selling aircraft, usually with operating leases in place, to investors, offering a return on their investment from a combination of future lease rentals, the aircraft residual value, and, in certain instances, tax benefits. Ancillary support for investors is also provided.

GPA conducts its core business through a range of joint venture companies and usually holds a 50 per cent equity interest. At the end of December 1992 the GPA fleet consisted of 476 aircraft, of which 357 were owned, 97 were leased from their owners and 22 were managed on behalf of their owners.

Development of GPA

GPA is a company operating in a dynamic external environment. Its headquarters is located at Shannon on the west coast of Ireland. Aviation is an unstable business. The company was founded by Dr Tony Ryan in 1975. He had worked for the Irish airline Aer Lingus, rising to middle management in the leasing department. The airline found itself with surplus planes. Tony Ryan worked out a deal whereby Aer Lingus planes would be leased to Air Siam together with support staff to operate them. From that grew the germ of an idea: an idea which in the 19 years since then has turned into a multi-billion dollar company.

GPA has diversified into activities such as aircraft maintenance, with facilities in the area as much to create jobs and opportunities as to build an empire. As Ryan recalls, "I felt there was an opportunity in the developing world where airlines would have great difficulty finding the capital to buy planes." It has evolved a long way since then. Aer Lingus baulked at Ryan's idea of a big push into a specialised aircraft (though it took a stake in the new company) but the London merchant bank Guinness Peat backed him and GPA was the result. Ryan started with £80,000 in capital. Throughout the group's history its level of growth and profit performance has been quite extraordinary. Its profits in 1992 were £268 million and it has more than half the world leasing market sewn up, twice the share of its only serious rival, the California-based ILFC.

The key to GPA's growth had been its ability to exploit Ryan's original observation of the demand for leases. Leasing was nothing new, but transferring the concept to aircraft was. When the company was founded, no more than 2–3 per cent of the world's planes were leased. Now the figure is nearer 20 per cent and expected to climb higher. "The separation between ownership and operation has happened very rapidly," says Ryan. GPA's core business is the leasing of aircraft to the world's airlines. Over the years this business has boomed, with GPA becoming the world leader in purchasing aircraft and renting them to airlines on leases of 3–7 years. The under-capitalisation of many airlines, coupled with the fact that such leases are off balance sheets are attractions for the airlines, while the residual value of the aircraft rests with GPA.

GPA in the early days found most of its clients in Africa, Asia and South America. A typical deal was a so-called "wet" lease, under which GPA provided full operational support, including pilots, engineering and maintenance. The growth in this area was fuelled in part by deregulation and rapid technological change. The demand from bigger airlines for leases without the operational back-up has also grown. Sixty per cent of GPA leases are with airlines from Europe and the Americas.

In 1979, the company began purchasing aircraft for its own account, concentrating on aircraft with wide customer acceptance and flexible operating characteristics. Since 1984 GPA has substantially expanded its aircraft portfolio. In 1986 GPA changed its legal status from a private company to a public limited company, the intention being to overcome problems the company might encounter in expanding its shareholders to more than 50, the maximum that a private company is allowed to have in Ireland.

Growth Patterns

For GPA the 1980s marked the group's greatest success. Between 1988 and 1992 pre-tax profit rose from $107 million to $276 million. In the two years to March 1990 GPA made more money out of selling aircraft than it did out of its core leasing business—$186 million in all, more than 40 per cent of its gross profits. In the year to March 1989, GPA sold $661 million worth of planes for a gross profit of $77 million. In the following year, sales soared to $1.48 billion at a profit of $109 million.

GPA had always been able to insulate itself against the market to some extent by finding tax-effective packages for its investors. In the mid-1980s GPA's finance department came up with an idea of raising money by selling off aircraft to investors while continuing to manage the leases on their behalf. The idea grew out of a deal with a group of Norwegian fishermen. A new division of the business called GPA Capital was founded, with Nigel Lawson, former British Chancellor of the Exchequer, as non-executive chairman. It soon became one of the fastest growing projects of the business portfolios.

Self confidence had never been short at GPA. Asked about its growth slowing down in the early 1990s, Ryan was quoted as saying that "no tree reaches the sky." Growth has slowed down all right: in the five years up to 1990, GPA averaged annual net profit growth of 70 per cent. Net profit in 1986 was $25 million, in 1990 it equalled $2.42 million. This trend could not go on indefinitely, and it did not.

GPA believed that the gloom which resulted from the invasion of Kuwait and the value of aircraft falling was an over-reaction: during this time, GPA had an enormous order book and a business based on growth. One of the major risks of GPA's business is that it has assets in the form of aircraft which it must ensure are permanently leased to maintain revenues rolling. Pessimism about the industry reached a peak early in 1991.

The Gulf War affected the company badly: international air traffic from the US slumped by 13.8 per cent and European traffic fell by 14.5 per cent. Strategic planning head Ken Holden, while acknowledging that air traffic fell 7 per cent in 1991 stated, "We have always planned for recession. We certainly couldn't predict the congruence of a world war, a credit crunch and an economic downturn, but we have performed in a very creditable fashion."

Tony Ryan tried to stick rigidly to his original philosophy of keeping the cash-hungry GPA fed by private funding arrangements with institutions and shareholders. However, it was clear that this was not feasible in the long run. The June 1992 flotation would have gone some way towards meeting GPA's voracious appetite for capital. In the four years to 1992, the number of aircraft owned or managed by GPA and its joint-venture companies had quadrupled from 101 to 409. The cash outflow for 1991, for instance, was $3.1 billion compared with the $2.13 billion the company spent on new aircraft. For the year ended March 1993, GPA was committed to paying $2.32 billion for new aircraft. It had cash in the bank of just $387 million. GPA and its joint-venture affiliates had orders for $11.9 billion worth of aircraft between 1992 and the year 2000, and there were options for a further $9 billion. GPA's decision to buy these aeroplanes was taken between 1985 and 1990 and was based on predictions that the huge growth in aviation over the previous two decades would continue through the 1990s, creating a shortage of planes, particularly the new types of fuel-efficient and less noisy aircraft. GPA needed capital, and a flotation was considered the best option open to them — the company estimated that between $600 million and $1 billion could be raised. Even after generating $1.57 billion from operations in 1991, GPA was still short $1.2 billion for its needs, and a flotation would have gone some way towards meeting these demands.

According to the financial press at the time, Tony Ryan was reluctant to make a move to a public quotation, mainly because it would have lessened his control of the group, and up to then the company had had no difficulty raising finance through both equity and debt fund issues. During 1990, GPA approached a number of companies to take a major stake in the company but discussions ended over the issue of price. There was a flotation attempt in August 1990 but it was postponed because of the depressed state of the airline industry. The effects of the Gulf War delayed the flotation beyond 1991. Also, the airlines — GPA's customers — were going through a rough time with financial results weak and profits very low. On a global basis, the world's airlines lost a cumulative total of $5 billion in 1990 and $4 billion in 1991, with such airlines as Pan Am going out of business, and TWA and America West — owing GPA $170 million — under chapter 11 protection. These factors were deterring many potential investors from lending to the aviation industry. Of the world's major airlines only three — British Airways, Cathay Pacific and Singapore — operated profitably in 1991.

GPA/GE's Business Activities

GPA's activities are organised in three principal business units: Leasing, Capital and Technologies.

Leasing

This area accounted for 31 per cent of revenue, and 30 per cent of gross profit. It acquired and managed the group's aircraft fleet, marketed the operating leases on a global basis, and sells new and used planes as operating assets to airlines worldwide. With a market share of 40 per cent, GPA is the world's leading provider of new aircraft on operating lease. Some of the business is conducted through joint-venture companies which purchase and lease specific aircraft. GPA manages these companies which are separately financed. Other shareholders include aerospace manufacturers, airlines, financial institutions and trading companies.

Capital

This area accounted for 68 per cent of revenue, and 60 per cent of gross profit. It marketed aviation-related products to individual and corporate investors, together with a range of related investment and merchant banking activities, including cross-border and tax-based financing. One major development was the ALPS (Aircraft Lease Portfolio Securitisation Aircraft Fund) 92-1 project launched in June 1992. It was widely acclaimed as an innovation in aviation financing. It was the first aircraft-related transaction to apply the techniques of asset-backed securities to open up new sources of finance for aircraft.

Other achievements by GPA Capital included a significant use of US foreign sales, corporation tax leases, and a further widening of customer and product bases in Gulf states, South East Asia and Latin America. The innovative "Eurofund" concept optimised general tax advantages for European companies using financial technology developed by GPA. Capital continued to be an important source of profit and liquidity for the company and very much a leader in the development of aircraft financing techniques worldwide.

Technologies

This managed GPA's investments in a number of businesses which provide a range of technical and support services to airlines. It is a division of GPA whose charter is to identify, develop and manage a portfolio of investments focused on businesses providing high-quality technical and infrastructural services for the aviation industry. A major objective of GPA Technologies is to sponsor and promote the Shannon area as a major aviation and support centre. A key element of this strategy is the development at Shannon of the GPA Aerospace Park, incorporating a range of aviation-related ventures that are profitable, mutually synergistic and provide infrastructural support for the company.

GPA Technologies was established in 1989 and it has invested in Shannon Aerospace, GPA Pacific Aero Support, GPA Expressair, and Shannon Engine Support.

Shannon Aerospace: GPA, Swissair and Lufthansa are partners in this maintenance joint venture whose chairman is Peter Sutherland, former EU Commissioner.

Pacific Aero Support is a subsidiary of Pacific Aviation Group, a company founded in 1983, which became a member of GPA in 1990 and has set up its European market and distribution base at

Shannon. The company supplies both new and used refurbished aircraft parts to airlines worldwide.

Expressair provides quality aircraft, painting services, cabin upgrading and refitting, and refurbishment to airline operations. Founded in 1984, it became a member of GPA in 1989.

Engine Support is a joint venture between GPA Technologies and CFMI, the manufacturer for the latest versions of Boeing 737 aircraft. The company makes spare engine coverage available to operators of these aircraft.

Shannon Turbine Technologies was founded in 1991, a venture between GPA (60 per cent) and Sulzer Brothers, specialising in the high-technology repair of jet engine components.

GPA conducts many of its business through joint ventures. Its partners in these ventures include major manufacturers of aircraft and their engines and certain financial institutions. The rationale for such arrangements is that they give GPA the opportunity to strengthen relationships with important industry participants, improve its competitive position and leverage GPA's own management expertise and capital by financing fleet growth on a non-resource basis. GPA typically holds 50 per cent of equity in the joint-venture company and provides the management expertise. Some of GPA's joint venture partners include: British Airways, Rolls Royce, Lufthansa/Swissair, Pacific Western and Midland Bank.

Shareholders and Directors of GPA/GE

Among the many shareholders in GPA are such notables as Aer Lingus which held a 19.6 per cent share up to 1988 but had to pull out because of its own internal difficulties, and Air Canada with a 15 per cent stake, and which pulled out of the company after the flotation confusion. Others include Bank of Ireland and the giant UK conglomerate Hanson, Chiyoda Finance of Japan and two Swedish companies — Gamlestaden and Nyckeln Holdings. The list of GPA directors reads like a who's who in politics and included a former government leader, a former Chancellor of the Exchequer, a former European Commissioner and the head of a major bank. They are not just figureheads.

- Dr Garret FitzGerald joined the board in 1987 and travelled extensively for the company on high-level missions.

- Peter Sutherland, the former EC Commissioner (1985–89) joined the group in 1989 but has since left to take over the role of Director General of GATT.

- Nigel Lawson, a former UK Chancellor of the Exchequer joined the board in 1990.

- Shinroko Morohashi the president of the Mitsubishi corporation came to the group in 1987 and was a director until 1992.

- Sir John Harvey-Jones is one of the most influential of the non-executive directors and is deputy chairman of the GPA Group. He is much regarded for his business and management development expertise.

GPA used these high-profile people for their door-opening ability, business contacts, business acumen and because they give the company considerable credibility internationally.

Financial Policies and Financial Performance

It is generally accepted that GPA has a detailed knowledge of aircraft and airlines. However, it has also used the most sophisticated financial weaponry and fiscal breaks available to give itself a competitive advantage. Successful financial planning and eliminating financial exposure as far as possible have been major ingredients in the GPA success story.

In particular, the following have been availed of:

- *Section 84 Financing*: GPA has been one of the major borrowers, sourcing Section 84 funds not only from Irish banks but also from abroad. While the advantages of Section 84 finance have diminished over the past few years, it still played a vital part in the financial policies of GPA.

- Another tax break was GPA Midland, formed on a 50/50 basis with Midland Bank, to provide long-term tax leverage finance leases. GPA Midland raises funds internationally to avail of double taxation treaties with Ireland, as it has with a number of other countries. However, the stamp duty imposed in 1985 on these loans was one of the reasons for the demise of GPA Midland.

- GPA itself is based in the Shannon Free Zone, which gave it tax-free profits to 1990. This tax-free status has been a very important ingredient in the financial success of GPA, by allowing it to retain substantial earnings while at the same time offering attractive tax-free returns to preference shareholders. These tax concessions should not be exaggerated in an industry where virtually all aircraft carry some tax advantage. All these opportunities were exploited to the full by GPA. Despite its huge leasing portfolio, GPA managed, up until recently, to emerge virtually unscathed from bad debts. When dealing with less-developed countries, GPA has been creative in its thinking in reducing exposures by using irrevocable letters of credit, guarantees and even deposits as circumstances dictate. On competition, deputy chairman Foley points out that: "humility is one of the strengths of GPA. Normally we don't have competition, we have contemporaries and it is very helpful to have such, they keep us on our toes."

- GPA has had a good credit rating: it could raise money more cheaply, and use it to buy planes which it then leased out to less creditworthy customers. It is much more efficient financially for the banks to lend money to GPA which passes it on in the shape of aircraft to less developed countries. As Foley states, "It required a mixture of good engineering, accounting and legal skills, but behind all that it fundamentally required good instincts for where money can be made and where it can't, and GPA have it down to an art form."

Table 19.1 below presents the financial performance of GPA for the years 1987 to 1992.

Profit Performance

In July 1988 at the height of the company's growth GPA was valued at $1 billion with net profit of $101 million and a doubling of its equity base in one year. The net profit of the group reached

$152 million in 1989, a compounded annual growth of 64 per cent in the five years to 1989. GPA continued to grow, and its gearing level of 200 per cent was heavy compared to other businesses in 1990 when it reached net profits of $242 million. The world recession saw a slowdown in the profits for the group, at $262 million (8.3 per cent growth) by 1991. The recession also hit the group lease rates (from 21 per cent to 13 per cent in 1992). Profits declined dramatically in 1993, and 1994 recorded a loss of $30 million. In 1995, the overall loss was $70 million.

Table 19.1: Financial Performance, 1987–92

	1987	1988	1989	1990	1991	1992	1993	1994	1995
	$m	$m	$m	$m	$m	$m	$m	$m	$m
Revenue	360	650	1,042	1,962	1,889	2,010	1,742	1,856	1,617
Gross Profit		123	161	222	308	306	15	30	70
Net Profit (Loss)	68	101.3	152.2	242	262	268	(64)	(26)	47
Shareholders' Funds	217	371	545	893	1,005	1,230	234	137	111
Total Aircraft Commitments	392	731	940	1,074	990	981	2,327	1,812	1,645
Permanent Employees	139	153	170	212	222	251	244	218	196
Earnings per Share	—	1.09	1.41	2.1	2.21	2.3	—	—	—

Gearing

For capital-intensive leasing companies the gearing ratio can be much higher than in other businesses, but the higher it is, the greater the interest burden on the company. In GPA's case this effectively was $225 million or 11 per cent of turnover in 1992. On closer inspection, $165 million (8.2 per cent of turnover) was directly related to bank loans, overdrafts and other loans wholly repayable within five years. Borrowings increased to $4.165 million by March 1992, compared to $2.712 million in 1991. In 1987 the company had secured a $1.2 billion loan with a further extension of $900 million in 1990 to support huge aircraft acquisition orders. The flotation was expected to raise up to $1 billion in fresh equity and reduce the gearing ratio from 3.4:1 to a more manageable 2.6:1, and strengthen the company's borrowing power. Its failure made borrowing much more expensive and the company's indebtedness increased to about $5 billion by November 1992, thus increasing the debt/equity ratio to around 4:1. The group's gearing ratio has increased from a manageable 1.8 in 1988 to 3.4 early in 1992.

Revenue Growth

GPA's turnover showed significant growth each year up to 1990. It was not until 1991 that the group saw an overall drop in revenue — 3 per cent — the first recorded in the company's 19-year history. For 1987 the group's revenue stood at $360 million, and by 1990 it had increased to $1,962.2 million. However, the 3 per cent drop in 1991 saw revenue fall to $1,889.2 million, but the 1992 figure saw a recovery with revenue totalling $2,010.5 million. There has been no growth in revenue since the beginning of the recession in 1990. Aircraft sales continued to be a great source of cash flow, contributing $1,284 million in 1991 and $1,127.4 million in 1992, but gross profit from aircraft sales fell by 5 per cent to $175 million in 1992. Since 1992, revenue has declined significantly and in 1994 stood at $1,856 million. In 1995, the figure was $1,617 million.

Earnings per Share

Earnings per share were up by 4 per cent in 1992 to $2.3 following a 5 per cent increase in 1991 to $2.21. In the five years to 1990 earnings per share had an annual compounded growth of 45 per cent. In 1988 earnings per share stood at $1.09 and by 1990 stood at $2.1. For the flotation, shares were offered at rates between $10 and $12 in June 1992, but because of its failure they had fallen to $8 in September 1992. At this time, GPA was worth approximately $800 million, down from the $2 billion in May 1992. Since 1992, it is difficult to establish a meaningful earnings per share figure because of restructuring.

Profitability

Between 1988 and 1992 there was a significant increase in gross profit. In 1988 gross profit stood at $123 million and by 1990 it had jumped to over $225 million. In 1992 it stood at $306 million. However, there was a significant fall in gross margins in leasing, from 21 per cent in 1991 to 12 per cent in 1992, indicating an increase in non-revenue-earning aircraft, and a downward pressure on lease rates. This trend resulted from the difficult trading conditions of the recession. The gross margin on aircraft sales was 17 per cent in 1992, compared to 18 per cent in 1991. Shareholders' funds continued to grow to $1,230 million in 1992. Return on capital employed — the return the owners receive for investing their money — was 21.5 per cent in 1992, down from 25 per cent in 1991 and 27 per cent in 1990. In the five years to 1990, return on capital employed had seen 40 per cent compounded growth.

The Internal Organisation of GPA

Management Team and Culture Base

GPA employees are highly skilled, mobile, highly motivated and very highly paid. The management team demonstrated this through superior growth rates and strategic shifts in its range of business activities. The team was able to identify a need in the marketplace for airlines to obtain aircraft without saddling GPA balance sheets with large debts.

As GPA points out, "it would be a great irony if we as a successful company, didn't tap into the very best human resources in Ireland. Why should bright young Irish people work internationally when they have a company in Ireland that can give them that dimension?" GPA recruits the best its salary scales and bonuses are envied, but the performance justifies the largesse. Despite the perception of being a company of young predators, the ratio of grey to non-grey hairs is fairly balanced, and all work together as a team.

According to Maurice Foley, the culture is international: "Small is good and Irish people have an attitude of neutrality when they go abroad and do not have an imperialist background. They adjust well." Foley makes the following points:

- It is not unreasonable to expect people to live near their work.

- No one takes holidays in March, June, September or December.

- People are driven by what has to be done.

- Everything is completely planned with forecasts for five years ahead, then annually, quarterly and weekly.

- GPA's high fliers work hard and long hours, but they are rewarded for their endeavours. It is not millionaires' playground, "more a corporate gymnasium for the advancement of the work ethic, with remuneration commensurate with effort".

According to the group: "one of the measures of our strength is our capacity to place aircraft around the world". GPA has the most skilled team in the world, the best portfolio of young aircraft, more than adequate financing contracted, and a global customer base in place.

Another cultural dimension is that the group has tried to encourage people to believe that there are no insoluble problems; that there are no countries or customers with whom business cannot on principle be done; and that it is necessary to vary techniques to a wide range of environments. "We send people to a wide range of customers without preconceptions, without bags of tricks thinking that this is the only way they can do it".

Extensive Knowledge of the Industry

GPA/GE's intelligence and knowledge of aviation are significant. With its computer system containing details of every aircraft in the world — its age, type, number of landings, flying hours and owner — this has enabled GPA to keep far ahead in the field: it just does not have a serious competitor. The company keeps constant tabs on its customers, relying mostly on industry gossip.

Take a Global Perspective

GPA tended to think big and think globally. Maurice Foley has said of its Shannon location:

> It may be an improbable place, but we consider it a very appropriate place to locate a global company because to think globally you need not have a substantial home market, or bring any baggage with you. We have avoided the conventional financial centres so as not to be trapped by the conventional wisdom.

The ethos is truly global.

Innovative Techniques

GPA's ability to ride the downturn in the airline industry was demonstrated in its 1991 figures, which showed a static level of profits rather than the dip that many had expected because of the recession and the war in Kuwait. This was mostly because of its ability to innovate itself out of trouble.

Structure and Attitude

Structure and attitude are very important to the way in which GPA is run. It has tried to build a business that is very innovative and that encourages people to identify opportunities, because: "a lot of what GPA does is doing things that other people aren't doing". An example is the creation of GPA Capital. Because uncertainty is at the heart of its business, it is the elixir that keeps it going: "One man's risk is another man's opportunity ... with a limit." This is basically the philosophy of the organisation.

Communication

GPA maintains that communication is one of the secrets of its success. Its people can contact each other, any time, anywhere. Tony Ryan even told an employee that he "could expect him to have a phone in his shoe, if that was necessary". The corporate culture at GPA makes for close bonds: "They depend a lot on each other for support." This has grown in spite of, and not with the help of, outside advice. "It is a company which believes in the myth of its invincibility." The whole history of GPA's success has been in not taking advice, in doing things that everyone said could not be done.

Business Ethos and Culture

Maurice Foley has identified a number of features of GPA's business ethos and modus operandi critical for achieving its objectives.

Most importantly, the company is market led, with its product tailored to the needs of the customer — thus everyone is focused on the customer. The company has assembled the strategic elements to enable it to tailor its products to the specific needs of customers.

GPA perceives its employees as the dynamic element in moulding the other raw materials to the customers' needs to turn specific commercial opportunities into profit-making deals. The aspects of the culture that provide the motivational framework for the company's human resources to be employed effectively are:

- People are challenged to their limits.
- Multi-disciplinary co-operation is given.
- Commitment — i.e. sacrifice, speed, etc. — is very high.
- Employees have the ability to handle change.
- Compensation is related to profits.

Planning is an essential element of GPA's ethos. GPA defines planning as the process of setting clear objectives for a range of horizons ranging from 15 years to the next quarter century. Maurice Foley points out that it is critical to develop the ability and the attitude to respond positively to new information and opportunity. This has led to an emphasis on flexibility.

GPA's culture is defined by its dynamic ethos rather than its structural characteristics: "Just do it — now!" "The immediate commercial exigencies, pulled, ad hoc, interdisciplinary teams together, and created temporary 'bootstrap' pragmatic lines of internal communication." GPA is very much geared towards clinching the deal, so to do this it is highly responsive, flexible, and innovative in its handling of potential customers.

Other facets of GPA's culture which contribute to the activity-oriented environment in which it operates are:

- The organisation is flat and fluid, so the net effect is that people are working with, rather than "for", colleagues. There is a focus on the job that has to be done, and an adaptability to change.

- High emphasis is put on entrepreneurial values. This is reflected in the procedural balance between facilitation and control, with an emphasis on the former. Authority is dispersed, with individual initiative, speed, and self-confidence in decision-making very much encouraged. Control exists but it is unobtrusive. The company is very much more concerned with achieving success than with preventing failure.

- There is a highly individualistic culture. Remuneration is related to profit but the share of the profit is individually determined. There are no collective agreements and each person's arrangements are private.

Completed commercial transactions are the only activities to receive applause. The company ideology praises the deal-doers and merely tolerates the controllers and administrators. While the need for people to "tidy up" is recognised and accepted, this is seen as an unfortunate, if necessary, cost, not as part of the value-creation process, and certainly not integral to the transaction process itself. Internal migration is a symptom of such a culture, and it is very much a trend in GPA.

A lack of a transcendent procedural framework, and established channels of communication transcending immediate commercial pressures, inhibited the pursuit of any activity which does not have an external commercial objective. This goes some way to explaining why the company resorts to external consultants to deal with internal problems. It has less to do with the lack of in-house expertise, and more to do with the lack of willingness on the company's part.

The effect of culture and contingencies define GPA as a market-led company whose core skills are reduced to selling, lacking the more sophisticated marketing strategy of being a creator of customer demand rather than simply satisfying it.

The GPA Flotation

For many years GPA had resisted pressure to float the company, yet capital requirements continued to grow, with the company committed to spending a phenomenal $12,110 million on 318 aircraft between 1992 and the year 2000. Shareholders wanted to make some money, and financial investors wanted the company's balance sheet strengthened. Bringing in more equity would have improved the group's gearing which was higher than the creditors wished. In April 1992 borrowings stood at $4.46 billion, which was 3.4 times more than shareholders funds. The flotation hoped to raise as much as $1 billion and bring the gearing down to 2. The decision to float the company was taken to finance the group's aircraft acquisition programme; to improve the company's equity structure; and to provide a global market for the company's ordinary shares.

The parties chosen to manage the flotation were Nomura of Japan as global co-ordinator; Goldman Sachs, Merrill Lynch and Saloman Brothers in the US; Schroders and BZW in the UK; and Nomura and Yamaichi in Japan. Under the offer, the company and the selling shareholders were to offer for sale 85 million ordinary shares representing 29.7 per cent of the enlarged-issue ordinary share capital of the company. This meant that the company would issue up to 59 million ordinary shares and the selling shareholders would sell up to 25.5 million ordinary shares. A global road show was set in motion with a specially appointed group working on the flotation for more than a year. The response was said to be great and the mood was optimistic. But the company could not have chosen a worse time to seek its international flotation. The world was still in the grip of the recession and the airline industry was in a state of shock after the worst year in aviation history. It would seem in hindsight that the result was inevitable.

The flotation was a spectacular failure that was cancelled the day the shares were due to start trading in London. The failure was attributed to a misreading of the stock market by the GPA board. The board was considered excellent at reading the aviation industry, but less good at determining the reactions of the investment community. Only 49 million of the 85 million total shares were bought up.

Almost half of the shares were sold not to major institutions but to private individuals, mainly in Japan, rather than institutions, with the result that GPA's shares would be hopelessly unstable on world markets. Cancelling the flotation was a last resort. It was the US investors who torpedoed the float. The company had come to the market against a backdrop of unparalleled decline in air traffic, falling aircraft orders, and a credit squeeze. Investors were looking for a reason not to invest, and in GPA they found it. What some considered as greed on the part of Tony Ryan did not help matters. He insisted on a $22 per share flotation price — had he accepted $15, the issue, according to experts, might have succeeded. There are many other views on why it all went wrong.

GPA appeared to have done a good job selling itself to the US. However, new issues had become an unpopular idea. Furthermore, the difficulties facing US airlines and the price war on which they had embarked did not help matters. The institutional investors were not impressed. Airlines were among the most unpopular stocks on the world stock exchange, and much of GPA's time was spent trying to explain to potential investors that the company was not an airline and, hence, did not follow airline trends. However, it seems that it did not get the message across. Added to this, the US election led to insecurity on Wall Street.

Other factors working against the company at the time included the fact that GPA buys almost entirely on spec without the comfort of pre-arranged leases for its planes. The company had a growing number of unleased aeroplanes on its books at the time. Furthermore, fund managers like to be able to see clearly what risks they are taking with people's money. In GPA's case, the risks were hard to quantify.

In 1990 Tony Ryan's share value in the company stood at $304 million and the company's shares were valued at $30 each. In September 1992 his share value had fallen to $75 million and share price stood at $8. By November 1992, the company's share price was less than $4. Before the flotation, Irish shareholders including Aer Lingus, GPA staff and Irish institutions owned about one third of the company. These holdings were worth about $1 billion in December 1989 when the price peaked at $32. They seemed to become paper millionaires. This so-called fortune fell 80 per cent because of the flotation failure. In monetary terms, the single individual loser was Tony Ryan himself whose share dropped at least $167 million in value. Other members lost about $18 million. Aer Lingus, the largest Irish shareholder which had seen its share decrease from $323 in 1990 to $49 million in 1992, has written down its investment but not the present share price. The advisors ended up getting none of their hoped-for $35 million share of the proceeds.

According to the financial press, the deal failed because of structures and people first, and the environment and story second. Successful global equity issues share a number of common themes. Many commentators pointed out that a successful flotation required a story that was well understood, a valuation agreed in all markets, a co-ordinated marketing effort and a clear home base, which was a problem for GPA. There is general agreement that the structures were not appropriate. If the structures had not been so inflexible and if the price could have been adjusted, things could perhaps have been different. The US was the most difficult market in which to sell the company; GPA was a complex story and it was difficult to make people comfortable with it. The US investors were also unsettled by adverse press comment. Throughout the transaction, the global co-ordination was absent. There was no high profile co-ordination of the marketing effort, no leadership in the battles over structure and price, and no attempt to rein in the rival advisors when their infighting threatened to undermine the entire transaction.

The failure of the flotation attempt was a shattering blow to GPA and the financial advisers who handled the issue. The initial reaction was that there was not an immediate need for the money to be raised by the flotation and that the business of buying, leasing and selling of aircraft would go on as normal. However, the reputation of Ireland's most successful company would never be the same again and the failure of the issue raised some serious questions about future financing, growth and survival of the group.

GPA'S Post-Flotation Fiasco: The Rescue Plan

Beginning in June 1992, the group's difficulties mounted. Already financially overextended, and facing a $12 billion bill for aircraft not yet delivered, not only did GPA not have the flotation proceeds, but its credit rating started to plunge and interest on debts began to rise.

Starved of fresh capital and with debts of $5.5 billion, GPA was forced to embark on a highly complex round of negotiations. By September of 1992, a survival package was being drawn up by the company, involving a rescheduling of its debts with its 100 bankers: a proposed $350 million share issue and the renegotiation of its commitments to manufacturers. It did succeed in cutting back its orders of new aircraft from over $11 billion at the time of the flotation, to $3 billion, and the agreement of a majority of its secured lenders to defer $1 billion of debt payments until 1996. However, the cost of winding up these contracts alone was significant.

GPA's bondholders, owed in total $2 billion, were due repayments of $200 million by 17 May 1993, and unless a reconstruction had been completed by then, GPA would have had to default. By April 1993, the company had abandoned efforts to raise fresh equity from its existing shareholders, after the majority indicated an unwillingness to invest. The shareholders effectively transferred control of the company to the banks. GPA had now to consider the unthinkable: court protection from its creditors in the form of examinership. This threat was seen by some as a way of forcing the hand of banks and bondholders who would not be keen on an outsider, answerable only to a court, running things. The move for examinership would have been very much triggered by the unsecured bondholders due payments by 17 May 1993. The advantages of an examinership were two fold: GPA would be instantly granted the $1 billion debt moratorium it had been seeking over the previous 6 months, without needing to raise further equity;

and the banks would have had little choice but to forego any hope that they might have entertained about controlling the company.

However, an examinership was sufficient protection because of GPA's worldwide operations. At this time, there were moves by some of GPA's bankers to sell on the company's debt to lessen their exposure to the troubled group. Five bank lenders to GPA bailed out of the company by off-loading debt into the market at heavily discounted prices. One bank dumped $50 million of company debt in a single transaction. At this stage, Air Canada also pulled out.

The only hope left was that a "White Knight" might come to the rescue and take a significant equity stake in the company, hence the discussions with such notables as General Electric, but it was more interested in buying GPA's aircraft assets on the cheap. General Electric, a giant American electronics and defence concern, was run by "Neutron" Jack Welch — a man with a reputation to match any of those who assembled in Shannon once a month for GPA's board meetings. With General Electric's financial depth and acumen, it could be very worthwhile for GPA. However, the price for General Electric's capital was effective control. Amidst speculation that the company would be forced to seek protection from creditors, the General Electric deal was offered, and GPA was in no position to refuse it.

The General Electric Deal

The arrangements with GE capital consist of the following principal elements:

Aircraft Transactions

(a) GE Capital or its associated undertakings acquired a mixed portfolio of 35 aircraft for an initial cash payment of between 75 per cent and 85 per cent approximately (and, in the case of two aircraft still to be acquired, 64 per cent) of the net book value at the date of sale. A further deferred consideration of approximately 15 per cent to 25 per cent (and, in the case of two aircraft, 36 per cent) of net book value at the sale date would be payable only if the aircraft was subsequently sold, or "deemed" sold, or upon the occurrence of certain deemed or actual casualty events, and only to the extent described below.

Upon a subsequent sale or deemed sale of an aircraft the amount of the deferred consideration which will be payable to GPA is determined as follows:

- GE Capital is entitled to a scheduled amount (which amount will recoup its investment in the aircraft together with an agreed upon return)

- To the extent of any remaining net proceeds GE Capital will pay to GPA an amount which is generally equivalent to between 15 per cent and 25 per cent approximately (or, in the case of two aircraft, 36 per cent) of the net book value of the aircraft.

Amounts equal to any remaining net proceeds will accrue firstly to GE Capital and thereafter, up to certain amounts, be paid by GE Capital to GPA on agreed terms.

In accordance with the accounting policy, investment in Aircraft, amounts of $nil in the year ended 31 March 1995, $28 million in the year ended 31 March 1994, and $38 million in the year ended 31 March 1993, were expensed in respect of the estimated residual value and related risks.

(b) In addition, in the event that GPA purchases up to eight A320 aircraft, they may be included in the GE transaction under similar arrangements conditional on certain future events. The sale of these aircraft would be subject to suitable lessees and lease terms being in place and GE Capital may reject any aircraft if it is not satisfied with the proposed lease or lessee.

Management of GPA's Aircraft Assets

In October 1993, GPA entered into a management contract with GECAS. Under the management contract, GECAS provides, on an exclusive basis, and in consideration for management fees, certain management services for aircraft assets owned or leased-in by GPA, and aircraft assets which GPA manages on behalf of its associated undertakings and third parties. Fees paid to GECAS in the year ended 31 March 1995 amounted to $45 million (1994: $17 million) of which $42 million (1994: $17 million) has been charged in the profit and loss account and $3 million representing a financing cost which is included in ALPS 94-1 deferred expenditure.

Assistance to GPA's ALPS Programme

GECAS will use reasonable commercial efforts to assist GPA in, and facilitate the implementation of, its future programme of ALPS sales. This assistance does not extend to any obligation of GECAS or any of its associated undertakings to underwrite or purchase any securities to be issued by GPA or any other person, including any ALPS vehicle, in connection with any ALPS transaction or to issue any guarantees or otherwise provide (or incur any obligations or liabilities to provide) any credit enhancement or support or to incur any other obligations or liabilities in connection with any ALPS transaction or take certain other specified action, including the execution of any registration statement or any similar document. In addition, GECAS's obligation to provide assistance with respect to any particular ALPS transaction is subject to GECAS's satisfaction with the terms and conditions of the relevant ALPS transaction (including indemnities with respect thereto to be given to GECAS). In addition, GECAS will participate in the structuring and marketing of the ALPS securities.

Equity Option

In consideration for the payment of $500,000 by GE Capital to the company, GE Capital has been granted an option to subscribe for B Shares representing 67.1 per cent ("GE Capital's percentage") of the enlarged diluted ordinary share capital of the company. The GE Capital Option must be exercised in full unless GE Capital is prohibited because of a legal or regulatory reason from so doing, in which case a partial exercise must be for the maximum number of B Shares permitted at that time by the law or relevant regulatory body.

The GE Capital Option is not transferable except to one or more majority-owned affiliate of General Electric Company or GE Capital. The B Shares issued upon an exercise of the GE Capital Option will be freely transferable. The GE Capital option may be exercised at any time on or prior to 31 March 1998, and the amount payable by GE Capital on exercise will be the par value of the B Shares subscribed by GE Capital on exercise of the GE Capital Option (not exceeding $1 million) plus an additional amount. This additional amount will be the higher of $113.2 million and an amount equal to GE Capital's percentage of 50 per cent of the value of the GPA's ordinary shareholders' funds as shown in GPA's latest quarterly financial statements prepared on the basis of Irish GAAP (as adjusted through a pre-arranged mechanism to (i) exclude the effects thereon of a change in accounting practice relating to FRS 5 which became effective for GPA in the year ended 31 March 1995, and (ii) reflect 50 per cent of any liabilities payable by the company which are conditional upon the exercise of the GE Capital Option or the GE Capital Call Option if then exercised (GE Capital's option to acquire all voting shares in GPA Group plc held by the Noteholders) including any incentive payments payable to directors and officers following exercise of the GE Capital Option and, if applicable, the GE Capital Call Option). However, the amount payable will not exceed $167.8 million.

The amount payable by GE Capital on exercise of the GE Capital Option will be allocated firstly to the company and thereafter to the holders of A Shares on terms specified in the agreements.

The GE takeover was a very shrewd and timely deal — the classic chance to buy cheap when company fortunes were low. GE was buying assets at less than cost, and it had four years to decide whether to buy into GPA at a price based on the company's then precarious position, rather than on any future recovery. At any time it could move to take over most of GPA at about $1 a share.

A restructuring of the company's management was now very likely. Tony Ryan had to fight to stay at the helm of the company he had founded 18 years previously. The bondholders and banks were demanding that Tony Ryan and the company's most senior staff be sacked as the price for their agreement, especially all those involved in the failed flotation. As experts have pointed out, after the flotation fiasco, the top team had only a few key decisions to make: when to float, at what price, and when to start talks with the banks. They got them all wrong. The irony is that over 12 months to December 1993, GPA had performed admirably in the business it knows best — leasing of aircraft. This was mainly because of a strong middle-tier management who kept things going during the mess. Middle management were angry at what they saw as a severe communications breakdown with the company's top executives, a feeling that the board was so concerned with refinancing that it had lost touch with the day-to-day operational efficiency of the company.

Changes in management have taken place with Dennis Stevenson coming in as Tony Ryan's replacement as chairman of GPA. In addition to the GPA chairmanship, he is a director of Blue Arrow Publishing Group, Pearson and J. Rothschild Assurance and Chairman of the management consultancy group SRU. Other changes at GPA included the departure of Dr Garret FitzGerald, Nigel Lawson and Sir John Harvey-Jones. Peter Sutherland quit on his appointment as Director General of GATT. Tony

Ryan was shunted sideways to chair General Electric Capital Aviation Management, which would be responsible for the aircraft leasing activities of both GPA and General Electric. Patrick Blaney would be chief executive of the old GPA. Others who survived the shake-up were finance director John Tierney and deputy chairman Maurice Foley.

The Future for GPA

While GPA is likely to face increased competition in the future, it still remains a world leader in the aircraft leasing business. Its growth will continue to be considerable. It still works with all the principal manufacturers, it has entered an exciting undertaking with Rolls Royce, and it has made moves into Eastern Europe. Deregulation and increased competition internationally have helped GPA, in that many airlines prefer to lease costly new planes, rather than buy them. GPA still has clear advantages over many competitors. It has built up many competencies and gained much experience over two decades in business. It has an impressive array of contacts and has influential contacts in both airlines and financial institutions.

In the coming ten years, the challenge for GPA will be to find enough money to finance the vast number of new aircraft needed. "In the last decade there was a shortage of planes," says Ken Holden, chief strategist at GPA, "this decade there will be a shortage of money." Tony Ryan goes further by suggesting that over the next 20 years $1.5 billion will need to be spent on planes for airlines to keep pace with the growth of passenger traffic. It is hoped that with the injection of new equity, GPA should be able to capitalise on all the new financing opportunities opening up in the industry in the future.

There is tremendous demand for new equipment and there is going to be a significant growth in the business as airlines focus on the heart of their operations, rather than simply the ownership of equipment.

APPENDIX

Figure A: Structure of GPA's Business Activities

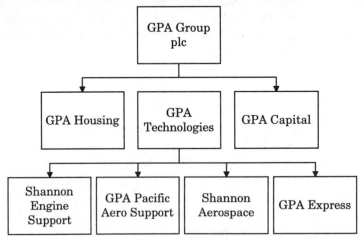

Table A: GPA Group plc and Subsidiaries

Subsidiary Undertaking	Holding of Ordinary Shares %	Nature of Business
Aero USA Inc.	100	Aircraft Leasing
Air Tara Ltd.	100	Aircraft Leasing
GPA Holdings (IOM) Ltd.	100	Investment Holding Company
GPA I Ltd.	100	Aircraft Leasing
GPA Airbus Ltd.	100	Aircraft Leasing
GPA Aero Citra Ltd.	67.5	Aircraft Leasing
GPA Capital Incorporated	100	Financial Services
GPA Corporation	100	Aircraft Leasing/Marketing
GPA Delaware Inc. Corporation	100	Financing
GPA Finance Ltd.	100	Aircraft Leasing and Aircraft Finance
GPA Fokker Ltd.	75	Aircraft Leasing
GPA Funding I Ltd.	100	Aircraft Leasing
GPA Holland BV	100	Financial Services
GPA Inc.	100	Holding Company for US Subsidiaries

Subsidiary Undertaking	Holding of Ordinary Shares %	Nature of Business
GPA Investments BV	100	Financial Services
GPA Jetprop Ltd.	100	Aircraft Leasing
GPA Leasing USA I Inc.	100	Aircraft Leasing
GPA Leasing USA II Inc.	100	Aircraft Leasing
GPA Netherlands BV	100	Financial Services
GPA Technologies Ltd.	100	Holding Company for Irish Technology Companies
Irish Aerospace Ltd.	100	Aircraft Leasing
Shannon Turbine Technologies Ltd.	60	Engine Overhaul

Associated Undertaking	Holding of Ordinary Shares %	Nature of Business
GPA-ATR Ltd.	50	Aircraft Leasing
GPA-Fokker 100 Ltd.	50	Aircraft Leasing
Shannon Aerospace Ltd.	30	Aircraft Maintenance
Shannon Engine Support Ltd.	50	Engine Leasing

Source: *Business and Finance* (various issues), company reports and interviews with company personnel.

Questions

1. Using your knowledge of business growth strategies, evaluate the main types of external growth in which GPA engaged during the 1980s.

2. How suitable were the internal culture and environment of GPA to the demands of its external environment?

3. Suggest reasons why the GPA flotation failed. How did the rescue plan deal with the financial situation that existed afterwards?

4. What advantages will the General Electric deal bring to GPA in the long run?

20

Analog Devices (Ireland)

Introduction

Analog Devices is a US company founded in 1965 and currently employing approximately 5,200 people worldwide. The company's corporate headquarters are located in Norwood, Massachusetts, in the US. The company has six divisions, four located in the Boston area, one in California, and one in Limerick in Ireland. Analog has manufacturing facilities in the US (Massachusetts, North Carolina, and California), Ireland, the Philippines, Taiwan and Japan. It also has arrangements with subcontractors, principally in the Far East, for wafer fabrication, assembly and testing of certain products. Analog Devices is a Fortune 500 company, which designs, manufactures and markets precision high-performance electronic components used in Analog and digital signal processing and measurement-control application. It is committed to the long-term integration of Total Quality Management (TQM) into the overall organisation and culture. In 1994, it had a turnover of $760 million.

Products

Analog Devices products include linear and mixed signal integrated circuits (ICs) used in Analog and digital signal-processing applications. These devices convert sensor information (temperature, velocity, pressure) into signals in digital form, which can then be read by a microprocessor or computer. The majority of the company's sales are in the standard functional devices. It also produces digital ICs for digital signal-processing applications, modular and board-level products and subsystems. The group's products come under three classifications:

- SLICs — standard functional linear and mixed signal ICs
- SPLICs/DSPLICs — special-purpose linear and mixed-signal ICs
- Assembly products.

Analog Devices' SLICs (category 1) continue to be the core products and the basis of the business. These are of a general-purpose type where the customer can incorporate them into a wide variety of equipment and systems. Category 2 devices, SPLICs and DSPLICs, require a higher level of integration, replacing similar devices, and because they are more specific in application, the customer base is smaller. Category 3, which consists of assembled products, comprises older products that have been in decline over the past number of years, partly because of obsolescence and replacement by newer models. The company is continuously developing new products. Since the markets that Analog serves are characterised by rapid technological change and advancement, the company makes significant levels of investment in the design and development of new products and processes.

Some of the company's main competitors include Harris Semi-Conductor, Texas Instruments, AT&T and Motorola Semi-Conductor. The diverse range of products offered by companies such as Analog affords scope for considerable market strength by ensuring that competition faced by one part of the product portfolio will not necessarily affect the overall product range. Most of Analog's sales are to original equipment manufacturers (OEMs) who incorporate them into a wide variety of end products. The group's relevant markets include laboratory and industrial automation, military/aerospace, telecommunications, computer peripherals, high-end consumer products, and automotive/transportation. All products are sold through direct-sales offices located throughout the US and in 14 other countries throughout the world. Also, the group makes use of sales representatives and industrial distributors in the distribution of its products.

The Irish Subsidiary

The Irish subsidiary, Analog Devices BV, was established in Limerick in 1976 and today represents 21 per cent of the company's total turnover, making it the corporation's largest facility. This subsidiary was set up to design and manufacture Complimentary

Metal Oxide Semiconductor (CMOS) ICs. Over the past 10 years the company has invested over £100 million in new plant and equipment facilities in Limerick where it caries out the higher-tech portion of production. It currently employs over 1,000 people, with a facility of 205,000 square feet. It designs, manufactures and markets its own products independently of the US corporate facility operation. In addition, it employs 50 people in various overseas locations in marketing and engineering roles. In 1991, the Limerick division branch was awarded the ISO9001 quality standard. Over 50 per cent of the staff have a third-level education, and over 200 of the staff are engineer and science graduates, and most are predominantly Irish. The company's key focuses include new product development, quality and customer service. Analog firmly believes that these objectives directly affect customer satisfaction, which in turn greatly impacts on long-term growth and profitability. Its market focus is computer peripherals (e.g. high performance PCs work stations, peripheral devices), communications (e.g. modern digital cellular phones), instrumentation (e.g. engineering, medical and scientific), and industrial automation (e.g. automatic test equipment). The company's key strengths include its employees, innovative design team, and technology development group.

Organisation Culture

Characteristics found in the most successful companies of the 1990s include those of flexibility and sensitivity to competitive markets, characteristics generally considered to be critical to the success of any organisation. In this context, the culture of Analog could be described as task oriented, in that it is extremely adaptable and responsible to immediate change. Essentially, there is an emphasis on problem solving, individual and team expertise, with a major focus on the organisation's goals. Individuals are allowed to exercise considerable control over their work, while informal communication channels are in place. Considerable emphasis is placed on performance appraisal and career development. Groups, project teams and quality improvement teams are set up to deal with specific problems that may arise, generally focusing on continuous improvement. Within departments, teams consist of a mix of operators, technicians, engineers, product supervisors, and administration. Participation is encouraged by all, and a flexible role is applied to job definitions. A cross-departmental team system of problem solving is used, while full training is provided to develop problem-solving techniques and presentation skills. Change, in general, is implemented quickly, and in the context of a wider organisational approach incorporating TQM.

In relation to TQM, it is worth noting that Analog's TQM principles include a focus on customer care, a focus in which Analog firmly believes, as customer satisfaction is the only way of achieving sustained business success in terms of long-term growth and profitability. A strategy for continuous improvement is also being implemented. This strategy has a number of key focuses for Analog:

- Systematic problem solving

- Focus on improvement to achieve results

- A step-by-step improvement of business processes, to achieve customer satisfaction and business success

- A focus on a few key activities which make a considerable difference to the organisation's performance.

Another TQM principle is that of Total Quality Involvement. This principle encourages employees to improve continuously those processes performed in an everyday work context. Accordingly, involvement is promoted generally by a management commitment to developing a mutual learning process involving individuals, teams, and the organisation as a whole. Significance is placed on teamwork capability, and more specifically, in respect of problem-solving capacities.

Organisation Structure

The Limerick branch is a multi-divisional management structure with a two-boss matrix configuration. The emphasis is on task achievement and results. The two joint general managers, who are also vice-presidents of Analog Inc. and Analog Devices BV, promote a policy of open management and genuine respect for each employee. By facilitating the achievement of employee goals and objectives, it is felt that the goals and objectives of the corporation as a whole will be met.

Corporate Strategy

According to Bob Marshall, President of A.D. Inc., and joint General Manager of Analog Devices BV, the corporate strategy of the company consists of the following key features:

Mission

The mission is to serve the real world signal-processing markets by being a market-driven organisation which aims to be the best at what it does in chosen market segments — the objective being one of sustaining profitability and growth. The path to profitability is through customer satisfaction via new product development, product quality and customer service. Employees are made aware of these objectives through quarterly plant-wide communication meetings, and through monthly meetings between department managers and employees. In the widely used Analog canteen, the key performance metrics, by which the success of the organisation is judged, are on display in an easily understood format. All employees are given a copy of the annual business plan.

The organisation structure of Analog Devices BV is characterised by dimensions that are fluid and flexible. Cross-functional problem-solving teams are a fundamental part of the company's participatory culture — over 45 teams are in place across all functional activities, with the responsibility for identifying the least costly, and most efficient solution for the company and customer. Over 50 per cent of the company's employees are members of one of these teams, forming one of the cornerstones of the company's TQM philosophy.

"To Achieve Customer Satisfaction"

The company takes the view that honouring customer commitment in respect of product deliveries, etc. is of prime importance. Customer satisfaction ratings are monitored by a cross-functional customer-service team, ensuring that the customer service provided by Analog is one of the main differentiating features of its products, and by extension, of the organisation itself. The importance of customer service is manifest, for example, in the assignment of the human resource manager to a cross-functional team for a number of months in order to imbue the team with the necessary interpersonal and human relations skills needed for such a role. The core competencies of the organisation include the high content of university graduates in employment in the organisation, and the fact that Analog Devices is a world leader in the market it serves. Continuous training and development are seen as essential for employee development throughout the organisation.

Strategy Formulation

A process of corporate strategy formulation exists within the organisation, whereby a defined corporate plan is produced annually at board level by a team of corporate strategy planners. This plan is then checked against performance metrics and market developments at six-monthly intervals, with adjustments made where appropriate. It is up to local management to interpret the overall corporate strategy in order to create a fit between their organisation and the strategic direction advanced by the corporate planners. The key determinants of strategic choice for the organisation include the achievement of an appropriate level of profitability to meet the high levels of capital investment required by the industry. Another key determinant is derived from the intensity of competition in those markets that are relevant to Analog.

The key competitive advantages of Analog Devices BV include the organisation's level of technology innovation, the extent of its technology, and the employment of effective recruitment strategies, thus ensuring a continuous supply of highly qualified and ambitious personnel. The company is market led, in that it adopts the market-in-concept, a concept which suggests that the purpose of work is to provide customer satisfaction. This process requires Analog to fulfil two requirements, namely the analysis of complex customer needs, and a willingness to consider what is "good" for the customer. Strategic alliances play a vital role in the company's continued success primarily because of the high level of capital investment required for new product development. Discussions are held on an ongoing basis with suitable firms in order to identify opportunities for mutual advancement. Generic strategies, as such, do not have a role to play in the Analog strategy-formulation process. Therefore, as a company, it operates in the market on the basis of sound technological leadership.

The human resource management function is generally viewed as a "consultant to the business" and has responsibility for organising cross-functional teams, thus providing essential key support to the organisation. HR is also responsible for setting guidelines to ensure that the reward systems in place are appropriate, and conducive to the achievement of the organisation goals. The function works to break down barriers that may exist in the organisation, enabling employees to perform their tasks in an effective manner.

Analog advances the need for the continuous assessment of organisational strategic direction in light of changing market conditions. Accordingly, it is felt that any chosen strategy must reflect the responsive and flexible dimensions of the electronics industry as a whole, dimensions held to be crucial to the success of any organisation within the industry.

Semi-Conductor Industry Overview

The semi-conductor industry was born in 1947 with the discovery of the transistor at Bell laboratories in the US. The transistor is the heart of the integrated circuit (IC), making the operation of the IC possible. This development started a microelectronics revolution, and helped to create a multi-billion dollar industry by the 1960s — an industry which, up to present times, continues to grow in size and technical sophistication.

Silicon Age — Integrated Circuits

The introduction of the first silicon transistor and its related processing, ushered in the silicon age, leading to the subsequent invention of the silicon chip or integrated circuit in 1959. Semi-conductor products consist of discrete devices (including resistors, diodes, and transistors) which are single-function devices, and integrated circuits. ICs are the primary product of the semi-conductor industry and, by definition, are circuits containing two or more components on a single piece of semi-conductor material such as silicon. The semi-conductor industry is estimated to reach $200 billion by the year 2000, and was rated the number one industry by the Dow Jones index in 1993.

In the early 1980s, Japan became the major international supplier of traded semi-conductor components, a position previously held by the US. In the early 1970s, the US held some 80 per cent of the global market, but by 1986 things had changed dramatically, with Japan gaining a 44 per cent share, compared to the 43 per cent share achieved by the US. One reason for the Japanese success was their willingness to commit greater expenditure in the area of research and development. US companies, by comparison, were losing out, not to smaller companies, but to large protected companies embedded in stable and co-ordinated alliances. The success of Japanese companies was also credited to the prevailing culture which rewards excellence in product design, manufacturing technology, and production efficiency. Policies of long-term investment in technology also played a key role in their success.

The Use of Integrated Circuits (ICS)

The PCB (Printed Circuit Board) is the main resting place for the ICs and a host of other electronic components. Minimisation is the nature of the industry — in other words, to reduce the weight and size of the PCB so that the net effect is to put as many functions as possible on a single IC and to package the JC in as small a unit as possible. This is reflected in the falling prices of personal computers from $5,000 in 1981 to $1,200 in 1994. Technology is developing rapidly in packaging the IC and the introduction and development of Surface Mount Packages has meant that packages can be placed in smaller areas and on both sides of a PCB — previously it was only on one side. As the industry develops, more and more functions are contained in a single IC. The fundamental competitive forces which exist in the international semi-conductor industry are concerned with technology strategy and the relative technological lead that the firms have over their competitors. Throughout its history, Analog has competed in markets not served by the billion-dollar companies, and competition from the Japanese in the market niches has also been limited. For Analog, the key focus has primarily been on three things:

- Technological innovation

- The scope of the firm's product line

- Vertical integration.

Competitive Factors Affecting Analog

Analog believes that competitive performance in the marketplace depends upon several factors including product price, technical innovation, product quality and reliability, range of products, customer service and technical support. It is worth taking a look at some of these issues.

New Products

In order to be competitive in the 1990s, a concerted effort is focused on improving the cost and quality of new products. With the product life span getting shorter and with costs increasing, Analog recognised the need for designing quality products with high yields, and improving on the organisation's manufacturing capabilities. Analog Devices' very existence depends on its ability to monitor the cost and quality of its products continuously.

Manufacturing Focus

The organisation operates in an environment that is highly dynamic and complex, and in order to succeed it continuously has to strive to develop innovative strategies aimed at keeping it ahead. It is recognised worldwide that the ideal integrated-circuit production facility must have a number of key features:

- The ability to manufacture at a competitive price

- The ability to cope with a variable product mix

- Short, predictable production-cycle times.

It was mainly as a result of these three major factors that Analog proceeded in 1987 to purchase a computer integrated manufacturing (CIM) system to keep track of its production process. This was a major manufacturing technology strategy for the company at the time. One step on from this is the recent purchase by the organisation of a knowledge-based "expert" CIM system to deal specifically with scheduling. It is through these strategies that Analog can maintain its distinctive competency and ultimately its potential competitive advantage. And maintaining a competitive edge usually comes about through developing in-depth skills, experience, innovation, market understanding, and information systems. Analog aims to advance this by focusing on service and short time to the market. For Analog, service includes product quality, reliability and technical innovation.

In the past, it was enough for a company to focus its business on specific end-product markets for it to succeed. But times have changed, as market boundaries have become more fluid and temporary in nature. It is within this context of change that companies have had to refocus their activities and create an environment that is capable of producing products that are beyond current customer expectations. In the short term, a company's competitiveness stems from the price/performance of its current product range. Yet in the longer term, this competitiveness derives from an ability to produce with a lower cost base, and more speedily than its competitors. Future growth and competitiveness for an organisation like Analog will depend on its ability to exploit its core competencies. Essentially, this means that the organisation must develop a depth of skill and expertise, particularly in respect of market information analysis. For Analog, this means becoming an "Intelligent Enterprise", developing and co-ordinating intellectual activities worldwide. The first step in this process has been the introduction of a single worldwide planning system, which is currently being implemented by a special planning council made up of representatives from all Analog sites. In the past, manufacturing, planning, forecasting, and distribution of raw materials and finished goods were controlled by a diffuse collection of systems. One single data base will now contain all this information.

The importance of manufacturing-technology strategies in relation to product and process technologies for companies such as Analog, is that strategies such as the introduction, for example, of a system like CIMs, will determine the nature and scope of the company's competency, and ultimately, its competitive advantage.

Strategies for Success

Manufacturing

Up to 1986, Analog did not have an overall operation/manufacturing system — that is, a system to control how the factory operates from when the raw materials come in, to when the finished product is shipped out. Hence, no one was really clear on the overall picture of the whole operation and how the various departments integrated and impacted on each other's performance. In the 1980s, Analog took a strategic decision to purchase a Computer-Integrated Manufacturing (CIM) system to suit its needs. This system was first installed in the water fabrication area (this manufacturing process crates the semi-conductor device or IC). But in recent times, the system has been extended to cover the entire manufacturing operation of the plant. The move to CIM across the plant, and the acquisition of a knowledge-based system in the manufacturing area will complement the organisation's new planning system. In the longer term, the system will help Analog to improve its competitive advantage. The large inventory (or long lead-time) concept was very much in evidence in wafer fabrication until the mid 1980s. All information was either written into logbooks and on cards, while scheduling was done through use of a wall chart. However, all of this changed with the purchase of the CIM system.

Benefits of Computer-Integrated Manufacturing (CIM)

With product life-cycles getting shorter, it is imperative to have a more effective functional integration between specialisms such as marketing, product design, and engineering so that new products and other modifications can be designed to meet customer demands, and can be quickly translated from the design stage into a clear set of instructions for immediate manufacture. A strong need exists for organisations like Analog to increase efficiency and lead times. This can be more effectively achieved through use of the computer. Accordingly, the CIM system has a number of features that afford the following benefits:

- The system improves the flow of information within a company

- It permits the establishment of a single data base for all manufacturing information

- It allows all personnel to have access and automatic feedback on all points in the process.

Analog recognised the importance of such a system and introduced PROMIS (Process Management Information System) in 1986, and by 1991 it had been implemented throughout the plant. This system was developed by I.P. Sharp (a Canadian company) and was principally designed for wafer fabrication, but was expanded to cover the entire manufacture operation. It is a real-time data-collection computer-based system that records all activity on the manufacturing floor concerned with process-flow, equipment, operations, etc. The core of PROMIS consists of a data base which defines plant facilities, products and manufacturing specifications. As lots are traded through the work area, data are collected and entered into the system through terminals located at each work station. In essence, PROMIS was another step towards achieving a competitive edge, and the benefits have been considerable for both Analog and its customers.

- There has been a dramatic improvement in yields, in which PROMIS has played a major role. The ability to tie together in a single data base information on every possible aspect has been a key factor in its success. The system allows Analog to get warnings of problems in their early stages, and its data-extraction capabilities allow for better understanding of day-to-day problems.

- PROMIS allows for more accurate control of all lot processing, with operating staff receiving direction on what to do at the right time, and the direction going to the right person.

- It has resulted in better feedback on any work-in-progress, thus enabling stoppages to be removed and inventory levels to be kept to a minimum.

- The system has improved communication between engineering staff and their production counterparts. The simple procedures for updating manufacturing processes have made it possible to keep detailed instructions up to date at all times.

- PROMIS has resulted in improved productivity because of its ability to generate accurate and timely information. The system's data-retrieval and plotting facilities allow engineering analyses to be undertaken on a routine basis.

- There is more efficient use made of all equipment.

- Accurate repeatability and tractability are possible, as each lot is recorded at every stage of the process.

- PROMIS allows for fast identification of problems.

- There is improved communication between different groups, and an interdependence which results from the system.

Artificial Intelligence

The CIM system allows people to manage work flow intelligently. However, it provides no decision-making aids for operators and engineers, only the data to allow them to complete their job effectively. Analog decided that a further project had to be undertaken to supplement the PROMIS system. Accordingly, an "artificial intelligence" expert CIM system was introduced, thus enabling PROMIS to function autonomously and to solve problems that it is not directly programmed to do. In order to optimise equipment usage, and because of the difficulty in keeping track of customers and suppliers while at the same time keeping lots on schedule, Analog needed a system that could digest all information currently existing on PROMIS regarding lots, equipment, the process flow, etc., together with the knowledge and intelligence currently residing only with experts in a certain area — namely, operators, production supervisors, engineers. As a result, the system introduced was a knowledge-based expert system called Logistics Management System (LMS) — a system developed by IBM. It is a form of artificial intelligence which can regulate the complex manufacturing tasks of an entire plant. It automatically picks up data, and using knowledge input by human experts, can reason and make corrections, the speed of which cannot be matched by an individual or group.

The introduction of any new system can be disastrous for any organisation if the "people" part is not managed properly. Analog was fortunate in that the management of change is planned for in a systematic way, well in advance of implementation, and considerate of employee contributions and involvement from the early stages of any new technology introduction such as, for example, the knowledge-based expert system, LMS. All the ground work was done by engineering personnel, production supervisors and operators, and it was because of this involvement and participation that the project became a success. Also, the total commitment by top management was of considerable importance in establishing an organisational climate conducive to the implementation of this and previous new technology.

Subcontracting

During the 1970s, manufacturing was very much labour intensive in nature, particularly in respect of the assembly process. In this context, it was not surprising to see the increased use of sub-contractors in assembly, a move principally driven by cost considerations. Yet many of these subcontractors have subsequently developed their capabilities by enhancing their skill and knowledge base, thus becoming highly competent at manufacturing, so much so, that some two decades later, they can be aptly described as "world-class" manufacturing employees. By the early 1990s, Singapore and Taiwan were rated as the world's sixth and seventh largest producers of electronic components, lagging behind the US, Japan, Britain and France. Because the semi-conductor industry is capital intensive, an outsourcing strategy allows a company to reduce investment risk, while still maintaining a smooth business cycle. Analog Devices BV first began to use subcontracted manufacturing in 1985 when internal assembly capacity became an issue. In 1986, it subcontracted work to a company called Anan in Korea, and again in 1993 when the group diversified into a major new market product line in order to maintain the high growth rates of the previous year's new product lines. Without the use of subcontractors, these product lines and other windows of opportunity, would not have come about. The use of outsourcing is especially suited to high-volume, low-weight ICs. At Analog, approximately 74 per cent of all assembly production volume is performed by subcontractors, with approximately 10 per cent of the company's total wafer-fabrication production volume subcontracted to locations in the Far East. Access to state-of-the-art technology without the immense capital investment is perhaps the main reasons for the use by Analog of subcontracting arrangements.

The pace of evolution within the semi-conductor industry is accelerating and the importance of new technology for new innovative designs is critical for competitive advantage. The high capital investment required, and the narrow market windows of opportunity have meant that the use of subcontractors is generally an attractive option. The pressures on Analog Devices to introduce the subcontractor management policy have come about for the following reasons: shorter product life cycle; increased competition; higher quality and reliability; lower costs and precise delivery times; customer demands; ISO9000 requirements

Internal reasons for introducing the subcontractor management policy include: to continue to design products to meet customer specifications; an ability to manufacture to the highest possible standard; to ensure that products are competitively priced, meet specific requirements and are reliable; to provide the organisation with a facility to exchange information with clients.

For Analog Devices, the subcontractor is regarded as an extension of the customer process. The organisation has a strategic policy in the management of the subcontract relationship, but this did not come about until 1990 following a bad and costly experience with one contractor — the case in question related to poor quality. With the implementation of the subcontractor programme, certain strategic and operational benefits have been realised by Analog:

- On a strategic basis, the policy of subcontracting has allowed the organisation to identify strategic subcontractors and to focus on them. As a result, management has been centralised, while risks associated with supply have been kept to a minimum. There has also been a reduction in product exposure.

- On an operational basis, the policy implementation has allowed for continuous improvement, improved communications through the building and support of an effective communications network, tighter processing controls, faster identification of problems and method of managing crises.

Table 20.1: Financial Performance

	1987	1988	1989	1990	1991	1992	1993
Domestic Sales	193.6	223.1	233.9	230.8	251.0	—	—
Int. Sales	176.8	216.0	219.5	254.3	—	—	—
Total Sales	370.4	439.2	453.3	485.2	537.7	567.3	666.3
Net Income	18.67	37.98	27.87	(12.91)	8.20	14.93	44.45
% of Sales	5	9	6	(3)	2	3	7
% ROI	6	11	7	(3)	3	4	10
% ROI Equity	7	12	8	(4)	2	4	11
Per Share	0.40	0.80	0.58	(0.28)	0.17	0.31	0.88
Equity per Share	6.29	7.07	7.57	7.31	7.47	7.79	8.78
No. of Employees	—	5,300	5,200	5,700	5,200	5,200	5,300

The company more than doubled net income for 1988 from $18.7 million to $38.0 million, and increased earnings per share from $0.40 to $0.80. Net incomes as a percentage of sales also showed a significant gain, increasing from 5 per cent to 8.6 per cent and reaching 9.7 per cent of sales for the last half of the fiscal year. Operating profit increased by 61 per cent during 1987 rising from $34.4 million to $55.4 million and as a percentage of sales rose from 9.3 per cent to 12.5 per cent. There was improved tight control over operating expenses, and as a result total operating expenses fell from 44.3 per cent to 41.7 per cent. Revenue also increased with growth of 19 per cent to $439.2 million.

In 1989 revenue grew by 3.2 per cent to $453 million — this was well below company expectations. Gross margins declined from 54.3 per cent in 1988 to 50 per cent, a decline caused by cutbacks in production and reduction in inventories. The company managed to contain growth of sales, marketing, and other expenses in aggregate to just 2.5 per cent over the previous year. R&D expenses were allowed to increase by 13.9 per cent over 1988 to 15.2 per cent in order to continue growth of new product. Net income declined 27 per cent to $27.9 million or $0.58 per share, yet at 6.1 per cent of sales net income was favourable compared to many semi-conductor companies. Revenue from new products introduced in 1986 and beyond, increased 76 per cent to $120 million or 26 per cent of sales for 1989. Total operating expenses increased by 6.3 per cent to 42.9 per cent of sales against 41.6 per cent in 1988. Non-operating expenses were $7.4 million or $3.6 million higher than the previous year. The tax rate for the year decreased to 23 per cent from 26 per cent in 1988 largely caused by a shift in the mix of worldwide income. The company continued to fund its operating requirements internally by generating cash flow from operations of $70.1 million or 15.5 per cent of sales. Capital expenditure for the year amounted to 451.0 million and total borrowing declined from $31.4 million in 1988 to $21.9 million resulting in a reduction in the debt to equity ratio from 9 per cent to 6 per cent.

In 1990, the company incurred a net loss of $21.9 million or $0.28 per share, compared to a net income of $27.9 million or $0.58 per share for 1989. For the first nine months of the fiscal year, the company reported net income of $10.7 million and for the last quarter, a net loss of $23.6 million. This last figure included an $18.5 million charge to operations for the company-wide restructuring and downsizing programme, an additional $12.0 million reserve against its venture-capital portfolio, and $3.0 million inventory adjustment for the acquisition during the year of Precision Monolithic Inc. (PMI) in the US which cost in total $60.5 million. Net sales increase 7 per cent to $485.2 million. Gross margins declined from 52.6 per cent of sales to 49.7 per cent to an end of year figure of 47.0 per cent. Operating income for the year prior to the $18.5 million restructuring charge and acquisition requirements was $27.7 million, or 5.7 per cent of sales, as compared to the 9.7 per cent for 1989. This decrease was attributable to the lower gross margin, and increased operating expenses as a percentage of sales. Non-operating expenses were up to $19.8 million compared to $7.4 million a year earlier. The company generated cash flow from operations of $82.2 million or 16.9 per cent of sales, yet despite this, cash balances fell from $30.1 million in 1989 to $8.3 million for 1990, a fall of $21.8 million. The $60.5 million purchase of PMI in

1990 was financed through a combination of cash in hand and bank borrowings. Borrowings as a result of this purchase increased by $22.8 million, but despite this the debt/equity ratio rose by only 10 per cent.

For 1991, net income generated for the year was $8.2 million or $0.17 per share, it was adversely affected by a $7.0 million restructuring charge taken in the last quarter of the fiscal year, which resulted in a $26 million or $0.06 share loss for that quarter. Net sales were $537.7 million. The revenue decline for the year was caused by a weakened worldwide semi-conductor demand. Gross margin for the year was 49.3 per cent of sales, compared to 49.7 per cent for 1990. R&D expenditure grew to $89.0 million from $80.3 million a year earlier, while as a percentage of sales, R&D remained constant at 16.6 per cent. Other expenses were 28.3 per cent of sales, slightly up on the 28 per cent of a year earlier. Operating income exclusive of the $7.0 million restructuring charge was £24.4 million or 4.5 per cent of sales, compared to $27.7 million or 5.7 per cent of sales in 1990. Operating income was $17.4 million or 3.2 per cent of sales. Liquidity and capital resources increased $8.2 million to $16.5 million, compared to a decrease of $21.9 million in 1990 because of the purchase of PMI The company generated cash from operations of $51.0 million or 9.5 per cent of sales compared to $82.2 million or 16.9 per cent of sales for 1990 — the fall resulting from higher working capital requirements. Capital expenditure for the year was $52.2 million for investment in capital equipment for new products. Total borrowings increased to $7.7 million, but the debt/equity ratio only rose slightly to 12 per cent, compared to 10 per cent for the previous year.

In 1992, revenues and bookings attained record highs in the latter part of the year, reaching $148.8 million and $152.0 million respectively. Gross margins as a percentage of sales increased to $7.05. At $0.31, earnings per share saw a significant improvement over 1991 with $0.17, which included a $7 million restructuring charge. Operating expenses fell from 44.8 per cent of sales to 41.1 per cent. R&D expenses were reduced from 16.6 per cent to 15.5 per cent, to a year-end figure of 14.7 per cent. New product growth totalled a record high of $23.6 million or 15.5 per cent of total bookings.

The year 1993 was very good for the company with progress made on many fronts. On the financial front alone, there was an increase in revenue of close on $110 million. Bookings and revenues both achieved record levels in every quarter, totalling $183 million, and $179 million respectively in the fourth quarter, and for the year end, they stood at $698 and $666 million — an increase of 20 per cent and 17 per cent respectively. Growth was achieved in all of the company' main markets: 125 per cent growth in Europe, 13 per cent in North America and 71 per cent in Southeast Asia. Operating profits also rose considerably during the year, representing 9.4 per cent of sales. Net income for the year was $44.5 million, a considerable increase on the pervious year's figure of $14.9 million, with the result that earning per share were $0.88 up from $0.31 for the previous year. The overall gross margin as a percentage of sales improved slightly. Operating expenses for the year declined to 37.9 per cent of sales, down from the previous year's figure of 42.2 per cent. There was an increase in expenditure on Research and Development by 7 per cent. Total employment for the company worldwide remained relatively static at 5,300. There has only been a 5 per cent increase in numbers employed since 1990. The return on equity at the end of year stood at 13 per cent. Also during the year, the company made changes to its senior management team and redefined its organisation and internal performance measurements in order to improve the alignment between organisational structure and business strategies. As a result of all these changes Analog has become more competitive and responsive with many potential future growth opportunities.

Source: Interviews with company personnel.

Questions

1. Using appropriate strategic management concepts and tools, evaluate the external environment within which Analog Devices (Ireland) operates.

2. How do the culture and structure of Analog Devices (Ireland) match the demands of its external environment?

3. What advantages does Computer Integrated Manufacturing bring to a company like Analog Devices? What demands does it

make of employees in terms of competencies and management practices?

4. Why is subcontracting a frequently used business strategy within the electronics sector? What factors need to be considered when managing subcontracting relationships?

21

Irish Distillers Group

Introduction

The name Irish Distillers is recognised worldwide as synonymous with Irish Whiskey, yet the group's activities are far more extensive and encompass a wide range of drink products at manufacturing, distribution and retail level. The essence of the company is captured in its logo:

> The Spirit of Ireland: Tradition and Quality

It is because of this tradition, quality and innovation that the company has been able to achieve its international reputation, making it one of Ireland's great national assets.

Evolution of the Group

Background

The company can trace its roots as far back as 1600 when Irish whiskey was first licensed to the "Old Bushmills" distillery in Co. Antrim, making it the oldest distillery in the world. The industry during this time was characterised by a simple and informal group structure with very little specialisation of tasks. Most were family-owned pot skills. The domestic market accounted for most of company sales. Finance was privately provided, while the basic strategy was one of general survival. There was specialised technology with tight control in place. The product produced was to meet market demand.

1966–70

Irish Distillers was formed in 1966 on the amalgamation of John Power and Sons Ltd. with Jameson and Sons Ltd. and Cork Distillers. These three companies were the main players in the distilling industry in the Republic of Ireland, with Bushmills being the main operator in Northern Ireland. The amalgamation move was very much prompted by a need to protect the home industry from foreign takeover and to pool resources so as to be capable of competing internationally. At this early stage, it was the group's belief that future growth would have to come from exporting. In fact, the economic environment at this point in time was geared towards export-led growth, with government policy encouraging more free trade. This free-trade policy became manifestly apparent with the appearance of some British operators who had become involved at the wholesale and distribution levels of the Irish drinks market. Thus a more open economy was being encouraged.

As with many amalgamations, and especially as this one involved three separate entities with their own way of doing things, a period of adjustment was required for Irish Distillers. In this case, it took some time for the three companies to mesh together from an operational point of view, because immediately after the merger each company continued to do more or less its own thing. All three had their own culture and had come to the merger with differing expectations about how they were to operate and cooperate after the merger had taken place. The biggest stumbling block to be overcome by the three companies concerned the Cork distillery, a family-run entity headed by Norbert Murphy, who had considerable control, and after the merger was reluctant to part with any of it.

New Management Team Structure

Frank O'Reilly, one of the people behind the merger, was appointed as chairman of the newly merged entity. He encountered many problems in those early days, least of which was the fact that other individuals seemed to think that they were running things. The problems for the group essentially existed at board level. To solve the issue, the company appointed an outside manager in 1968 as managing director. Kevin McCourt was not seen to have divided loyalties and was appointed on a 10-year contract basis. He came with valuable sales and marketing experience, having spent many years working in the Irish tobacco industry.

McCourt had also previously held the post of director general of RTE. The O'Reilly/McCourt team proved to be a very effective combination in making the merger work, not least because they brought to the job a new level of professionalism at senior management level, with a strong focus on three strategic areas — marketing, finance and production. They did not solely rely on their own knowledge but recruited other expertise in the areas of marketing and finance, and an end objective was to integrate the two functions.

Along with changes to management, the industry characteristics had also changed considerably by this time. The company's structure required a complete overhaul with an emphasis on rationalisation, while professional management was introduced to allow for greater specialisation of tasks — finance, marketing, planning etc. The strategic focus was one of rationalisation and international expansion. The changes did not stop here —on the distribution side there was forward integration so as to allow the company to deal directly with the retailer. This move was also aimed at reducing the company's reliance on the traditional distribution network which was becoming more and more controlled by large British enterprises.

Strategic Focus

The strategy formulated by this new management team for the group's growth and development was two-fold in its emphasis: to secure the company's position on the home market; and to use the funds generated from the domestic market to forge an attack on the international market. Thus marketing becomes a key focus, and to emphasise this new strategic focus, the company acquired a 65 per cent interest in Edward Dillons, an independent spirit merchant, which allowed for a broadening of the group's marketing base. Moreover, new product development became a major focus, partly as a result of declining whiskey demand in the 1960s and 1970s, and a new series of gin, vodka and rum drinks and a new blended whiskey were launched. Through the use of market research undertaken in the US, new lighter blends of whiskey were also developed.

1970–79

This period was characterised by an organisation focused on markets and sales. The company increased its marketing by focusing on such countries as France, Holland and Belgium through its newly created export company, Irish Distillers International. On the home front, between 1970 and 1974, the company embarked on a programme of acquisitions, resulting in the purchase of the Irish Whiskey Blending company, which allowed it to diversify into liqueur products. It was during this period also that the company embarked on its programme of production rationalisation, while in 1975 the most modern of facilities were opened in Middleton, Co. Cork, the main reason for these new facilities being the need to meet market demands which at this time were considerable and more sophisticated, with requirements for more subtle blends of whiskey than previously. Also, high-volume production allowed for greater economies of scale.

Irish Distillers felt at the time that some of the existing facilities did not possess the flexibility necessary to allow it to develop new products, hence the only alternative was to construct new facilities while closing any inefficient plants. International consultants A.D. Little were brought in to assist in the design of the new distilling facilities, and the Cork location for the plant was chosen not least because of the area's long tradition of distilling. The group's original estimate for these new facilities was put at £2 million but it ended up costing close to £9 million, mostly because of rather unfavourable inflation movements during the period. Also, further difficulties for the group came in the form of the 1973 oil crisis, which had impacted greatly on the company's plans because the new facilities were energy-intensive rather than labour-intensive. Furthermore, Middleton was to prove in the coming years that it was tough with regard to industrial relations, something which the group could not possibly have anticipated at the time.

By 1977, the company was focusing on gaining control of the Irish whiskey industry, and to this end, entered into an agreement with Seagrams of Canada, the world's largest distiller. Originally Seagrams was intent on gaining ownership and control of the company, but Irish Distillers was not interested in such a plan, and in the end Seagrams settled for a 15 per cent stake in Irish distillers, with an upper limit of 20 per cent. As a result of this new alliance, Irish Distillers acquired a 25 per cent stake in "Old Bushmills", which was part of the Seagrams portfolio, and in 1974 Irish Distillers increased its stake to 80 per cent. The move meant that Irish Distillers had acquired access to a vast distribution network in the US, as well as a strong financial base. The group's objective at this stage in its development was to gain total control of the Irish whiskey market, and then to build on the strengths of the various brands, while increasing overall volume sold.

Besides the ultimate control of the Irish whiskey industry, there were other benefits accruing to Irish Distillers from this acquisition, not least of which was the fact that the Bushmills brands were long established on international markets such as the UK and US. Bushmills plant facilities are the oldest in the world and this brought with it a certain amount of prestige, and the plant is highly efficient because of an extensive modernisation programme undertaken by Seagrams. Bushmills also provided Irish Distillers with an additional production facility. In 1977, the group raised its holding in Bushmills to 100 per cent. The arrangement with Seagrams was also entered into in order to help the Irish group to make greater inroads into the US market, and to this end, the group in 1977 spent £3 million on promoting whiskey in the US alone. The year 1977 was also when Kevin McCourt retired from the management of the company. By 1978, the company's efforts were paying off with profits increasing by 50 per cent (a 20 per cent increase in sales on the home market and a 50 per cent increase in the US). The following year, 1978, saw the group launch a new liqueur, "Irish Velvet".

On Kevin McCourt's retirement, a replacement was found in the form of Richard Burrows, who previously had spent a year as an apprentice for his future job under McCourt's guidance. He came from an accountancy background with family connections in the industry, and was first recruited by Seagrams as managing director of the newly acquired Bushmills. He is credited with turning the company round, and so it is perhaps understandable why he got the top job in Irish Distillers when he was just 31 years old. Although he had his own way of doing things, his appointment was very much a reinforcement of the McCourt style that had been so effective. Frank O'Reilly continued in his post as chairman of the board until 1981, and Kevin McCourt remained a member of the company board until 1982.

By the end of the 1970s, the company had achieved record levels of sales on the home market and was making good inroads into the international market. So it was fitting for the group to end the decade by embarking in 1979 on further expansion with the investment of £30 million in two new large distilleries. An expansion programme was envisaged to take place over a five-year period with

a target of increasing production by as much as 50 per cent, with
the ultimate aim of capturing a larger slice of the US market.

1980–85

The strategy for the 1970s was the conversion of three family-
owned businesses into one modern business corporation, and the
strategy for the 1980s was very much in keeping with this and the
further expansion through exports. However, the 1980s marked
the first period in the group's history of any degree of setbacks. To
start with, there was a recession in the early part of the 1980s
and a dreaded increase in excise duty, something for which an export-oriented company like Irish Distillers did not wish. Also
there was increased competition, with greater imports now coming into the market. The end result of all of this was a reduction
in group profits, with a 29 per cent drop in 1980, a development
which meant that many workers had to be put on short-term. The
year 1982 by comparison, was no better, with sales declining by 17
per cent. The Canadian company Seagrams added to the group's
troubles by reducing its holdings in Irish Distillers to 15 per cent.
The company was adversely affected by the excessive excise duty
that it had to pay. It was not until 1984 that the government saw
fit to do something about it, reducing the duty by 20 per cent, a
move which immediately resulted in an improved sales performance. However, the good times did not last for very long because in
1986 the government reversed its decision and increased excise
duty again, with the result that by 1987, Irish Distillers' domestic
sales were 20 per cent slower than in 1981. This was detrimental
for a company whose export strategy success depended on the
amount of funds generated on the home market.

From a financial perspective, until the 1980s the group had
been very much privately financed — bank loan etc. — without
resource to its shareholders. However, this changed in March 1983
when the group raised £10 million in equity from its shareholders
in order to reduce borrowings and to finance its export growth
programme. It was around this time also that the company responded to the many changes that had been taking place over the
previous number of years, especially as regards its distribution
network in operation. Previously, the main outlet for the company's product was the public house, but this was changing with
the appearance of off-licences and supermarkets. And while the
major customers dealt directly with the company, many of the

smaller businesses were more likely to deal with the cash-and-carry wholesalers. By the 1980s, this was the most popular mode of distribution.

In line with these changing trends, the group in 1984 undertook some vertical integration to combat the deteriorating situation at home. By acquiring BWG Foods for a total cost of £10 million, Irish Distillers had access to a publicly quoted food, pharmaceutical and engineering company, with an extensive network of cash-and-carry outlets. The acquisition of BWG meant a change of the group's structure, one that would lend itself to more specialisation and complexity, but more importantly, allowed the company to exert more control over the distribution network and marketing of its products in the home market. The BWG acquisition received a considerable amount of criticism from all quarters, with much of it focused on the substantial mount of money that Irish distillers spent on acquiring the company, and the fact that the investment was undertaken in a market that had been stagnant for some time. To many onlookers, this was not a positive indication of a management interest in pursuing a viable export strategy. Accordingly, the perception of the company took a change for the worse, with investors loosing faith in the ability of the company's management to manage it.

The 1980s were not good times for Irish Distillers. Along with the stagnant domestic market, there was also a noticeable decline in other markets, especially in the company's main export market the US. The new wave of health, fitness and healthy eating was impacting on the drinks market, with people becoming more interested in non-alcoholic beverages. Between 1979 and 1987, there was a 13 per cent drop in spirit consumption, while the share of whiskey fell from a high of 76 per cent in 1960 to 40 per cent by 1986. But even with these declining sales, there still existed in the US a vast market for the company's products, into which the company up to now had not managed to tap. The US represented 40 per cent of the 68 million cases per annum market, and of this the group had only half a percentage. By increasing sales to the US by a mere 1 per cent, the company would have experienced a considerable increase in its turnover. By the 1980s, the company had increased its exports to the US to 0.35 million cases, a favourable improvement considering that at the time of the merger in 1966, the total amount was 0.04 million.

Matters were not helped by the fact that the company's marketing efforts were being hindered by problems within the organisation. In

1982, the new marketing director who was hired proved to be unsuitable, and the company's strategy for distribution in the US was not working out. The company had allocated its main brands to different importers for distribution — for instance, Seagrams handled Jameson, while Brown-Forman looked after Bushmills. In order to establish a stronger local presence, new agents were appointed to get the right marketing mix and to work more closely with these importers on the marketing and distribution of the various brands. As a result of these efforts, the exports to the US did expand up until 1984. However, after that, sales levels stagnated at 0.3 million cases, and with an increase in taxes, this figure had fallen to 9.27 million by 1987. In 1985, in an attempt to reverse the situation, the company undertook an extensive review of its marketing strategy, which resulted in a slight change in emphasis. Accordingly, the European markets were to be given greater attention, while in the US, market efforts were to be concentrated in only five main states, with an emphasis on two brands — Bushmills and Jameson. For the group, the future strategy continued to be consolidation of the group's share of the home market and greater market penetration abroad through a process of new product development. The programme got underway in 1985 with the launch of "West Coast Cooler", which in present times is a brand leader in Australia. Along with changes to the marketing strategy, the culture of the company was also changing, becoming more task-oriented.

1986–88

The year 1986 saw an increase in profits for the domestic market, but things were not so good in the US where sales were down 20 per cent. Things did not improve when in June 1987, because of a lack of confidence in Irish Distillers, the Canadian company Seagrams sold its remaining stake in the group. Even through Irish Distillers had a strong emphasis on quality, it was not achieving the level of market penetration and brand development that big investors believed possible. The company throughout the 1980s had undertaken extensive programmes in order to make it more competitive. It had reduced overheads, invested close to £1.5 million on modernising the transport system, and in 1987 some £10 million was spent on an extensive rationalisation programme with staff numbers reduced by one third, a move which the company hoped would result in a 25 per cent increase in pre-tax earnings. All of these changes meant that Irish Distillers became a leaner and more profitable organisation. Yet all of these changes were not enough, as the group was operating in an industry where most of the big players were achieving growth through acquisitions. The spirits market had become very consolidated with more of the business in the hands of about six players. In the whiskey segment of the market, consolidation was even more pronounced, with the main players accounting for almost 60 per cent of the global market.

By 1987, Irish Distillers, with its generic brands' under-exploited market potential, was vulnerable and susceptible to takeover. In October 1987 speculation grew when FII Fyffes, the large fruit importer, acquired a 20 per cent stake in the group. But the group's management acted promptly to dampen such speculation by calling a number of meetings with its main investors, many of whom had become disheartened with the lack of success the company was experiencing with its export strategy. These investors were a little reassured when the half-yearly results showed that the rationalisation programme and the marketing strategy were beginning to show positive results. But the threat of a takeover raised its head again when in May 1988 a new consortium, GC&C, launched a takeover bid for the group. This consortium consisted of the Irish subsidiaries of some of the largest players in the drinks industry, including many British-based companies such as Gibney's of Grand Metropolitan and Cantrell and Cochrane of Allied Lyons (51 per cent) and Guinness (49 per cent). This bid was viewed with some hostility by Irish distillers which saw it as a move by the big players to take control of the Irish whiskey market. They were also trying to reap the benefits of the rationalisation and marketing programme which was just beginning to show positive results for Irish Distillers. But the main objection to this particular bid was focused on the intention of the consortium to split the brands between them, as opposed to retaining them within the existing entity. When this bid was made, Irish Distillers had a market value of £176 million. The GC&C bid put the value to £198 million or 315p per share. In the end, it was white knight Pernod Ricard, the French drinks company, which eventually took over Irish Distillers in September of 1988. Under this ownership arrangement, Irish Distillers was allowed to operate independently, with collaboration in areas where synergy could be achieved.

Events Leading up to the Takeover

For Irish Distillers several factors were prevailing at the time of the takeover bid, and these were working against the group:

- *A Heavy Dependence on the Home Market*, which in 1987 was 67 per cent. The home market was in a steady decline owing to a combination of increased excise duty and a contraction in GNP growth which had resulted in the dramatic fall of spirits sales since 1979. No great recovery was in sight.

- *Limited Success with Product Development.* Irish Distillers had shown itself over the years to be unable to produce new products with names that would have gained substantial segments of the market.

- *Industrial Relations Problems.* The group had been dogged by industrial relations problems, particularly at its main Middleton plant. In 1985, a seven-week strike prevented the group from reaping the full benefits of the reduction in excise duty, and in 1987 it had to shed up to 200 jobs.

- *Overseas Marketing Policy.* Because of an unsuccessful overseas marketing policy, the group was very susceptible to a takeover bid from any large multinational that could offer shareholders a good return on their investment. The group's export sales were not as had been hoped — for instance, total sales in 1987 were £230 million. Of this, Ireland and the UK accounted for 89 per cent, North America only 4 per cent, Continental Europe 5 per cent, and others 2 per cent.

- *Poor Operating Performance.* In the five years prior to 1987, the profits, earnings per share and dividend for Irish Distillers had been very erratic in their performance. For example, in 1984 profits were £11.2 million, but by 1987 they had plummeted to £2.7 million. There had been no substantial increase in turnover.

- *Management.* It can be argued that management resources within the group had limited the growth of the organisation. There has been considerable indifference on the part of management to developing the organisation, and this indifference was a contributing factor to the poor performance in the five years prior to the takeover.

- *Finance*. Up to 1983, the group financed all its activities through bank loans and retention of profits, but from this period on, interest rates on borrowings were so high that the group had to dilute its equity to cope with cash-flow problems. The group's gearing ratio fluctuated greatly up to 1987 when it was 30.22, up from a figure of 25.81 five years previously. Profit margins and return on capital employed reached an all-time low in 1987.

Other factors working against the group at this time included:

- *Maturation Time of the Whiskey*. Irish Whiskey requires seven years to mature, compared to Scotch whiskey which only requires three.

- *Control of Distribution*. The group lost control of its market because it could not adequately control distribution. However, it did manage to rectify this to some extent in the US by reducing the number of distributors from fifty in fifty states to five in five states, focusing attention on two premium brands, Jameson and Bushmills.

- *Family-Run/Owned Business*. Irish Distillers changed from being a family-run business to being a modern business corporation, but did so with great reluctance. Much of the resistance was manifest in management's unwillingness to change as the organisation changed ownership.

The Company Takeover: May–September 1988

It was a combination of events that led to the takeover of Irish Distillers in 1988. The first interested party to step into the ring was the GC&C consortium (Grand Metropolitan/Allied Lyons/Guinness) on 30 May — a consortium that was greeted with considerable hostility by the group. A more favourable candidate in the form of Pernod Picard, put its name into the hat on the following day, 31 May. Thus the bidding had begun in earnest.

Founded in 1975, Pernod Ricard company resulted from the amalgamation of two of France's leading producers of anise-based spirits. It is the largest spirit manufacturing company on the European mainland, but only half the size of the smallest of the big five drink producers:

Company	Sales	Brands
IDV	£53m	Smirnoff, Bailey's, Piat D'Or
Seagrams	£44m	Seagrams Martell
Guinness	£40m	Johnnie Walker, Bells, Gordons, Dewars
Allied Lyons	£28m	Teachers, Harvey's, Tia Maria, Canadian Club
Suntory	£25m	None
IDG	£23m	Bushmills, Jameson

Pernod Ricard is 45 per cent owned by the Pernod and Ricard families, and France itself accounts for 90 per cent of its wine, spirit and drinks sales. Initially it was thought that Pernod Ricard might buy FII Fyffes' 20 per cent stake in Irish Distillers and become a minority shareholder. The view of this company as the great white saviour is not one that is universally shared as it has been described by some critics as a multinational strategy held back by a family board. The firm is indeed tightly controlled by the family who retain just over 50 per cent of the shares. It also currently has a millstone around its neck in the form of a group debt of £443 million.

Irish Distillers managed to persuade its investors that the GC&C bid was not a favourable one. It also managed to have the bid referred to the European Commission on the issue of "concerted practices" which the EC subsequently verified as being one. Not to be deterred, however, GC&C came back two days later, now 100 per cent owned by Grand Metropolitan, and offered 400p per share, putting the value of Irish Distillers at £235 million. Much to the latter's dislike, Grand Metropolitan was allowed to put in a bid on its own, a step that was unusual in that the procedure usually was that a consortium that had failed in a bid was not allowed to bid again within a 12-month period. This new bid was allowed because it was made by a consortium that consisted of one major layer, Gibney's of the Grand Metropolitan Group. However, this second bid was rejected by Irish Distillers.

The only possible defence tactic left open to Irish Distillers was a counter offer from some other contender, and it seemed possible that the group had one in mind — while all of these offers were flying about, the group's managing director Richard Burrows and Pernod president Thierry Jacquillat had been engaging in extensive discussions. The result of these talks was that Pernod Ricard was willing to enter the ring, but only on condition that its offer of 450p per share would be accepted by Irish Distillers. It would not enter on the basis that it would have to go rounds with GC&C in order to win the fight. Following discussions with the group's main shareholders and also with FII Fyffes, who had its 20 per cent interest, management secured agreement that would guarantee Pernod Ricard over 50 per cent control of Irish Distillers. However, not to be outdone, GC&C came back with a counter offer of 525p per share. It also tried to help its own case by engaging in some smear tactics, producing statistics reflecting Irish Distillers' poor sales performance on the home market. The Irish group denounced these statistics as not being a true reflection of the state of the company. The proceedings were to enter a final phase with further court proceedings before Pernod's bid was finally accepted, enabling it to become the new owner of Irish Distillers.

Implications of the Takeover

Throughout the whole proceedings, Irish Distillers' management, under the direction of Richard Burrows, fought very strongly to keep the company as a single entity, and by succeeding in its efforts, this period marked an important watershed in the company's history for two very important reasons:

- If Irish Distillers had accepted the GC&C offer, the price would have been 525p per share instead of 450p. It would have been part of a large multinational group and have access to an extensive distribution network. The downside of the deal would have been that Irish Distillers would have been split on a 50/50 basis between Gilbey's and Cantrell and Cochrane, resulting in a loss of product identity between these two large organisations. Bushmills would have been sold, thus severing the last remaining link between the Northern Ireland and the Republic of Ireland. A change in management would have taken place and autonomy would very much be with GC&C.

- On accepting Pernod's offer of 450p per share, the group was going to remain more or less intact, as would management and autonomy. With Pernod Ricard's dominance of its home market and with a strong position in Europe, it would allow for greater promotion of Irish whiskey on the Continent. The market strategy of "keeping the spirit Irish" would remain intact.

Post Takeover

Since the takeover, pre-tax profits at the group have increased from £18 million to £30 million, with sales increasing from £244 million to £302 million. Other changes that have taken place at the group include the strong emphasis on cost-competitive management and the implementation of a rationalisation programme throughout the group, all of which have considerably reduced costs, resulting in improved profitability. The increased profitability of the group is also caused by the utilisation of its parent company Pernod Ricard's extensive distribution network, with most of the bottling process now taking place in Ireland. The importance of this change is that it allows the group to add value to the product. The importance of the access to Pernod's extensive distribution network cannot be over stressed in allowing the Irish group to establish itself on the European market. It has been the policy at Pernod to establish distribution companies in all of its markets including Japan, Korea, Singapore, the Far East, and of course in Europe. It has not been a burden to the Irish group to have a parent company that understands what it is about, and that is willing to support it in its endeavours.

Irish Distillers in its earlier days of operation, very much focused on the US market as an area of growth and expansion. This has now been replaced by a focus on the European market, owing in part to its European-based parent company, Pernod. Europe, excluding Ireland, is now a larger market for the group, and while the home market still has a major part to play in the company's success, more than half of the group's sales and profits come from outside Ireland. Britain is another market to which the group has given major focus, and this has not changed, with Jameson being one of the best-performing whiskey brands in Britain today.

Distribution of Brands

One year after the takeover there was an increase of 13 per cent in Irish Distillers' exports. In this context, 1989 was very much a transitional year for Irish Distillers. The company moved its brands in many of its market to its new parent company. For instance, Jameson was moved to Ricard in France with its own sales force of over 600. Bushmills was given to Pernod which helped the brand to take off dramatically. Tullamore Dew went to Cusenier, and Powers went to champagne specialists Besserat de Bellefon, while Paddy stayed with Sovedi, a Grand Metropolitan company.

In Japan, Pernod Ricard Japan was established, with responsibility for Jameson and Bushmills, while Suntory has responsibility for Tullamore Dew. These moves were seen as being very important for the future growth of Irish whiskey, because Irish Distillers' sister companies within Pernod have an interest in seeing the Irish company achieve its objective, and any future growth will come as a result of the commitment of the parent company. In the UK market, Matthew Clark distribution had been used since 1982, and had done a great job in helping Irish Distillers to carve out a niche for itself. However, Irish Distillers decided to go to fellow subsidiary Campbell Distillers, which handles Pernod, Dubonnet and Clan Campbell Scotch whiskey. In Germany, Italy, Spain and Switzerland, Jameson was moved into the Pernod Ricard group of companies, while a mix of arrangements is in place on the remaining brands. Australia has played a big role in the success so far. In 1989, 1 million cases of West Coast Cooler were sold in this market, which has a 70 per cent share of the carbonated bottled cooler market.

The Australian market has great potential for Irish Distillers, with 30 per cent of the population of Irish extraction. In 1991, the group consolidated its brands into Pernod Ricard Australia. The US market also holds much potential and possibility for the group. The others, in order of size, are Britain, Germany, France and the Netherlands. Duty free is also an important sales earner. One of the major benefits of its link-up with Pernod is that the Irish group now has an extensive international network available to it, allowing it to reach new consumers. The group's efforts to crack the US market have not changed much since Pernod took over, with sales stuck at 250,000 cases. Where Pernod has helped though is in Europe. After switching distribution to Pernod, company sales increased by some 30 per cent, with the French market putting in the best performance. Membership of Pernod has been good for Irish Distillers, not only because it has helped with European distribution, but because it has allowed the group to boost its advertising to £16 million.

In December 1993, Irish Distillers announced the sale of one of its brands, Tullamore Dew, to the UK-owned Cantrell and Cochrane. This move effectively amounted to the break-up of the monopoly hold that the group had on sales of Irish whiskey. The sale of the brand was effectively an exchange, because C&C's UK parent company, Allied Lyons, was handing over its Royal Canadian brand to Irish Distillers' parent company, Pernod Ricard, along with a substantial payment to Pernod in recognition of the considerable potential that Tullamore Dew had to offer. The Royal Canadian brand had been very much confined to the US market, and it was the intention of Pernod to develop the brand internationally. Furthermore, C&C joined forces with Irish Distillers in a whiskey-supply agreement. It was C&C's intention to spend up to £20 million on the promotion and marketing of Tullamore Dew, and the brand would be distributed by Allied Lyons' distribution channels. From Irish Distillers' viewpoint, Tullamore Dew was not a core brand, as most of the group focus was on the other major brands in its portfolio, including its flagship brand, Jameson. The group saw the move as having positive implications for the future development of Irish whiskey in world markets. That is not to say that Tullamore does not have a loyal following. It is in fact, the leading Irish whiskey in Germany, selling some 60,000 cases each year.

Management Changes and Restructuring

From a management perspective, the senior management team of Irish Distillers is much more involved with the day-to-day business than it was. But Irish Distillers still operates as an autonomous unit making all its own decisions. Pernod Ricard has certainly honoured its promise to prevent the dismemberment of the Irish whiskey industry. With the exception of the departure of a number of directors from Irish Distillers' board, the corporate structure has remained very much intact. The top positions in the group are filled by Richard Burrows as managing director, Michael Cummins as sales director, and Camilus Dwane as marketing manager. Yet the company would be quick to point out that, while the people have not changed, there has been considerable change in the jobs that they perform.

The year 1993 saw the restructuring of both Irish Distillers and its parent company, Pernod Ricard. Irish Distillers' legal affairs director, Bernard Rogan, was promoted to executive vice-president of Pernod Ricard in France. He was also appointed as personal assistant to Pernod chairman Patrick Ricard. Other changes that took place included the assignment of Francesco Taddonio, the budget planning director at Pernod, to the position of continental European director of sales and marketing at Irish Distillers. He would operate from a Dublin office reporting to Irish Distillers' chairman and chief executive Richard Burrows. His appointment, it was hoped, would help the group to establish itself in Europe with the help of Pernod Ricard companies. Also Michael Cummins retired as Irish Distillers' managing director of sales, but still continues on a consultancy basis to oversee marketing plans in Ireland.

New Marketing Strategy

Since the group's inception, its marketing policy has been focused on the promotion and development of a few major products, namely Jameson and Black Bush (part of the Bushmills family), with the former aimed at the premium end of the spirits market and Black Bush at the super premium end of the market. The reason for this two-brand focus is simply that Irish Distillers lacked the resources necessary to back all brands. So with few resources available, it was perhaps the best policy to focus on what the group considered to be its best two brands. In its alliance with Pernod, Jameson and Bushmills still have top priority within the group's portfolio of international priority brands. But as previously in Irish Distillers, Jameson is getting much of the attention by getting the primary brand treatment in all of the export markets. Bushmills is also given special treatment in selection markets, as is Powers. The group spends up to £16 million on the promotion of its products, but of this more than half would be spent on the promotion of its flagship product, Jameson.

The group's new marketing strategy since the takeover, with Jameson as the flagship, is promoting a commonality of brand, a move which essentially means that the products will be promoted using the same format and packaging worldwide. The advertising and promotions campaigns will be much the same everywhere. Irish Distillers feels that it has finally achieved the desired marketing mix for the future growth of the company. It is a premium marketer in that it utilises a two-brand investment strategy in most of its key markets, and in all of these markets the company works 50/50 with a partner in the investment and promotion of its brands. Irish Distillers has not deviated from its export strategy, with strict control of marketing investment, partnership on a 50/50 basis, and major investment in the markets that offer the greatest potential. The main thrust of Irish Distillers' marketing strategy as before is Jameson as the premium brand, with Black Bush as the de luxe brand. The reasons for the market success of Irish whiskey are as follows:

- The taste of the product — the most important and distinctive selling point

- Very high texture and quality

- Long heritage and history of the product — it has a longer history than Scotch whiskey

- Ireland's image as being environmentally clean and natural — this assists the marketing effort considerably

- Association with natural ingredients which make it very appealing to many of its customers especially the German and Dutch customers.

There are several factors associated with the company which have been criticised from a good business point of view. Principally, the market is an ageing and declining one, with the product perceived as being somewhat staid. Management is also regularly berated for its lack of marketing dynamism. It is this latter point that has received the greatest amount of criticism.

Irish Distillers does not have to worry about the quality of its product — Jameson is Jameson. What it has had to concentrate on, however, is how it brings that product to the market, on both the domestic and international fronts. The failure of Irish Distillers' management to capitalise on the opportunities available to the company was one of the main arguments put forward by the hostile GC&C consortium in presenting its takeover bid in 1988. Part of the problem for the group could be the lack of any significant competition on the home market. Irish Distillers has close on 75 per cent of the whiskey market in Ireland and has traditionally cohabited comfortably with the Scottish imports. However, overall volume sales of Irish whiskey fell significantly in the early 1980s, and one of the main reasons for this was the high excise duties which resulted in a major programme of redundancies being undertaken at the company. Since 1984, with a lowering of the government's tax take, the company has been able to restructure its operations, with sales rising again as a result. Irish Distillers is currently engaged in a major revamp of its marketing. In 1989, the group entered a joint venture with Bass Ireland, the largest wine and spirits company in Northern Ireland, to distribute wine and spirits there, with a new company called Dillon Bass being created for the purpose. Based in Belfast, the company employs Peter Greaney as its managing director.

The clearest sign of change on the home market was the launch of the multi-brand advertising campaign in 1992. Traditionally, Irish Distillers in promoting individual brands had focused the appeal in its advertisements on the traditional core market: middle aged and middle class. The multi-brand campaign took a different approach and featured four new full-colour advertisements with fashionable young people in modern locations. Five of the brands were discretely featured through the use of bottle tops. The clear aim of the advert was to spread the base of Irish whiskey consumers so as to include the young and upwardly mobile. The investment in this campaign alone was in excess of £500,000, with the intention of creating an interest in Irish whiskey among new consumers without offending existing customers.

This new approach to marketing was very much prompted by research undertaken by the company which showed that, while the brand image of the individual products was strong, the image of whiskey was not of the same calibre.

Sale of Subsidiary

In December 1992, Waterford Liqueurs, the liqueur manufacturer and contract bottler which is owned by Irish Distillers, was put up for sale. It employed some 20 people and was located outside Waterford city. At one stage, it manufactured the well-known Waterford Cream Liqueur, but with declining sales and increased competition from some new arrivals such as Emmet's, O'Darby's, Carolan's, and in particular, Bailey's, production ceased a few years ago. It now manufactures two products for Irish Distillers, Irish Velvet and Snug, a whiskey-based drink used in Irish coffees. It also manufactures West Coast Cooler for both the home and export markets. A major part of its business was in the contract-bottling business for other drinks companies. A management buyout led by its managing director Dayrell Gallery has been suggested, and some foreign parties have expressed an interest in its purchase.

Cooley Distillery Takeover Attempt

In October 1993, the group announced that it had acquired a 51 per cent share in the Louth-based Cooley distillery, with a further intention of acquiring the remaining interest. The talks between the two companies had begun in June 1993, and the total cost if

Irish Distillers had been successful would have been around £22 million: £9.5 million for the acquisition; £1.5 million for Cooley's bank debt; and an undertaking to acquire £11 million of matured whiskey over the next four years. Involved were some 22 million bottles of whiskey, maturing at a rate of 180,000 bottles a week. Cooley whiskey is sold under the Tyrconnell, Locke's and Kilbeggan brands. Cooley Distillery, an independent Irish whiskey manufacturer, opened in 1987. The takeover bid by Irish Distillers for Cooley's did not go smoothly from the start as it was delayed by the Competition Authority which expressed considerable concern over the implications of such a takeover, particularly in respect of Irish Distillers' monopoly on Irish whiskey manufacturing. Many were of the view that the move by Irish Distillers was an attempt to cancel out any rivalry in the Irish whiskey market. Cooley's whiskey brands are the only Irish competition to Irish Distillers' whiskey brands. From Irish Distillers' viewpoint, such a move was a "defensive one", designed to protect the reputation of Irish whiskey abroad. Irish Distillers considered Cooley's whiskey to be of an inferior quality.

Essentially, it was Irish Distillers' plan to take over Cooley's, with the intention of subsequently closing it down. The then Minister for Enterprise and Employment, Ruairí Quinn, hoped that another company would come forward to buy all or some of the distillery, running it as a going concern. Examples here would include Gibney's of Grand Met. The Competition Authority decided to investigate the move to determine whether or not it contravened Section 4 of the Competition Act, 1991. This section relates to anti-competitive agreements, decisions and concerned practices. Section 4 prohibits any agreements that have as their "object or effect" a "restriction or distortion of competition in trade in any goods or services". Despite considerable effort over the past two years by the company's chairman, John Teeling, Cooley's has not managed to come up with a buyer. The company also failed to receive much needed grant-aid from the IDA or CTT. It would appear that a number of submissions were made to the Competition Authority from various interested parties — including Cooley itself, Irish Distillers, former employees of the company and of two overseas distributors — each of which was willing to invest some £1.5 million in the company. The Cooley distillery by this point had run out of money and could not afford the multi-million pound marketing required to promote its products. The company's 30 staff, seven of whom were full-time, accepted the redundancy terms. If the Irish Distillers deal was to be blocked by Ruairí Quinn, on the advice of the Competition Authority, speculation suggested that either Cantrell and Cochrane or Grand Metropolitan would be interested in taking up the company.

During February of 1994, in contemplation of its intentions to take over the company, Irish Distillers announced a £50,000 investment in the Cooley distillery, bringing the total amount spent by the group in its attempts to acquire whiskey stocks in Cooley to £1.7 million. Of this figure, £1.5 million was spent in 1993, with a further £200,000 spent in 1994. Irish Distillers invested a further £100,000 to prevent the company from being put into receivership. These separate payments were made because Irish Distillers would not have been allowed to make a straight cash injection into the company because of its proposed takeover of Cooley's, which at this time was still under review by the Competition Authority. In the end, all of the group's efforts came to nothing, because in March 1994, the proposed takeover of Cooley's was blocked by the Competition Authority. Irish Distillers at this stage had spent between £2 million and £3 million on the aborted deal, but the money was not lost as the group will be able to recover it by selling off the whiskey stocks it had bought from the group. The effect of the failed takeover by Irish Distillers had been to strengthen Cooley's balance sheet, by removing debt and cutting its weekly interest bill by 75 per cent. Irish Distillers were said to be disappointed by the Competition Authority's blocking of the takeover.

Financial Performance of Irish Distillers

For the year 1985, pre-tax profits were £7.57 million, a fall of one third on a year earlier with £11.23 million. A prolonged industrial dispute was felt most severely in the first half of the year when a net loss before tax of £577,000 was recorded. This took account of an exceptional item amounting to £1.47 million because of rationalisation and redundancy costs. Pre-tax profits in the second half of the year came to £8.15 million, compared to £6.06 million a year earlier, following a five-year spirits decline between 1979 and 1984. Present times have seen an increase of 15 per cent. Profits before interest, tax and exceptional items declined by over 4 per cent from £13.99 million to £13.37 million. Interest charges rose by almost 57 per cent from £2.77 million to £4.33 million, reflecting the cash shortage caused by the industrial dispute and the cost of acquisitions. Profit before tax and exceptional items fell by 19.5 per cent to £9.04 million; the cost of rationalisation alone was £1.47 million. Earnings per share after exceptional items came to 10.28p, compared with 17.28p for the pervious year.

In 1986, record pre-tax profits of £12.94 million were achieved representing a 70 per cent increase on the previous year with £7.57 million. Turnover declined by just over £1 million, but sales rose from 14.7 per cent to 20.8 per cent because of changes in the profit mix, and there was reduced capital expenditure. The improved trading performance of the company, plus the disposal of its share in United Drug plc, led to a reduction in the group's net gearing of 34.7 per cent from 39.4 per cent. Fixed asset investment for the year amounted to £5.56 million and earnings per share were 16.28p from 190.28p a year earlier.

1987–89

In 1987, the group met with difficult trading conditions but it managed to produce trading profits of £13.1 million. Turnover decreased to £230 million from £240 million a year earlier. The cost of rationalisation was £10.4 million, earnings per share improved to 17.42p, and the dividend was 5.65p. A 4.6 per cent decline in the home market for spirits was the most disappointing feature of the year. Trading profit before exceptional charges was £13.1 million, an increase on the profit level a year earlier of £12.9 million. Redundancy costs came to £4.8 million, and borrowing rose to a net figure of £38.2 million, because of rationalisation outlays. The year 1989 was the first full year of operation for Irish Distillers as part of the Pernod Ricard group, and the results achieved by the group showed a significant improvement in performance. The benefits of the takeover were clearly reflected in the progress Irish Distillers made in developing its European markets. The link-up has led to substantially higher marketing investment and to higher profits. Turnover for the year amounted to £257 million, profits before tax rose to £244.6 million, and after a tax charge of £4.4 million after-tax profits were £20.2 million. In the export market, sales grew by 13 per cent mainly as a result of the many changes in distribution that the Irish group made, utilising the strength of sister companies within the Pernod group to assist in the growth of Irish whiskey. Market sales at home were maintained. Sales in the French market rose 31.3 per cent. In this market, Ricard handled Jameson; Pernod handled Bushmills; Besserate de Bellefon had Powers; Cusenier distributed Tullamore Dew; Sovedi distributed Paddy.

1990–92

Sales in France grew by 65 per cent, while sales in other key markets such as Germany, Holland, and Italy were also significantly up on 1989 figures. The company recorded pre-tax profits of £218.7 million, up 16.7 per cent. Turnover only showed a small increase — 2 per cent to £262 million, and if one strips away the 9.4 per cent sales advance at cash-and-carry subsidiary BWG Foods to £129 million, it quickly becomes clear that sales from the core sprits business actually fell for the year from £139 million to £133 million. This represented a 55 per cent increase on the £18.5 million pre-tax profit recorded for the year to September 1988, Irish Distillers' last year as an independent company. However, for the £4.50 a share that Pernod paid for the company in 1988, the French company only earned a pre-tax return of 10.07 per cent on its investment. After tax the return slipped to only 8.56 per cent.

In 1992, the group saw profits drop 8 per cent to £24.2 million for the year. Turnover increased 5.4 per cent to £3.02 million but its profit margins were reduced. The previous year's profit had been boosted by a £508,000 exception gain. Sales of its brands Jacob's Creek wines and West Coast Cooler grew significantly in Ireland during the year. Irish Distillers paid an increased £25.4 million dividend to its French parent company. Payment of this dividend saw Irish Distillers transferring a net £1.2 million loss into its retained profits which stood at £85 million. Turnover in the Irish market — Irish Distillers' largest market — increased by 8 per cent to £220 million. Exports also grew strongly from £47 million to £50 million. Earnings per 25p ordinary share were 37.43p compared to 39.86p in the previous year. These results were considered very satisfactory given the uncertain conditions and the pressure on the margins in the last quarter because of the devaluation of sterling.

For 1993, Irish Distillers reported strong growth for the year with pre-tax profits of £34.1 million compared to the £30 million profits for 1992. Irish Distillers accounted for up to 18 per cent of the 1.58 billion French francs (£191 million) profits of its parent company, Pernod Ricard. Before an exceptional charge of £2.8 million which related to the closure of its Waterford bottling plant and the group's aborted attempt to take over Cooley's, Irish Distillers had profits of £36.9 million, which represented a record for the group. The closure of the Waterford plant cost the group £800,000. Of the exceptional charge incurred by the group, £1.3 million related directly to the Cooley bid. There was a write-down of £2 million worth of stock purchased from Cooley. The whiskey that Irish Distillers retains from Cooley will more than likely be sold on the international market over the coming years. Turnover for the year was up 12.5 per cent to £34.0 million; of this, 30 per cent of sales were in Europe, 41 per cent in the Irish market, 4 per cent duty-free and 15 per cent in the remaining markets, especially the US.

Trading profits showed a £4.8 million improvement; there were interest savings of £1.7 million mainly resulting from lower debt and interest rates, and a £400,000 profit boost from the BWG cash-and-carry subsidiary. Volume sales also grew during the year, with overall sales in the Republic up 6 per cent and Irish Whiskey sales up 10 per cent. In Northern Ireland sales were up by 20 per cent. Ireland is still the group's main market, even though over the past five years Irish sales as a percentage of turnover have fallen 5 per cent to 41 per cent. Europe, the UK and the US along with duty-free account for up to 59 per cent of sales. On the international markets, sales grew by 19 per cent, with strong demand coming from France, Greece and Italy. Jameson and Bushmills sales grew by 19 per cent. The US has still not shown the results that the group would like, with only modest growth for the year, with a shift away from hard liquor to wine and beer. In total, Irish Distillers would only have about 1.5 per cent of the US market, which in bottle terms means about 3 out of every 200 bottles sold in the US. Scotch whiskey has a much better share, accounting for up to 60 out of every 200 bottles sold.

Note: Since 1989, Irish Distillers have not published any accounts.

Strategy for the Future

For the future, the group's business will very much hinge on the growth and promotion of Jameson and Bushmills. The aim is to try and establish various brands with a loyal customer following, with Irish Distillers starting to utilise a concept being used by some of their competitors, called "trade up". For example, within the Jameson family of whiskeys, consumers will in the future be able to trade up from Jameson to Jameson 1780 (a 12-year-old whiskey). The Bushmills range also has this concept available to its customers, whereby in the standard process market, Bushmills is available, Black Bush in the premium blends sector and Bushmills Malt (a 10-year-old single malt whiskey) is aimed at the de luxe premium sector. Irish Distillers would also be aiming in the future for a seat in the world's top 100 spirit brands. At present, Bailey's is the only Irish company making the list, registering in at number 15.

The alliance with Pernod is proving to be fruitful, with sales in France alone more than tripling since the takeover to 120,000 cases of whiskey per year. The focus for the brands such as Jameson and Bushmills will be on markets such as continental Europe and the Far East, and Pernod's financial muscle will help Irish Distillers to break into the real markets for the future — the Far East and China. But in Europe and Asia, as in the US, Irish Distillers is up against some considerable competition from Scotch and Canadian Whiskey, along with American Bourbon. These brands are owned by giants such as Grand Met. and Guinness which have the resources to move into new markets while holding their own in existing ones.

Source: Company reports and interviews with company personnel.

Questions

1. What relationships between strategy and structure are evident from the Irish Distillers Groups case?

2. From the Irish Distillers Group perspective, what advantages and disadvantages followed from the takeover?

3. Evaluate the branding and marketing strategies utilised by Irish Distillers Group.

4. How would you assess the financial performance of Irish Distillers up to 1993?

22

Jefferson Smurfit Group

Evolution of the Group

The Early Years

Jefferson Smurfit was born in 1909 in Sunderland, in the north of England. A tailor by trade, he started his own business in 1934, and in the same year was offered a stake in a small badly-run box-making business in Dublin, owned by his wife's family, the Magees of Belfast. His initial involvement was that of advisor, concentrating most of his efforts on developing his own tailoring business, which consisted of four shops. At this stage, he came to recognise the potential of the Dublin plant and set about improving his knowledge of packaging technology. By 1938, he had made the move to Dublin to take full control of the ailing company.

The 1930s were good years to be in the packaging industry, with industrial production rising steadily. However, all was interrupted in 1939 by the Second World War, which caused a scarcity of many things, including paper. To overcome this, Jefferson Smurfit built his own machine to use on the only material available, waste paper. Unlike some companies which expanded their manufacturing base, Jefferson Smurfit stuck to corrugated packaging and, with the upturn in business after the War, the company prospered more than most. By 1950, the Dublin company was five times its original size. Because the company was a family concern, the boss brought in his four sons, who included the present chairman and eldest son, Michael. All four sons learned their trade by starting on the factory floor. Michael's first working period was with Continental Can in the US, concentrating on plant management. This was followed by a period spent with Associated

British Consultants. In 1958, he opened his own corrugated box business in Lancashire, and within four years its turnover was greater than £2 million, supplying companies such as Heinz, Kellogg's and United Biscuits. In 1962, he returned to Dublin to manage the now vibrant family business.

The 1960s — Acquisition Strategy

In 1964, Jefferson Smurfit and Sons Ltd. became a public company on the Irish stock market and set about raising capital. Its first investment was in a new corrugated and conversion plant followed by a new paper-machine company and the acquisition of an interest in a waste-paper company. The Irish print and packaging industry at the time was very fragmented and coming under threat from free trade. Therefore, Smurfit decided on a diversification programme, by acquiring other companies.

In 1968, several companies were acquired and a joint venture was entered into with the UK-based Reed Industries to manufacture paper sacks. In the same year, the company acquired Temple Press Ltd., a public company that produced cartons and boxes. In 1969, the company took over Browne and Nolan Ltd., a company specialising in the packaging, printing and publishing of educational products. Also in 1969, the company got its quotation on the London stock exchange. In 1970, it was still on the acquisition trail, taking over the Hely Group, a conglomerate with interests in packaging, printing, radio and television assembly, distribution, education and office supplies. In a very short period, the company had doubled its assets and had substantially diversified.

The 1970s — Acquisition Strategy

In 1970, the enlarged company was consolidated and re-organised as the Jefferson Smurfit Group. More rationalisation followed and opportunities for growth in the UK were sought. In 1972 the group bought W.J. Noble, a Yorkshire-based company manufacturing cartons and general print material. The same year, the family business in Lancashire was integrated into the group, and Continental Can was brought in as holder of 10 per cent of the enlarged company, raising it to 20 per cent later that year, and providing cash for further acquisitions. These included the UK Tremletts Group, a company having a wide range of packaging interests including plants in Nigeria, and costing £1.0 million in 1973. By this time, the company had extended its activities into the area of flexible packaging and paper merchanting. This period also saw a new direction in strategy, with the group opening an office in the US to test the growth opportunities there.

In the UK, over a two-year period, some £11 million was spent acquiring Alliance Alers, a paper and packaging company with paper mills, corrugated plants, and sheet plants located from London to Glasgow. Smurfit's US tests showed fruition when in 1974 the group acquired 40 per cent of stock of Time Industries, a Chicago-based manufacturing and marketing company of paper board and packaging products, with nine plants producing £321 million annual sales. By 1977, the group had acquired the remaining 60 per cent and renamed the company Smurfit Industries Inc.

Diversification Strategy

In Ireland the group undertook new investment in plastic packaging, corrugated packaging, and printing. Around this time, it extended its involvement in publishing, by acquiring Creation Group followed by further diversification into printing and the creation of Richview Browne and Nolan as a large export-oriented printing company. In 1977, Jefferson Smurfit senior died and Michael took over as chairman and chief executive, ensuring the continuity of strategy and leadership. Back in 1973, the energy crisis had increased paper prices and created a scarcity, but Smurfit Group managed to overcome this with an innovative idea: in 1978, it sold 49 per cent of its UK and Irish corrugated packaging interest to Svensca (SCA) in exchange for cash of £16.5 million and a contract to supply 75 per cent of the group's Irish and UK Kraft liner requirements. Around this time, Continental Can gave up its 20 per cent interest in the group to investors in the UK. Further expansion for the group was achieved by acquiring 27 per cent of Alton Box Board company of the US, and by 1979 Smurfit had managed to become majority shareholders, purchasing the remaining shares over three years. Renamed Alton Packaging Corporation, it was an integrated producer and seller of paper board and packaging, with many plants throughout the US and sales of £300 million.

In 1979, the entry into Ireland of the US packaging company, Union, brought about an excess supply which affected prices and profits. Difficulties in the publishing field led to the closure of

Vision Magazine, followed in 1982 by the withdrawal from participation in the *Sunday Tribune* and ventures entered into in
1980 by the group. This was followed by more divestment in 1981,
with a withdrawal from the office-equipment business. The company did, however, invest in natural resources, with a minority
stake in Aran Energy, an oil exporting company, also in Woodfab, a
producer of forest products, and Norish, the Irish food storage
company Consolidating its commitment to Ireland, a new world
corporate headquarters was built in Clonskeagh in 1979, close to
the original operation.

The 1980s — Integration and Reorganisation Strategy

The 1980s was a decade of general economic decline in the UK.
Economies of scale were working against the group in the corrugated business, with the result that, in 1983, the company merged
its UK corrugated business with Canadian company, Macmillan
Bloedel, a company that had a larger share of the market. The US
remained an area of great potential, with the operations of
Smurfit Industries and Alton integrated into one organisation. In
1982, Quality Packaging Materials was added to the group, which
later on included Southern Fibre Corporation, a paper tube manufacturer. A cash-flow problem for Sir James Goldsmith of Diamond
International, Corporation, a US packaging company, was capitalised on by Smurfit who bought four paperboard and packaging
divisions of the company. The group also entered into a joint venture with Clarke Holdings whose interest could be bought out the
following year. The Diamond acquisition consisted of twelve
plants and annual sales of £2.0 million.

In 1983, the group acquired a 50 per cent interest in Diamond-
Match corporation, and the US operations were reorganised with
the US holding company and renamed Jefferson Smurfit Corporation, with Smurfit Industries, Alton and Smurfit Diamond as
subsidiaries. This was followed by a further reorganisation of
these subsidiaries into product divisions to allow for maximum
operational synergy. Twenty-two per cent of Jefferson Smurfit
Corporation was floated on the New York Stock Exchange to raise
funds. In all, by 1983, the group's US operation consisted of 78 per
cent of J.S. Corporation, 50 per cent of Diamond Match, 100 per
cent of Dinagraphics Inc., 34 per cent of Sequoia Pacific Holdings,
and 50 per cent of Amir, a US venture-capital company. By 1984,
the holdings in Diamond Match were up to 10.9 per cent. It did not

stop there, for in June 1984 the group purchased a 9.3 per cent stake in a fortune 500 company, Southwest Forest Industries.

By 1984, the Smurfit Group was the number one Irish company, with capital employed amounting to £442 million, turnover at £685.9 million, and pre-tax profits at £12,827 million. It was also the year that saw Michael Smurfit appointed chairman of Telecom Éireann. It was a boom period for the group in the US. The home market showed a profit of £4.2 million or 6.7 per cent of sales. In 1985, the group continued on the acquisition trail with the purchase of Sharick Packaging and J&S Manufacturing, while joint ventures were arranged with Panasonic in Ireland and Sonoco in the UK. The US continued to dominate both Smurfit sales and profit performance as over 74 per cent of sales and 71 per cent of profits were earned there, while Irish profits were boosted to £6.2 million. The group also decided to become a shareholder of the *Sunday Tribune*, and pulled out of its takeover bid for Southwest Forest. The 9.3 per cent stake in Southwest paid Smurfit "Greenmail" to forget its bid, so instead of losing, Smurfit came out almost £10 million ahead.

The group also acquired an 80 per cent interest in Publishers Papers, a subsidiary of the Times Mirror Group, costing £133 million. This increased the group's geographical spread, but more importantly, it gave the company access to new markets — namely, in the lucrative newsprint sector of the paper industry. The company was renamed Smurfit Newsprint. The group also purchased a 76 per cent stake of Executive Travel, a company specialising in business holdings, and a controlling 51 per cent share in US-based Visalia Packaging Corporation. Profits stood at £45.5 million, while turnover rose by 13 per cent to £678.1 million, with sales breaking the £1 billion mark. In 1986, Smurfit achieved a billion-dollar coup with the purchase of the Container Corporation of America from Mobil. Smurfit operated over 90 mills and plant facilities, while Container Corporation had 65 facilities in the US and 63 outside the US, including operations in Columbia, Mexico and Venezuela.

Smurfit was also acquiring plants in the Netherlands, Italy and Spain, giving it the significant European presence it had long wished for. This major achievement was accomplished in association with New York bankers, Morgan Stanley in a 50/50 venture. In this context, it is not surprising that 1986 was viewed as the year of the takeover. Jefferson Smurfit Group exercised its option to buy out the European Subsidiaries of CCA for £14 million, it also had the option to purchase CCA's South American subsidiaries. In May 1987, it sold its 5 per cent share in Aran Energy because investment in the oil business was no longer seen to be appropriate. Net profits stood at £19.8 million and sales doubled to £645 million partly because of the performance of Publishers Paper, but mainly as a result of the group's continued capital expenditure in plants and equipment. The year 1987 was a prosperous one for the paper industry, as pre-tax profits increased by 156 per cent to £154 million, of which CCA earned £66 million.

Because of the CCA investment, the group now had three regions of activity — Europe, US and Latin America. Of these, Europe was the area in which the group concentrated its activities, allowing the organisation the scope to balance the profit sources more evenly. In the US, the group now had three major profit centres — 78 per cent of Jefferson Smurfit Corporation, 80 per cent of Smurfit Newsprint Corporation, and a 50 per cent stake and management contract with CCA. The main strategy for Smurfit was to control costs and improve operations in the US. By 1988, turnover had reached £1,660 million and pre-tax profit stood at £245 million. Acquisitions for the year included Dinagraphics for £33 million, the Cundell Group, and a joint venture was entered into with Tembec Inc. of Montreal. In addition, a total of £2.5 million was given towards various education institutions in Ireland. Also acquired were Industrial Cartoners SA in Spain, which contributed £2.9 million to profits, and Smurfit Natural Resources was created to manage a significant afforestation programme in Ireland. The year 1989 saw the most significant event since the purchase of CCA, with the restructuring of the US operation — which essentially meant the remortgaging of it. The group acquired its first German company in 1989 with the purchase of C.D. Haupt, thus allowing the group access to a major market. Smurfit also purchased Ondulato Iimmolese and Euronda in Italy and major expansions plans were undertaken in Holland.

The Spanish company Manyibor was acquired and expanded, and as before, capital expenditure was increased in order to bring all the plants to international standards. The full effect of the group's restructuring was reflected in the 1990 pre-tax profits which fell from £245 million to £173 million. However, the profit/turnover ratio increased from 14 per cent to 17 per cent, while earnings per share increased, highlighting the success for the restructuring. Acquisitions during the year included UK Corrugated and Townsend Hook Group Ltd. and the repurchase of Smurfit Corrugated Ireland. In France, three companies were acquired, including the country's second largest waste-paper collector, Centre de Dechets Industries.

Slow-Down in US Growth

For the year ending January 1992, Smurfit in the US turned in a pre-tax profit of £157 million and earnings per share (EPS) of 48.7p. The pre-tax figure was down 9 per cent on the previous year, while EPS was off 6 per cent. At the same time, four other operating regions — Ireland, UK, the Continent and Latin America — saw their operating profits increase. In the US and Canada, profits tumbled by 71 per cent from £28 million to £8.1 million.

The outlook for 1993 was bleak, with some analysts reckoning that JSC/CCA would do well to maintain losses at the 1992 level. Also, operating profits in Europe fell by 30 per cent, and in Latin America increased by 5 per cent. While Smurfit watchers tended to focus on the US, the biggest generators of operating profits for the group in 1993 were Columbia with £24.4 million, Venezuela with £21.5 million, Ireland with £19.3 million, and Mexico with £15.5 million.

While profits in the US and Europe were lower then expected, the group's performance in Latin America has continued to show good results. In fact, the group at present is relying to a considerable degree on Latin America for the majority of its profits. In the 1992 results, for instance, Latin America accounted for £63 million or 58 per cent of the profits before interest, tax and exceptional items. In 1993, although the figure had fallen to £54 at present entering a period of upturn with the packaging industry emerging from a severe recession, with Smurfit set to benefit more than most. Since 1993, Latin America has been the mainstay of the group, but things should change with the US and Europe making a larger contribution.

Flotation of JSC in the US

In March 1994 the group announced that Jefferson Smurfit Corporation (JSC), the US paperboard and packaging company, which is 50 per cent owned by Smurfit Group, was planning to raise up to $2.5 billion through a new recapitalisation plan. The company was floated on the New York Stock Exchange in April 1994.

Losses for the company amounted to $174.6 million before ex-
traordinary items and cumulative accountancy charges. The recapitalisation plan was made up of an offer of $14.65 million new
shares in the company at a price of $20 per share, and was ex-
pected to raise as much as $3 million for SIBV/MS Holdings Inc.,
JSC's parent company, which Smurfit Group jointly owns with
Morgan Stanley. Smurfit International BV the Smurfit Group's
holding company for its 50 per cent share, subscribed $100 million
for new shares. SIBV/MS subsequently changed its name to Jefferson Smurfit Corporation before the flotation, and JSC became
known as Jefferson Smurfit Corporation (US).

Container Corporation of America, a wholly-owned subsidiary
of JSC, raised $600 million in loan note offerings, the remaining
$1.05 billion was raised through new term loans. The story goes
back as far as 1986, when JSC, a US public company 78 per cent
owned by Smurfit, joined Morgan Stanley (MS) to raise huge
sums of money to buy Container Corporation of America (CCA).
The CCA assets were owned by a company called JSC-CCA. In
1989, after JSC-CCA had enjoyed some years of great performance, it was restructured, with Smurfit Group taking over JSC.
Virtually all of Smurfit's other US operations were merged with
the JSC-CCA assets.

Despite a weakening of investor interest, in April of 1989 the
group managed to do what GPA was unable to achieve, and
raised $250 million from American institutions to mark the dé-
but of Jefferson Smurfit Corporation on the US stock exchange.
It was a job well done. This was part of a £2 billion programme
which would see Smurfit's US business totally restructured by
the end of 1989. The group now claims to be one of the largest
producers of paperboard and packaging products in the US and
the nation's single largest producer of recycled paperboard and
packaging products. In the end, JSC got $13 a share from inves-
tors, when it had originally looked for $20. It also had to invest
$150 million of its own money, rather than the $100 million it
had planned. From the group's viewpoint, the price was disappointing, but the important thing was to get the issue underway.
Undeterred by a weakening in the market, Smurfit took a difficult decision and did what was necessary to complete its
planned programme. As a result, the group has improved its
position. The decisiveness of the group in completing what it set
out to do contrasts sharply with the indecisiveness of GPA in its
initiative to raise capital from a flotation in 1992. Even though

Smurfit originally wanted a $20 share price, it was pleased to settle for $13. GPA, on the other hand, was not so willing to lower its asking price, and ended up getting nothing.

The Company's Success

A number of key factors can be identified as having made a significant contribution to the group's success to date.

Basic Strategy

From Smurfit's viewpoint, the only way for any company to grow significantly in this country in the short term is through a strategy of acquisitions and mergers. Ideally, a consistent 25–30 per cent growth rate is achievable through such a strategy. Fundamentally, an acquisition strategy will diversify the source of a company's profits, thereby providing greater financial security for shareholders by spreading their risk. An acquisition rather than a merger strategy is preferred by Smurfit, because the latter involves some compromise, and less commitment to dynamic new ideas and internal policies. Smurfit is also keen to stay within its core business, a factor that is considered when new acquisitions are being sought.

The policy is to buy underperforming assets, to turn them around, and to make them profitable once again. As the group stresses, the key to competitiveness and long-term success is to become the lowest-cost producer. In order to become more effective, considerable investment has been made in modern equipment. A major factor that has helped the group to remain focused in its activities has been the relative permanence of its senior management personnel, many of whom have been with Smurfit since the group's first acquisition in 1970 of the Hely Group in Ireland, to the more recent one — that of the Container Corporation of America.

Investment in Assets

A major strategy of the company has been to invest in plant and equipment. Some of the companies that Smurfit Group has acquired, such as Alton Packaging Corporation and Jacksonville Mill, have equipment that is very much outdated, yet with adequate investment, the potential exists for above-average output in this sector. However, when acquiring Publishers Paper, Smurfit was fortunate in that the previous owners, the *Los Angeles Times*, had invested heavily in equipment. In addition, the previous owners of CCA Mobil Oil, invested $800 million in the company over five years, giving the Container Corporation some of the most modern and efficient plants in the world. With this investment in equipment, the white-collar payroll was trimmed back.

Along with trimming costs, another feature of the CCA turn-around has been its gain in productivity. By increasing its production by just 10 per cent, it became possible to increase profitability by 30 per cent. Thus Smurfit has become a significant international company by acquiring underperforming plants at competitive prices; and, by applying top management expertise, it has achieved high-performance capabilities in its core business, while managing to remain relatively competitive.

Organisation Structure

In most organisations, the founder has a significant influence on the general scope and direction of business activities. This was very much the case with Jefferson Smurfit. Yet when the organisation began to grow during the 1940s, and 1950s, functional specialisation was introduced to alleviate the difficulties associated with the developing organisation structure. Accordingly, management specialists were allocated to functions such as accounting, engineering and sales, while the owner, Jefferson Smurfit, concentrated efforts on efficiency and customer service. This simple structure remained in place until the company embarked on an acquisition strategy in the late 1960s. A problem often associated with family-owned companies is that the decision-making process is concentrated at higher levels in the organisational hierarchy. An added problem is that of deficiencies in professional management expertise. Yet Smurfit managed to overcome these difficulties by employing suitably qualified individuals in key business areas. For example, in 1986 the former head of the Investment Bank of Ireland, C.F.M. Rawlinson, was appointed as the group's new financial controller, while Alan Jeffers was recruited to plan financial and organisational strategy. He was later replaced in 1972 by Howard Kilroy, who was made responsible for planning and implementing the finance and organisational strategy of the group's overseas expansion.

In 1970, two years into the group's acquisition strategy, Smurfit introduced a multi-divisional form of organisation structure along the same lines as Du Pont and General Motors. It was within this particular structure that Smurfit gave the personnel and training department corporate-level status under the direction of one of Ireland's few professional training executives, the late Bill Lazenby. Personnel managers were recruited for each division of the organisation, while management in general was improved through the greater integration of corporate objectives and key management personnel.

When the group expanded into the UK during the years 1973–76, three extra regional product divisions were created. On acquiring Time Industries in 1975, management consultants McKinsey's were brought in to design a new organisational structure, a structure that would emphasise synergy, and decentralise responsibility and accountability. In the process, strategic weaknesses were identified and individual business life cycles were redefined according to growth earnings. These divisions were then grouped within product divisions, which in turn were classified as strategic business units (SBUs) for maximum synergy. In total, 25 SBUs were formed within nine divisions. Some Irish companies were regrouped into UK divisions and vice versa, but US and other operations were organised on a geographical basis. With expansion, the SBU concept was modified, with dividing lines based along national boundaries and product or service divisions.

In addition to redefining the organisational structure, McKinsey's recommended a review of the role played by the group's managing director. Essentially, the consultants recommended the separation of strategic planning from the operations management function, which led to Howard Kilroy being appointed chief operations director, leaving Michael Smurfit to focus on corporate strategy. In 1987, Jim Molloy was recruited to head Alton Packaging as chief operations officer, and later to head Jefferson Smurfit Corporation, its main subsidiary in the US. Integration within this structure was provided by a hierarchy of common superiors. Each of the divisional managing directors forms an executive management committee in each national region, to focus on issues such as government regulations, industrial relations and capital expenditure. The overall effect is one of simplicity in product divisions, supported by a lean corporate staff of 35 worldwide.

Control Systems

As with most companies, in the early years, the Smurfit group was only concerned with its profit and loss statements, and the cost of manufacturing. With experience, and the introduction of its own machinery, cost-efficiency became a priority, along with a strong focus on customer requirements and expectations. Smurfit had a tight financial control system in place when it commenced its acquisition programme, a control system that was extended to each of the group's more recent acquisitions. Tight financial control is very much part of the company philosophy, in that each strategic business unit is its own profit centre. Each SBU has its own managing director, who has complete autonomy in day-to-day activities, and who is responsible for reporting within a tightly controlled budget. This philosophy was applied in each of the group's acquisitions, and, where deemed necessary, management consultants were brought in to help to introduce more efficient systems of production, planning, materials, etc. With the Hely acquisition and the use of a federally decentralised structure, a corporate planning department was set up to develop long- and short-term planning strategies for the group as a whole. This development very much complemented the tight financial control system in place.

The same financial control and corporate planning systems were introduced into the company's UK, US and South American acquisitions, which proved to be a great way of integrating a widely dispersed company. Tight financial control was only one feature of the company's overall policy of controlling costs. Profits have been sustained over depressed periods through cost reduction programmes implemented on a plant-by-plant basis. In 1978, Smurfit Group demonstrated its commitment to the concept of planning and control systems by endowing a Chair of Corporate Planning at UCD for 10 years.

Management Reward Systems

Smurfit recognises the importance of incentives as a means of developing desirable management attributes such as commitment, entrepreneurial flair and excellence. For the senior executives of the company, a stock option scheme was introduced after the Hely acquisitions, while profit incentive schemes were developed in the 1970s for company executives. Smurfit wanted its executives to link their future to the company — in a decentralised structure, this is essential if profit is to be produced. The group's personnel department brought in a salary review system linked to performance appraisal. Training and development schemes were also introduced. The success of such programmes depends very much on management attitudes and their level of interpersonal skills. Where necessary, management consultants were brought in to develop training programmes to remedy any problems that may have been present.

Managers do not work by financial incentives alone. They are also interested in career development. The SBU system gives managers ample opportunity to gain executive experience relatively quickly. Good performance never goes unnoticed, and there is no limit placed on career development. Smurfit is a result-oriented company where good performance is rewarded generously. The formula for motivating managers is no different from the one that the group traditionally has applied — namely, incentives. And because executives at plant level can more than double their salaries, it means that people identify with their own success.

HRM Strategies within the Company

Entrepreneurial and Professional Management

In total, the company employs some 37,000 people worldwide in more than 300 operating units, in 14 countries. Its record indicates a very successful approach to expansion, blending entrepreneurial and professional management in a way that will achieve the desired results. Operations are governed by a set of strict, unvarying principles. The basic tenet of these principles is that of decentralisation in a multi-divisional organisation. Each division has been structured on a product basis around the concept of strategic business units. Staff are kept to a minimum, and each company operates independently, under tight financial control.

The managing director has full day-to-day autonomy. Incentive schemes ensure adequate rewards for performance. Any capital expenditure required has to be competed for, while the actual expenditure will go through the group and not the subsidiary. In this context, the role of management is not one of control, but rather one of facilitation — to listen and eliminate those obstacles to good performance. The adopted management principle, known as "the Smurfit way" is to manage for continuous improvement. Smurfit's main management philosophy is to remain within its core business.

The Smurfit group can be classified as an organisation with drive, a characteristic highlighted by the company's track record to date. The group's plans are aggressive in their approach and focus, while the ultimate goal continues to be one of delivering value to the stockholder. It is part of the group's management strategy to distribute its power base throughout the group, which will enable workers to contribute in a meaningful way to the organisation, as though the business were their own. Smurfit is an organisation that believes in profit-centre responsibility and the creation of a highly decentralised structure, within which people feel good about operating the business for which they are responsible. The Smurfit Group will continue to grow because it possesses the vital combination of financial and management resources, but perhaps more importantly, it has the necessary will to succeed.

The focus for the future will be to create a company that is resourceful and driven by a hunger to succeed in its business. Smurfit could be described as a family in that the concept of "family" is evident in the broadest sense of he word. Not only are there Smurfits, but there are Kilroys, Molloys and sons and daughters of other managers working in the business. It is something that the company encourages and is viewed as a positive feature in its development. Since the CCA purchase, the group has undergone considerable reorganisation, with joint deputy chairman Dermot Smurfit moving to London to take charge of UK operations, and brother Alan, also deputy chairman, going to Miami to oversee the Latin American interest. St Louis remains the headquarters of JSC, while in Europe, John Coleman is in charge from offices in Monte Carlo. However, Dublin, as far as its chairman is concerned, remains the centre of operations.

Strategy for Investment

The group believes in investing in people to secure its future. There are clearly defined roles and the group operates on the organisation theory of providing its employees with a sense of participation that will increase productivity in excess of that elicited by incentive pay. Accordingly, employees are no longer viewed as an extension of technology, and with a strong family presence, the company is prevented from becoming a faceless "monolith". The company has a broadly based commitment to the education and training of its employees, and is involved in various educational projects in those countries in which it operates. Continuous training for employees at all levels is seen as essential if the company is to remain competitive in an environment of improved quality and cost control. Training schemes include in-house and external programmes ranging from a single discipline or product course on management and team skills development, basic production techniques and training, to industry-awareness seminars, and in some countries, such as Mexico, primary/secondary education for factory employees. Wherever it operates, the group is involved in the education and development of people. The following examples attest to the group's commitment to education:

- University of St Louis funded by Jefferson Smurfit centre for entrepreneurial studies

- Washington University: John M. Olin School of Business funds three MBA scholarships to be awarded to the dependants of Smurfit employees

- Jefferson Smurfit forum at the Colombian Institute of Higher Education

- In 1989, the Jefferson Smurfit Group gave £2.5 million to Irish Universities of which £1.5 million was to be used to develop the Dr Michael Smurfit Business School in UCD.

Strategy for Total Quality Packaging

The driving force behind every company within the packaging division over the past number of years has been the emphasis on quality. It can boast the fact that every plant within the division has achieved ISO9000 standard, and that they have very much been leaders in the quality race within the packaging industry. Since 1992, close to £8 million has been spent on improving the facilities at the various plants, specifically through installing more innovative and top-of-the-range technology. The group is currently undertaking a further £12 million capital investment programme. Because of this investment, the overall capacity of the plants has been increased by some 25 per cent. The Dublin plant, for instance, can boast fully computerised state-of-the-art technology.

Over the next four years a further £4 million will be spent, with part of this being allocated to the Cork plant to bring it up to the standard of its Dublin counterpart. This investment is not being undertaken for aesthetic purposes, but to meet the ever-changing demands of its customers. The Smurfit plants are the only ones in Ireland to offer their customers the facility of four-colour printing on Corrugated packaging. In fact, it was Smurfit who pioneered this process in the early 1980s, and because of its commitment to quality, is the industry leader. The equipment, coupled with expertise, allows the group to meet its customer demands. Image is very important, and companies are always looking for more attractive packaging to promote their products. The company designs and manufactures a wide variety of different packaging styles and sizes, including display cases, regular slotted cases and easy-erect packaging. A more recent innovation for the group has been a packaging called Aqua-guard, which is a packaging product incorporating pre-laminated polyester film, giving it a water-resistant quality. The Cork plant is a major supplier of the dairy sector and the Dublin plant, located in Walkinstown, is currently celebrating 25 years in the business, with 50 per cent of its output sold to the food and drinks sector. In fact, the group would consider itself an expert in this area because of its long association with the sector.

The attainment of the ISO Quality standard is only one rung on the quality ladder. Total Quality Management is the ultimate aim for the group. As part of its current drive for quality, Jefferson Smurfit Corporation is spending about £11,000 per employee on training in order to increase quality awareness and to improve standards. The ultimate satisfaction comes from knowing that the group is looking after its customers' needs on time, and delivered to perfection. The group has always been environmentally conscious, with much of the paper produced recycled at mills in Dublin, and the finished pack is also 100 per cent recyclable.

The year 1990 was a highlight for the Smurfit group, with major financial restructuring of US operations. Total shareholder funds of £850 million were achieved, as were record pre-tax profits of £245 million. There was also an increase in diluted earnings per share of 8.5 per cent. Sales grew at a compound rate of 15 per cent and pre-tax profits at a rate of 28 per cent per annum. EPS increased over 500 per cent from 8.1p in 1980 to 51.0p by 1990, a compound rate of 20 per cent per annum. Capital expenditure totalled £144 million and consolidated sales amounted to £1.7 billion, 21 per cent higher than the previous year. A major gain of £325 million was achieved as a result of a net profit on the recapitalisation of US interests.

Total shareholder funds more than doubled from £1.46 to £3.28 per share, and the company ended the year with net liquid funds of £464 million, compared with net borrowings a year earlier of £195 million. In Ireland, sales were £157.2 million, or 9.5 per cent, and profit before interest and tax were £16.0 million, or 5.8 per cent.

Table 22.1: Financial Analysis of Jefferson Smurfit Group since 1990

| | 1990 | 1991 | 1992 | 1993 | January 1994 | Dec * 1994 |
	£m	£m	£m	£m	£m	£m
Turnover	1,600	992.6	1,227	1,259	1,467	1,710
Operating Profit	158.9	114.1	133.2	104.2	75.01	110.6
Profit Before Tax	245.5	173.1	157.5	65.8	47.80	317.0
Profit After Tax	144.0	131.34	122.50	46.7	42.48	297.0
Dividend	4.7	5.05	4.87	2.50	5.99	13.0
EPS	51.0p	52.0p	48.7p	24.4p	7.2p	59.1p

* In 1994, the company changed its year end to December. The financial statements for the period ended 31 December 1994 therefore include results of certain subsidiaries for 1 month and others for 12 months.

For 1991, pre-tax profits were £173.1 million, compared to £245.5 million the previous year, because of capital restructuring in the US. Diluted earnings per share increased from 51p to 52p and a dividend of 3.48p per share was paid. Total cash at year end was £845 million and borrowings stood at £548 million, with net cash of £306 million. Assets per share increased from 3.28 to 3.43 and total shareholder funds grew to £884 million. Capital expenditure amounted to £133 million, with acquisitions and investments amounting to £196 million. Consolidated sales of £992.6 million were down 40.2 per cent on the previous year's figure of £1,660.5 million, as a result of JSC in the US becoming a 50 per cent associate company instead of a subsidiary. Gross managed sales amounted to £3,788 million, compared to £3,969 million a year earlier, representing a reduction of 5 per cent. Ireland accounted for sales of £156.6 million, or 15.8 per cent, with profit before interest and tax amounting to £18.8 million.

In 1992, gross managed sales came to £4.2 billion compared to £3.8 billion a year earlier. Group sales were up from £993 million to £1,227 million, representing an increase of 24 per cent. Price erosion affected growth leaving profit before interest and tax at £142 million, down 3 per cent. Interest income stood at £103 million up 5 per cent, and there was an extraordinary charge of £25 million caused by a write-off of investment in Brent Walker. Assets per share grew from 3.43 to 3.65, and total shareholder funds amounted to £945 million. A dividend of 48.72p was paid and free cash amounted to £825 million. Capital expenditure for the year totalled £198 million, and there were four acquisitions costing £50 million. The group's diluted EPS was 54 per cent and pre-tax profits were £158 million compared to £173 million for the previous year, a decline of 9 per cent. Interest payable was £88 million, up from a year earlier when it was £72 million — the increase was because of additional local borrowings. The overall tax charge was 22 per cent. Operating cash inflows were a very healthy £202 million, up from £182 million a year earlier. Borrowings, which were mostly medium term were £680 million. The Irish performance brought in profits of £19.3 million on sales of £175 million. Ireland accounted for sales of £175.4 million or 14.3 per cent and profit before tax and interest was £19 million or 6 per cent.

In 1993, gross managed sales came to £4,111 million compared to £4,189 million in the previous year. Group sales (consolidated turnover) were £1,260 million, up from £1,227 million, representing an increase of 2.7 per cent, which reflects some volume and acquisition growth offset by price erosion and weakness in some of the company's trading currencies. Profits before exceptional charges and taxes came to £123.9 million, a reduction of 21.3 per cent on the previous year's figure of £157.5 million. Earnings per share were 11.8 (24.4p), with dividends standing at 2.509. Investment totalled £54 million, with an allocation of £10 million to an enterprise fund for Ireland to help develop employment opportunities. The year 1993 was considered the most difficult year for the company since it went public 30 years previously, but as usual the company used these difficult times to review operations and to consolidate its position. Thus, in the year's results, provisions were made for a restructuring charge of £29.6 million.

The year 1994 was a year of resurgence and growth for the paper industry worldwide. Following the damaging recession of the previous four years, Smurfit managed to stage a recovery in its profitability Profit before interest, taxation and exceptional items rebounded from £75.6 million in the previous year to £128.5 million on consolidated sales, which increased from £1,468 million to £1,710 million. The 17 per cent increase in sales was driven mainly by strong growth in the group's continental European business. Before exceptional items, profits of £118.8 million represent a 39 per cent increase over the 1993 figure of £85.4 million. Gross managed sales increased by 13 per cent from £4.5 billion to £5.1 billion for the period.

Source: Company reports and interviews with company personnel.

Questions

1. Critically evaluate the diversification strategies of Jefferson Smurfit Group in terms of their type and effectiveness.

2. Evaluate the human resource strategies used by Jefferson Smurfit Group and comment on how they may facilitate it in achieving its strategic objectives.

3. What strategic options are now available to Jefferson Smurfit Group in terms of future expansion and growth?

23

Irish Chemical Industry

Introduction

The chemical, healthcare and pharmaceutical sector has been one of the success stories of the Irish economy during the past 20 years. The IDA's intensive promotion and marketing of Ireland as a location for the globalising healthcare, pharmaceutical and chemicals industry, started in the 1970s, has born substantial fruit and benefits to the economy. In 1991, for example, the IDA calculated that employment in the sector — broadly defined — amounted to over 17,000 people employed in 300 companies.

An important distinction must be made at the outset of this case regarding the particular niche under consideration. Principally, it will examine the bulk pharmaceutical chemical (or BPC) manufacturing facility. This is the manufacturing plant responsible for producing the active drug substances — usually milled solid powders — in bulk, to supply what are known as "formulation" plants or pharmaceutical manufacturers. These in turn combine the active substances with "excipients", or ingredients that make the drugs more palatable, to produce the finished products that consumers buy in pharmacies. All of the companies examined in this case study fall into the BPC category. Each of the companies, in one way or another, is involved with a series of chemical processes or "reactions" whereby the active drug substances — the products — are synthesised from chemical raw materials in solvents or aqueous media. Only a small number of firms which can accurately be described as chemical companies have manufacturing facilities in Ireland. These companies can be included here since they are involved in the synthesis of raw materials and intermediates used by the BPC companies.

[459]

Industry Economics

The Irish chemical industry is extremely small by comparison with the industry in the major European industrial countries. It is estimated that in 1989, Ireland accounted for only 1.2 per cent of the industry in the EU. Only Denmark accounted for a smaller proportion of Community turnover. Yet the turnover of the chemical industry is more important, relative to GDP, in Ireland than in any other EU country except Belgium and Luxembourg. Taken in this context, the value of output in chemicals in Ireland is exceptionally high relative to other industries.

The industry is very much export-oriented. In 1989, exports amounted to just 75 per cent of the value of industry turnover. This compares favourably with the 60 per cent export/turnover ratio for all other industries. Exports of chemical products accounted for 16 per cent of all exports in 1975; this proportion has risen to 20 per cent of all exports, or 42 per cent of all exports of manufactured goods. However, Ireland's trade in chemical products is two-way in that imports of chemical products are also significant, amounting to 20 per cent of the value of all imports in 1991. Yet despite continuing recession throughout 1992, exports of chemicals grew by almost 21 per cent to exceed the IR£3 billion mark for the first time. Imports of the industry's raw materials and of chemicals generally showed no change on the 1991 level, to yield a record net trade balance in chemicals of £1.5 billion.

The scale of Irish firms in the chemical industry is extremely small by European standards. There are six European companies employing 10,000 or more, whereas total employment in the industry in Ireland is only 37,500. Employment in the industry amounts to 6.1 per cent of industrial employment in Ireland, compared with the EU average of 7 per cent. The average income in the industry is significantly higher than in other manufacturing industries. While this is partly a result of the high level of graduate and professional employment, the income of general operatives is also higher than in general industry. Most of this employment is in multinational companies attracted here by the IDA incentive package. However, the indigenous sector is in itself a relatively significant employer, employing more people than the indigenous textile, drink and tobacco industries. The greater part of the industry is composed of multi-purpose manufacturing plants of the multinational firms whose investment is from the United States (companies like Pfizer, Eli Lilly, and Merck, Sharp and Dohme) though Japanese investment (Yamanouchi, for example) has also become important. Significant mainland European players — such as Sandoz — have also been attracted to locate in Ireland.

Fifteen of the top US pharmaceutical companies and 12 of the top 16 pharmaceutical and healthcare companies in the world now have substantial manufacturing operations in Ireland. The first companies — Pfizer and Smith-Kline, for example — located here as a consequence of the industrial promotions environment consisting of capital grants and tax incentives such as the Export Sales Tax Relief Scheme. At the time — the early 1970s — full employment was the norm in many of the industrialised countries of the west, and hence the availability of skilled labour was also an attraction. This was further boosted when Ireland joined the EEC, and the desirability of a physical presence within the Community became important to US companies, and lately to Japanese firms. In more recent times, there has been an oversupply of labour in the industrialised countries, while capital grants have become relatively less important. Consequently, the tax situation — even after the substitution of a 10 per cent manufacturing tax rate for Export Sales Relief — and EU membership are the major determining influences for locating plants in Ireland. The cost of labour in Ireland is not seen, initially at least, as an important influence, since the physical plants are among the most capital intensive in the country.

One popular misconception about the industry is that it is primarily a warehouse or import/export operation designed to facilitate tax-avoidance via transfer price mechanism. However, the size of the physical investment, the volume of local expenditure and the control exercised on the plants by regulatory authorities, both fiscal and healthcare, quickly dispel this view. New US tax legislation which may remove the transfer pricing mechanism could have a negative effect on the industry here.

Another view is that the plants in Ireland are simply satellite production units selling to a captive market. While it is true that the plants are primarily production units, they are not just that. Most plants undertake significant process development after applying quite considerable resources to this task. The existence of a number of numerically large development teams, such as at Syntex, Pfizer, Schering Plough etc., attests to this fact. In addition, some of the plants provide support services — engineering, development, quality standardisation — to other locations within the multinational organisation. Indeed, in many cases, senior management in Ireland is not just concerned with the Irish operation, but has a corporate role in relation to worldwide operations. It is also worth noting that the primary incentive to locate production in Ireland — namely, the tax régime — makes it unlikely that firms would locate basic research facilities here since to do so would not be tax-effective.

Generally speaking, while most of the production may be sold to affiliates, the market is by no means captive. The Irish plant is often just one of several within the firm capable of producing the material (Syntex Ireland is one of five), and corporate headquarters has the option of sourcing elsewhere within the group, at any time.

The Environment

During the late 1980s in Ireland, the image of the chemical industry changed from that of an industry which contributes to an increasing standard of living to one which lowers living standards by polluting the environment. This image-change was blown out of all proportion by media-attention given to the *Hanrahan* v. *Merck, Sharp and Dohme (Ireland) Ltd.*, and the *Merrell Dow* cases.

Formulating policy on environmental responsibilities and performance levels has become a critical concern for many of the firms in the chemical industry. For example, Schering-Plough has sought to develop a standard which must be maintained and made applicable to all Schering-Plough sites worldwide. Environmental policy is developed in Good Environment Practice (GEP) documents, which take account of the varying types of operations at different sites. These documents provide a uniform environmental standard for all locations, and take into account local regulatory and legislative requirements. Environmental considerations are built-in at the R&D stage for new products or processes to eliminate the use of environmentally undesirable materials. Waste production is also minimised by process optimisation and recovery or recycling of process materials. Older processes are continuously examined to minimise emissions by installation of new or improved recovery systems or process modifications. Such changes have not only significantly reduced environmental emissions, but have also led to substantial cost savings and reduced use of materials. Waste disposal in an environmentally acceptable manner is strictly controlled and total waste-reduction programmes, including packaging and other industrial waste, as well as hazardous waste, are an integral part of overall company policy. Auditing of environmental compliance with company policy and local or state regulations is carried out regularly at each site and by an independent corporate audit function. Environmental and safety considerations are closely related, and an integrated approach to their management is taken. Schering-Plough in Ireland is using the FICI (Federation of Irish Chemical Industries) Responsible Care programmes to improve the overall levels of health, safety and environmental protection in its operation. Its experiences show that such an integrated approach to environmental protection best serves the needs of employees, the public and the environment.

In environmental terms, the Sandoz pharmaceutical facility in Cork harbour will be one of the most tightly controlled in the country, and in Europe for that matter. Sandoz has committed IR£35 million to environmental management expenditure out of a total investment cost of IR£175 million. In addition to what appears to be a basically eco-friendly concept in terms of operation, the company is also making a major investment in landscaping and in the development of its 100-acre site. Essentially, the environmental management plan for the Sandoz family focuses on a number of priority areas. Resources will be recycled wherever possible, with used solvents directed to a solvent-recovery plant where in excess of 95 per cent will be recovered for re-use. No waste water, even rainwater, will leave the site without being checked and treated. All plant emissions will go through a three-stage cleansing, scrubbing and incineration process. The general plant (domestic-type) refuse will be reduced in a separate trash incinerator to about 10 per cent of its size, before going to landfills. Sandoz currently is on track to create, by the time it is ready for commercial production in 1996, a factory for the year 2000 — a grass roots design on a "greenfield" site incorporating up-to-the-minute technology to set and reach ambitious environmental standards.

Merck Sharp and Dohme (Ireland) Ltd., consumes approximately 300,000 gallons of water a day from the River Suir, and waste from the plant is treated in an activated sludge waste treatment system, capable of handling a throughput of 1,000,000 gallons a day. The purified water is then used for processing, generating steam and cooling reaction vessels, as well as for human consumption. Discharges are tested every day and the results are sent to the county council, which also carries out independent spot checks to ensure the integrity of the company's results. This is a common practice of most local authorities with responsibility for monitoring a chemical plant in their area. An independent survey of the River Suir is also carried out each year by Trinity College and Forbairt (formerly Eolas). Merck, Sharp and Dohme's planning permission licence for the river discharges is 181 kg of chemical waste per day. The company says that by any standards this is a very tight limit, and that in the course of its operations total discharge to the River Suir has only been 40 per cent of that allowed by its planning permission. This upgrading has led to a 40 per cent reduction in daily chemical waste to the waste-water treatment plant between 1987 and 1990, as well as a 16 per cent reduction in waste-water volumes between 1989 and 1991. In this context, the company has set out a number of key environmental objectives. These include water minimisation and the conservation of energy and resources. Merck has also recently installed two new basins for the treatment of waste, and has spent £500,000 on the installation of cross-flow filtration for solids/liquids separation. One of the objectives of this project is to reduce the solvent usage in certain processes.

Jansen Pharmaceuticals Ltd. in Cork feels that the pharmaceutical industry is now one of the cleaner industries in this country. In 1983, Jansen installed its biological treatment plant employing extended aeration followed by clarification. The effluent has a design capacity of 467 kg DOB per day, equivalent to a production of 6,800 people, and operates at a greater than 90 per cent chemical-waste reduction. The treated effluent discharges from the Little Island plant, via a sewer, to Lough Mahon, where the effluent from Cork City is also discharged.

Cork-based Pfizer Chemical Corporation is also committed to the Responsible Care initiative. Staff monitor effluent discharges daily to ensure that they comply with a licence issued by Cork County Council under the Water Pollution Act. Almost £1 million is spent each year on environmental control, and the company is becoming heavily involved in waste-management projects that will eliminate some wastes, and reduce solvent waste by over 60 per cent. Pfizer has spent £16 million to provide its own boiler house, effluent-treatment plant, and laboratory facilities, following the sale of its food chemical business (ADM) in 1990.

Profile of Industry Performers

Merrell Dow

In September 1989, *Script*, the world pharmaceutical news journal ran two stories on under the headings "Merrell Dow Cancels Irish Plant" and "Sandoz Plans New Irish Plant" (*Script*, 1989b). In hindsight the accounts of these two companies serve to illustrate the best- and worst-case scenarios of the establishment of bulk pharmaceutical chemical manufacturing facilities in Ireland. Earlier in 1989, in July, the pharmaceutical subsidiary of Dow Chemical, Merrell Dow, and Marion Laboratories announced an agreement in principle under which Dow would take a 67 per cent stake in Marion, and Marion and Merrell Dow would merge. The expanded company, called Marion Merrell Dow (MMD) is based in Kansas City, US. In 1988/89 Marion was forty-sixth and Merrell Dow thirty-fifth in terms of sales in the Pharmaceutical Leagues Table, and the new merged company rose to twentieth in 1991. In 1992, MMD's turnover reached $3.3 billion, an increase of 16 per cent from $2.85 billion in 1991.

The decision of the company not to proceed with the construction of its proposed bulk terfenadine manufacturing plant in Killeagh, Co. Cork was attributed to the merger with Marion, which the company stated would create new opportunities for meeting future production requirements. An evaluation of the combined assets and needs of the merged company took almost a year. The company planned to meet its projected product demands through expansion of existing facilities in the US, France and Italy, along with the process-efficiency improvements.

According to *Script*, the local opposition to the plant does not appear to have been a factor in the decision. The High Court in Dublin had ruled against an appeal lodged by community groups against the planning permission, effectively clearing legal obstacles against construction of the plant. The objectors, who were local farmers and members of the Womanagh Valley Protection Agency, had taken legal action against the decision by Cork County Council and An Bord Pleanála, alleging that Merrell Dow had not complied with an EEC Directive of 27 June 1985 (85/337/EEC) requiring certain data on the environmental impact of the plant. Justice Barron ruled that the Directive was not legally binding on the domestic legislative process, as it had not yet been incorporated into Irish law. Merrell Dow had spent IR£1 million on a comprehensive environmental impact study. The plant had also gained planning permission for producing finished formulations of terfenadine, although that was not part of its immediate plans for the plant, the company told *Script* at the time (*Script*, 1989a).

Script also reported that MMD might well re-apply for planning permission to build the plant should the merged company still require it, and commented at the time that despite the local opposition to the Killeagh plant, Ireland was still a very attractive location. MMD's major products include the calcium antagonist, Cardizem, sales of which rose by 16 per cent to over $1 billion in 1992. Sales of the non-sedating antihistamine, Seldane (terfenadine), rose by 13 per cent to an estimated $865 million. Sales of MMD's nicotine products for smoking cessation, the Nicoderm patch and Nicorette gum also rose and Carafate (Sucralfate) sales were unchanged (the latter is a gastrointestinal system regulating agent).

However, in May 1993, the company reported substantially lower than expected sales and earnings for the first quarter of the year, and announced plans to cope with the tougher business climate. These will include taking a close look at staffing levels and cutting operating expenses. MMD said that it planned to continue a high degree of commitment to R&D but would focus resources on getting key near-term products to the market as quickly as possible.

Sandoz

Sandoz is one of the top 15 largest pharmaceutical companies in the world. With headquarters in Basle, Switzerland, the company has been manufacturing chemicals for over 100 years. Sandoz employs almost 50,000 people in 170 locations around the world. Currently, Sandoz has approximately 2 per cent of the total world drug trade, and a 2.5 per cent market share, translating to $4.41 billion in sales of the worldwide market prescription drugs in 1992. Between 1990 and 1995, Sandoz was ranked eighth in terms of pharmaceutical sales in *Script*'s annual league table. The pharmaceutical division accounted for 47.6 per cent of overall sales, which rose by 8 per cent over the previous year. Sandoz's biggest-selling product is the immunosuppressant, Sandimmum, used in the prevention of organ-transplant rejection, which was ranked nineteenth top-selling product in 1992 by Pharma Forum and accounted for an estimated $738 million in sales. The company also manufactures fine chemicals used to make anti-depressants, sleep-aiding drugs, and antihistamines as well as peptides to fight osteoporosis and growth regulations. The anti-schizophrenic Clorazil (clozaphine) became one of Sandoz's five top-selling drugs in 1992.

Sandoz in Ireland

In August 1989, Sandoz announced its plans to build a pharmaceutical manufacturing plant at Ringaskiddy, in Cork Harbour, and began a local information campaign on the project. Commenting on reports at the time that the future of the plant was in doubt after Merrell Dow's decision not to proceed with its plant in the area, Colin Preston of Sandoz in Basle told *Script* that Sandoz considered Ringaskiddy to be the ideal site. He also noted that it differed greatly from the Merrell Dow plant, which was to be built on a greenfield site rather than an industrial site. Mr Preston said that the company was encouraged by the response that it had from the information campaign, which included a series of meetings with local residents' associations, civic leaders, trade unions and media. He added that they were not "over-confident" and that it would be premature to predict that Sandoz would go ahead with construction of the plant before the completion of a planned environmental impact study, which should answer many questions about the facility.

In a cover story in *Business and Finance* magazine, published at the time (*Business and Finance* 1989), Winfred Pedersen, vice-president of Sandoz's pharmaceutical division and the project director at Ringaskiddy plant (and currently general manager), was quoted as saying that the final decision to locate in Ringaskiddy would depend entirely on the amount of opposition it got to the plant. "We do not want a re-run of Merrell Dow" he said.

> We feel that nowhere in the world can we get as good a package as Ireland and have already spent £4 million drawing up plans and we would like to follow these through. However, If Ireland says no to Sandoz, we will have to go elsewhere.

Fortunately Ireland said yes, and the company has been manufacturing in Ringaskiddy since 1994. Sandoz Ringaskiddy involves a total investment of £175 million and will employ 250 people, many with technical qualifications. The plant includes three production units, consisting of a Sandimmum (ciclosporin) purification facility, a peptide synthesis facility, and a multi-purpose synthesis facility. To monitor environmental matters, a number of specialist employees will be recruited by the organisation — specifically, an environmental chemist (reporting to the safety and ecology manager), two technicians, four supervisors and eight operators who will look after environmental controls such as a waste-water treatment plant, a liquid/vapour incinerator, a trash incinerator, a tank farm and solvent recovery plant.

Sandoz Environmental Initiatives

Sandoz corporation places a very high emphasis on clean technology. The *Sandoz Safety and Environmental Protection: Principles and Strategies* document outlines the company's objectives to "Avoid, Reduce, Reuse and Recycle" as part of an ongoing process. Top management is committed to strong environmental awareness and managers are measured on their performance in this area. Waste minimisation programmes will commence with production. Detailed inventories of waste from each area will be maintained and used as a basis for seeking reductions.

Sandoz and Community Relations

Sandoz actively encourages an open policy with regard to the public. Regular on-site and off-site meetings between Sandoz senior management and the local community have taken place and the company has already held one open day. Currently, community relations are excellent, and the opportunity for the general public to have access to environmental emissions information is certainly unique. Local residents have always adopted a pragmatic approach — unlike the protesters at the proposed Merrell Dow site in Killeagh, the Ringaskiddy Residents' Association stated early on that they would not make any decisions about Sandoz until they had received as much information as possible. Their then chairman Joe O'Driscoll was quoted in *Business and Finance* (1989) as saying:

> We will take every case on its merits and will not be led by any industrialist or environmentalist. We will make our own decisions based on the advice given by the experts we appoint to examine Sandoz.

Subsequently, those experts examined the possible effects of air, water and noise pollution as well as the "chemical mix" in the area caused by the addition of Sandoz emissions to those of the existing plants. A visit to Sandoz headquarters in Basle by a group of residents and their advisers took place, all at Sandoz's expense. Mr O'Driscoll stressed that his group was pro-industry if it could be shown to be good industry.

Yamanouchi

Yamanouchi is a Japanese company with an ever-increasing presence in the global pharmaceutical industry. During the years 1988–90, the company moved from position 36 to becoming the twentieth top R&D company in the *Script* league table, with a total of 65 R&D drugs in its research pipeline of which 21 were licensed. In the year ended 31 March 1993, Yamanouchi's non-consolidated sales were up by 7.9 per cent to Yen 243,671 million ($2.2 billion). Ordinary and net profit were down by 6.5 per cent and 13 per cent to Yen 57,125 million and Yen 27,224 million respectively. On a consolidated basis, sales were static at $3.2 billion, ordinary profit rose by 3.1 per cent, and net profit fell by 8 per cent. Sales outside Japan accounted for 19.7 per cent of the total. The company employs 7,500 people worldwide and 5,500 of these in the pharmaceutical business.

Cardiovascular and respiratory products continue to be the main contributors to Yamanouchi's business, although topical/dermatologicals showed the greatest sales gain in the fiscal year. There was steady demand for the H_2-antagonist, Gaster (famotidine), during the year, which remained the company's leading prescription product. Other products which showed strong sales growth included Intron-A (DNA interferon alpha-2b, licensed from Schering-Plough), in the new indication of hepatitis C, and the anti diabetic, Euglucon, and Novo Nordisk's insulin and human growth hormone preparation.

Yamanouchi Ireland Co., Ltd. (YICL)

YICL was established in 1986 and commenced production in July 1988. The company currently employs 35 people plus three permanent maintenance contractors. YICL also employs security, cleaning, and catering contractors on a permanent basis. Many maintenance functions/services are contracted also. In the environmental department, the company employs two operators on a permanent basis. Other technical staff who have responsibility in the environmental area would account for a further two or three man-years.

Yamanouchi and Community Relations

YICL has an excellent relationship with the local community in Damastown, Mulhuddart, Dublin 15., where it is located. The company actively encourages visits by groups or individuals, regardless of their purpose. To date, YICL has facilitated residents' associations, schools, IFA, colleges, career guidance teachers, and a variety of local, national and international media, professional bodies, and other pharmaceutical companies. At present, Yamanouchi Ireland Co. Ltd. is developing a formal programme for liaising regularly with the local community as part of its Responsible Care/Environmental Management System programmes.

Yamanouchi Environmental Initiatives

Company policy states that protection of the environment is a key strategic issue for sustained commercial success. It must rank alongside the traditional principal functions of a site such as YICL — namely, quality control and production. Environmental management and performance are considered high-priority issues. Yamanouchi environmental protection policy is communicated to all employees. A formal annual programme takes place to heighten the basic training in environmental operations. Technical staff are encouraged to attend seminars in order to keep up to date with current best practices and technology. There is a core team of five operators who are fully trained and experienced in the routine operation of all environmental-protection facilities. At any one time, two of these are assigned to the environmental area. This means that they are working in the processing area, which provides an environmental perspective on processing issues/incidents. YICL finds this very beneficial. These operators also receive additional external training.

In 1989, YICL won the Irish "Good Environmental Management Award" for the industry, and it subsequently won the European award in 1990. YICL actively participates in the Responsible Care Programme, and their manufacturing director, Dr Pat Macken was a member of the FICI committee which set up the programme in Ireland. YICL was one of the 17 companies from throughout the European Community, invited to participate in an ECO Adult Pilot Programme (October 1992 to March 1993). Arising out of this, the company has established a group to work towards developing a comprehensive environmental management system and compliance with ECO/BS 7750.

The CEO, Joseph Harford, is very proactive in the environmental area and has devoted a lot of time both internally and externally to promoting a positive approach to addressing environmental issues. He has delivered numerous presentations at both national and international level on these and related subjects to a wide variety of audiences. This proactive attitude has permeated the company. Other members of staff participate in FICI working parties on environmental, health and safety matters.

The company's environmental policy statement is displayed throughout the site alongside the company quality policy and the statement of commitment to responsible care. Policies and strategies are primarily site-driven. Core values include disposal of own waste-on-site; to be open and honest with the public and try to explain true environmental impacts to interested parties; to aim for more than minimal compliance with regulatory requirements; and to implement best industrial practice.

Merck, Sharp and Dohme (MS&D)

Merck and Company had 16 products with sales of more than $100 million in 1992, according to the company's annual report. Total worldwide revenues were $9,662.5 million, up by 12 per cent on 1991. Net income was $2.24 billion, an increase of 15 per cent. R&D spending in 1992 was $1.1 billion (13 per cent of human healthcare sales), up from $987.8 million in 1991, and Merck planned to increase this to $1.2 billion in 1995. Merck employs over 34,000 people worldwide and has consistently been the top-selling pharmaceutical company for the past 10 years or more. Merck's human and animal health products fall into the following therapeutic categories: cardiovascular, anti-ulcers, vaccine/biological, ophthalmologicals, anti-inflammatories/analgesics as well as other human healthcare and animal health/crop protection products.

MS&D Ireland

MS&D Ireland is a BPC-manufacturing site exporting intermediates and finished products to other Merck plants in Europe and

the US. Merck came to Ireland in 1973 and commenced production in its Ballydine, Co. Tipperary plant in 1976. Since then the
number of employees has grown from 165 to 280. Eleven are directly involved in environmental matters.

Environmental Surveys and Waste Management Practices

A corporate environmental audit of the Irish plant is carried
out every three to four years. The plant must conform to both
US (worldwide) and EU legislation. The Ballydine plant has
its own environmental audit procedures which are currently
under review.

Merck currently holds two environmental licences: one for air
emissions, and the other a waste-water licence. The company
has an excellent relationship with the local authority which
sends a representative to the site each month to monitor air and
water emissions and to carry out regular spot checks throughout
the year. Air emissions are minimised using a state-of-the-art
scrubbing system and a newly installed thermal oxidiser. Almost
all liquid waste is sent to a bio-treatment plant, and aqueous
waste is clarified before being released to the River Suir. The
plant maintains that the water released back into the river is
purer than that removed. Planning permission legislation allows
land-filling of activated sludge which is considered non-
dischargeable to the river. MS&D also has an incinerator on-site
with a destruction efficiency of 99.99 per cent for non-
chlorinated solvents. All chlorinated solvents are sent off-site for
incineration.

MS&D Community Relations

MS&D actively encourages local people, community representatives, schools and colleges to visit its site. An average of 30 groups
visit the plant each year. Once a year, neighbours are invited to
attend a presentation by senior management. During this informal session any problems encountered in the plant's operations
are explained and details of any recent investments in new environmental technology are outlined. The meeting also provides an
opportunity for those living in the locality to have their questions
answered. The company supports local community projects and
initiatives as well as sponsoring a third-level student from the
vicinity.

MS&D Environmental Initiatives

As a member of FICI, Merck is actively involved in implementing the Responsible Care Programme. To date, Merck has been responsible for the development of both the distribution and safety codes of practice in the programme. In 1992, MS&D won the "Good Environmental Management Award" in an Eolas-run scheme. All Merck plants are actively involved in the US EPA SARA programme. The object of this programme is to quantify solvent emissions to the atmosphere by performing an overall plant-mass balance. One of Merck's corporate goals was to reduce emissions of all solvents by 90 per cent before 1996. To this end, a number of projects were placed very high in the priorities of senior management at Merck. Equal importance was attached to safety and quality issues. Each week an environmental status meeting is held. MS&D is also a partner in the Clean Technology Centre, Cork RTC, a forum for the investigation and dissemination of state-of-the-art technology and waste minimisation methodologies.

MS&D currently has an environmental policy statement that is widely read and understood by all employees. The corporate environmental policy specifies the following goals within the stated time-frames:

- By the end of 1991, to reduce worldwide air emissions of carcinogens or suspected carcinogens by 90 per cent

- By the end of 1993, to eliminate the above air emissions completely, using the best available technology

- By the end of 1995, to reduce all environmental releases of toxic chemicals worldwide by 90 per cent.

The company reports that it achieved its objectives by the target dates set.

Syntex Ireland Ltd.

Syntex Corporation is an international healthcare company of about 11,000 employees involved in the research, development, manufacturing and marketing of human and animal pharmaceutical products and medical diagnostic systems. Net sales worldwide in 1991 were $2.09 billion, up 15 per cent on the previous year. Founded in the US in the 1940s, with headquarters in Palo

Alto, California, Syntex has grown from a small research institute dedicated to the discovery and production of steroid hormones into a leading healthcare company with operations in more than 23 countries.

Today, Syntex's prescription products include medicines to treat arthritis, pain, inflammation and allergies; cardiovascular, cerebrovascular, gynaecological, viral and skin disease; and oral contraceptives. Syntex's major product, Naprosyn, a non-steroidal anti-inflammatory drug was the eleventh top-selling pharmaceutical product in the world in 1992, with sales alone estimated at just over $1 billion. Worldwide sales of newer human pharmaceutical products — Toradol, Cardene (nicardipine hydrochloride), Cytovene, Synarel and Tielid grew 66 per cent to $400.7 million.

Syntex Ireland Limited (SIL)

Syntex Ireland was established in 1974 and currently employs 270 people who are engaged in manufacturing, engineering, research and development, quality control, finance, administration and environmental control. SIL is one of five manufacturing sites in the corporate chemical division. The remaining four are located at Cuernavaca, Mexico; Springfield, Missouri; Freeport, Grand Bahamas; and Boulder, Colorado. The environmental health and safety department is staffed by a team of 13 people. The department is headed by a full-time manager with extensive experience in the areas of safety and environmental protection. It is divided into three main areas, namely safety and loss prevention, environmental and industrial hygiene laboratory, and waste-water treatment plant.

Waste Management Practices

Syntex has its own waste-water treatment plant, which treats all waste water generated on site to a standard acceptable for discharge into the adjacent River Fergus. The waste from the production building is transferred from double container sumps via overhead drains to the waste treatment plant. This plant produces very high-quality effluent, consistently to twice the standard required by licence on such major parameters as BOD and suspended solids. Discharged contents are issued to SIL by Clare County Council for discharge of treated aqueous effluent within the terms of the local government (Water Pollution) Act, 1977.

Waste solvents and other wastes unsuitable for biological treatment are sent off-site for incineration. The off-site disposal facility is regularly monitored by Syntex and has been audited on occasion. Back-up facilities are constantly under review.

SIL Community Relations

SIL currently enjoys excellent relations with its neighbours in the local community in Clarecastle and with the wider community of Ennis and environs. Meetings are held with the local parish council every three months at which the environmental, health and safety (EH&S) manager outlines recent developments. Local people are kept informed of imminent changes, and any complaints relating to odours are dealt with immediately. Visitors to the plant are actively encouraged and a number of "open days" have been held over the years. Tours of students and other interested groups have been held on numerous occasions. The EH&S manager meets every six months or so with EH&S managers in other chemical/pharmaceutical plants in the Mid-West and South-West regions to share ideas and developments in environmental, health and safety matters.

SIL Environmental Initiatives

SIL believes that the two factors which are most critical to the success of its environmental management function are exercising responsible care and practising waste minimisation. Under the responsible care concept, to which SIL subscribes, the company is committed, in all aspects of safety, health and protection of the environment, to seek continuos improvement in performance, to educate all staff, and work with customers and communities regarding product use and overall operation. In 1987, Syntex won Ireland's Good Environmental Management Award for its outstanding contributions to environmental protection, which included the establishment of a novel "catch and release" system for waste treatment and the incorporation of an on-site nature zone.

Creating Competitive Advantage in the Irish Chemical Industry

The Irish chemical industry, in its search for competitive advantage, has a choice in those strategies that it has the potential to implement. The choice of strategy is determined by each company's relative level of competitiveness within its specific business environment. Yet at a generic level, there are several strategies which manufacturing firms within the industry have used. Many organisations have identified the need to develop their core competencies. They see how the increasing complexity of the business environment can be managed only by reducing the scope of activities conducted and by concentration on the core activities of each individual business. It is this core that must be maintained and developed, and which should attract the bulk of managerial activity. By concentrating on the core, firms may get closer to their suppliers who can share the risks and opportunities associated with core business activities. Using such an approach, organisations can minimise their management and resource allocation to non-core activities, and thereby maximise their competence contribution to bottom-line performance. Many organisations also incorporate flexibility into their manufacturing operations. Flexible manufacturing facilities allow companies to respond quickly to both long- and short-term influences.

Short-term influences include variations in product and volume mix, which are a direct consequence of the greater variety of products demanded by the marketplace and the competitive intensity within the market itself. Longer-term effects include overshortening product life cycles, requiring the need to modify old, or introduce new, manufacturing processes. Flexible manufacturing techniques include Total Quality Management, Statistical Process Control and Just-in-Time manufacturing methods. Competitive advantage may also be achieved through the speed of new product innovation and introduction to the marketplace. In addition, the use of greater speed involves a trade off between inventory levels and distribution costs. This will not have universal applicability in all sectors of the chemical industry, but will be critical to those companies supplying or manufacturing products for the fast-moving consumer goods sector.

The role of people is also of significance in achieving competitive advantage. By focusing on core competencies, flexibility and speed, organisations will acquire new skills and techniques enabling them to develop an organisational culture capable of delivering and sustaining competitive advantage. In this context, training and development become of strategic importance, as will new approaches to workforce management.

Workforce Management Policies

Decentralising management responsibility by reducing the number of layers in the managerial hierarchy creates an organisational form that is flexible, more responsive to change and less functionally oriented. Individual managers are given more responsibility in achieving the desired standard of product quality and cost performance, and are encouraged to integrate more closely the manufacturing function with customer needs and expectations. The notion of decentralisation of responsibility also asserts the importance of teamwork, and of how line managers should incorporate staff and human resource management activities into their everyday management concerns. Organising work on a teamwork basis facilitates multi-skilling and making work practices flexible. By blurring the traditional boundaries between roles, organisations can be framed in a way that integrates new technology and flexible work designs. The process in achieving this transition to the "new" organisation is one that requires a reassessment of traditional structural and cultural forms — a process that can only be driven by a leadership vision that is strategically compliant with procuring competitive advantage in complex and turbulent market conditions.

Training Needs of the Irish Chemical Industry

Management development at a general level, and more specifically at a specialist functional level is necessary if organisations are to acquire new skills and competencies to secure corporate objectives successfully. At senior-management level, skill development in strategic planning can help to focus attention on cost competitiveness, product quality and market responsiveness. The manufacturing function will principally be supported in any strategic reformulation because of its importance to Irish subsidiaries of multinational companies where competition is both within their own organisation and in the wider marketplace. Developing a first-class manufacturing facility is primarily the means by which Irish subsidiaries create the conditions for an increased allocation of resources and production within a global organisation structure. Training in general management is also a requisite for organisations that source their management from specialist functional areas. This is further reinforced by the need to manage organisations with managerial levels in which the lines of demarcation between different functions are increasingly less clear. Essentially, organisations should develop training programmes that enable managers both to become proficient in managing change and to integrate business processes within the overall corporate strategy. Production management is another area within which management and supervisory training is necessary if organisations are to be equipped with the skills to achieve higher levels of output with lower costs, while maintaining sufficiently high levels of customer service and quality. In this instance, training should focus on formulating manufacturing strategy in an overall business context. Performance measurement and the management of manufacturing technologies should also be included in any proposed training programme.

Total Quality Management is increasingly becoming of strategic importance to manufacturing organisations seeking to achieve competitive advantage through continuous process improvement. In terms of skill development, management and supervisory training should concentrate on techniques such as statistical process control and on achieving the performance standards required for ISO9000 accreditation. Health and safety considerations also form part of an overall management-development programme. Because of the legislation which set up the Health and Safety Authority, employers are required to train personnel at all levels in the organisation, specifically in developing a public awareness of both environmental and workplace health and safety issues, and in establishing safe manufacturing practices. Moreover, organisations need to acquire environmental management skills in order to develop an environmental protection policy. Because the detailed technical application of environmental control regulations is usually the responsibility of engineering personnel, it is unlikely that all managers from the production and quality control functions receive adequate training in this area. Yet if organisations are successfully to develop an awareness of environmental issues, training opportunities should be extended to all functional personnel.

The development of skills at supervisory level is necessary if firms are to strengthen their business performance at operative level. The advent of team-working, continuous process improvement, and increased employee involvement will fundamentally alter the nature of the supervisory role. In this context, supervisors are charged with designing work for the best motivation and utilisation of talent. By empowering employees to manage their performance in support of business objectives, supervisors become less directive and more facilitating of the work group they serve. Training efforts will be directed at building collaboration in the work group, gaining commitment through involvement, managing group dynamics and developing more appropriate leadership skills.

References

Business and Finance (1989): 3 August: 12–15.
Script (1989a): 1438, 16 August: 4.
Script (1989b): 1448, 20 September: 10.

Questions

1. What disadvantages are experienced by the Irish chemical industry in comparison to those of other countries?

2. Analyse the external environment of the chemical industry in terms of its complexity and stability.

3. What implications does the greater awareness of environmental issues among the general public have for business strategies within the chemical industry? What types of environmental management initiatives have been adopted to date? Comment on their overall effectiveness.

4. What factors will help give the Irish chemical industry sustainable competitive advantage?

24

Kerry Group plc

Introduction

Until 1972, Co. Kerry was considered the most underdeveloped part of Ireland in terms of milk production. There had been plans to build a milk-processing plant in the region, but nothing ever came of them. With over a million acres of land, and 50 per cent of this acreage considered to be of good or excellent grass land, the area had great potential. The structure of the dairy industry in Kerry at the time was such that the state, through a dairy disposal company, handled 70 per cent of the milk produced, but most people in the area believed that the influence was only one of stagnancy. The first breakthrough for what was then known as North Kerry Milk Products came in 1971 when a company called Erie Casein came to Ireland to source supplies of casein (milk protein used in the food industry). All that was required by Kerry was a licence from the Department of Agriculture, and in 1972, Kerry Co-Op was formed, with Denis Brosnan, Hugh Friel and Denis Cregan as key management strategists. A production plant costing £742,000 was built, with production commencing in June 1972. Profit for the first year of operation was £110,000. By 1980, Kerry Co-Op had paid up subscriptions of over £1 million.

A number of developments during the early years affected the formative growth of the co-operative. The development of the Shannon region and, in particular, two major projects at Aughinish and Moneypoint, saw shifts from an agricultural to an industrial wage base in the south-west of the country. In a more direct way, the decision by the Irish government to introduce a brucellosis eradication scheme to Co. Kerry meant that the co-operative was forced to consider growth options other than dairy processing. As a result, a diversity strategy was developed, with many new products introduced. The first venture out of the dairy industry came in 1982, when Kerry Co-Op acquired two pigmeat plants, Denny's and Duffy's. The pigmeat industry was not in good shape at the time, and because Kerry intended its acquisitions to become low-cost producers, considerable capital expenditure was required. Furthermore, because this was a new departure for the company, expertise had to be imported from Denmark and Sweden. Great progress was made in a very short space of time, as within four years, these plants were turning in a profit.

Flotation of Kerry Co-Op

In order to realise Denis Brosnan's ambition of Kerry becoming an international food company, and because the company did not have sufficient venture capital to expand successfully into world markets, the company decided that a stock-exchange flotation was ultimately the best capitalisation option. Others in the co-operative movement felt that this approach was selling out on co-op principles, but for Kerry it was quite simply a means of generating added revenue, and a way of earning a return on investment for its shareholders and farmers. The articles of association of the proposed plc stipulated that a 52 per cent shareholding was to be held by Kerry Co-Op, and that this was not to be reduced without the agreement of at least 75 per cent of the co-op's shareholders. This stake ensured that the people of Kerry, who had helped to build up the co-operative over the previous 15 years, would continue to have a key contribution in the future direction of the group.

The transition from co-op status to that of public limited company went relatively smoothly, though many political and legal barriers had to be overcome. Thus, by October 1986, the former Kerry Co-Op had successfully acquired its new status as a publicly quoted company. This was the first step in becoming an Irish multinational company. The corporate objectives were redrafted, with higher trends set for group growth, much of which was to be achieved through acquisitions both at home and abroad. The group's mission statement was made quite clear — to build a major international food ingredients corporation and a sizeable food supplier business in Europe. Specifically, the statement asserts that Kerry will be a leader in selected markets through technological creativity; superior product quality; superior service to customers; and the unique wholehearted commitment of each employee. With the necessary capital investment in place, the company set off yet again, on the acquisition trail.

Kerry Group Diversification Strategies

Diversification into the Beef-Processing and Pigmeat Markets

In 1986, the group moved into the beef-processing business, purchasing the IMP beef-processing plant at Middleton and its sister company, Convenience Foods, in Tallaght. Using the same approach as in previous acquisitions, Kerry invested heavily to make it the lowest-cost producer using imported specialists and retraining strategies. It was a good move on the part of the company because 1986 was one of the better years for the Irish beef industry for some time. The beef division in that year generated some £255 million of the Kerry group turnover. In October 1988, the company acquired South West Meats from Unigate for stg£4 million, and in so doing, secured access to the UK and continental European markets. South West Meats was a food-processing and distribution business, marketing beef and lamb to major UK and European retailers.

Another diversification for the group was into the pigmeat market. In 1987, the Denny plant at Portadown was purchased, and since then it has made a significant contribution to the pigmeat sector. It also affords the company a degree of versatility in terms of both product form and packaging variety, with new additions to the range being successfully test-marketed and introduced. The group strengthened its position in this market in 1988 when it acquired McCallum Meats in Portsmouth. McCallum gave Kerry considerable access to a wide range of markets in the valuable catering sector, a sector that includes specialist catering companies, restaurant chains and hotels. Because of its customer focus, the catering sector is scrupulous in demanding portion control, exacting specifications, fast and efficient service. Growth potential for Kerry in this area is considerable, and McCallum meats will be able to capitalise on the ready availability of all types of meat from Kerry Group's other facilities.

Diversification into the Poultry Market

In June 1988, the company diversified into the poultry market by purchasing Grove Farm and Ballyfree, the largest producers and

processors of turkeys in Ireland, with processing plants at Smith-
boro, Co. Monaghan, and Glenealy, Co. Wicklow. With the most
modern of facilities in the industry, they produce a wide variety of
fresh, frozen and value-added products to the highest standards.
The acquisition took Kerry into a new and fast-growing food area,
as turkey had been identified as the fastest-growing meat product
internationally. Kerry wanted to expand its range of breaded and
portion products and, to this end, put the weight of its marketing
and distribution network behind the acquisition, in order to
maximise the potential for further increased growth of these critical value-added products. At Grove Farm, over 6,000 turkeys are
processed each week, 35 per cent of which are exported, with the
balance sold at home. It employs 320 people, plus 100 more on a
contract basis. The factory gets 25 per cent of its supply from its
own two units, and the rest from contract growers. Grove has 85
growers, supplying 75 per cent of total requirements.

The factory supplies the grower with the poultry, feed and electricity, while the grower supplies the houses and labour. So, in effect, the farmers are working exclusively for Grove, and are paid a
management fee for looking after the birds — a fee that is fixed in
terms of price per pound. The farmer/grower is left with the cost of
the growing houses, roughly about £70,000. The grower gets an
interest-free loan, and no income is earned for the first seven
years, as any return is used to cover bank and company repayments. After the loan is repaid there is a return of about £12,000
per house per annum. Most growers have about two sheds, housing
some 14,000 birds. Grove has a strict selection procedure for growers, where attention to every aspect of the process is important. Because the growers have invested so much, they are highly
motivated to produce consistently high-quality products.

Kerry Group as a Multinational Organisation

By the end of 1988, Kerry had come a long way in its development, with record profits recorded. Pre-tax profits were 52 per
cent up on 1987. Internal cash flow was at a record £19.1 million,
while funds generated from share issues amounted to £26.9 million, with sales in the UK and Europe reaching £135 million. The
acquisition of the Grove Farm and Ballyfree brands had significantly strengthened the company's position in the Irish market.
In 1989, the foods division introduced new products in response to

a changing and far more discriminating consumer base, examples of which included Low-Low butter spread, Dawn Light butter, and a whole range of low-fat products. Many of these new products made major progress in Ireland, the UK and Europe, much of which has been sustained through ongoing monitoring of changes in market structure and population demographics.

In the bottled powders area, the market was in decline, but through product reformulation and new packaging, Kerry managed to maintain its market strength and position. In 1990, the group acquired UK food companies Robirch and W.L. Miller, both of which have strong traditions of excellent service, manufacturing a wide range of sausages, pies, savoury products, and other consumer-oriented meat and pastry products. The distribution structures afforded by these two acquisitions have provided Kerry with additional market-entry points for the introduction of new food-product lines. In the beef sector, further inroads into Europe were made, particularly in Germany, where many outlets were specifying Kerry as their primary beef source. In 1991, two further strategic acquisitions were made in this sector — Meadow Meats in Rathdowney and Tunney Meats in Clones. Meadow Meats, at the time, was one of the better processing and packaging plants in Ireland, and had a number of valuable UK retail meat contracts. In pork, Denny performed well, increasing its market share and strengthening its product portfolio. New forms of packaging were introduced, facilitating stronger market penetration for specialist products. The poultry division made great progress because of the emphasis placed by Grove Farm and Ballyfree on quality. Through a process of consumer re-education, new products such as escallops, fillets and nuggets were introduced, thereby increasing the group's market penetration and customer base. In its agribusiness division, the group experienced restrictions on growth because of static milk-volume intake, but products such as High Bloom performed well, and the sale of feed and fertilisers reached considerably higher levels than before.

Most significant of achievements for the group at this time was the decision to explore the international food-ingredients sector acquisitively. In 1983, Kerry constructed an indigenous food-ingredients plant in Listowel, Co. Kerry. Following on from this, the group in 1986 purchased a drying plant in Jackson, Wisconsin in the US, for $10 million. Tentatively, these developments contributed to the group's progress in achieving its objective of becoming an international food and food-ingredients organisation.

Diversification into the Food-Ingredients Market

Market Overview

The international food-ingredients industry can be broken up into product categories like dairy ingredients, bakery ingredients, flavourings, seasonings, to name but a few. Generally, each sector is dominated by a small number of major manufacturers. In 1995, apart from Kerry Ingredients, the other major global players included Universal Foods, Monsanto, McCormicks, IFF and Unilever. As the international food-ingredients market is highly competitive, thousands of new products flood on to the market every year, making research and development and new technologies pivotal to the success of any company operating in the market. The ingredients market is driven by high margins, with relatively modest global sales.

Food-Ingredient Acquisitions

In 1988, Kerry acquired Beatreme Foods in the US for $130 million. This was the largest acquisition to date and was financed mainly through borrowings, causing the group's gearing to go through the roof. To put the acquisition in context, Beatreme at the time was larger in size than the then Kerry group, contributing in part to the group's record 1989 results. Beatreme is the leading speciality food-ingredients company in the US, and the newly acquired technology allowed the technical teams from both organisations to maximise market penetration in the food-ingredients business worldwide.

The group made a series of add-on acquisitions to Beatreme in the late 1980s and early 1990s, an example of which included US company Primas Foods plc. This particular purchase widened the choice of milk-drink alternatives that the group could offer its customers. In 1993, the group, through its subsidiary Kerry Ingredients (UK) Ltd., spent £10 million on acquiring Tingles, a specialist food-ingredient manufacturing company based at Portsmouth. This company operates from one of the most modern production facilities in Europe and is a leading flavourings supplier in the UK and European snack-food industry. Kerry's existing flavourings business at Eastleigh, when combined with Tingles, made Kerry one of the leading flavouring companies in Europe. In September 1993, the group acquired Research Foods in Canada. Combining Research Foods with Malcolm Foods, which was acquired in March 1993, Kerry established itself as a principal supplier to the snack-food industry in Canada — a move which will assist the group's global business-expansion programme in this sector.

Strategy for the Future of Food Ingredients

The move into food ingredients can account for a considerable proportion of the group's strategic success and growth. The success of Kerry Food Ingredients is very much linked to trends in the global food market where value-added prepared foods are growing at a rate of 6–8 per cent per annum. In 1994, the group made significant progress in achieving its corporate objective, with the purchase of DCA in the US, and its British offshoot, Margetts. Also acquired in 1994 was UK ingredients company, Matteson Walls. In particular the DCA acquisition, which cost Kerry £250 million, catapulted the group into the top five food-ingredients groups in the world. DCA specialises in the manufacture of coating systems. This involves the development of batter mixes and systems, clear crisp systems, and Japanese and American bread crumbs. With the coatings market in the US worth about £300 million annually, Kerry is poised, through its DCA acquisition, to capture an estimated 40 per cent market share in this sector. While the DCA acquisition has given Kerry Ingredients 21 manufacturing facilities in Canada and the US, there is still plenty of scope for developing and expanding the business into Central and South America. For example, in 1994 the company ventured into Mexico with the $20 million acquisition of Productos VPM in Irapuato. Apart from the purchase of the Mexican manufacturing facility, Kerry has also opened sales offices in Argentina and Puerto Rico. Chile is also being carefully evaluated as a possible future acquisition area. Also considered are a number of acquisition opportunities in the Far East and Pacific Rim. In Japan, Kerry Ingredients has a joint-venture operation with the MIYOSHI Organisation in Tokyo. Recent European acquisitions by the ingredients division include the purchase of Milac GmbH in Germany, a food ingredients business with a strong customer base. Kerry Food ingredients in 1994 accounted for £343.4 million or 42 per cent of the group's turnover and, by giving the highest margins, it is the fastest-growing part of the business.

Because the food ingredients sector is growing quite rapidly, Kerry hopes to capitalise on this growth by doubling in size within the next few years. The group is hoping to achieve this growth in three ways — by expanding its existing businesses; through major investment in new technology; and by expanding geographically. The group's commitment to doubling in size will involve an anticipated growth in turnover approximating some £1.5 billion by 1997, with the major impetus for this growth coming from the expected expansion of the food-ingredients sector.

Business Strategies Implemented by Kerry Group

A range of strategies has been successfully implemented by the group.

Achieving ISO9000 Accreditation

In 1990, the Kerry subsidiary Dawn Dairies was rewarded for its efforts in achieving standards of quality and excellence in its production process. Each of the five dairies in the Dawn Group was awarded the International Quality standard ISO9000. This was a major achievement for the organisation and has since strengthened the Dawn brand and Kerry's international market presence.

Restructuring Programme

Because of a worldwide slump in agricultural prices during the early 1990s, the group has significantly modified its pricing structure. The group has additionally embarked on a major restructuring programme in all of its divisions, resulting specifically in a radical overhaul of its bulk-feed distribution process, a process that now affords a substantial improvement to farm services. The pig-breeding service was similarly modified and was further developed with an added emphasis on leaner meat that is disease and antibiotic free. Denny extended its product range in pork and bacon, while continuing to research for further new product launches. It also continued to enhance the perception of bacon as a frequent-consumption consumer product. In the poultry area, continued market emphasis was placed on the Ballyfree brand and on cooked turkey products, and as a result of sustained marketing efforts by the company, the dietary benefits of poultry continued to grow. Also, greater production and processing sources are affording Kerry the continued strategic alternatives to expand its distribution.

Kerry's entire beef and lamb processing facilities have, since the 1991 acquisition of Meadow Meats Ltd., been merged under the Meadow Meats identity. Initially supplying a range of quality value-added beef and lamb products to the European consumer market, Meadow Meats in the 1990s became susceptible to a subdued demand for beef, and was losing out to perceived cheaper and healthier white-meat products such as poultry and pork. In addition, margins in the beef business became wafer thin because of factors such as the high price of cattle and the relative strength of the Irish pound against sterling. A considerable overcapacity in the European beef industry also affected demand for products. Turnover for Meadow Meats fell from £204 million in 1992 to £194 million in 1993. In 1994, sales dropped by £46 million to £148 million. Faced with this scenario, Kerry decided to refocus its beef processing operations so as to increase the value-added content of Meadow Meats' business. This strategy included the sale of its Middleton processing plant in 1994. In 1995, the group sold its processing plants at Rathdowney and Waterford, and also divested its slaughtering facility at Clones. Also considered for future divestment are the group's beef-related businesses in the UK.

Implementing a Total Quality Management Programme

Total Quality Management (TQM) was adopted by Kerry as the guiding principle in its drive to transform its Beatreme food-ingredients plant in the US when it was acquired by the group in 1988. This approach has been successful in securing vital customer confidence and in increasing medium-term profitability. In addition, the company has made extensive use of its research and development capability in responding to variable market trends. In the US, the divisions have operated profitably, while in Europe the acquisition of Milac GmbH in Germany and Simmons Taylor in the UK, brought valuable new business to the group's expanding portfolio in the food-ingredients sector. The emphasis on quality continued to pay off with Dell flavours, an arm of Beatreme, when it was awarded "Supplier of the Year" in 1994, by a major US food conglomerate.

The Group's Success

There is no one specific factor that can be focused upon as an explanation for the group's success. Rather, it has been a combination of many factors that has helped Kerry to become a successful organisation. The group has a dedicated, innovative and experienced management team. Since its beginning, this team has been to the forefront of group decision-making. Not restricted by traditional business boundaries, it has been willing to break new ground with purchases such as Limerick Dairies in 1979. In the same year, it masterminded a rights issue, and in 1986 it was the first Irish co-operative to raise capital through a stock-exchange flotation. The group has also invested considerably in its research and development activities, and currently has three research sites located in Ireland, England and the US, with a total annual research budget of approximately £3 million. The significance Kerry attaches to its research and development has established the group as a key supplier to some of the leading convenience and snack-food producers in the US who, in recent years, have cut back on their own R&D expenditure. For Kerry, research and development has resulted in much new product development.

The history of Kerry has been characterised by high-risk acquisitive growth, a strategy that can be very much attributed to the competence and experience of the group's key management strategists. In its appraisal of prospective acquisitions, group management looks for a fit between the prospect and the overall corporate objectives of the Kerry Group. More specifically examined is the relative similarity between the profit criteria used by Kerry and those of the prospective acquisition. Some of the more excellent decisions taken by the group include its move into food ingredients in the US; the taking over of local milk distributors; and going public.

The group has excelled in its financial management by consistently sustaining its profitability in the 1990s. Confidence in the group is high, with profit levels and earnings per share well above average. The group's high tax rate, owing to profit repatriations from overseas investment, is evidence of the group's successful acquisition programme, a factor reflected in increased shareholder confidence. In harnessing the energies and capabilities of its suppliers, employees and management, the group has become more responsive in meeting the needs and expectations of its customers. Since the foundation of the organisation, much emphasis has been placed on training and development. By developing employee skills and competencies, and by maintaining a highly motivated and stable workforce, the group has managed to create an organisational culture capable of generating competitive advantage in indigenous and international markets.

The group operates a successful graduate recruitment programme, employing and developing graduates of many disciplines. Because the group's overall strategy remains one of expansion through acquisition, graduates are afforded personal and professional growth opportunities as they familiarise and socially integrate themselves with the various operations of the Kerry Group conglomerate.

Culture and Structural Aspects of Kerry Group

The culture of the group and the role of Denis Brosnan are inextricably linked. On its formation in 1972, the group exhibited an entrepreneurial-type structure and, at the time, was critically dependent on the direction of Denis Brosnan. He harnessed the "Kerry pride" and made the suppliers and employees of the business the owners of the co-op. After buying out state interests, the suppliers (farmers) had to be convinced that they owned the assets and therefore were responsible for funding the development of Kerry Co-Op. Accordingly, they were required to make a levy contribution to the organisation. Brosnan felt that this approach was necessary for the future success and development of the company. It was a good strategic move, as capital inflows subsequently became apparent. On gaining the support and flexibility of suppliers and employees, Brosnan was now in a position to promote a more supportive and creative organisational culture, one that was encouraging of teamwork and co-operation between the various stakeholders of the business. The cultural transition was a success in that it gave a great sense of belonging and urgency to all of the group's activities. Having developed from an entrepreneurial-type organisational form, the co-op rapidly matured into a more bureaucratic-type structure, with an objective of utilising the potential of the Kerry milk supply. The state was bought out and six privately owned co-ops were acquired, giving Kerry an expanded range of butter and milk products. At this stage, a divisional structure was beginning to develop.

In 1979, the organisation was pushed by external environmental factors from a divisional-type structure into a multi-divisional one. Until that year, the group had always fully complied with Irish Government and EEC agriculture and food regulations. The group,

Figure 24.1: Kerry Group plc Organisation Structure

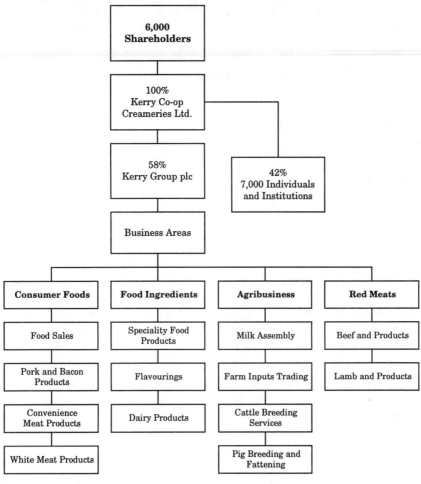

however, now accepts that this approach was a short-sighted and foolhardy way to run a business, because if Irish or European policy were suddenly to change, the group would have been left out to dry. This was precisely the case in 1979, when the Irish Government decided to introduce its Brucellosis eradication scheme to Co. Kerry, a move which resulted in a 20 per cent drop in the county's cattle and milk supply. Because the group had, up to this point, exclusively devoted itself to milk processing, a radical reformulation of strategic direction was now required. There followed a change in strategy — a change which redirected the group beyond the geography and tradition of Co. Kerry. Through a process of hard canvassing, and by offering attractive milk prices to a more broadly defined customer base, Kerry became a proactive, multidivisional-type organisation, determined in its approach not to be solely dependent on milk in the future.

Denis Brosnan's Role and Management Style

Strong Personality

No other major Irish quoted company is as closely identified with its chief executive as the Kerry Group is with Denis Brosnan. Over the years, Brosnan has slowly, and in a calculating and strategic fashion, positioned the group as the foremost food combination company in Ireland. Phlegmatic by nature, Brosnan is not one to give much away in personal terms about his role in bringing Kerry group to its current position internationally. However, in explaining the phenomenal growth of the group, he attributes in part his personal ambition and management philosophy as factors significant in the formation and development of the group's organisational culture. Brosnan's style of management directs individuals to seek out any opportunities that may present themselves. His supporters describe him as a talented manager, a strategic thinker, one who does not shirk tough decisions. He is not overly concerned with what people think, taking the view that if something is right, one should go ahead and do it regardless of what others might say. Despite his detractors, Brosnan has managed to create the country's largest and most profitable food organisation. Considered by some to have the Midas touch, Brosnan's entrepreneurial flair has had a significant bearing on the operations and performance of the group to date.

It was Brosnan who transformed the Kerry Group from a small regionally based co-operative into Ireland's largest food company. But while the sheer force of his personality is one of the reasons for Kerry's meteoric rise, the market is yet wary of the company being perceived as a one-man-band type operation (it did not help Tony Ryan and GPA in their bid for plc status in June, 1992). While Kerry can be criticised for its critical dependence on Brosnan, his tough, no-nonsense management style has delivered results. The success of Beatreme in the US, and the turnaround at Irish-based pigmeat operations illustrate the powerful capacity of Kerry Group management, and the endless anecdotes on this tough, aggressive management style attest to where much of this motivation is sourced. Brosnan's steely determination comes across in everything he does. His management style, whether it's as chief executive of Kerry Group, as chairman of the Racing Board, Leisure Holdings, or of Kerry Airport, has always been of the hands-on variety.

Commitment

Brosnan's ability to elicit commitment from his staff is an important factor in the overall success of the business. Commitment promotes enthusiasm and constancy of purpose, features which help develop a vision and drive that is commonly shared by all stakeholders in any organisation. Yet many of Brosnan's early decisions and ideas upset the well-entrenched traditions of the Irish Co-operative Organisation Society (ICOS). Many in this organisation felt that he was a maverick figure, caring nothing for the traditional approach to co-operative management. However, his detractors were to be proven wrong. Brosnan operated in the dairy industry, but felt the need to diversify beyond the scope of this particular industry. Having initially diversified into poultry and pork, Brosnan sourced supplies, expertise and technology outside Ireland. His final break with tradition was in 1986 when he decided to go to the stock market with his business. Now Brosnan sits atop a diversified food organisation with an annual turnover of £882 million and a pre-tax profit which has grown to some £39.7 million.

Strategic Approach

From 1979, the group devised and implemented a five-year corporate plan to build a food and agriculture business. Research and development was fundamental to the success of the plan, as was the development of overseas offices and a programme of strategic acquisitions. The overall objective of the programme was to develop a self-directing organisation capable of achieving both organic and acquisitive growth in the longer term. In this context, Denis Brosnan set parameters for real growth, return on capital, and on borrowing to equity. His efforts surpassed all expectations as the organisation managed to increase its sales from a modest £23 million in 1974 to an impressive £882 million in 1994. Because of Brosnan's strategic approach from the outset, Kerry has achieved technological leadership, excellent product quality, and has earned critical international respect for its quality of customer service.

Clear Vision of the Future

Denis Brosnan's aim to make the food-ingredients division of the business the dominant power within Kerry Group is a medium-term objective. On ingredients, the group stresses its ability to deliver on flavour, and, to ensure this, an assurance of consistency and product quality is given to customers. Kerry Ingredients core technology is well acknowledged in creating and producing the most innovative and versatile ingredients systems in the food industry. Given the near absolute scope of the food industry, it is therefore not surprising that Brosnan views food ingredients as a major force within the Kerry Group. In time, Kerry plans to make food ingredients the flagship business of the organisation.

Group Financial Performance to Date

Kerry Group was initially listed in 1986. In that year, trading profits were £16.2 million, operating profits were £11.2 million, profit before tax was £6.3 million, and earnings per share (eps) were 6.01p. Since then, there has been an unbroken record of eps growth. This sustained growth rate reflects the success of the diversification policy pursued and the quality of group acquisitions. The quality of acquisitions can be devised by their capacity for organic volume growth and for relatively high and stable margins. In general, the growth in companies acquired has been impressive. For example, the growth of Beatreme since its acquisition in 1988 has been exceptional.

Table 24.1: Trading Record of Kerry Group

	1990 £m	1991 £m	1992 £m	1993 £m	1994 £m
Turnover	584.0	755.0	827.0	879.9	882.7
Profit before tax	19.3	24.1	28.7	35.0	39.7
Dividends	2.7	3.4	3.5	4.1	4.6
Retained Profit	16.2	18.9	21.1	24.8	27.6
Earnings per Share	12.6	14.5	15.8	18.5	20.5

The year 1990 was an excellent one for the company. Pre-tax profit increased by 12.5 per cent to an all time high of £19.26

million, and earnings power share increased by 10.7 per cent to 12.6p. Turnover increased from £560 million in 1989 to £584 million. Two acquisitions — Robirch and W.L. Miller resulted in borrowings amounting to £15.6 million, but the business acquired from these acquisitions equalled £40 million, with capital expenditure totalling £18.7 million. Considerable growth was achieved in all areas despite the collapse in commodity prices in world dairy markets.

The year 1991 was yet another excellent one for the company, with pre-tax profits rising by 25 per cent from £19.268 million to £24.143 million. Turnover increased from £584 million to £755 million while earnings per share increased by 15 per cent to 14.5p. Growth in sales was very much caused by the company's success in increasing its operating profit margin to 5.6 per cent Investment amounted to £62 million, with acquisitions costing £340 million, and fixed asset expenditure of £22 million.

In 1992, group profits before tax increased by 19 per cent from £24.143 million to £28,718 million, and earnings per share increased by 9 per cent to 15.80p. Group turnover increased by £827 million in a year noted for currency fluctuations and difficult trading conditions in many of the company's export markets. Sales of consumer foods amounted to 36 per cent of turnover, and Kerry Ingredients accounted for 35 per cent of total group sales. Cash flow from operations increased to £62.4 million, and net debt amounted to £109 million, which represented a decrease of £15 million on the previous year.

For 1993, Kerry Group reported a 28 per cent increase in pre-tax profits on an unchanged turnover for the first six months of 1993. The apparent absence of turnover growth was the result of currency movement and a number of small acquisitions and disposals. However, operating margins widened from 5.25 per cent to 5.4 per cent, and the interest charge was down as a result of debt pay down and lower interest rates in both the US and the UK. The food-ingredients business continued to be the main area for growth in the group, which at this time was building a European business base to rival its highly successful operation in the US. End-of-year results saw a 22 per cent increase in pre-tax profits to £35 million. The results were slightly better than market expectations, but there was one element of surprise. The debt figure had risen to £142 million from the 1992 figure of £105 million — this despite the fact that only £16.9 million was spent on acquisitions. This increase was caused by larger working capital requirements (up £16 million on 1992, which, considering the effects of currency translation, was up £13 million).

Kerry borrows a significant amount overseas to cater for the geographical spread of its business. However, the key debt/ shareholders funds ratio (gearing) is 56 per cent. The interest repayments to the banks were covered 4.2 times in 1993, compared to 3.1 times for 1992. The interest bill declined, reflecting the decline in interest rates from £13.89 million in 1992 to £10.99 million. At £879.8 million, Kerry's turnover was 6 per cent higher, and earnings per share, after goodwill, were 17 per cent up at 18.5p. Shareholders' funds stood at £255 million, compared with £217 million for the previous year. Group operating profit, before annual goodwill write-offs and interest charges, amounted to £50.18 million; the operating profit margin increased from 5.58 per cent to 5.7 per cent. The board paid a final dividend of 1.69 per cent per share, up nearly 15 per cent on the previous year.

In 1994, pre-tax profits amounted to £39.7 million, an increase of 13.5 per cent on the 1933 level. Group operating profit in 1994 increased to £55.9 million, up from £50.2 million, thereby significantly increasing operating profit as a percentage of sales, from 5.7 per cent to 6.3 per cent. Earnings per share after goodwill increased by 10.8 per cent to 20.5p. Shareholder funds stood at £307.8, a considerable increase on the previous year's figure of £255.3 million. Group turnover amounted to £882.7 million, of which the ingredients division accounted for 42 per cent. With the acquisition of US ingredients company DCA in 1994, group turnover is expected to increase to £1.2 billion in 1995, with ingredients accounting for 55 per cent of sales.

Interim results for 1995, when published in July of that year, showed a 38.3 per cent rise in group turnover from £419 million at the half-way stage in 1994, to £580 million at the 1995 interim stage. Kerry Ingredients reported a 72.9 per cent increase in turnover to £299 million, while Kerry Foods reported a 41.5 per cent increase in turnover to £196.8 million. The contributions from DCA, DCA's British offshoot Margetts, and Mattesson Walls were largely responsible for the 61.2 per cent jump in operating profits, from £23.1 million at the half-way stage in 1994 to £37.3 million at the interim in 1995. These acquisitions were also responsible for boosting Kerry's overall operating margin from 5.5 per cent to 6.4 per cent, its highest ever. This is the highest operating margin reported by any of the quoted Irish food companies for quite some time.

Future Strategic Options

According to the 1994 Kerry Group annual report, there is a growing demand throughout the world for quality convenience foods with broader taste profiles, creating an increased momentum for new product development and affording existing opportunities to food-ingredient suppliers. Through Kerry's continuing investment programme and expansion of its existing specificity ingredients business, the group is poised to expand its position in existing ingredient markets. The recent establishment of worldwide ingredients sales offices will no doubt facilitate this expansion. In 1994, Kerry's consumer foods businesses performed well, while maintaining a strategy of business expansion, sales growth, brand investment and improved operating efficiencies. Despite intense market conditions, the Kerry Foods division improved operating efficiencies and made strong progress in all of its business units. Sales of the division increased by £21 million to £322 million, which in 1994 represented 36.5 per cent of total group sales. However, turnover in the meat division declined by £46 million to £148 million following the reorganisation of its beef processing activities. In the context of this decline, it is not surprising that Kerry divested its Irish beef-processing facilities in 1995.

The year 1994 was a hectic one for the group. It spent a total of £274 million on acquisition, primarily DCA and Mattesson Walls. The group's acquisition strategy over the past number of years and particularly in 1994, has left it with considerable debt. At the end of 1994, debt amounted to over £370 million. Despite this, it has been able to fund most of its acquisitions by way of a mixture of cash-flow and debt, without having to reduce Kerry Co-Op's shareholding below the stipulated 50 per cent level. Thus, for the first six months of 1995, the emphasis was on integration of acquisitions and consolidation of existing businesses.

Kerry Group plc is committed to developing new businesses and increasing its profitability. It has an excellent management team and has established long-term relationships with many major customers, providing them with a wide variety of value-added goods. In terms of strategic direction and growth, the group will probably continue on the acquisition trail, as major acquisitions in the US have resulted in Kerry becoming a prominent supplier to the snack-food sector there, a move which the group hopes to emulate in Britain, Canada and Mexico. With the exception of Africa, Kerry now has a presence in every continent, and moves are afoot to expand this presence in places like the Far East and South America.

There are several factors which could obstruct or support Kerry in becoming an international food conglomerate. Obstacles to its future success include the public perception of the group as being linked to Denis Brosnan. The markets, in evaluating prospective flotations, generally prefer an organisation that is not inextricably linked with one individual. EU subsidies are also an issue of consideration. Kerry's main dairy products, casein and butter/spreads are both heavily subsidised. Casein is the major input in many of Kerry's food-ingredient products. Excessive dependence on such a heavily subsidised product could create a precarious base for the group's ambitions of becoming a major international food company. Factors in its favour include the group's proven ability to choose and dominate niche food markets; its commitment to product development and technology, particularly in respect of its rapidly expanding food-ingredients division; and, of course, its high-powered management style.

Source: Company reports and interviews with company personnel.

Questions

1. Evaluate Kerry Group's diversification in terms of type and overall success.

2. Critically evaluate the management style of Denis Brosnan.

3. In your opinion, does Kerry Group plc meet the definitional requirements of a multinational or global organisation? Explain your answer.

4. What factors have contributed to the overall success of Kerry Group plc?

25

Kentz Corporation

Overview of Kentz Corporation

Activity

Kentz Corporation, formerly M.F. Kent, has been in business since 1919. Originally founded at the electrical contracting company operating in Ireland, M.F. Kent in the early 1970s diversified into the mechanical and instrumental services area. In 1977, the company carried out its first overseas contract. Over the years it has greatly expanded and diversified, and is at present divided into five disciplines: electrical, mechanical, control and instrumentation, civil and building, and management. Kentz runs its business through four operating divisions:

- Management Engineering and Construction Division: Kentz MEC

- Contracting and Management Division: Kentz C&M

- Technologies and Management Division: Kentz T&M

- Resources and Management Division: Kentz R&M.

The combination of the operating business divisions and the operating market sectors has produced a matrix within the organisation of activities. For example, project management or engineering work on an assembly plant in the commercial and light industrial sector would be carried out by the MEC divisions, whilst the building services for the same project would be carried out by the C&M division.

Status

Kentz Corporation's world headquarters are situated in Clonmel, Co. Tipperary. The corporation is structured in such a way that the MEC division is Clonmel based, the C&M division is subsidiary based in geographical locations, the T&M division is Cork based and the R&M division is Clonmel based. All Kentz offices (worldwide) report to the operating sector manager, who in turn reports to the operating business division director (who is also a main board director). Situations do arise where personnel based in the same branch may be reporting to different sector managers or divisional directors, depending on the work with which they are involved.

Size and Ownership

Kentz currently employs about 4,000 worldwide. The number of personnel peaked at approximately 6,000 in mid-1992. Kentz is an Irish-owned private company/corporation. Until 1988, the company was a family-owned private company, but it was the subject of a management buyout by six of the then directors of the company, all of whom remain the main board directors of Kentz Corporation.

Production Process Technology

Kentz is not a manufacturing company. It could be described as a "construction" or "construction services" company, capable of putting all of the elements of a project together with a team of highly qualified and experienced personnel employing the latest technology to produce a quality product on time and within budget.

External Environment

Product Market

As Kentz is a multi-disciplined, multi-sectoral, multi-locational corporation, it is not possible to detail the internal/external environmental and personnel policies for every element. For example, the MEC division in the commercial and light industrial sector is currently involved in projects all over the world, including Ireland, Scotland and Nigeria. This is a relatively new (young) branch of the overall organisation, and competition from international companies and organisations is high in this field. Within Ireland, the product market is low because of diminished investment from abroad, combined with aggressive competition and tight margins from more traditional construction companies. As regards external forces, Kentz engages in either reactive or proactive changes. Reactive organisational changes came about with the fall in demand for the company's products in 1992, and resulted in a slimming down of operations. It was done through natural wastage, redeployment and the expanding international division, layoff of operatives, and through the employment of staff on a contract basis. Other reactive changes were to develop Kentz technologies as a facilitating department to Kentz Ireland, and also to make the marketing manager a director to highlight his importance and that of the marketing role which has become more intensified in recent years. Data/information collection is facilitated by the company's policy of achieving the ISO9002 quality standard. Standardisation and the setting up of a data base, in conjunction with the publication of a manual entitled *Project Construction Management — Detailed Construction Procedures*, has led to more efficient and effective data control.

Labour Market

As a dynamic company, Kentz needs to have a flexible structure, a strong emphasis on the market/customer-service role, and a public relations department. This flexible structure and its effects on the personnel/HRM polices are brought about through the following means:

- A centralised personnel department facilitating all divisions including Kentz Ireland. The basic function of this department is to manage the personnel function within the company with regard to policies/activities in the areas of recruitment and selection, training, wage and salary structure, safety, and industrial relations as they affect the company.

- A marketing and information/data system to note any changes in the labour market. The management team and workforce must be flexible enough to move from job to job on a continuous basis, and they have to be skilled enough to undertake and complete a project. Motivation towards the achievement of rewards and incentives is also of importance in handling disruption. The human resource department must be aware of different political information, union requirements, accommodation levels, technological levels and pending labour arrangements. Kentz has a strategic policy relating to personnel above the basic line-manager level, which is monitored and reported on monthly to Gus Kearney, chief executive of Kentz Corporation. It relates to the successful management of resources in management, engineering, professional and supervisory areas to meet the long-term organisation plans and goals. In addition to the personnel brought in from the external labour market, in Kentz MEC, for example, experienced and management-oriented personnel are brought in from other sectors of the Kentz Corporation. Similarly MEC staff members are sometimes seconded to other sectors within the corporation for specific projects.

Technology

Kentz MEC is involved in project and construct management. It endeavours to keep up-to-date with the latest developments and advances in technology. Where possible, MEC provides its staff with experience in relation to existing or new technologies through in-house experience (i.e. site experience). Where this is not possible, external bodies are employed to provide the necessary experience and development. In general, when MEC is employing new personnel it does so to fit specified profiles — education and experience, for example. As technology advances to higher levels, MEC provides the necessary training to ensure that the organisation keeps pace with any changes in the environment. A similar policy is employed in all the other divisions.

Other External Factors

These include the other sectors/divisions that are internal to Kentz but external to MEC. Such factors include:

- Temporary demand in this division for management personnel from other areas within the organisation

- The availability of temporary or permanent suitably qualified people from other areas within the organisation

- In-house involvement in projects being carried out by other sectors/divisions.

Whilst there is some autonomy for each division within the Kentz Corporation, corporate policies on all areas of business are developed and driven from the top. It is not always possible for each division to pursue the course of action which it feels may be of most benefit to it, but as a subsystem of Kentz, it must pursue policies that are in keeping with the goals of the corporation as a whole.

Internal Environment

Management Values / Culture

Taken as a whole, the Kentz Corporation is a strong culture in so far as it has a single individual (51 per cent shareholder) who is the main driving force of the organisation. This person is largely responsible for determining the goals and objectives of the organisation, and the policies and the means for achieving them. There exists a reluctance to delegate power (that is, a desire to keep control at the centre of the organisation). Within the MEC division for example, operation is more along the lines of a flexible culture, in that there is a flatter structure, it is flexible, and it operates in a dynamic/complex environment where the emphasis is on role definitions as opposed to "tight" job descriptions. Other divisions also differ in culture, primarily because of their difference in requirements.

Organisation Structure and Size

Kentz is a formalised organisation with functional and facilitating departments, showing definite lines of authority. This structural form is related to the technology and size of Kentz, as are the roles and lines of authority. Many functions are centralised whereas others are decentralised to the different regions.

Personnel is one function that is centralised in the group, and is located at head office. The internal environment takes cognisance over external factors and may include such things as managerial ideology, workforce profile, established HR policies, size/culture. The organisation is divided into divisions, each of which is headed up by a main board of directors. The divisions are also further divided into operating sectors. For example, in the mechanical division, the structure is based on projects and the management of these projects. Each project is controlled by a

project manager to whom a variable number and type of staff will
be allocated relative to the size and complexity of the project.
Project managers report to project directors who will have overall
responsibility for two or more projects, depending on size, etc. The
project directors report to the operations sector manager. In the
separate organisations under the MEC division, for example,
there exist service sectors such as engineering design, finance and
accounting, each of which provides essential back-up services to
the mechanical division.

Figure 25.1: Kentz Group

Operating Business Divisions

Management, Engineering and Construction (MEC)	Contracting and Management (C&M)	Technologies and Management (T&M)	Resources and Management (R&M)
Project Management	General Contracting (Building/Civil)	Instrumentation Control and Automation	Financial Services
Engineering	Industrial Plant Contracting (Mechanical/ Electrical/ Instrumentation)	Communication	Business Services
Procurement		Information Services	Human Resources
Construction		Systems Integration	Travel and Leisure
Management Construction	Building Services Contracting (Mechanical/ Electrical/ Instrumentation)	Business Management Services	
		Maintenance and Facilities Management	

Organisation Climate

Any move that a personnel manager makes to change a policy or
technique, must be made in the context of their understanding
of the organisation's culture and climate. Kentz carries this out
through its personnel policy, a policy which encourages advance
planning and a system of preventive maintenance tailored to the
particular project. This is achieved through research of local

custom and practice and a planned programme of recruitment and selection aimed at integrating suitable individuals onto project sites.

Management Style

Within the Kentz Corporation, management objectives are set down and agreed at project-validation meetings. Various monitoring techniques are carried out periodically, and the necessary machinery is in place for prompt collective action in cases where problems arise. The style of each individual manager is different, thus making it difficult to identify and describe any single technique. However, elements of a task culture prevail, particularly within the project-management structure, but, in general, a formal culture pervades the organisation, i.e. procedures and techniques are carried out, not through collective reasoning but through position and influence. Accordingly, position, as opposed to expert or personal power, is used as a source of power.

Corporate Objectives

Kentz Corporation's objectives are set out in the company's mission statement, which states that the organisation's goal is to remain at the forefront of its industry by providing a quality service second to none, developing innovative strategies for the future and continuing to build upon the engineering and technical excellence long associated with the company. The ultimate objective of Kentz is to achieve an organisation status on a par with international organisations such as Becled and Jacobs, offering a multidisciplinary service to clients in project management and associated fields. This will be achieved by developing and expanding the business within the corporation in order to provide "turn-key" capabilities and projects to a variety of possible clients.

Workforce Characteristics

As Kentz developed and expanded, it progressed from its original situation of consisting of a handful of electricians with a working foreman, to a situation where, on occasion, some areas have had up to 2,200 personnel operating on a single site, and whilst the majority of these personnel are of an operative status, most projects necessitate a management structure. Within the core business of mechanical and electrical contracting, Kentz takes its apprentices in at school age, trains them to operative status and promotes from within. It is not unusual to find a project manager who has been with the organisation for over 15 or 20 years, and who started "on the tools". With the exception of Kentz mechanical, technologies and instrumentation sectors, the workforce profile within the organisation is very similar to that of any large contracting organisation with a committed core of "company men" in line-management roles supervising operatives who are contracted on a project basis (in other words, if there is no other work available at the end of a project, the operative will be let go).

Figure 25.2: MEC Division

Typical Project Organisation Chart

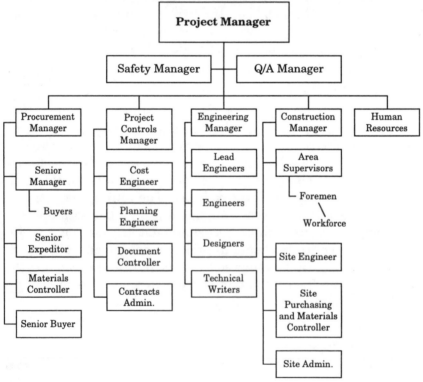

For skilled labour, the age groups are from early twenties to late fifties. Knowledge and skill are generally obtained through on-the-job training and experience. In this labour market, employment is generally short-term, with training only given to apprentices, or as a reactive policy for a specialised contract that needs more people. Because of the promotional and experience policies of the company, junior to middle levels of management, and right up to project-management levels, tend to consist of young graduates, with some graduates having up to 10 years' experience. Senior management tends to be sourced from the more experienced project managers/financial management grade.

Established Personnel/Employee Relations Practices

At operative level within the organisation, people are largely governed by traditional personnel management policies, are paid above minimum unionised rates, and work agreed unionised hours. The urge to get the job done and a flexible approach to working have been transmitted to the operative levels who are aware that the company will look after them in so far as possible by endeavouring to provide continuity of employment. Above operative level there are no established personnel practices or policies, in that new staff are generally employed by the managers to whom they will be reporting, and any problems that arise are dealt with on an individual basis. The organisation would like to believe that it has a HRM approach to the management of its personnel. However, in reality, it is evident that an ad-hoc approach is deployed. Kentz holds an operational focus and has a collective approach to agreements. The construction Industry Federation outlines what the payment rates and terms should be, and performance-related pay is sometimes given, based on output. HR practices apply more to management where Kentz adopts a strategic approach. The job is defined more as a role description than as a role definition, and is reasonably flexible. Kentz has its own recruitment arm, European Ltd., which specialises in recruitment, selection and induction.

Kentz Ireland organisations have multiple short-duration contracts and are broken into six areas — Dublin, Cork, Clonmel, West Derby, UK and London. Flexibility and mobility are very important and it is an accepted feature of employment that employees will have to travel. Personnel has a policy of trying to minimise travel disruption by picking project personnel from among those who live near the particular project where possible.

It is Kentz personnel policy to hold company-induction

courses to explain to new employees how the company operates, its objectives and the opportunities with the organisation. The company has a policy of supporting staff social and sporting activities. It also carries out evaluations of job content and environment factors affecting staff.

It is a company policy to draw up a hiring plan which will expand the manpower-needs forecast to identify exact requirements by category of skill, salary, grade etc., and also to develop a policy of how this is to be achieved.

The industrial relations policy has been developed over many years of contracting experience on both unionised and non-unionised projects. The Kentz policy relates to planning, personnel responsible for IR, liaison procedures with area trade union officials, welfare facilities, skill levels, union membership, contracts of employment, company rules and discipline procedures, etc. Kentz adheres to all legal and social requirements. Personnel policy choice will vary from operative/supervisory level to the middle/senior management levels.

It is Kentz policy to keep staff/employees aware of what is happening through company circulars, induction courses, education courses, memos, periodic meetings, etc. Kentz also considers the following in its personnel policies relating to communications:

- Informing staff of progress, policies and plans

- Involving staff in managing the business on a team basis giving them all relevant information

- Gaining commitment from people by letting them know what they have to achieve

- Having a policy for all staff not to divulge certain information, especially main board topics.

At project-team level, good communications are vital to the success of the project, and regular weekly team meetings are held to achieve the following:

- To ensure that team members are conversant with the requirements of the client/project as outlined by the project manager

- To co-ordinate the efforts of all team members towards the progression and completion of the project

- To resolve difficulties and problems through team involvement or through intervention of the project manager/director.

The project manager will not only have the responsibility for keeping the team up to date on client/project requirements, but will also be a direct link to the other activities within the sector. Effective communications is the only means by which an organisation such as Kentz can survive and operate.

The reward-system policies of Kentz consider as significant factors motivation, job satisfaction, increased responsibility, job title, etc. The intrinsic motivating factors, such as job content, variety, challenge, etc. are used to reward management and those involved in management or decision-making. Extrinsic factors are more related to operative-level employees. Here reward systems are predetermined by collective agreements. This type of system, which relates to the degree of skill, does not itself relate to performance — hence the use performance-related pay systems such as bonus/incentive schemes. Furthermore, it usually pertains to the blue-collar or skilled/unskilled labour sector of the organisation. As reward is linked to performance, Kentz also considers such things as the level of supervision, sense of achievement, or success in a job/task. Performance is seen as an equation including individual attributes and work effort, all with organisation support. Kentz views the education and advancement of its employees as a reward policy affording benefits both to workforce and to the organisation as a whole.

Recruitment is based upon short- and long-term strategic policies. With high unemployment levels a feature of most societies in present times, Kentz would have no problems filling unskilled general operative positions. The company has no policy regarding filling positions relating to this category of employment. Supervisory and management employee levels are part of a more long-term strategic plan. These positions are filled from teams which have finished, or are about to finish, another project. With up-to-date files, it allows Kentz to consider whether positions can be filled from within, through education, or whether they need to go outside the company to source labour. Advertising for positions is very rarely undertaken within Kentz Ireland, unless it is for a management position that will affect the company in the short term. It is Kentz policy to employ and educate people for positions, which instils loyalty and keeps the Kentz philosophy within the organisation.

Countdown to Collapse

The Kentz Group was placed in receivership by AIB in January 1994, but successfully applied to the High Court to have the receiver removed and an examiner appointed in his place. Following the collapse of the Kentz Group, the impression was given that it was a highly successful multinational company that was brought to its knees by some of its creditors who were a little nervous about their money. In fact, Kentz itself gave assurances to anyone prepared to listen that it was a company with a bright future, and was only going through some temporary difficulties. It was these assurances which helped the company to persuade the powers that be to have Hugh Cooney installed as examiner, a move which mollified the powers of Rory O'Farrell, the receiver appointed by the banks. This examinership move, however, did not guarantee a future for Kentz, but it did give the examiner a short period of time to make an assessment of the company. The original receiver told the High Court that the group's overall deficit could amount to close on £50 million. This figure turned out to be a slight underestimation of the true extent of the problem. Creditors of the troubled company were owed in the region of £100 million, a figure contradicted by Kentz itself which has claimed that the company deficit was somewhere in the region of £9 million to £10 million. Perhaps one of the reasons for this confusion over the actual true state of the group is the complex treatment of accounts for contract work and the group's inter-company arrangements around the world. The last financial statements available are for the year to end 1990.

Reasons for Collapse: Overview of the Group's Development

It could be argued that the group was an indirect casualty of the Gulf War, as the group's business opportunities in the Middle East came virtually to an end as a result. The group then turned to Europe for business, which was not a very good move because this region was suffering from its own problems — a deep recession affected most of Europe at this time. One notable contract that the group did win in Europe was to assist in the building of a £400-million hotel complex in Barcelona in preparation for the 1992 Olympics. This project, however, was late in its completion, went way over budget, and embroiled Kentz in litigation against the property's developer, the American hotelier, G. Ware Travelstead. The project was finally completed 18 months behind schedule, and it is estimated to have cost Kentz some £6 million. It was this bad deal that altered the attitude of the banks to the group's problems. Accordingly, they requested that the group's seven board members be joined by four non-executive directors. Among those selected were former Waterford Foods managing director Stephen O'Connor, and former CRH executive Diarmuid Quirke.

Between 1979 and 1986, the AIB Group, through Allied Irish Investment Bank, made five substantial loans to the group, while the Dublin office of Banque Nationale de Paris gave the group smaller loans. Following the Barcelona problems, the group had to look elsewhere for financial assistance, and it managed to raise more substantial loans this time in Germany and the United Arab Emirates, and currencies from AIG Europe, totalling £9 million. On obtaining these funds, the policy for the group was to refocus, with certain markets being targeted, particularly in Africa, the Middle East, the Far East, Ireland and the UK, as well as expansion into engineering procurement. In line with this policy, some operations in the Netherlands, Germany and Belgium ceased trading or were wound up. Because the group was perhaps overly keen to acquire contracts, it began a policy of making low bids. It has been suggested that the bids made were excessively low so as to win contracts and improve current cash flows. In the Irish market for instance, the group pursued an aggressive strategy to win projects which included the Custom House Docks, Bolands mill and the Intel computer plant at Leixlip in Co. Kildare. Accusations in respect of the Intel project were centred on the competitiveness of the Kentz bid. It was suggested, for example, that the bid was some £750,000 lower than its nearest competitor — a charge that the group vehemently denies.

With these stories of under-bidding circulating, it is perhaps understandable that the new refocus strategy did not turn out as the group had intended. Matters were not helped by the fact that, in 1992, the group was badly affected by interest-rate fluctuations. In 1993, it withdrew from a project in Singapore, resulting in a fall in turnover of £20 million to £320 million. By 1993, only the Middle East and South African operations were doing well, with all others suffering from serious cash-flow problems. In Belgium, the group got the contract for the construction of the Morgan Bank headquarters, with the estimated cost put at £7.95

million. However, it ended up costing twice that amount, with resulting losses of £2.7 million for the group. Yet write-off of losses was not something new for the group, because in 1992 it had to write off £0.5 million for an East German project. In the UK, the group experienced serious financial problems with two projects they were involved with — one was the Ministry of Defence armaments plant at Aldermaston near Reading, the other was a British Gas research building in Loughborough. In fact, one of the group's subcontractors on the Loughborough project, Flue-Stock Engineering, petitioned for its winding up over an unpaid debt. However, it was later repaid. Late payments were becoming yet another feature of the group's operations as it was receiving numerous complaints from both Irish and UK sub-contractors over delays.

The other main project in the UK where the group experienced major financial trouble, and, according to the group, the reason for the payment delays, was the Guys Hospital project. Like other projects this was beset with problems and huge cost overruns. The project was estimated to cost £22.6 million but ended up costing £37.4 million, with Kentz losing £6 million. It led in the end to a petition being put forward by the Inland Revenue for the winding-up of Kentz's UK subsidiary, Kentz C&M. The Inland Revenue was joined in the action by five unsecured creditors, subcontractors on the Guys hospital extension project. It appears that Kentz C&M were in dispute with Guys Hospital over claims that the hospital owed over £5 million for work that Kentz C&M had carried out, and Kentz wanted its money. The Guys Hospital project was estimated to cost £80 million, but over two years later the final cost was closer to £140 million. In the end, Kentz C&M was given 28 days to meet its obligations or else face closure, but it would appear that the company ran out of money because senior management did not, in the end, contest the winding up. This winding up was a serious move from Kentz's point of view, because it could have had a domino effect, with the group's creditors, around the globe seeking payment for some 250 projects in which the group was involved. This move in the UK to appoint a receiver to Kentz C&M forced the Irish bank to move, and within a matter of hours, receivers were appointed on both sides of the Irish Sea.

Since 1991, the Kentz corporation has lost a total of £10 million in various projects that it has undertaken, and it could also be argued that among other things, the group's financial problems were not helped by the fact that group management was dispersed around the world. Accordingly, the issues highlighted by the collapse of the Kentz group posed very serious questions on the way in which the business of the group was managed.

The Group's Debts

The following represented the main debts of concern:

- The banks were owed close to £17 million, while the deficit between Kentz assets and liabilities is between £9 million and £50 million.

- Telecom Éireann was owed debts of £350,000.

- The Revenue Commissioners were owed about £8.5 million. This was made up of a preferential debt of just under £3.9 million and another debt of £4.6 million which is not ranked as preferential.

- The company faced a $25 million claim against it by the developers of a major commercial, retail and leisure project in Singapore. The Suntec City project developers' claim against Kentz related to considerable overruns both in the time scale and the budget allocated for the project. Because it was not able to meet its contractual and financial obligations, and thus wished to cut its losses having worked on the project for two years, Kentz sold its interest to its other partners, the Australian contractors O'Donnell Griffin and Tyco-Grinell. The Suntec City development included two five-storey office blocks and an 18-storey office tower, as well as a retail and hotel complex. The contract was estimated to be worth $70 million to Kentz.

- M.F. Kent was owed a total of £14 million from the group's European subsidiaries and £7.9 million from UK subsidiaries. There exists little or no chance of recovering this money. In January of 1994, M.F. Kent has fixed assets of £985,000, with current assets of £3.255 million made up of work-in-progress (£2.42 million), debtors and pre-payments (£800,000) and cash (£35,000). This gave the company total assets of £4.24 million. However, the deficit of the company is £14.54 million after taking into account total liabilities of £18.78 million — trade creditors are owed £4.1 million, the banks £5.83 million, the Revenue Commissioners £4.95 million and inter-company creditors £3.9 million.

Figure 25.3: Kentz Group World Business Locations

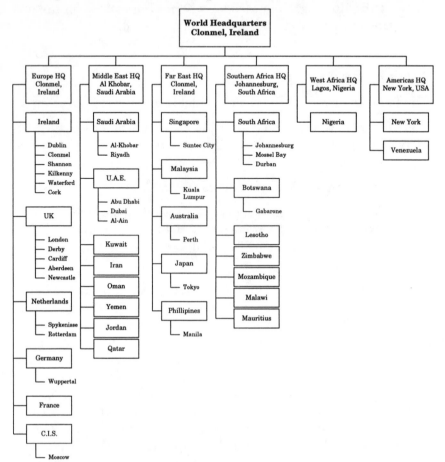

Workforce

The 4,000-strong workforce is split as follows:

- *Middle East* — Where the company has between 1,600 and 1,700 working on an oil refinery in Kuwait. Similar work is being carried out in Saudi Arabia and a power station in Abu Dhabi in the United Emirates. Up to 300 of these workers are Irish.

- *Africa* — Kentz has some 400 workers in South Africa and Botswana on similar oil-refinery projects, and about one quarter of these are Irish.

- *South East Asia* — Up to 150 people are working on a gas-producing plant in Malaysia, and of these some 50 are from Ireland.

- *Ireland* — The total Kentz workforce in Ireland is between 650 and 900, and this figure may be closer to 1,000. Because of the complexity of operations, and the multitude of divisions, it means that total employment at the company is close to 4,000.

Companies Wound Up

Hopes for the survival of Kentz faded fast because seven of the 19 companies in the group were taken out of examinership. Seven Irish subsidiaries of the group and its UK operation have gone into receivership. In the UK division, the total number of people involved was 500, and all have been let go. The Kentz group's UK receiver, Terry Carter of Ernst and Young, estimated that the UK subsidiary was owed between £2 million and £5 million by the parent company. In the Irish subsidiaries, between 60 and 70 people lost their jobs, but many of these have been taken on in other group companies. Other group companies that have been wound up include Kent Travel Ltd. and Kencam. These companies had been part of Holidair Ltd. and 18 related companies. Kent Travel Ltd., located in Tipperary, had nominal share capital of £1 million. Kencam, located in Clonmel, which was set up to organise building projects, has a staff of 40 and nominal share capital of £32 million, and could be facing a deficit of nearly £10 million.

Other companies in doubt over their survival include: Kent Technologies; Kentz Data Systems (Ireland) Ltd.; Kent Technical Services Ltd.; and Kentz Patents Ltd. Kent Technologies Ltd. is the parent company of the other four which are subsidiaries. It specialises in computer software in which its own parent company, Holidair Ltd. has a 25 per cent stake. Kent Technologies, which employs 28 people, could be facing a combined deficiency of close to £3 million.

The management of the Kentz Kilkenny-based subsidiary, Mahon and McPhillips, has expressed an interest in buying out the company which would have a price tag of around £2 million. This company highlights the level of inter-company indebtedness that exists within the Kentz group. Mahon and McPhillips is owed £2 million by M.F. Kent International, and the latter, which is the most profitable subsidiary of the Kentz group, is in turn owed in excess of £30 million by other group companies, many of which have now been put into receivership.

Issues Causing Concern

After the collapse of the company, many issues came to light regarding Kentz management, which have caused considerable concern not only for Kentz creditors, but for the business community at large. The main issues of concern were as follows:

• Apart from the very high level of inter-company indebtedness, the other serious issue of concern for the group's creditors was the presence of a group of Channel Island registered companies which have become known as the Chandler group of companies. These are groups outside the Kentz group but which share the same shareholders. It would appear that these companies actually own contracts that were won by one of the companies within the Kentz Group and M.F. Kent International, in Saudi Arabia and Nigeria. It is one of these companies which owns the Digital plant in Clonmel, and which has received grants from the IDA for setting up a technology division there. What is not clear, however, is whether or not profits earned by these external companies have been given back to the Kentz group. It would also appear that many Kentz Group employees would have worked on these contracts.

It is possible that revenue generated by various Kentz projects was not paid to Kentz itself but to the Channel Island companies not owned by the group. One of these external companies is said to be at least partly beneficially owned by Kentz shareholders, so money may not have been paid into the Kentz group accounts in order to pay the group's various creditors and banks. On why such companies were set up, Kentz itself has argued that it was necessary to establish companies outside the group itself in order to carry out certain projects and because clients requested such a move. They did not wish to be caught up in any problems that would affect the group as a whole. After the project was completed, it was Kentz's intention to bring these companies back within the group, an assurance that has been given by the group's solicitors. If they are brought within the group, then the banks have to be provided with security in relation to them.

- Another claim being made is that these other companies outside the Kentz group were left to choose the best contracts for themselves by bidding excessively low for them.

- Also of concern to the banks and creditors is the fact that Kentz gave some of its directors interest-free loans of such large amounts, that there is the possibility that they may be in contravention of the Companies Act, and of the group's agreements with its various banks. Loans totalling £1.3 million were paid to directors of the group, and have yet to be repaid. Group accounts for 1992 show that chief executive Gus Kearney owed in excess of £590,000; director Sean White owed more than £125,000; director Paul Lloyd owed almost £104,000; and company secretary Michael Campbell owed over £81,000. These loans are reported to be interest free, unsecured and with no fixed term of repayment.

- Investigations have also revealed other transactions involving many millions of pounds, which took place between the Kentz group and companies connected with the group's chief executive, Gus Kearney. Some of his private companies were involved with Kentz in transactions worth over £5 million for 1992 alone. One company of which he is a director, Westgate, which is involved in the electrical-equipment supply market, was paid £4.5 million by the Kentz group. Westgate is said to have connections with another company, Poamako, in which Gus Kearney and his son hold a joint 50/50 partnership. The end-of-year accounts for 1992 show that Westgate is owed a total of £455,325 by the Kentz group, and another company connected with Gus Kearney repaid a bill of £417,000 to Kentz earlier in the year. It is maintained that the Westgate company relied on the Kentz group for 50 per cent of its Irish business and up to 80 per cent of its UK and international business.

- There is the question as to why a company experiencing very serious financial difficulties paid dividends amounting to £11.5 million to company shareholders, with these payments being made in two tranches. The first payment of £7.5 million was made during 1990, while the second payment of £4 million was paid out in 1992. These dividends relate to the management buyouts which took place over a two-year period and which were later given back to the company in the form of shareholders' loans. In 1988, there was a management buy-out of MF

Kent with the group's name being changed to Kentz, because in
that year and 1991, chief executive Gus Kearney paid almost
£7 million for Frank Kentz's share.

- Another claim against the group is that it took on projects that
  it had not properly costed, and which ended up running excessively over budget; and with little cash in the bank to fund
  various projects, Kentz still went ahead with work costing millions of pounds. The end result was that the group was relying
  on its clients to provide the funding for the work, and very often this funding was delayed or disputed. Because of the vast
  size of some of these projects, it would have taken only one to
  wipe out the whole group. The Barcelona project highlights
  this fact — it ran excessively over budget, with the client dis-
  puting the extra spending. Kentz faced financial ruin as a result, even though the client was forthcoming with most of the
  money.

- In its endeavours to become a large multinational, Kentz undertook many projects on excessively low profit margins. In fact,
  many of the projects taken on were loss-makers.

The Rescue Plan

A rescue plan was proposed by the group's examiner, which proposed that the Kentz group with the assistance of a Malaysian
investor would form a new Dutch holding company to control the
group. However, the Revenue Commissioners rejected the Kentz
rescue plan drawn up by the group's examiner, Mr Hugh Cooney,
but the group's main banks, AIB and BNP accepted the deal offering them 50p in the pound, which will give them £4 million of the
£8.6 million owed to them. The ICC bank, which was owed £2.5
million by the Kentz subsidiary, M.F. Kent for work done on an
office block in Clonskeagh, Co. Dublin, accepted the rescue plan.
An arrangement was worked out whereby more than £2 million of
the debt would be transferred to property companies within the
Kentz group for which ICC holds primary security, and M.F. Kent
will then be released from liability.

The Revenue Commissioners were offered 50p in the pound for
the preferential debit and 35p in the pound for non-preferential
debt — that is, if they accepted the plan. The unsecured creditors

— mainly subcontractors — were offered between 20p and 50p in the pound, and a very small number of the unsecured creditors, such as the pension fund, former employees, and leasing companies received 100p in the pound. If this rescue plan were approved by the court, then Kentz could come out of examinership. The Malaysian company, Renong, was then willing to pay close on £8 million for a 40 per cent share in a new Kentz holding company which will be registered in the Netherlands, Kentz would hold the remaining 60 per cent. Three separate schemes of arrangement were up for approval, concerning M.F. Kent, its subsidiary Mahon and McPhillips and Holidair, the parent company of the Kentz group. The banks were being offered £0.45 million by both Mahon and McPhillips and M.F. Kentz, while Holidair would pay AIB and BNP a total of £3.1 million. If this scheme of arrangement were accepted then it was understood that Kentz would apply to the High Court under section 17 of the Companies Act to have the assets and liabilities of M.F. Kent International transferred to this new Dutch holding company in order to secure large contracts held in the Middle East. Kentz's core businesses, if they are to survive for the immediate future, require working capital in the region of £700,000 per week, if not more, with the company's wage bill alone standing at £500,000 per week. If the group could not come up with this money, the future of the remaining twelve companies in examinership was in doubt. However, in 1994, the company's main banks, AIB and Banque Nationale de Paris, were not very positive in their response. If the money was not forthcoming, the only alternative was to sell off some of the group's other businesses.

There were intense negotiations between Kentz management and a former senior manager of United Engineers of Malaysia (UEM) to secure a deal for the troubled Irish engineering group. In these talks with UEM, Kentz management agreed to part with at least a further 20 per cent of the restructured company in order to swing a deal. In earlier discussions it appeared that EUM would take a 40 per cent share of the Irish subsidiaries and 60 per cent of Kentz international operations. Negotiations between Kentz and UEM, a subsidiary of Renong, collapsed following the delivery of a report on the Kentz operations. The High Court was told that the new investor was seeking to acquire 60 per cent of the group.

If the deal went through, the group was set to benefit from an injection of £10 million in funds, including a £1.5 million loan which was being arranged. Around £2.625 million extra would be allocated to the group, with the remainder used to pay off creditors. Kentz management had agreed to put up a further £815,000 on top of around £1 million pumped into Chandler Enterprises during the examinership. Not all of the £2.625 million would be available to the group because an unspecified sum had been set aside for legal and examinership costs. Under the new corporate structure, the ultimate Kentz parent would be a Malaysian-controlled investment company called Kerbett, which would hold a 60 per cent stake in the new joint-venture company, Pinacere, with the Irish holding the remaining 40 per cent, most likely through the original Kentz holding company, Holidair. Opposition from trade creditors to the scheme of arrangement emerged. The Revenue Commissioners indicated that they had objections to the scheme. The Revenue Commissioners would get back 80 per cent of what they were owed instead of the 40 per cent provided for in the Cooney scheme. On a more positive front, plans for the survival of eight companies in the Kentz Group were confirmed by the High Court. The eight companies which are the subject of the seven schemes of arrangement are Holidair Ltd; M.F. Kent and Company Ltd; Clonmak Ltd; Europlan Ltd; Mahon and McPhillips CEM Ltd; Kent Properties Ltd; Guy Properties Ltd; and Venice Enterprises Ltd.

Conclusion

Kentz is still operating as a going concern. The restructuring resulted in an investment of IR£75 million by way of share capital and loans. The new investors have taken a 60 per cent share holding in the group and, as a consequence, hold majority voting rights on the restructured board of directors.

The group continues to operate in Ireland, Kuwait, Saudi Arabia, Abu Dhabi, Botswana, South Africa and Malaysia. It continues to provide a full range of engineering and construction services.

Source: Company reports and interviews with company personnel.

Questions

1. Evaluate the main factors within the external environment that influence the business strategies of Kentz Corporation.

2. Analyse the internal strengths and weaknesses of Kentz Corporation and explain their implications for future strategic initiatives.

3. Evaluate the recruitment and employee relations of Kentz Corporation in terms of their effectiveness and general type.

4. What strategic options are open to Kentz Corporation given the present financial state?

26

Allergan Pharmaceuticals Ireland Ltd.

Introduction

The pharmaceutical industry, and specifically the eye-care industry, in Ireland has grown significantly in the past 20 years. There are currently 300 companies employing 20,000 people directly, with further major indirect employment. Since 1988, the industry has proven a boom for the Irish economy, with exports now totalling over £3 billion per annum — representing one fifth of total manufacturing exports. Twelve of the world's top pharmaceutical companies now have major plants in Ireland.

Ireland remains one of the most attractive locations in Europe for eye-care and pharmaceutical industries. The rise in popularity of Ireland as a strategic location looks set to continue, despite the country's position on the periphery of Europe. The availability of a highly educated, trained and skilled workforce commands instant attention for the country. Ireland's corporation tax rate for manufacturing companies remains at 10 per cent until the year 2010, which offers a significant element of certainty for foreign companies.

Allergan Pharmaceuticals (Ireland) Ltd. is one of the leading eye-care manufacturing companies in Ireland. It is ranked 103 out of the top 1,000 companies in Ireland, with Bausch and Lomb ranked 127, Johnson and Johnson ranked 367, Smith and Nephew ranked 602, and Ciba Geigy ranked 436. Allergan Pharmaceuticals (Ireland) Ltd. expanded its operation in Westport, Co. Mayo, in 1995 with a new 25,000 square foot facility for the production of two new eye-care products, "Botox" and "Vitrax", which were launched on the Irish market in September 1995.

Vistakon, a division of Johnson and Johnson Vision products Inc., invested £130 million in a major new health-care operation located at the National Technological Park, Plassey, Limerick, in 1995. Vistakon plans to create 450 new jobs over the next three years, in the manufacture of disposable contact lenses. This is the largest investment to be announced by any company in the manufacturing sector in Ireland, and is among the top investments ever in the health-care industry in this country.

Background to Company

Allergan Pharmaceuticals was founded by Gavin Herbert in 1948. In a small room over Mr Herbert's pharmacy in Los Angeles, he and his son began compounding ophthalmic products for physicians according to sterility rules. The firm added ear, nose and throat products. The compound used in these products was also used as an anti-allergy eye drop, and thus the product was named "Allergan". After achieving success in the Los Angeles market, the product's name became the company's name. Allergan has now emerged as a major eye-care/pharmaceutical manufacturing company, with strong positions abroad in its speciality market. It is engaged primarily in quality pharmaceuticals which include, preparations for treatment of diseases in the eye, and for use with contact lenses. The company's headquarters and plant offices are located in Irvine, California. It operates through 26 subsidiaries, one of which is Allergan, Westport, Co. Mayo. Allergan Inc. is a world leader in developing, manufacturing, and marketing eye-care products. The head manufacturing office is in Waco in the US. Allergan Westport is its biggest manufacturing plant. It began operations in 1977, with a small office located at Westport, Co. Mayo. The company was founded in Westport by Jim Kierly and Gavin Herbert. It consisted of an 18,500 square foot plant with 15 employees. The entire operation then was confined to the manufacture of one product, "Hydrocare".

Colm O'Neill, Managing Director of Allergan Ltd. suggests three reasons for establishing a plant in Westport:

- In the mid-1970s the Irish government was actively campaigning to attract foreign companies, to set up manufacturing facilities in economically depressed areas of the country, by offering them major tax incentives.

• The quality of the tap water in Westport was and still is extremely high, and therefore requires very little treatment for use in manufacture. This was a very important factor for Allergan since almost all its products are aqueous solutions.

• Westport as a town had a strong industrial tradition, a high-quality environment and a range of facilities that set it apart from other towns of similar size.

The Westport operation concentrates on ophthalmic products, 60 per cent of which are contact-lens care products and 40 per cent eye-care products. All production in Westport is exported. The plant is the single largest manufacturing plant in the Allergan group. Allergan currently produces a basic 300 products, which can be expanded to a product range of approximately 1,100. It employs over 600 people in the following departments: plastics, sterilisation, filling, packaging, tableting, kits, lab, warehouse, shipping, maintenance, administration offices, quality control and management.

Allergan Ltd. operates two principal systems of sterilisation: Ethyl Oxide Gas, and Gamma Irradiation. Allergan has its own sterilisation chambers, where components are sterilised and all bacterial contamination removed.

Gamma irradiation is used on the majority of components, and is performed by Dutch company Gammaster, which is located adjacent to the Allergan plant. Allergan launched a new product onto the Irish market in May 1995, namely a "complete" all-in-one, contact-lens care solution, which has enhanced Allergen's foothold in both the conventional and the disposable contact-lens care market in Ireland.

In 1994, production began at a new Allergan plant known as Allergan (Botox) Ireland. This new development facility will manufacture two new product lines: "Botox" and "Vitrax". The new £6 million plant will be in full production by 1998.

Allergan's Products and Quality Standards

The main products manufactured and supplied by Allergan include contact-lens care products and eye-care products. These are divided into two product lines:

• Pharmaceuticals consisting of steroids, anti-viral drugs, prescription and over-the-counter eye-care products;

- Contact-lens care products (CLCPs) consisting of cleaning, wetting, soaking and disinfecting solutions and other products for contact lenses.

The new botox facility now in operation manufactures two new product lines:

- Botox: a powerful muscle relaxant used to cure squints, involuntary eye closure and facial disorders

- Vitrax: an eye-fluid replacement product.

Like all health-care products quality standards have to be very high. The Federal Drug Administration (FDA) in the US carries out a major inspection at least once every two years. The FDA checks standards on a selected number of product lines. If specified standards are not upheld, this can result in the withdrawal of that product off the market. For example, "Tylenol" produced by Johnson and Johnson Ltd. was withdrawn from the Irish market in 1993 because it did not satisfy specified standards.

Allergan successfully obtained the ISO9002 Quality Award in 1992. This is a recognised internationally Q mark which has enhanced Allergan's foothold in the worldwide market. Allergan undergoes an ISO inspection once every three months. This standard has conferred a number of benefits on the company:

1. It operates as a control function. All standards and procedures must be documented. All procedures in all departments must be documented, copies taken and back-ups made for record. To maintain the ISO Q mark involves a lot of work and dedication. The ISO inspectors investigate whether or not documented procedures equate with procedures applied in practice. The ISO places great emphasis on customer service.

2. The ISO Q mark elevates the perception of product quality.

3. Being the proud holder of this Q mark means quality across all international boundaries, without any questions.

4. It guarantees quality to Allergan's customers, and it also helps customers to appreciate the strict quality control that exists within the company.

5. At the end of each ISO inspection, Allergan is provided with a list of ISO recommendations on how procedures and standards can be improved.

EU Regulation of Pharmaceutical Industry

As part of the effort to harmonise trading conditions within the EU, the European Commission has been working on a number of directives aimed at harmonising standards in the manufacture of pharmaceutical goods. The Medical Devices Directives were proposed by the European Commission under article 100a of the Treaty of Rome, with the objective of regulating the safety and marketing of medical devices throughout the European Community. Such directives are to replace national systems in each member state and are seen as an integral part of the drive to complete the single market.

Each directive concerned has a defined scope and lays down essential requirements and procedures for checking that all pharmaceutical products comply. The requirements make it clear that devices must not compromise the health or safety of patients or users, and they must also achieve their intended and claimed performance. Devices meeting these requirements will be entitled to carry the CE Mark. When this mark is displayed on a device, it indicates that the safety of the device can be presumed and that the device may be placed on the community market without further restrictions. In general, devices carrying the CE Mark can be marketed anywhere in the EU without future control.

The Minister for Health has designated the National Standards of Ireland as the notifying body for issuing approval of the CE Mark to manufacturers, and it also ensures that manufacturers conform to the requirements and standards set.

Allergan Ltd. was the first eye-care product manufacturer in Ireland to obtain the CE mark EN460002 in December 1994. Allergan Ltd. will now gain approval for new and forthcoming products on the European market without delay. The CE Mark applies only to new products and is of no relevance to existing products on the market.

Marketing and Distribution Efforts of Allergan

As Allergan enters its fifth decade of operation as a global provider of specialised products, it remains the leader in the ever-growing and developing world markets. Allergan Ltd. exports to 74 countries worldwide by air freight, courier and by road. It ships to over 50 countries per month. The normal practice for transporting products for export is via courier or haulage to the appropriate airport or dock in Ireland. In countries like the UK and France where Allergan Ltd. has a large market share, the products are distributed through distributors and agents such as wholesalers. In countries where Allergan Ltd. has a low market share, products are distributed to depots and distributed from there.

The level of Allergan stock held at any one time is restricted in each given market. Each Allergan subsidiary is requested to store a month's supply of critical items which have an 80 per cent selling rate.

Allergan Ltd. delivers every three days to Western Europe, while the normal lead time for an order is approximately five months.

Promotion

Allergan Ltd. distributes over 300,000 free starter kits to its customers per month. Allergan has found from experience that a person using eye-care/contact-lens care products for the first time tends to stick to the brand of product they start with. The potential user of eye-care products is offered a free starter kit, which is quite an attractive package for the patient. This promotional idea is a very tactful marketing ploy on Allergan's part and has contributed greatly to its success in increasing its share of the Irish market.

Allergan Ltd. promotes itself through association with leisure, health and fitness. The majority of people who play sports or keep fit and who suffer from bad eye sight wear contact lenses. Many of Allergan's promotional leaflets associate people with sports.

Packaging

Colour is a very distinctive feature of Allergan's form of packaging. Each product line is given a specific colour scheme so as to identify the product in question. The size of packaging depends on the product and the market in which it is being sold. Every country has its own culture, and its own regulations with regard to packaging requirements. A unique feature of Allergan's packaging, which is not included in competitor-brand packaging is that of "special dosage indicator caps", on a selected number of its eye-care drops. This idea evolved in response to customer requests, and is of considerable benefit for old people who may not recall taking the required dosage.

Allergan Ltd. has recently introduced multi-language packs,

enabling one product line to be shipped to four or five countries. A new feature of Allergan's packaging takes the form of a peel-off label known as "an affixaform label". It is placed on bottled products, and instructions are inserted under the peel-off label for users to adhere to. Suck screening is another new feature of Allergan's packaging — this involves printing details of products permanently on the bottles.

Retail Outlets

The Allergan brand was the first brand of eye-care products to be sold through chemist shops. Allergan's products are widely available on the Irish market because of the large number of pharmacies throughout the country.

Opticians

There are approximately 280 opticians practising in Ireland. Opticians recommend different brands to different patients depending on suitability of the brand for the patient in question. Many opticians stock Allergan products.

Doctors / Surgeons / Private Practices

Allergan supplies doctors, surgeons and private practices mainly with pharmaceuticals consisting of steroids, anti-viral drugs and prescription eye-care products.

Major Chain Stores

Allergan supplies the following major chain stores in Northern Ireland and the UK: Boots, Donan and Atkinson, Tesco, and Safeway. There are several reasons why Allergan supplies the major chain stores:

- Because of the high recognition and popularity held by major chain stores as opposed to ordinary retail outlets in general, they attract a large proportion of the consumer market and therefore Allergan has the opportunity to get a high percentage of that market.

- Allergan does not supply supermarkets because it believes that this would reduce the patients' perception of the product — they may no longer regard it as a medical product and become careless in adhering to users' instructions.

- Allergan is now involved in private labelling for "Boots" and "Donan and Atkinson". A potential risk attaching to this market idea is that all Allergan's products are sold under the "Boots" and "Donan and Atkinson" brand names as opposed to Allergan's own brand name.

Allergan's Key Competitors

There are five major competitors in the Irish market.

Johnson and Johnson

Johnson and Johnson, one of the world's leading health-care corporations has 168 operating companies in 53 countries, and employs approximately 80,000 people worldwide. It has two plants located in Ireland: Janssen Pharmaceuticals Ltd. Cork, employing 128 people, and Johnson and Johnson (Ire) Ltd., Tallaght Co. Dublin, employing 114 people in the production of toiletries and health-care produces. Research and development of new products and processes is important to the company's success in all areas of its business. The competitive environment in the eye-care industry requires substantial investments and continuing research. Thirty-four per cent of Johnson and Johnson's 1993 sales of $14.14 billion came from new products introduced during the previous five years and from existing products launched onto new markets during the same period.

Vistakon, a division of Johnson and Johnson Vision Products Inc. has established a major new health-care operation in Limerick. The official announcement of this new venture was made in December 1993 by the then Minister for Enterprise and Employment, Mr Ruairí Quinn, who stated that "this is the largest investment announced by any company in the manufacturing sector in Ireland and is among the top investments ever in the health-care industry in this country". As a result of securing this new investment, Ireland will become the dominant supplier of contact lenses in Europe. Vistakon revolutionised the contact-lens industry when it introduced "Acuvue", the world's first disposable contact lens, in 1987. In 1991, the company introduced its "Surevue" contact lens, and then in June 1993, it broke another contact-lens barrier with the introduction of 1-day Acuvue — the first daily disposable contact lens to be launched on the worldwide market. Today, Vistakon holds 80 per cent of the worldwide disposable contact lens market, and its Acuvue lens is the number-one selling contact lens worldwide. The key factor which influenced the decision of Vistakon to locate in Limerick was access to the University of Limerick, which incorporates Ireland's largest college of engineering, and the infrastructure at the National Technological Park.

Bausch and Lomb

Bausch and Lomb is representative of a number of multinational companies operating very successfully in Ireland. Its Irish operation manufacturing contact lens is based in Waterford and employs over 600 people. B&L has been described as "a new 135-year-old company". It is a household name in the health-care and optics industry. B&L set up in Waterford in 1981 and it was the company's first overseas manufacturing source. It is now the principal overseas production facility, capable of manufacturing 100 per cent of European needs. Within the eye-care industry, sales for B&L's contact lenses are growing at approximately 20 per cent per annum worldwide. Over 95 per cent of soft contact-lens wearers in the US have started on a regimen of chemical disinfectants. B&L's ReNu multi-purpose contact-lens solution is the most advanced product in this category. It is used as a daily cleaner, rinse and disinfectant, and is similar to Allergan's "Oxysept one-step solution", and its more recent all-in-one "complete" solution. This convenience is highly valued by consumers and its efficiency is well respected by eye-care professionals both in Ireland and worldwide. B&L ReLu solution achieved a revenue mark of $150 million in 1994.

B&L sales of rigid gas-permeable contact-lens solutions increased by 30 per cent in 1994, reflecting excellent market-share gains in the UK, Holland and Japan. It is a market leader in Sweden, Hong Kong, Mexico, and Taiwan. B&L holds the number-two position in Japan, the world's second contact-lens care market with seven million wearers. B&L holds the number-one position in worldwide contact-lens sales and is ranked first or second in virtually every important local market. Bausch and Lomb's "Quantum 2" lens and the "Boston Envision" lens are two of the company's most successful lens products, which were launched onto the European market in 1992. Europe accounts for more than 40 per cent of the ophthalmic/pharmaceutical business. For example, "Betamann" a glaucoma drug manufactured by B&L holds the number-two position in Germany.

Ciba Geigy / Ciba Vision

Through innovation, research and development Ciba Geigy has taken its place as one of the top five pharmaceutical companies worldwide, and is market leader in most of its business sectors. More than 90,000 people are employed by Ciba Geigy in over 60 countries worldwide. Ciba Vision is primarily engaged in research, development, manufacture and marketing of contact lenses and eye-care products. As a result of its innovations in product design, sophisticated manufacturing technology and good marketing strategy, Ciba Vision has grown from a concept in 1980, to its current position as number two in the worldwide contact-lens and eye-care market. A major factor attributing to its strong performance in 1993/94 was its high-volume contact lenses, "New Vues" and "Focus". In the lens-care sector "Aosept" defended its position as the world's leading contact-lens disinfectant solution.

"Instacare" and "Solacare", two new lens-care products for one-step cleaning and disinfecting, received a positive response on their launch in several European countries. Ciba Vision doubled its production capacity in 1993/94 for disposable lenses, in response to the dramatic increase in demand.

Sauflon and Alcon

These are two foreign eye-care manufacturing companies which engage in similar activities to those of Allergan Ltd., and whose products are sold on the Irish market.

Conclusion

The pharmaceutical eye-care industry is currently in a period of growth. It is a highly competitive industry, with a significant number of competitors operating in Ireland. Allergan Pharmaceuticals, one of the leading eye-care manufacturing companies, operates successfully in Westport, Co. Mayo. The success of the company is primarily as a result of high-quality products, effective marketing and innovation, in terms of new products and uses for products.

Source: Company reports and interviews with company personnel.

Questions

1. Evaluate the competitive environment within which Allergan Pharmaceuticals Ltd. operates.

2. Evaluate the marketing strategies used by the company. How effective are they?

3. What advantages and disadvantages does an internationally recognised quality mark confer on a company like Allergan Pharmaceuticals Ireland Ltd?